REBEL
DAUGHTERS

PUBLICATIONS OF THE UNIVERSITY OF CALIFORNIA
HUMANITIES RESEARCH INSTITUTE
Mark Rose, *Director*

ANNOTATION AND ITS TEXTS
Edited by Stephen A. Barney

REBEL DAUGHTERS

Women and the French Revolution

EDITED BY

Sara E. Melzer
Leslie W. Rabine

New York   Oxford
OXFORD UNIVERSITY PRESS
1992

Oxford University Press

Oxford   New York   Toronto
Delhi   Bombay   Calcutta   Madras   Karachi
Kuala Lumpur   Singapore   Hong Kong   Tokyo
Nairobi   Dar es Salaam   Cape Town
Melbourne   Auckland

and associated companies in
Berlin   Ibadan

Published by Oxford University Press, Inc.,
200 Madison Avenue, New York, New York 10016

Oxford is a registered trademark of Oxford University Press

Library of Congress Cataloging-in-Publication Data
Rebel daughters : women and the French Revolution / edited by Sara E.
Melzer and Leslie W. Rabine.
p. cm. (Publications of the University of California
Humanities Research Institute)
ISBN 0-19-506886-6
ISBN 0-19-507016-X (pbk.)
1. France—History—Revolution, 1789–1799—Women.
2. France—History—Revolution, 1789–1799—Literature and the revolution.
3. Women revolutionaires—France—History—18th century.
4. Women in public life—France—History—18th century.
I. Melzer, Sara E.   II. Rabine, Leslie W., 1944–
III. Series.
DC158.8.R44   1991
944.04′082—dc20   90-49604

2 4 6 8 9 7 5 3 1
Printed in the United States of America
on acid-free paper

ACKNOWLEDGMENTS

To commemorate the Women's March on Versailles in October 1789, we organized a conference on Women and the French Revolution that took place in October 1989 at UCLA. Essays, based on those papers, are now collected in this volume.

Our conference was part of *1787/1989 The French Revolution: A UCLA Bicentennial Program*. We wish to thank Robert Maniquis, director of that program, for his support, as well as the University of California, Los Angeles, especially Chancellor Charles E. Young, former Executive Vice-Chancellor William D. Schaefer, and Executive Vice-Chancellor Andrea Rich. Our project was funded by a grant from the National Endowment for the Humanities. We would especially like to thank the Florence Gould Foundation, which provided the major support for all our activities.

The initial impetus for the conference came from Karen Rowe, founder and former director of the UCLA Center for the Study of Women. We owe her a special thanks, as well as to the staff of the Center for the Study of Women, which helped organize the entire project from its inception to its completion. Emily Ooms and Marjorie Pearson were the backbone of the sturdy support staff, and Susan Barnes, Van Do-Nguyen, and Carole Collier Frick gave more than generously of their time at crucial stages of the process.

The University of California Humanities Research Institute helped fund the project and provided administrative assistance. We particularly wish to thank its former director, Murray Krieger, and the current director Mark Rose for their support. Julia Van Camp provided crucial administrative aid.

From yet other corners came much appreciated help. The French Consulate, especially Cultural Attaché Alexander Tolstoi, helped us bring distinguished scholars from France. The Los Angeles League of Women Voters helped publicize the conference.

Editing the papers for publication was an essential part of our task. The editorial board deserves a very special mention for their perceptive comments on the essays in this volume. We wish to thank Suzanne Gearhart, Kathryn Norberg, Mark Poster, Karen Rowe, and Domna Stanton.

S. M.
L. R.

CONTENTS

CONTRIBUTORS

HARRIET APPLEWHITE, Professor of Political Science at Southern Connecticut State University, is the author of *Political Alignment in the French National Assembly, 1789–1791* (forthcoming, Louisiana State University Press, 1992). She and Darline Levy are co-editors of a collection of documents, *Women in Revolutionary Paris, 1789–95* (University of Illinois Press, 1979, 1980), and an anthology of essays, *Women and Politics in the Age of the Democratic Revolution* (University of Michigan Press, 1990). They are presently completing a book, *Gender and Citizenship in Revolutionary Paris* (forthcoming, Duke University Press, 1993).

DOMINIQUE DESANTI is a historian, novelist, and journalist residing in Paris. Her books include *Flora Tristan: La Femme révoltée* (Hachette, 1972) [translated as *A Woman in Revolt: A Biography of Flora Tristan*] (Crown, 1976), *Flora Tristan: Oeuvres et Vie Melées* (U.G.E., 1972), *Les Socialistes de L'utopie* (Payot, 1971), and numerous other fiction and nonfiction works. She is presently working on her memoirs.

MADELYN GUTWIRTH is author of *Mme. de Stael, Novelist: The Emergence of the Artist as Woman* (University of Illinois Press, 1978) and a further study, *The Twilight of the Goddesses, Women and Representation in the French Revolutionary Era* (Rutgers University Press, 1992). She is retired from Westchester University, where she was Professor of French and Women's Studies. A former ACLS and National Humanities Center Fellow, she remains an active participant in the MLA and the American Society for 18th Century Studies.

MARY JACOBUS is John Wendell Anderson Professor of English at Cornell University. She is the author of *Reading Woman: Essays in Feminist Criticism* (Columbia University Press, 1986), the editor of *Women Writing and Writing about Women* (Croom Helm, 1979), the author of two books on Wordsworth—*Tradition and Experiment in Wordsworth's Lyrical Ballads, 1798* (Clarendon, 1976) and *Romanticism, Writing, and Sexual Difference: Essays on the Prelude* (Clarendon, 1989)—and co-editor of *Body/Politics: Women and the Discourses of Science* (Routledge, 1990). She is currently working on a book about psychoanalysis, feminism, and the maternal body.

JOAN B. LANDES is Professor of Politics and Women's Studies at Hampshire College in Amherst, Massachusetts. She is author of *Women and the Public Sphere in the Age of the French Revolution* (Cornell University Press, 1988), and of numerous articles on feminism, political philosophy, critical theory, and cultural history. Her current research focuses on political imagery in the graphic arts of eighteenth-century France.

DARLINE GAY LEVY teaches French and European intellectual and cultural history at New York University. She is the author of *The Ideas and Careers of Simon-Nicolas-Henri Linquet. A Study of Eighteenth Century French Politics* (University of Illinois Press, 1980). With Harriet Applewhite, she has edited an anthology of documents, *Women in Revolutionary Paris, 1789–1795* (University of Illinois Press, 1979, 1980) and a book of essays, *Women and Politics in the Age of the Democratic Revolution* (University of Michigan Press, 1990). She and Harriet Applewhite are presently completing a study *Gender and Citizenship in Revolutionary Paris* (forthcoming, Duke University Press, 1993) that expands and synthesizes their collaborative work.

SARA MELZER, co-editor of this volume, is Associate Professor of French and Women's Studies at the University of California, Los Angeles. She is author of *Discourses of the Fall: A Study of Pascal's Pensées* (University of California Press, 1986). She is writing a book on the harem as an erotic and political fantasy (1660–1905).

ANNE K. MELLOR is Professor of English and Women's Studies at the University of California, Los Angeles. She is the author of *Blake's Human Form Divine* (University of California Press, 1974), *English Romantic Irony* (Harvard University Press, 1980), *Mary Shelley: Her Life, Her Fiction, Her Monsters* (Routledge, 1988), and *Romanticism and Gender* (Routledge, forthcoming), and is the editor of *Romanticism and Feminism* (Indiana University Press, 1988). She is currently writing on the leading women writers of the English Romantic period.

CLAIRE MOSES is Associate Professor of Women's Studies at the University of Maryland at College Park and editor and manager of *Feminist Studies*. She is author of *French Feminism in the 19th Century* (State University of New York Press, 1984); and co-author, with Leslie Rabine, of *The Word and the Act: French Feminism in the Age of Romanticism* (University of Indiana Press, forthcoming).

KATHRYN NORBERG is an Associate Professor in the Department of History at the University of California, Los Angeles. She is the author of *Rich and Poor in Grenoble, 1600–1814* (University of California Press, 1985) as well as of articles on women in seventeenth and eighteenth-century France. She is currently Director of the UCLA Center for the Study of Women and is writing a book on prostitution in seventeenth and eighteenth-century French culture and society.

LINDA ORR is Professor of French at Duke University. She is author of *Headless History: 19th Century French Historiography of the Revolution* (Cornell University Press, 1990).

LESLIE W. RABINE, co-editor of this volume, teaches French and Women's Studies at the University of California, Irvine. She is author of *Reading the Romantic Heroine: Text, History, Ideology* (University of Michigan Press, 1985) and co-author with Claire Moses of *The Word and the Act: French Feminism in the Age of Romanticism* (University of Indiana Press, forthcoming.

NAOMI SCHOR is William Hanes Wannamaker Professor of Romance Studies at Duke University. Her most recent books include *Reading in Detail: Aesthetics and the Feminine* (Methuen, 1987) and *Breaking the Chain: Women, Theory and French Realist Fiction* (Columbia University Press, 1985). She's currently completing a book, *George Sand and Idealism*. She is author of over 40 articles on 19th-century French fiction, feminist theory, and literary criticism. She co-edits with Elizabeth Weed *differences: A Journal of Feminist, Cultural Studies* (Indiana University Press).

JOAN W. SCOTT is Professor of Social Science at the Institute for Advanced Study. She is author of *Gender and the Politics of History* (Columbia University Press, 1988) and editor, with Judith Butler, of *Feminists Theorize the Political* (Routledge, 1992). She is currently writing a book about feminist claims for political rights in France, 1789–1945.

MARIE-CLAIRE VALLOIS, Associate Professor at Miami University, is the author of *Fictions féminines: Mme de Stael et les voix de la Sibylle*. She has written on both eighteenth- and nineteenth-century authors (Montesquieu, Diderot, Chateaubriand, and Hugo). She is currently completing a study to be called "Changing Places: Women, Fiction, Revolution (1735–1848)."

MARGARET WALLER is Assistant Professor of French at Pomona College. Her publications include *The Male Malady* (Rutgers University Press, forthcoming) and the English translation of Julia Kristeva's *Revolution in Poetic Language*. Her new book project, *Consuming Fashions*, studies fictions of gender identity and social mobility in fashion journalism and realist literature under the July Monarchy.

REBEL
DAUGHTERS

1

Introduction

The further one delves into the subject of gender and the French Revolution, the less one can validate François Furet's contention that "the French Revolution is over."[1] Our attempts to talk about the revolution, even at a distance of 200 years, are strangely haunted by its most famous patrimony—the institutionalization of the Universal Rights of Man. Implicit in this doctrine is the notion of "man" as ungendered and universal, on the one hand, but also gendered and exclusive of women, on the other. The liberal discourse of the rights of man thus institutionalized the implicit assumption of "woman" as particular, excluded from universality. Women had of course always been on the periphery of Western culture, but never before within the closed conceptual framework of universal rights to liberty, equality, and fraternity.

The liberal discourse of the rights of man places all writing by and about women in a double bind, from which even the subtitle of this work, *Women and the French Revolution*, cannot escape. A collection of essays that criticize and take us beyond the discursive category of "women" as inherited from the liberal discourse of the French Revolution, must by necessity name itself within that category. Its connotations of "women" as essentially tangential, excentric, supplementary, and incidental to the revolution reverberate in the subtitle even as the chapters herein dissect the historical and cultural processes that constructed these connotations. These chapters demonstrate that the critical study of women and gender does not exist in some remote no-man's-land, but impinges on all human understanding. It alters the basic terms through which we understand the revolution, or any historical and cultural phenomenon within the liberal tradition. Yet these chapters must speak in a language that denies the power of their critique by naming women as marginal. Where a subtitle like *Men and the French Revolution* (or worse still, *The Role of Men in the French Revolution*) would sound ridiculously redundant, our subtitle is both necessary to our endeavor and condemned to signify the very connotations it intends to refute.

Of course the asymmetry of gender that connotes man as central and primary, woman as peripheral and secondary predates the French Revolution by centuries if not millennia. So what changes with the French Revolution? It marks a new era that holds out to women the promise of inclusion in its universal community of equal human subjects only to snatch that promise away when women rise up to actively claim its fulfillment, as they have done ever since the first days of the 1789 upheavals. They have been, in the words of our main title, "Rebel Daughters" of their father, the Revolution. This title, like the subtitle, is caught within the same double bind. In order to seek inclusion within its community, women had to rebel against that community and its ideology. Or, to put the matter another way: In order to win rights and freedoms, women had to, and still must, rebel against a revolution that ultimately rejected and excluded them, but they could, and can, justify and articulate their claims only by virtue of the principles established by that revolution.

The title of this book comes from the title of one of the chapters herein, Dominique Desanti's "Flora Tristan: Rebel Daughter of the Revolution." Tristan, the noted nineteenth-century writer and pioneer socialist feminist organizer recognizes, as Desanti says, "the source of her ideas in the French Revolution," which she also "criticizes and at times rejects . . . because of its inadequacies." Yet the phrase "rebel daughter" also fits the other women written about in this volume: the crowds of Parisian women involved in fighting in the revolution from 1789 to 1793 that Darline Gay Levy and Harriet Applewhite present; the flamboyant revolutionary feminist Olympe de Gouges, whose *Declaration of the Rights of Woman* and other writings Joan Wallach Scott analyzes; the writer Germaine de Staël, who saw her own father as the central figure of 1789, and whom Linda Orr writes about in terms of her struggles to reclaim her family legacy; the Saint-Simonian feminists of the 1830s whose social utopianism and sexual radicalism Claire Moses documents; the English feminists Mary Wollstonecraft and her daughter Mary Shelley, whose ambivalent writings about the French Revolution are interpreted by Anne Mellor; and even, unlikely as it may seem, Chateaubriand's romantic heroine Atala, interpreted in different ways by Naomi Schor, Margaret Waller, Marie-Claire Vallois, and Madelyn Gutwirth. Although the anti revolutionary, royalist Chateaubriand described Atala as his faithful daughter, she is a rebel daughter in that this character became a popular icon who, along with Chateaubriand's hero René, provided the vehicle through which the rebellious gender ideology of the revolution was absorbed into the self-identity of post-revolutionary generations. The phrase "rebel daughters" applies even to the authors Joan Landes, Kathryn Norberg, and Mary Jacobus, whose chapters explore the representation of woman by male writers and artists. For as feminist scholars in the West today, we are all ambiguous heiresses of the paternal revolutionary legacy.

The double bind of this legacy extends even to the conjunction "and" in *Women and the French Revolution*, since conjunctions suggest the bringing together of separate entities. But in fact, women always belonged inseparably to the revolution, which could not have existed without them. While working to assemble this book, we have had many people ask us if we were surprised to "discover" that women participated in the French Revolution. A feminist scholar might be surprised by the question, since the experience of feminist historiography would lead us to expect that women would have of course participated, and that their apparent absence would be a product of traditional historiography. Thus any study of this subject must begin by establishing the basic fact that women and the French Revolution are not distinct entities—although their union, as expressed in patriarchal language, is a contradictory one.

Women's active participation from 1789 to 1793 was necessary to the revolution's success. Women demonstrated and fought to establish the new order, demanded bread for their families, and pressured the government to defend the new republic and regulate the economy. But like women in social movements since that time, they found themselves fighting on two contradictory fronts: with the men to bring about a new society based on "liberty, equality, fraternity," and against the men to claim those very rights for themselves. Although the masculine leaders of the revolution continually withheld from women the rights of citizenship, they also, as Darline Gay Levy and Harriet Applewhite show in their chapter, needed the women's active militant participation to secure the tenuous existence of their infant state. These men, then, also faced a contradiction: how to unleash the women's activity yet prevent them from being the conscious agents of that activity. As Levy and Applewhite point out, the women's demonstration that they could act as citizens in the same way as men threatened to overturn the gender boundaries upon which the men's identity depended.

In June of 1793, women were explicitly excluded from citizenship, and in the autumn of that year women's political clubs and organizations were banned, and women were prohibited from speaking before the legislative body. Although Joan Landes, Darline Gay Levy, Harriet Applewhite, Marie-Claire Vallois, Naomi Schor, Joan Wallach Scott, and Mary Jacobus analyze the prohibition placed upon women in 1793 in intriguingly different ways, all show that it was not an isolated incident but rather a turning point in the development of modern structures of personal, sexual, and political identity.

Women's exclusion from the public realm calls forth yet another, this time perhaps apparent, contradiction. At the same time that women were expelled from the public sphere, Woman as an allegorical figure came more and more pervasively to stand for Liberty, Equality, republican virtues, and the Republic itself in the men's representations of their new political order. Several of the chapters in this volume discuss the nature and significance of replacing active women with Woman as allegory, analyzing how it provided the new culture with representational forms through which it could construct mirrors of masculine self-identity.

The execution of Louis XVI at the end of 1792 brought to a head what Hunt calls a "crisis of representation."[2] In the Old Regime the body of the king represented what Lynn Hunt calls the "sacred center" of the representational system that relates self to world. The body of the king, as Hunt has shown, is replaced by the figure of woman, but denuded of autonomous agency, providing a mirroring center in which the male individual can find his idealized reflection. This change, however, did not occur suddenly during the revolution, but was an ongoing process traceable to eighteenth-century art and literature. It represents a change in the structure of the masculine psyche. Whereas in the Old Regime men experienced themselves essentially as members of a hierarchical community centered on the king, they now needed to find a way to represent their selves as autonomous individuals. The female allegorical figures in republican revolutionary iconography, embodying the male values of Liberty and Equality, exemplify earlier attempts to construct such mirrors of self-identity. But the self-sacrificing romantic heroines of the early nineteenth century, beginning with Chateaubriand's Atala and Amélie (in *René*), succeed in this, perhaps because of their apparently apolitical nature, at a much deeper and more internalized level.

Recent publications on the revolution suggest the extent to which these structures of identity inherited from the revolution persist in shaping our own thought. While many do not challenge this heritage, others, like this volume, participate in current attempts to question and even change gendered psychic structures. As an example of the former, the monumental *The French Revolution and the Creation of Modern Political Culture*,[3] does not include among the twenty-seven articles of its first volume, *The Political Culture of the Old Regime*, a single one that expressly takes up the significance of women and gender in the prerevolutionary process. The second volume, *The Political Culture of the French Revolution*, contains one such essay "Le Citoyen/la citoyenne: Activity, Passivity and the Revolutionary Concept of Citizenship" by William H. Sewell.[4] Such volumes do little to question the discursive legacy that both rests upon and hides the work of asymmetrical gender. On the other hand, conferences at University of California, Santa Barbara, and Hofstra University,[5] to name only two, make gender analysis an integral part of the included scholarship.

Whereas feminist criticism can rewrite the history of the French Revolution only in a language that marks "women" as a specialized category, books about men and the revolution offer titles that synecdochally substitute the masculine part for the bigendered whole, like *A Cultural History of the French Revolution*.[6] While the title would suggest a study of humanity on both sides of the gender divide, it contains, as Sara Maza says, "nothing . . . about attitudes toward women and femininity."[7] By contrast, a book subtitled *Women and the French Revolution* cannot help but engage extensively and profoundly in questions of men and masculinity. Seen in terms of gender, both books evince a gap of incompatibility between the title and its content. But when the two books are juxtaposed in this light, the irony attending the feminist discourse of "women" turns around and now sets the masculine discourse of generality against itself.

In order to understand this shift and its effect, we need first to review briefly the various masculine discourses on the revolution and then ask what feminist analyses would add to them. Among those discourses are the following: For Tocqueville and subsequent Tocquevillians, the revolution consolidated the development of the modern, centralized state; for Marxist social historians, as exemplified by Albert Soboul, it marks the end of the feudal order with its aristocratic rule and the beginning of the capitalist order under bourgeois hegemony; in the frame of post-structuralist historiography, as first applied to the revolution by François Furet, it institutes not a real social change but the ideologies and discourse (which Furet rather naively opposes to the "real" as "imaginary") that have led to modern totalitarianism; and for the revisionist historians who have followed in the wake of Furet it marks the creation of modern political culture.[8] In debates between the various schools, the revolution thus presents itself as a cataclysmic rupture in historical time, of inescapable significance, one which must be confronted and cannot be bridged or filled in, but exactly what it separates from what remains a subject of endless debate.

The inclusion of feminist scholarship in these debates would not end them. On the contrary. But it would certainly change their terms. The body of feminist re-readings of the revolution does not comprise another position alongside these. Rather, it permeates them all as their ironic undercurrent. It points to the gap between the abstract universals of the "state," the "socioeconomic order," "ideology," or "political culture" and their gendered objects of analysis. It constantly asks how a recognition of the gender politics founding these objects as well as awareness of its concealment in discourse would transform the analysis of all these schools and the language of their analysis.

In providing this undercurrent to French Revolution scholarship, these chapters also demonstrate that political power relations, economics, and culture cannot be understood simply as that which goes on within the state or public economy, as they do not in fact exist in isolation. An understanding of politics, economics, and culture would come from taking into account both the public space and that which it has repressed to a "private" space in order to form itself, as well as the relation between the two.

In creating this new vision, this volume belongs to a second wave of feminist studies in this field. It builds upon the work of a first generation represented by such books as *Women in Revolutionary Paris, 1789–1795* by Darline Gay Levy, Harriet Bronson Applewhite, and Mary Durham Johnson, and *Les Femmes et la Révolution* by Paule-Marie Duhet.[9] These texts of the 1970s did the necessary work of unearthing and making accessible the hidden story of women's participation in the events of 1787 to 1795, as well as the masculine leaders' contradictory and ulitmately repressive response to it. A second generation of feminist scholarship includes, along with the essays presented here, such books as *Women and the Public Sphere in the Age of the Revolution* by Joan Landes and *The Body and the French Revolution* by Dorinda Outram.[10] Like the chapters in this volume, these two books demonstrate that gender is not an external, supplementary category, but a founding category of modern politics, culture, and ideology.

The chapters in this volume contribute to that second generation in yet another way. Like the discipline of women's studies, in whose development most of the contributors have participated, this collection is creatively interdisciplinary in two senses. First, as a collection, this book joins the work of historians and literary critics, allowing readers to see how scholars from different disciplines approach the same set of problems with different viewpoints and methods. Second, each chapter, whether primarily historical, literary, or cultural, borrows in different ways from its sister disciplines to further feminist and critical theory. The essays thus also allow readers to see disciplinary methods combined in strikingly different ways to create diverse interpretations and readings of cultural and historical process.

The first chapter analyzes the use of woman as sign and symbol in the production of a new ideology. In Joan Landes's study, "Representing the Body Politic: The Paradox of Gender in the Graphic Politics of the French Revolution," she contrasts the goddess Liberty as symbol of popular sovereignty with the image of the king as symbol of divine authority. Gender difference in the revolutionary period is, according to her, mapped onto a new hierarchical system of interaction between visual representation and more abstract forms of linguistic representation.

While Landes examines the "graphic politics" of revolutionary imagery, Kathryn Norberg, in "'Love and Patriotism': Gender and Politics in the Life and Work of Louvet de Couvrai," examines the sexual politics of this bestselling author of the revolutionary period who was also a Girondist deputy to the National Assembly. Reading together his fictional and political writings, she uncovers the discursive construction of a gender system that attempts to contain within secure bounds the feminine sexuality considered threatening to men's republican virtue.

In "Incorruptible Milk: Breast-feeding and the French Revolution," Mary Jacobus then combines iconic and textual analysis to study the semiotics of the maternal breast for revolutionary theory and practice. She draws relations between texts by Rousseau and Marie Anel Le Rebours advocating maternal breast-feeding, historical changes in its practice, allegorical figures of the Republic as nursing mother, and psychoanalytic interpretations of the role of the introjected maternal breast as phantasm in the development of wish-fulfillment mechanisms. Her chapter analyzes the political discourse of the revolutionaries as phantasmatic and wish-fulfilling with respect to their material practices.

Following these chapters on figures of femininity in masculine discursive practices come studies of the words and actions of women as participants in the revolution. In Darline Gay Levy and Harriet Applewhite's "Women and Militant Citizenship in Revolutionary Paris," we see the women of the popular classes acting against the formation of a republican ideology that requires their containment, while the masculine leaders veer between co-opting and repressing their active agency. Where Levy explores the collective political practice of sans-culotte women, Joan Wallach Scott and Linda Orr focus on women who left their imprint upon history as individuals.

For Scott a reading of writings by the flamboyant revolutionary feminist Olympe de Gouges provides material for a theoretical reflection upon the paradoxical relation of feminism to masculine liberal philosophical systems, symbolic constructs, and political discourses both then and now. Her chapter, "'A Woman Who Has Only Paradoxes to Offer': Olympe de Gouges Claims Rights for Women," questions whether any feminism can avoid paradox.

By contrast, Orr's analysis of the influential romantic writer and political figure Germaine de Staël, "Outspoken Women and the Rightful Daughter of the Revolution: Madame de Staël's *Considérations sur la Révolution française*" allows us to reflect upon the writing of history. In discussing the many implicit ways that De Staël's text offers a culturally defined feminine and original perspective on the revolution, Orr is led to speculate on why possession of the meaning and memory of the revolution must continue to elude the grasp of historians even until now.

De Staël's book has unjustly received the same kind of exclusion from the historical canon that women have received from the public space of liberal society. And the chapters in the third section of the book unravel the processes of cultural construction in the aftermath of the revolution that make this multileveled exclusion invisible. Within these analyses, the fiction of Alphonse-René de Chateaubriand, the first great writer of the postrevolutionary period and the most influential in producing new forms of cultural and literary representation, finds a privileged place. Feminist rereadings of *Atala* and *René* challenge traditional interpretations of Chateaubriand and show, in the words of Vallois, how the texts "traduce in a symptomatic sense the work of repression and of the reorganization of [a] cultural imaginary."

Schor takes up in a different way from Landes and Jacobus the thorny problem of feminine allegory in "*Triste Amérique: Atala* and the Postrevolutionary Construction of Woman." She argues that Atala has been misread as a realist rather than allegorical figure. Thus transforming our view of this heroine, Schor leads us to see that through an allegorization of the feminine body, which actually decorporializes women, Chateaubriand's text resolves the crisis of representation opened by the revolutionary destruction of the old symbolic order.

Margaret Waller's chapter, "Being René, Buying Atala: Alienated Subjects and Decorative Objects in Postrevolutionary France," shifts our attention from the texts themselves to the paired figures of Atala and René as icons of a new post-revolutionary popular culture. Atala as consumer object and René as object of identification help to engender the gender system and ideology of liberal capitalist culture.

Marie-Claire Vallois's chapter, "Exotic Femininity and the Rights of Man: *Paul et Virginie* and *Atala*, or the Revolution in Stasis," pairs *René* with the prerevolutionary exotic text *Paul et Virginie* to analyze the relation between exotic femininity and domesticated femininity in the "ill-accomplished" effort to permanently repress the feminine from a universalist postrevolutionary language that unsuccessfully attempts to freeze language in fixed meanings.

In Madelyn Gutwirth's "The Engulfed Beloved: Representations of Dead and Dying Women in the Art and Literature of the Revolutionary Era," *René* appears with a host of literary texts and paintings that suggest a masculine fascination with female sacrifice for love and/or family. Throughout this broad overview of literature and art from the revolutionary era, Gutwirth finds a consistent gender politics in which women are repressed as subjects in order to become the objects of masculine desire.

By repressing women for the sake of forming a homogenous public and symbolic space while establishing a doctrine of universal rights and liberties, the new masculine-centered social order ensured that it would always harbor within itself a subversive force: modern feminism. Although feminist ideas had circulated in the centuries before the revolution among the elite, 1789 gave birth to feminism as popular movements actively engaged in the political arena to win women's rights and change patriarchal society. The chapters in the final section of this book analyze the significance of the feminist thought that emerged during the revolution and in the following generation.

Claire G. Moses's historical comparison between the revolutionary feminists and the Saint-Simonian feminists of the period from 1830 to 1848 calls into question the categorization of feminism into schools of sexual "equality" and sexual "difference." Her chapter, "'Equality' and 'Difference' in Historical Perspective: A Comparative Examination of the Feminisms of French Revolutionaries and Utopian Socialists," thereby challenges our association of specific attributes (e.g., "radical" or "conservative") with philosophies of either equality or difference.

Anne Mellor's chapter, "English Women Writers and the French Revolution," allows us to make comparisons between the French feminists of the revolutionary and romantic generations and English feminists of the same periods, as her chapter finds a very different influence of the revolution upon English feminists. Three of them, Mary Wollstonecraft, Helen Maria Williams, and Mary Godwin Shelley, experienced first hand the revolution or its aftermath in France. They found in the revolution a disturbing contradiction, both a possibility for greater freedom for women and the potential for unleashing monstrous evil, in part because of this repression of women. Their critique of the revolution is articulated explicitly in Wollstonecraft's *A Vindication of the Rights of Women* and allegorically in Shelley's *Frankenstein*.

With Dominique Desanti's "Flora Tristan: Rebel Daughter of the Revolution," we return to the France of the 1830s and 1840s, this time to examine the life and thought of a feminist only loosely connected to the Saint-Simonian group, who nevertheless transformed their ideas into a theory of class struggle. Desanti shows us how one of the foremost socialist feminist writers and activitists of this period acknowledged the liberal thought of the revolution but could criticize its limitations and go beyond it.

This final chapter brings us back to our own feminist methods, as yet another generation of rebel daughters of the revolution. While women have been excluded historically from the universality of human rights, this discourse of universal rights and freedoms alone provides the ground upon which we can pursue our feminist critiques and thereby continue to claim equality and freedom. Like the feminist writings engendered both positively and negatively by the revolution, we can proceed only by pulling out from under us the ground on which we stand.

December, 1991   S. M.
Los Angeles, Cal.   L. R.

Notes

1. François Furet, "La Révolution française est terminée," in *Penser la Révolution française* (Paris: Gallimard, 1978), 13–109.

2. Lynn Hunt, *Politics, Culture, and Class in the French Revolution* (Berkeley: University of California Press, 1984), 88.

3. Keith Michael Baker, ed., *The French Revolution and the Creation of Modern Political Culture*, vol. I, *The Political Culture of the Old Regime* (New York: Oxford University Press, 1987).

4. William H. Sewell, Jr., "Le Citoyen/la citoyenne: Activity, Passivity and the Revolutionary Concept of Citizenship," in *The French Revolution and the Creation of Modern Political Culture*, vol. II, *The Political Culture of the French Revolution* (New York: Oxford University Press, 1988).

5. *Revolution '89: Perspectives on the French Revolution*, a Bicentenary Conference, University of California, Santa Barbara, May 12–13, 1989; *The French Revolution and its Impact*. Bicentennial Conference, Hofstra University, October 5, 6, 7, 1989.

6. Emmet Kennedy, *A Cultural History of the French Revolution* (New Haven: Yale University Press, 1989).

7. Sara Maza, "After the Revolution, the Arts Lived On . . . ," *The New York Times Book Review*, July 9, 1989, 12.

8. Alexis de Tocqueville, *L'Ancien Régime et la Révolution*, 2nd ed. (Paris: Michel Lévy frères, 1856); Albert Soboul, *La Révolution française* (Paris: Gallimard, 1962); Furet, *Penser la Révolution française*; Baker, *The French Revolution and Political Culture*.

9. Darline Gay Levy, Harriet Bronson Applewhite, Mary Durham Johnson, *Women in Revolutionary Paris, 1789–1795: Selected Documents Translated with Notes and Commentary* (Urbana: University of Illinois Press, 1979); Paule-Marie Duhet, *Les Femmes et la Révolution, 1789–1794* (Paris: Julliard, 1971).

10. Joan B. Landes, *Women and the Public Sphere in the Age of the French Revolution* (Ithaca: Cornell University Press, 1988); Dorinda Outram, *The Body and the French Revolution: Sex, Class, and Political Culture* (New Haven: Yale University Press, 1989).

I

Women and the Formation of Revolutionary Ideology

2

Representing the Body Politic: The Paradox of Gender in the Graphic Politics of the French Revolution

JOAN B. LANDES

Even under optimal circumstances, the trial and execution of a king as occurred in France in 1793 would not be a trivial matter. To the king's supporters, the revolutionaries were guilty of the most awful form of parricide and a capital crime against the whole community. The Convention's action was predicated upon a striking inversion: The king's once sacred body had to become first a criminal body; one condemned according to a new, higher morality of crimes against the public's liberty and the state's security.[1] Any judgment implies both a judge and the law. Indeed, in this unusual proceeding, a new (popular) sovereign, its representatives, and its legal code were in evidence. In this sovereign's name the regicides acted. Standing behind, empowering, authorizing, and legitimating the decisive vote of the Convention was a sovereign power whose claim to authority was no less absolute than that of either God or King, the twin pillars of Old Regime France: In the name of the people and its liberty, the nation and its security, justice was being done. In the words of Jean-Jacques Rousseau, the most uncompromising eighteenth-century theorist of popular sovereignty: "sovereignty is inalienable, it is indivisible." Indeed, like its predecessor, this new sovereign power is "entirely absolute, entirely sacred, and entirely inviolable."[2]

According to the doctrine of kingship by which Louis XVI and his ancestors ruled France, the king possessed two bodies: A material body subject to corruption and decay, and a spiritual body symbolic of the life of the community.[3] It was natural and expected that a king should die. But the trial and execution of this king exceeded nature and ancient law. It struck at the heart of the central metaphor of Old Regime France. By decapitating the sacred, corporate body of the ancien régime, necessarily its "head," the fraternal band of revolutionary brothers who wanted to start anew, to create a new community predicated on equality and virtue, risked the continued life of the body politic.[4] Yet, in the political imaginary of the new nation, in the language of the social contract from which the new republic derived its legitimacy, the central trope of the body politic lived on. Even earlier, Rousseau had refused to cede the old metaphor to his political opponents. In *The Social Contract*, for example, he writes, "Just as nature gives each man absolute power over all his members, the social compact gives the body politic absolute power over all its members. . . ."[5] Rousseau's sovereign is nevertheless extremely abstract. His body politic exists symbolically in the law. His effort to anchor political representation in the concept of the general will bequeathed a troubling legacy to his followers.

The project of redefining and representing the body politic with the nation and its populace, not the king, at the now vacant, sacred center proved vexing from a visual as well as a political standpoint. Virtually all eighteenth-century republicans exhibited a deeply felt, iconoclastic hatred of political and religious idolatry.[6] As Thomas Paine protested: "The old idea was that man must be governed by effigy and show, and that a superstitious reverence was necessary to establish authority. . . . The putting of any individual as a figure for a nation is improper." Perhaps more striking is John Quincy Adams's formulation: "Democracy has no monuments. It strikes no medals. It bears the head of no man on a coin. Its very essence is iconoclastic."[7] In France, Rousseau's formulation of the general will encouraged revolutionaries to resist the very notion of political representation; not only in terms of the revolution's symbolic repertoire, as Quincy Adams and Paine recommend, but in the constitutive practices of politics itself.[8] "The instant a people chooses representatives," Rousseau states, "it is no longer free; it no longer exists."[9]

There now exists an extremely rich account of revolutionary and old regime political culture from the perspective of language or political discourse.[10] On the other hand, students of the revolution are beginning to appreciate the considerable role played by visual imagery.[11] Still, there is room for a continuing exploration of the interaction between visual and political argumentation in this age. No more compelling site exists of what I would like to term a "graphic politics" than that of the representation of the body politic. In France, moreover, we are confronted by the often noticed, but still perplexing substitution of the goddess Liberty for the body of the king.[12] A closer investigation of body imagery in revolutionary popular prints in light of political thought and practice may help to identify a series of paradoxes within the territory of iconic and symbolic practice. One way to frame the discussion that follows, then, would be to ask the question how does Rousseau's vision of an absolute, sacred, and inviolable new sovereign power fare once it is embodied in the allegorical figure of a woman?

We need to observe initially something of the improbable origins of the democratic body politic as articulated by Rousseau and his revolutionary admirers. Over a century before the French Revolution, Thomas Hobbes had devastated the naturalistic and organic underpinnings of medieval, corporate rule, only to save the body politic for other uses. Through the metaphor of the social contract, Hobbes linked the issue of political authority to that of personation and representation. His Leviathan, a living god, amounts to a grand artifice, an artificial person, created through a contract by which the members of the commonwealth are made complicit in the sovereign's absolute power and authority. As individuals, according to Hobbes, are nothing more than impersonators, actors, bearers of masks, it is entirely consistent that the "feigned person" of the sovereign be an extension of each individual subject's will.[13] By contracting together, they have represented, authorized, authored, and engendered the sovereign. A multitude has "made *One* Person. . . . For it is the *Unity* of the Representer, not the *Unity* of the Represented, that maketh the Person *One*."[14] Hobbes's subjects are not born into natural submission as hapless creatures in the old order of social station, they have the privilege of *willing* their own domination.

The image on the frontispiece of the 1651 edition of *Leviathan* and in whose creation Hobbes is said to have had a direct hand, says it best: The authorizing members of the (artificial) body politic are seen from the back, their bodies literally compose the sovereign's armor. All leveled, none more equal than any other, the members of the body politic are figured as awed spectators of this terrifyingly absolute sovereign whose justification to rule is depicted in the pastoral image of a peaceful, prosperous, and protected countryside. He exists for their "common benefit." Although he himself doesn't care to dwell explicitly on these matters, it is of some import for a study of the ways in which gender inflects politics that only decades after the end of Elizabeth's reign and the more immediate experience of civil war, the person of Hobbes's imposing sovereign is decidedly male.[15]

Rousseau is equally anxious about the effects of political and social division; though unlike Hobbes he sought a democratic, not an authoritarian solution to these problems. His myth of the social contract takes Hobbes's argument one step further. If Hobbes's metaphor requires a metamorphosis, Rousseau asks for nothing less than a transubstantiation. By willing the good and the general, each member of the political body is at one with the whole. Mysteriously, the members not only authorize and legitimate the sovereign, they become the sovereign as well: "Each of us puts his person and all his power in common under the supreme direction of the general will; and in a body we receive each member as an indivisible part of the whole."[16] The end result of all of this willing, then, is not a person, but the popular sovereign, the evanescent body of the people and its laws. Rather than follow Hobbes in the direction of a theatrical theory of representation, Rousseau refuses the assistance of all masks and the representations. He evokes instead a transparent, natural basis of power, forgetting, as the revolutionaries themselves ruefully discovered, "the theatrical is the political."[17] Despite their own keen ambitions to call into question the legitimacy of all representations, the revolutionaries were never able to impose a strict Rousseauist program either in the area of politics or culture.[18] The need to achieve a new representation of the altered body politic remained a pressing concern of the leadership and the revolutionary publics. As for the specific instance of visual imagery, Rolf Reichardt reminds us of the importance of illustrated broadsides, which were produced in vast numbers for a predominantly illiterate population:

Illustrated broadsides fulfilled a more than supplementary function. Together with the nonwritten media of public speeches and songs, they approached the man and woman in the street in the terms of their own oral or semioral culture. They not only rendered the revolutionary message accessible but also drew ordinary people into the communication and opinion-making process of a widening public sphere, with its tendency toward democratization. These prints were at once a means of political education and testimony to popular ideas.[19]

The dynamic process by which the French nation broke with past symbols and images and struggled to create new ones can be examined from three distinct, but constantly overlapping perspectives. First, the manner in which a body politic was refigured; second, dismembered; and, third, re-membered. As the movement from the masculine visage of the monarch to the goddess Liberty underscores, the logic of representation in the revolution is also gender coded. In the earliest years of the revolution, a plethora of prints were produced that referred, typically in allegorical terms, to the reorganization of the old corporate body of France, the Estates General, into a modern parliamentary body, the National Assembly, under a constitutional monarchy. The people are triple—not yet subsumed under a single, abstract personification. In contrast (Figure 2.1), *Adieu Bastille* is a much less optimistic rendering of the course to be taken by the new body politic. A member of the Third Estate stands playing a bagpipe. This representative of the new nation causes two marionettes dressed as a nobleman and a clergyman to dance to his tune as the

Figure 2.1 Anonymous, *Adieu Bastille*, 1789. Etching with hand coloring on blue paper. *Source*: Library of Congress.

Bastille, the hated symbol of the old despotic regime, is dismantled in the background by patriots with pickaxes.[20] The presence of the Bastille, the print's one realistic element, reinforces the dominant message of the otherwise allegorical image that, as Sieyès proclaimed, the Third Estate is everything; "nobody outside the Third Estate can be considered as part of the nation." There is no longer any purpose to be performed by the idle, useless, privileged appendages of the old body politic. The popular allegory of a world-upside-down is joined to the theatrical space of the fairs and little theatres. The people, represented as a great puppeteer, now control political space and their own destiny. As for the monarchy, its despotism is tamed. Not the Third Estate— whom Sieyès described as being "like a strong and robust man with one arm still in chains"[21]—but the monarchy (symbolized by a lion) lies in chains at the feet of the people's representative.

In the many versions of a commonly reproduced popular allegorical rendering of the taking of the Bastille, the armed citizenry is depicted decapitating the many-headed Hydra of either despotism or aristocracy. More menacing still are the representations of severed heads of victims paraded on pikes as in (Figure 2.2) *Triomphe de l'armée Parisienne réunis au Peuple à son Retour de Versailles le 6 Octobre 1789*, one of numerous depictions of the October days. In this celebration of the people's return from Versailles, the aristocracy and clergy are completely offstage, replaced by women from the popular classes, national guardsmen, and soldiers. The women are far from passive. This is an affirmative image of emancipation—the women and soldiers

Figure 2.2 Anonymous, *Triomphe de l'armée Parisienne réunis au Peuple à son Retour de Versailles le 6 October 1789. Source*: Library of Congress.

Figure 2.3 Anonymous, *Les Couches de Monsieur Target*, 1791. Etching and mezzotint. *Source*: Bibliothèque Nationale.

carry liberty trees—not a representation of Edmund Burke's vile furies.[22] Still, the women in this print show unsettling signs of possessing strong sexual and martial appetites. They carry bread and heads on pikes. One woman straddles a cannon, whose barrel comes between her legs; another woman is caught in a compromising posture with a soldier whose intentions are evident.[23]

The issue of gender is encoded forcefully in a series of royalist caricatures of the birth of the constitution of 1791. *Les Couches de M. Target* (Figure 2.3) is a rather explicit image of the *engendering* of the new body politic.[24] The lawyer Target, deputy of the Third Estate from Paris and member of the committee charged with drafting the new constitution, is seen sitting with his legs spread apart having just delivered a baby (the new constitution). Three males allegorizing the three estates and the female revolutionary Théroigne de Mericourt witness the baby's baptism. Lynn Hunt presents this etching as an almost unbelievable confirmation of Carole Pateman's argument that "the story of the original contract tells a modern story of masculine political birth . . . an example of the appropriation by men of the awesome gift that nature has denied them and its transmutation into masculine political creativity." For Pateman, modern contract theory represents a particular version of the masculine genesis of political life, "a specifically modern tale, told over the dead political body of the father."[25] Hunt observes that the mother of *la nation* has no threatening feminizing qualities.[26] Rather, Mericourt is reduced to an assisting role. On the other hand, as Langlois stresses, the royalists habitually allied Mericourt with the populace both symbolically (for her support of the Constituent Assembly) and because of her alleged loose morals (she was a courtesan before 1789). Behind this casual joke, then, there resides an obsession with the theme of the world-turned-upside-down. "La Révolution non seulement pervertit l'ordre politique, mais plus profondément elle renverse celui de la nature."[27] Surely, then, Mericourt's appearance functions as a satirical accent with respect to the forces that have engendered this new political body. There is certainly something laughable also about a man caught in the compromising and unnatural scene of birth.

There is little doubt about the satirical intent of the royalist lampoon (Figure 2.4) *Grand Débandement de l'armée anti-constitutionelle*. Mericourt, "la demoiselle Teroig" as she is called here, shows up as a general leading her troops—all aristocratic women (Madame de Sta[ël], Madame Condor[cet], Madame de Dondon, Madame Silles (de Genlis, the marquise de Sillery), Madame de Calo[nne], and Madame Talmouse (de Laval-Talmont) who openly supported revolutionary ideals. Mericourt frightens the emperor's troops by revealing her "république." Likewise, the women each present a "villette"—a reference to the ardent revolutionary the Marquis de Villette. The print bitterly mocks the cowardice of the counterrevolutionary armies arrayed against a poorly outfitted contingent of women with their few sans-culotte and jacobin supporters who are carrying nothing so terrible as pikes topped with hams and sausages; what the editors of *French Caricature* term "the phallic spoils of war."[28] The real power of the revolutionary forces as portrayed here lies in their "sex." This provocative image achieves a humorous but deeply disturbing condensation of political and sexual anxieties. Taking a leaf from the book of enlightened and republican criticism of absolutism with its constant complaint against the emasculation of would-be virile male citizens, the anonymous artist cleverly represents *royalist* opposition to the revolution as a fear of the emasculating, voracious appetites of the women which the revolution has now unleashed.

We are now firmly within the transgressive territory of revolutionary caricature whose most pronounced examples can be aggregated under the category which I referred to earlier as that of the body politic's dismemberment. What is being dismembered is the carefully articulated sacred body politic of Old Regime France, whichi culminated directly in removal of its head.[29] The basic theory of kingship had its roots in the Middle Ages wherein intermediate groups stood in a kind of graduated order between the supreme unit and the individual; a political and individual body that necessarily repelled any hint of monstrosity:[30]

> "On the analogy of the physical body, to avoid monstrosity, finger must be joined directly, not to head but to hand; then hand to arm, arm to shoulder, shoulder to neck, neck to head . . . 'the [medieval] constituencies are organic and corporatively constructed limbs of an articulated People.'"[31]

Moreover, under royal absolutism, the spectacular figuration of power was tied ineluctably to the masculine subject of the monarch. All circuits of desire

Figure 2.4 Anonymous, *Grand Débandement de l'armée anti-constitutionelle*, c. 1792. Etching with hand coloring on blue paper. *Source*: Bibliothèque Nationale.

pointed in the direction of the king's body. Accordingly, visual representations of power dominated all other forms of communication.[32] In the elevated genres of history painting and royal portraiture, classicizing artists found their ideal subject matter. Indeed, engravings after painted portraits of the royal family circulated widely. They ran the gamut from those which were produced at a relatively low cost and were made available to a wide public for display in their homes to gilded and polychromed works aimed at a more prosperous, elite audience. But, following conventions congealed in the metaphor of the well articulated and sacred body politic, representations of royalty—indeed, all expressions of official high culture—took the form of a classical body. Radiant and transcendent, the classical body is what Mikhail Bakhtin terms a finished and completed body.[33] The dismemberment of the classical political body involved the transgressive symbolic practices of grotesque realism through which king's body was made to appear gargantuan in its physical appetites; cuckolded by a sexually avaricious and disloyal queen who also appeared as a harpy or a panther; parodied as a low form of barnyard of wild animal; and, at the extremes, where material reality and satire literally converged, disembodied.[34] In (Figure 2.5) *Matière à réflection pour les jongleurs couronnées/ qu'un sang impur abrueve nos sillons*, the artist Villeneuve's medusan image of the king's severed head dripping blood, raised up by a disarticulated hand, contemporaries witnessed the most horrible grotesque reversal of the king's

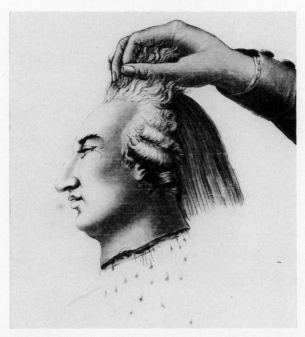

Figure 2.5 Villeneuve, *Matière à réflexion pour les jongleurs couronnés/qu'un sang impur abreuve nos sillons*, 1793. *Source*: Bibliothèque Nationale.

classical body. As Ronald Paulson argues persuasively, during the revolution "dismemberment itself became an obsessive notion."[35]

The dismemberment of the royal body was a long, involved process. Jean-Pierre Guicciardi, for instance, locates its origin in what might be referred to as the "sexual reign" of Louis XV; proposing that "The king's sex, that fabulous phallus, was one of the major instruments of *political* subversion in France toward the end of the ancien régime.[36] Certainly, the extensive political and sexual pornography in printed and visual matter directed at the aristocracy, the clergy, and above all, the royal family in the last years of the old regime and the early years of the revolution were a major factor in the symbolic process of political dismemberment.[37] In any event, Louis XVI's supposed impotence was a topic of general discussion, made worse by rumors of the queen's infidelities. A series of prints from the period of the royal family's flight and capture at Varennes in June 1791 are especially revealing.

In a bizarre representation of a paralyzed, two-headed monster (Figure 2.6), *Les Deux ne font qu'un*, the king wears the horns of a cuckold, the body of a ram, while the queen is caricatured as a hyena wearing a medusan headdress, snakes flying forth, punctuated by ostrich feathers, a pun on her Austrian heritage. Other etchings of the period depict the royal family as pigs en route to market, or, to slaughter. They all seem to echo Edmund Burke's haunting prophecy of 1790 that once "the decent drapery of life" is torn off, "A king is

Figure 2.6 Anonymous, *Les Deux ne font qu'un*, c. 1791. Etching with hand coloring on blue paper. *Source*: Library of Congress.

but a man; a queen is but a woman; a woman is but an animal; and an animal not of the highest order."[38]

The bestial is closely adjoined to the theme of sexuality, as in (Figure 2.7) *Enjambée de la Sainte famille des Thuilleries à Montmidy*. A grotesquely disproportionate queen, in a low-cut dress and ostrich plumes, uses her body to form a bridge from the Palace to Montmédy on the northeastern frontier. Looking particularly ridiculous and effete, the (diminished) king rides on the queen's back, whose infidelities and counterrevolutionary intentions are reinforced by the presence in the print of several notorious emigrés and personalities from the infamous Diamond Necklace Affair. The monarchy's demise is satirically attributed to the queen's enormous appetites, sexual and otherwise. In (Figure 2.8) *Bombardement de tous les trônes de l'Europe/et la chûte des tyrans pour le bonheur de l'univers* the king's mouth and anus serve as the grotesque openings for a marvelous scatological caricature. Three tiers of bare-bottomed deputies (literally sans-culottes) to the National Assembly are shown defecating "liberty" and the notorious revolutionary song, the "Ça ira,' on the crowned heads of Europe. Liberty stands on top of the deputies; igniting a cannon that fires into the posterior of Louis XVI; forcing him to vomit vetoes that rain on the crowned heads, the pope, and William Pitt, England's prime minister. A monstrous, bare-breasted Empress Catherine II rises above her fellow monarchs, trying to humiliate them into attacking France.

In contrast, what first appears to be a more benign representation of the king in 1792 (Figure 2.9), *Louis Seize, Roi des Français: Bonnet de la Liberté*, partakes as well of the transgressive dynamic of dismemberment whereby the

Figure 2.7 Anonymous, *Enjambée de la Sainte Famille des Thuilleries à Montmidy*, c. 1791. Etching with hand coloring. *Source*: Library of Congress.

categories of high and low are exchanged. By placing a red cap of liberty on a familiar image of the king based on a painted portrait of the period by the artist Joseph Boze just prior to July 1789, the print recasts the king's classical body. He reappears as simply another citizen of the French republic. After all, the king had first to be symbolically leveled before he could be beheaded.[39] This print also conveys the fact that by this point in the revolution the king has been made a captive of the people. Other representations of the king in a liberty cap show him toasting the nation—no longer even in control of his own speech—as he had been made to do by the Parisian crowd during their demonstration at the Tuilleries Palace in August 1792. By representing the king in republican costume, this anonymous artist violates all of the iconographical conventions of royal portraiture. And, in the gap opened up between representations of the once sacred father-king and the people's friend, there lies the possibility for further caricature and ridicule.

The political body of the king is a corporate body whose upper limbs are composed of the clergy and the aristocracy. Numerous scatological and pornographic prints of the period caricature the members of the two privileged orders as feeding on the nation, in dire need of an emetic; sexually promiscuous; in league with the devil. Animal-like noses bring the aristocracy and the clergy down from the ethereal, spiritual realm to the material order of the lower body. Reiterating grotesque themes already observed in anti-royalist imagery, the pornographic cartooning directed toward the privileged orders

Figure 2.8 Anonymous, *Bombardement de tous les Trônes de l 'Europe et la Chute des Tyrans pour le Bonheur de l 'Univers*, c. 1792. Etching with hand coloring. *Source*: Library of Congress.

further weakened the sexual and political potency of the Crown. Under these circumstances the king could no longer be the "erect member" of the body politic of France.[40] Not surprisingly, the literature of the bourgeois republican opposition under the late old regime and during the revolution was rife with gender-laden metaphors. Not only did powerless men feel themselves to be "unmanned" by the absolutist power of the monarchy; but, Louis XVI himself was said to be impotent and cuckolded. Moreover, the entire old regime was excoriated by its republican critics for encouraging women in their exercise of sexual and political power.[41]

A series of images show the sexualized body of the aristocracy as a female body. *Le Corps Aristocratique sous la figure d'une femme expirant dans les bras de la noblesse* (Figure 2.10) drives home the extent to which the revolutionaries were intent on excising the excessively feminized and feminizing dimension of the old body politic.[42] Although no direct reference is made to the monarch, the representation of the corporate body as a dying feminine body symbolizes the internment of the monarchy's patriarchal and sacred claims to absolute rule. This print also exploits one of the great themes of the revolution's ribald literature, that of health. As de Baecque points out: "its purpose is to contrast the healthy patriotic body and the diseased aristocratic body. It

Figure 2.9 Anonymous, after painting by Joseph Boze, *Louis Seize, Roi des Français: Bonnet de la Liberté*, 1792. Stipple engraving with hand coloring. *Source*: Metropolitan Museum of Art, The Elisha Whittelsey Collection, The Elisha Whittelsey Fund, 1962.

Figure 2.10 Anonymous, *Le Corps Aristocratique sous la figure d'une femme expirant dans les bras de la noblesse, etc.* Etching with hand coloring. *Source*: Library of Congress.

Figure 2.11 Louis Charles Ruotte, after Louis-Marie Sicardi, finished by Jacques-Louis Copis, *La Liberté Patronne des Français*, after Boizot, c. 1795. *Source*: S. P. Avery Collection, Miriam & Ira D. Wallach Division of Art, Prints, and Photographs, The New York Public Library, Astor, Lenox and Tilden Foundations.

gave rise to an explanation and justification of the 'political and moral rebirth' of the Revolution—a rebirth that would purify the sexual act and bring it under the purview of the new government."[43]

Finally, there is the topic of re-membering. In (Figure 2.11) *La Liberté Patronne des Français*, an allegory of Republic appears as the patroness of the French people. This is merely one of myriad images of Liberty, who became an important republican and national symbol during the nineteenth-century and down to the present day.[44] Attached to her tricolor sash, she wears a lion-headed sword, attesting symbolically to her triumph over superstition, despotism, and the monarchy. Syncretically combining Christian and republican symbols, this virginal figure wears the phrygian cap, yet is surrounded by an aureole. She is figured as young, innocent, and pure; precisely the kind of transparent, natural representation that a reading of Rousseau inclined the revolutionaries to adopt. Happily, the sinful female body, the corrupt aristocratic or royal whore, is made over into a virtuous (and virginal) republican body. As opposed to the sexually threatening images of the female aristocratic body, this feminine representation of the reinvented body politic seems almost to call out for the protection of virile republican men.

There is, however, something odd about a female figuration of the body politic in the context of a revolution that enfranchised men but not women.[45] Yet, as Marina Warner cautions, "Liberty is not represented as a woman . . . because women were or are free."[46] Lynn Hunt concurs, stating, "the proliferation of the female allegory was made possible, in fact, by the exclusion of women from public affairs. Women could be representative of abstract qualities and collective dreams because women were not about to vote or govern."[47]

Indeed, Liberty seems to satisfy the foremost requirement of the new symbolic system: To achieve an abstract, impersonal representation that carried none of the connotations of monarchical rule. In the old body politic, any and all representations of an individual king operated as a metonym for the corporate populace of the realm: Part stood for whole, precisely because a recognizeable individual who occupied society's premier role was in turn endowed with mystical qualities that allowed his person to substitute for the entire body politic. In contrast, the female representation of the nation works best because it effaces the identifiable features of any known female person. Because of her generality, Liberty stands as a metaphor—not a metonym—for the whole social community, free from any and all divisions.[48] Even before the revolution artists and writers depicted France, as well as justice, liberty, force, truth, and science as female allegories, but their aim was to personify abstract principles or virtues, not to depict real, living subjects.[49]

In her provocative recent study, Dorinda Outram argues persuasively for a strong link between the middle-class domination of political, social, and cultural space, on the one hand, and the expulsion of females (and lower-class traits and characteristics) from public life, on the other. Ironically the men of the late eighteenth-century body politic, like the kings before them, were expected to be absolutely sovereign—in absolute control of their bodies—in a physical and a political sense. A kind of redistribution of the divine body took place leading to an intensification of the interaction between public men and their audiences. The virtuous heroic man, *homo clausus*, was an individual who exhibited remorseless control over his body and his emotions. But, if male virtue required a certain stoical, public self-exhibition, women's virtue was tied to chastity and fidelity within marriage. "Virtue, far from being the linchpin of a monolithic 'discourse of the Revolution,' in fact bisected the apparently universalistic discourse of the general will into distinct destinies, one male and the other female. Both were part of *le souvereign*, but somehow one half of *le souvereign* could function only at the price of the sexual containment of the other."[50] In this light, we might want to view Liberty as a symbol of an entire public culture, but one that hides the extent to which the values of rationality, universality, autonomy, and emancipation were predicated upon a gendered division between public and private, male and female domains.

Moreover, the re-membered body is an internally contradictory thing, pointing forward and backward at the same time. Even as the revolutionaries sought an absolute rupture wiht the past, they suffered from what Mona Ozouf tellingly calls a "horror vacuii."[51] Their iconoclastic passion to purge all memories of the past, to empty out the sacred contents of everyday life, was accompanied by efforts to resacralize the present by way of a primitive model of Roman and Greek antiquity. Like all the female goddesses who graced the new republic, Liberty appears in antique dress.[52] She is an emblem of the revolutionaries' desire to bypass their own national history, to institute an ideal, nondespotic Republic, in which personal liberty and communal togetherness would be reconciled joyously. Like her sister goddesses, she is a tutelary figure: Her virtue is meant to serve as an example to all who would banish selfish private desire in order to serve the whole. For women, her discipline involves their socialization into a virtuous domestic routine. For men, Liberty teaches the virtue of civic action and universal sociability.

But on whose behalf? Even though there was a strong taboo against erecting any symbol that would revalue the patriarchal polity, it may be that Liberty's innocence and purity functioned to her benefit as a talisman: Not against masculine politics in itself but against the historically tainted form of the old body politic. For, ultimately, the re-membered body is another fatherland. Strikingly, Mona Ozouf confirms just this point in the conclusion to her pathbreaking study of festivals.

> Never shown, the invisible fatherland was nonetheless the focal point of the whole festival: the altar was the altar of the fatherland; the defenders were the defenders of the fatherland; the battalion of children was the hope of the fatherland; the duty of every citizen, as every speech hammered home, was to be worthy of the fatherland; and the injunction on all the banners was to live and die for the fatherland.[53]

The body of the nation, the re-membered body politic, is a deeply gendered construction; like its predecessor, it privileges the masculine. An invisible construction, says Ozouf. An absolute sovereign who possesses no human face, according to Rousseau. This sovereign hides behind universal law, universal reason, the nation. But, if Ozouf is right, and I believe she is, how are we to account for the paradoxical fact that the new body politic appears in the guise of a female goddess? The Republic even acquired a female name, Marianne.

Ozouf directs attention to the proliferation of speeches and banners (with texts), commentaries on the proper interpretation of images, and extensive written directions to festival participants and organizers. She writes of a transfer of sacrality from the old religion and state to such objects as the Declaration of Rights, the Constitution, patriotic anthems, civic sermons, and constitutional oaths. Above all, she proposes that visual allegories and, indeed, the entire spectacular realm of the festival were areas of concern for the pedagogically minded festival organizers. Ozouf points out, for example, a contradiction between the (masculine) forms that symbolized the festivals and the fact that they were populated by female figures. She cites one protester's anguished observation. "'Women everywhere, when what we need is a vigorous, severe regeneration!'" Ozouf also notices the suspicion the organizers held of the public: They doubted the people's ability to properly decode images, and they feared the emotional charge of images. Accordingly, she states, "The Revolutionary festival was certainly verbose . . . [It] said more than it showed."[54] The horror of exhibition and show was balanced by an utterly unqualified fascination with words. "The Revolutionary sensibility expected words to have an immediate contagious effect."[55]

I have sought to establish the logic by which the old iconic order of France was disestablished and reconstructed. I have charted the passage away from the masculine iconography of the absolutist body politic to a female representation of Republic. The visual order of (political) representation had indeed become feminine. Yet, as I have argued elsewhere, the revolution marks the point of a dramatic shift away from the iconic, visual order of representation of the absolutist public sphere to a new masculine, symbolic, discursive order of writing, the law, speech and its proclamation. The system of visual representation was not abandoned, nor was it entirely powerless and irrelevant; but it was certainly dethroned. In the new symbolic order wrought by the bourgeois revolution, the old hierarchy between icon and sign was reversed. As Ozouf's observations on the power of words within the revolutionary festival make clear, visual images by themselves were suspect; they were becoming textualized, made increasingly responsive to legal forms of public discourse.[56] The existence of a female representation within the new masculinist order of representation is paradoxical, then, only at the level of visual/aural perception and action. Whereas the place of women is preserved in the visual realm, re-membering does not occur strictly at that level. Marianne is *nothing but a picture.* She neither reflects nor authorizes the public actions of actually existing women in postrevolutionary society. Nor is she the only expression of nationhood. At a higher level of abstraction in the newly dominant symbolic order of representation, the invisible fatherland need not be and ought not be pictured. It is spoken and written. The nation's body is a discursive body.

Intellectually, the way for this change in the order of political representation away from an anthropomorphic representation was prepared by Hobbes and Rousseau. The relationship between a nation and its citizens exists on a higher level of abstraction than that between the monarch and his subjects. Even though Hobbes authorized an anthropomorphic image for the frontispiece of his book, he gave a rational not a mystical version of the body politic wherein subjects are cells not functional members of an organic body. In truth, too, the Leviathan is not a person but a symbolic construct: The residual outcome of a series of verbal contracts entered into by each of the nation's subjects. Rousseau confirmed Hobbes's break with sensuous representations. His sovereign bears no human face. The law is not pictured, but written.

The re-membered body politic is not, then, a simple, one-dimensional construction. In the more differentiated and hierarchical modern order of representation, the lower functions of sensuous, concrete, visual perception are accorded an inferior status to the higher, more abstract, symbolic functions of logic, mathematics, symbolic reasoning, writing/authoring.[57] In the new age of reason, the rational mind was to become a wholly male preserve and the public sphere a realm of male discourse. In the real world of postrevolutionary Europe, women were judged to be chatterboxes and gossips, not serious, purposeful, rational thinkers. The new symbolic head of the republican body politic, not a king's head, belongs to the realm of the higher functions. Insofar as this head rules through a feminized body, it is a body of a very particular kind: Liberty, it will be recalled, was not figured as a mother, but as a virginal, chaste daughter; a sister to other goddesses and sometimes to Hercules, the masculine representation of popular strength. She has a decidedly emotive force, but one purged of all unruliness and sexuality. She cohabits an imagined community with an abstraction called the nation or the people, whose power flows directly from words.

Notes

1. See the Convention's decree in Marie-Hélène Huet, *Rehearsing the Revolution: The Staging of Marat's Death, 1793–1797*, trans. Robert Hurley (Berkeley: University of California Press, 1982), 6. Cf. Albert Soboul, *Le procès de Louis XVI* (Paris: Collection Archives Juillard, 1966); Carol Blum, *Rousseau and the Republic of Virtue: The Language of Politics in the French Revolution* (Ithaca: Cornell University Press, 1986), 169–81; David P. Jordan, *The King's Trial: Louis XVI vs. the French Revolution* (Berkeley: University of California Press, 1979); *Regicide and Revolution: Speeches at the Trial of Louis XVI*, ed. and intro. by Michael Walzer, trans. Marian Rothstein (London: Cambridge University Press, 1974).

2. Jean-Jacques Rousseau, *On the Social Contract; with Geneva Manuscript and Political Economy*, ed. Roger D. Masters, trans. Judith R. Masters (New York: St. Martin's Press, 1978), 59, 63; *Oeuvres complètes*, vol. 3, eds. Bernard Gagnebin and Marcel Raymond (Paris: Gallimard, 1964), 369, 375.

3. Ernst Kantorowicz, *The King's Two Bodies: A Study in Medieval Political Theology* (Princeton: Princeton University Press, 1957).

4. Not surprisingly, many have noticed that these actions ushered in a profound genealogical crisis. In the space opened up by the death of the king, who would be his heirs? See Lynn Hunt, *Politics, Culture and Class in the French Revolution* (Berkeley: University of California Press, 1984).

5. Rousseau, *The Social Contract*, 62; *Oeuvres complètes*, 3:372.

6. See Ronald Paulson, *Representations of Revolution (1789–1820)* (New Haven: Yale University Press, 1983); and Norman O. Brown, *Love's Body* (New York: Vintage, 1966).

7. Cited in Brown, *Love's Body*, 114.

8. As Keith Michael Baker remarks in his excellent review, "It is one of the paradoxes of the French Revolution that the revolutionaries, in repudiating the old order they saw as the feudal regime, and embracing the principle of popular sovereignty inherent in the concept of the general will, nevertheless fell back upon the practice of representation so explicitly condemned by Rousseau." "Representation" in *The Political Culture of the Old Regime*, ed. Keith Michael Baker (Oxford: Pergamon Press, 1987), 469.

9. Rousseau, *The Social Contract*, 103; Rousseau, *Oeuvres complètes*, 3:431. "Sovereignty cannot be represented for the same reason it cannot be alienated. It

consists essentially in the general will, and the will cannot be represented. Either it is itself or it is something else; there is no middle ground. The deputies of the people, therefore, are not nor can they be its representatives; they are merely its agents. . . . The idea of representatives is modern. We get it from feudal government, that wicked and absurd government in which the human species is degraded and the name of man is dishonored. In the ancient republics and even in monarchies, the people never had representatives. The word itself was unknown." *The Social Contract*, 102; *Oeuvres complètes*, 3:429–30.

10. See François Furet, *Interpreting the French Revolution*, trans. Elborg Forster (Cambridge: Cambridge University Press, 1981); Regine Robin, *La Société française en 1789: Sèmur-en-Auxois* (Paris, 1970); *The Political Culture of the Old Regime; The Political Culture of the French Revolution*, ed. Colin Lucas (Oxford: Pergamon Press, 1988). Lynn Hunt is an exception in that she looks at visual as well as verbal symbols. See Hunt, *Politics, Culture, and Class*, and "Hercules and the Radical Image in the French Revolution," *Representations* 1, no. 2 (Spring 1983):95–117. One finds much the same discursive emphasis in the writings of political theorists J. G. A. Pocock, Quentin Skinner, H. Mark Roelofs, John Brigham, Michael Shapiro, William Connolly, and Murray Edelman.

11. See especially Emmett Kennedy, *A Cultural History of the French Revolution* (New Haven: Yale University Press, 1989); Maurice Agulhon, *Marianne into Battle: Republican Imagery and Symbolism in France 1789–1880*, trans. Janet Lloyd (Cambridge: Cambridge University Press, 1981); Hunt, *Politics, Culture and Class*; Hunt, "Engraving the Revolution: Prints and Propaganda in the French Revolution," *History Today* 30 (1980):11–17; Michel Vovelle, *La Révolution Française: Images et récit*, 5 vols. (Paris: Editions Messidor, Livre Club Diderot, 1986); *La Révolution Française—Le Premier Empire* (Paris: Musée Carnavalet, 1982); *Premieres Collections* (Vizille: Musée de la Révolution Française, 1985); Robert Darnton and Daniel Roche, eds., *Revolution in Print: The Press in France 1775–1800* (Berkeley: University of California Press, in collaboration with the New York Public Library, 1989); Antoine de Baecque, *La Caricature Revolutionnaire* and Claude Langlois, *La Caricature Contre-Revolutionnaire* (Paris: Presses du CNRS, 1988); *French Caricature and the French Revolution, 1789–1799* (Grunwald Center for the Graphic Arts, Wight Art Gallery, University of California, Los Angeles, 1988); Joan B. Landes and Sura Levine, eds., *Representing Revolution: French and British Images, 1789–1804* (Amherst, Mass.: Mead Art Museum, Amherst College, 1989).

12. At the inaugural meeting of the National Convention on September 21, 1792, delegates demanded the conscious extirpation of all images of royalty. Defying the iconic conventions of royalist patriarchalism, they adopted a female allegorical figure for the seal of the first French Republic. Yet, on Jacques-Louis David's recommendation, in 1793 the radical Convention voted to substitute Hercules for Liberty on the seal of the Republic. Even during the revolution, then, there was no stable solution to the problem of representation, only a continuing struggle over its appropriate content and form. Hercules himself was supplanted by female representations of Liberty and Republic. See Hunt, "Hercules and the Radical Image in the French Revolution."

13. On the theatrical dimension of Hobbes's political theory, see Christopher Pye, "The Sovereign, the Theater, and the Kingdoms of Darknesse: Hobbes and the Spectacle of Power," in *Representing the English Renaissance*, ed. Stephen Greenblatt (Berkeley: University of California Press, 1988), 279–302; Brown, *Love's Body*; Hanna Fenichel Pitkin, *The Concept of Representation* (Berkeley: University of California Press, 1972); Bryan Turner, *The Body and Society* (Oxford and New York: Basil Blackwell,

1984). For a seminal discussion of the overlap between bodily metaphors and mechanical imagery in the political thought of Hobbes, Rousseau, and other early modern thinkers, see Otto Mayr, *Authority, Liberty and Automatic Machinery in Early Modern Europe* (Baltimore: The Johns Hopkins University Press, 1986).

14. Thomas Hobbes, *Leviathan*, ed. C. B. Macpherson (Harmondsworth, England: Penguin Books, 1968), 220.

15. Louis Adrian Montrose observes that in her discourse Elizabeth "dwelt upon the womanly frailty of her body natural and the masculine strength of her body politic." "'Shaping Fantasies': Figurations of Gender and Power in Elizabethan Culture," *Representations* 1, no. 2 (Spring 1983):77.

16. Rousseau, *The Social Contract*, 52; *Oeuvres complètes*, 3:361. Rousseau also admonishes his readers: "Whoever refuses to obey the general will shall be forced to do so by the entire body; which means only that he will be forced to be free." (*Social Contract*, 55). Furthermore, "the general will is always right, but the judgment that guides it is not always enlightened. . . . Private individuals see the good they reject; the public wants the good it does not see. All are equally in need of guides. The former must be obligated to make their wills conform to their reason. The latter must be taught to know what it wants. Then public enlightenment results in the union of understanding and will in the social body; hence the complete cooperation of the parts, and finally the greatest force of the whole. From this arises the necessity for a legislator." *Social Contract*, 55, 67; *Oeuvres complètes*, 3:364, 380.

17. Brown, *Love's Body*, 104–5. On the topic of revolution and theater, see Huet, *Rehearsing the Revolution*; Mona Ozouf, *Festivals and the French Revolution*, trans. Alan Sheridan (Cambridge, Mass.: Harvard University Press, 1988); and Frederick Brown, *Theater and Revolution: The Culture of the French Stage* (New York: Viking Press, 1980).

18. On this subject, see Ozouf, *Festivals*; Marie-Hélène Huet, "Le Sacre du Printemps: Essai sur le sublime et la Terreur," *MLN* 103, no. 4 (September 1988):782–99; Baker, "Representation."

19. Rolf Reichardt, "Prints: Images of the Bastille," in Darnton and Roche, *Revolution in Print*, 223–49, quote on 224. Cf. de Baecque, *Caricature Revolutionnaire*; and Langlois, *Caricature Contre-Revolutionnaire*.

20. In fact, as Antoine de Baecque observes, the print combines allegory, popular imagery (of the world-turned-upside-down), and realism, *Caricature Revolutionnaire*, 148.

21. Emmanuel-Joseph Sieyès, "What is the Third Estate?," trans. M. Blondel, in *The Old Regime and the French Revolution*, ed. Keith Michael Baker (Chicago and London: The University of Chicago Press, 1987), 154–79, quotes on 157, 156.

22. Burke described the return from Versailles in the following provocative manner: "heads were stuck upon spears, and led the procession; whilst the royal captives who followed in the train were slowly moved along, amidst the horrid yells, and shrilling screams, and frantic dances, and infamous contumelies, and all the unutterable abominations of the furies of hell, in the abused shape of the vilest of women." Edmund Burke, *Reflections on the Revolution in France* (Garden City, N.Y.: Doubleday, 1961), 85.

23. In the literature and visual imagery of the day, the market women are routinely referred to as heroines and "modern Amazons." For example, compare the text of another print *Journée Memorable de Versailles le lundi 5 Octobre 1789*, which reads "Nos modernes Amazones glorieuses de leurs Victoire revinrent à Cheval sur les Canons avec plusieurs Messieurs de la Garde Nationale, tenant des branches de Peupliers au

bruit des cris réiterés de Vive la Nation, Vive le Roi." François-Louis Bruel, *Collection de Vinck: Inventaire analytique*, vol. 2, no. 2999 (Paris: Imprimerie Nationale, 1914).

24. See Langlois, "Counterrevolutionary iconography," in *French Caricature*, 41–54, and "La fille à Target" in *Caricature Contre-Revolutionnaire*, 65–69. Vivian Cameron provided an excellent account of royalist caricatures of Targinette in "Reading the Constitution: Contradictory Images in the French Revolution," paper presented at The American Society for Eighteenth-Century Studies Twentieth Annual Meeting, New Orleans, March 29–April 2, 1989.

25. Carole Pateman, *The Sexual Contract* (Stanford: Stanford University Press, 1988), 102, 88. On this issue within republican theory, see Hanna Fenichel Pitkin, *Fortune is a Woman: Gender and Politics in the Thought of Niccolò Machiavelli* (Berkeley: University of California Press, 1984); and more generally, Mary O'Brien, *The Politics of Reproduction* (Boston: Routledge and Kegan Paul, 1981).

26. Lynn Hunt, "The Many Bodies of Marie Antoinette," lecture delivered at Hampshire College, Amherst, Mass., September 26, 1988.

27. Langlois, *Caricature Contre-Revolutionnaire*, 69. For a recent, generally unsympathetic discussion of Théroigne de Mericourt's participation in the revolution, see Simon Schama, *Citizens: A Chronicle of the French Revolution* (New York: Alfred A. Knopf, 1989), esp. 873–75.

28. *French Caricature*, 213.

29. Ronald Paulson observes: "In the model of the Body Politic the king is the 'head' of state, and so it is appropriate, indeed necessary, that his removal should be accomplished by decapitation." "The Severed Head: The Impact of French Revolutionary Caricatures on England," in *French Caricature*, 58. Or, as Danton stated at the time: "Kings are struck only at the head." Cited in Huet, *Rehearsing the Revolution*, 5.

30. In early modern Europe, as Bryan Turner (following R. H. Tawney, *Religion and the Rise of Capitalism*, 1938) accurately observes, "the teleological purposiveness of the body was employed to legitimate political and social divisions in society. 'Society, like the human body, is an organism composed of different members. Each member has its own function, prayer, or defence, or merchandise, or tilling the soil. Each must receive the means suited to its station, and must claim no more.'" Turner, *The Body and Society*, 177.

31. Ibid., 138. Cf. Otto Gierke, *Political Theories of the Middle Ages*, trans. Frederic William Maitland (Boston: Beacon Press, 1958), 66.

32. For a more detailed discussion of this point, see my *Women and the Public Sphere in the Age of the French Revolution* (Ithaca: Cornell University Press, 1988); Louis Marin, *Portrait of the King*, trans. Martha M. House (Minneapolis: University of Minnesota Press, 1988); idem, "The King's Body" in *Food for Thought*, trans. Mette Hjort (Baltimore: The Johns Hopkins University Press, 1989), 189–241.

33. See Mikhail Bakhtin's magisterial study, *Rabelais and His World*, trans. Hélène Iswolsky (Cambridge: The MIT Press, 1968). Cf. Peter Stallybrass and Allon White, *The Politics and Poetics of Transgression* (Ithaca: Cornell University Press, 1986); Barbara Babcock, ed., *The Reversible World: Symbolic Inversions in Art and Society* (Ithaca: Cornell University Press, 1978).

34. See, for example, catalogue section, "The Royal Family," in *French Caricature*, pp. 178–98.

35. Ronald Paulson, "The Severed Head: The Impact of French Revolutionary Caricatures on England," in *French Caricature*, 55–56, quote on 59. For an essential, related account, see Neil Hertz, "Medusa's Head: Male Hysteria under Political Pressure," *Representations* 4 (Fall 1983):27–54. On the scatological side of grotesque revolutionary

imagery, see Albert Boime, "Jacques-Louis David, Scatological Discourse in the French Revolution, and the Art of Caricature," in *French Caricature*, 67–82.

36. Jean-Pierre Guicciardi, "Between the Licit and the Illicit: The Sexuality of the King," trans. Michael Murray, in *'Tis Nature's Fault: Unauthorized Sexuality during the Enlightenment*, ed. Robert Parks Maccubbin (Cambridge: Cambridge University Press, 1985), 88–97, quote on 96.

37. See James Cuno, "Introduction," esp. figures 3 to 6, in *French Caricature*, 13–22; Robert Darnton, *The Literary Underground of the Old Regime* (Cambridge: Harvard University Press, 1982); and Hunt, "The Many Bodies of Marie Antoinette."

38. Burke, *Reflections on the Revolution in France*, 90.

39. As Hunt remarks, "Representations of the king wearing the cap of liberty and drinking to the health of the nation showed that he was no longer a distant, regal figure. He was now more familiar, more accessible, more like a good bourgeois and much less like a father." "The Political Psychology of Revolutionary Caricatures," in *French Caricature*, 33–40.

40. Norman O. Brown comments on the link between the sexual and the political "A king is erected, *rex erectus est*. A king is an erection of the body politic." Brown, *Love's Body*, 133.

41. On this theme, see my *Women and the Public Sphere*.

42. On the other hand, royalists and counterrevolutionaries were not loathe to borrow republican themes when it came to exploiting issues of gender as we saw in (figure 2-4) *Grand Débandement de l'armée anti-constitutionelle*. In a particularly mordant series of satirical prints, Targinette (an allegory of the Constitution) is portrayed as dying. Indeed, Langlois prefaces his discussion of the dying Targinette with a reproduction of the print *Le Corps Aristocrate sous la figure d'une femme . . .* , see *Caricature Contre-Revolutionnaire*, 96–100.

43. Antoine de Baecque, "Pamphlets: Libel and Political Mythology," in Darnton and Roche, *Revolution in Print*, 173. On anti-aristocratic discourse, see Patrice Higonnet, "'Aristocrate,' 'Aristocratie': Language and Politics in the French Revolution," in *The French Revolution, 1789–1989: Two Hundred Years of Rethinking*, ed. Sandy Petrey, a special issue of *The Eighteenth Century: Theory and Interpretation* (Lubbock: Texas Tech University Press, 1989), 47–66.

44. Witness the centennial celebration of the Statue of Liberty, gift of France to the American nation; as well as the press discussions of the gigantic "Liberty" statue erected by Chinese students at Tiananmen Square, Beijing. In France, Chanel model Ines de la Fressange, descendant of an old aristocratic family, has been elected by the Mayors of France to be the new Marianne. She succeeds Brigitte Bardot, who held the honor in the 1970s, and Catherine Deneuve, in the 1980s.

45. My purpose here is not to attempt a full account of how the exclusion of women from the public sphere is related to the representation of Republic as a woman. On this topic, see my *Women and the Public Sphere*, esp. chaps. 4–5; and Geneviève Fraisse, *Muse de la raison: La démocratie exclusive et la différence des sexes* (Aix-en-Provence: Alinéa, 1989). On the symbolic representation of Liberty, her different postures, and some of the reasons inclining the French to choose a female representation of Republic, see Agulhon, *Marianne into Battle*; Lynn Hunt, *Politics, Culture and Class*; Marina Warner, *Monuments and Maidens: The Allegory of the Female Form* (New York: Atheneum, 1985); and, Stéphane Michaud, *Muse et madone: Visages de la femme de la Révolution française aux apparitions de Lourdes* (Paris: Seuil, 1985). Finally, Madelyn Gutwirth has wrestled with the important issue of allegorical female representations in her "The Rights and Wrongs of Women: The Defeat of Feminist Rhetoric by Revolu-

tionary Allegory," paper presented at The Revolutionary Moment: A Bicentennial Conference on Representations of the French Revolution in Literature, Art, and Historiography, Dartmouth College, Hanover, New Hampshire, July 13–15, 1989.

46. Warner, *Monuments and Maidens*, xix–xx.

47. Hunt, "Political Psychology," in *French Caricature*, 39.

48. I am grateful to Eva Feder Kittay for helping me to clarify this point. For a wide-ranging discussion of this issue, see her "Woman as Metaphor," *Hypatia* 3, no. 2 (Summer 1988):63–85.

49. Nevertheless, old regime artists sometimes did depict their female subjects as muses, and aristocrats amused themselves by play-acting at being gods and goddesses. But, the purpose of all this artifice was to mimetically enhance the character of the subject of representation. Moreover, these artists and performers addressed a privileged audience of initiates who pleasured in distinguishing the known model from the artful imitation.

50. Dorinda Outram, *The Body and the French Revolution: Sex, Class and Political Culture* (New Haven: Yale University Press, 1989), 126; cf. 175–84.

51. See Mona Ozouf, *Festivals*, 267 and 262–82.

52. Of course, the revolutionaries did not invent the allegorical tradition to which Liberty belongs. Still, as I am arguing they made particular use of Liberty as a symbol of their break with the monarchical past. Marina Warner observes that there are two outstanding rationales offered for the strong link between allegory and the female form: (1) linguistic gender—in the Romance languages, absolute concepts are for the most part feminine; (2) classical myth allotted considerable importance to goddesses, personifications of various virtues. *Monuments and Maidens*, 87 and passim. On the Renaissance tradition, see Cesare Ripa, *Iconologue*, trans. Jean Baudoin (New York: Garland Press, 1976); and the discussion by E. H. Gombrich, "Icones Symbolicae: Philosophies of Symbolism and their Bearing on Art," in *Symbolic Images: Studies in the Art of the Renaissance* (London: Phaidon, 1972).

53. Ibid., 280.

54. Ozouf, *Festivals*, 212–13.

55. Ibid., 214.

56. On the impact of legal discourse and the print media on public opinion prior to and during the revolution, see Sarah Maza, "Le Tribunal de la Nation: Les Mémoires Judiciares et l'Opinion Publique A La Fin De L'ancien Régime," *Annales ESC*, no. 1 (January–February 1987):73–90. Maza also addresses the paradox of a female allegory for the (postrevolutionary) public world of men in her extremely valuable study, "The Rose-Girl of Salency: Representations of Virtue in Prerevolutionary France," *Eighteenth-Century Studies* 22, no. 3 (Spring 1989):395–412.

57. As in so many other matters, G. W. F. Hegel offers a stunning philosophical condensation of the principle of a gendered, differentiated Mind. See my "Hegel's Conception of the Family" in *The Family in Political Thought*, ed. Jean Bethke Elshtain (Amherst: University of Massachusetts Press, 1981). For two important perspectives on the late eighteenth- and nineteenth-century science of the female, see Thomas Laqeur, "Orgasm, Generation, and the Politics of Reproductive Biology," *Representations* 14 (Spring 1986):1–41; and Londa Schiebinger, *The Mind Has No Sex? Women in the Origins of Modern Science* (Cambridge: Harvard University Press, 1989).

3

"Love and Patriotism": Gender and Politics in the Life and Work of Louvet de Couvrai

KATHRYN NORBERG

I was at Nemours near my dear Lodoiska, when the astonishing news made its way to us. They said the Bastille had fallen, but this victory had cost over 100,000 men to the patriots. At that very moment, I put on the tricolor cockade which had been won at such a bloody price. How can I paint the emotional transports with which this cockade was given me and with which I adopted it? I was at the knees of my tender friend [amie]. With my tears I drenched her hands which I then placed upon my furiously beating heart! It was a mixture of patriotism and love which is difficult to describe.

Louvet de Couvrai
Mémoires sur la révolution français[1]

"Love and patriotism"—the "mixture" invoked in this passage might at first seem strange. Historians of the Revolution of 1789 have long been prisoners of the distinction between private and public, a distinction largely created by the revolution itself. They have been wont to ignore the "private" (that which pertains to women and sexuality) in favor of the "public" (that which deals with factional struggle). This division obscures more than it reveals. Gender and politics, we now know, are inextricably entwined and their relationship at times of political upheaval, like the French Revolution, is particularly problematic.[2] When, to paraphrase Carole Pateman, the "social contract" is renegotiated, then inevitably the "sexual contract" will be redefined and restructured, too.[3] A few historians—among them Darline Levy, Harriet Applewhite, Mary Johnson, Sara Maza, Joan B. Landes, Dorinda Outram, Ludmilla Jordanova, and Lynn Hunt—have begun to construct a "gendered" history of political thought and action during the revolution.[4] My purpose in this paper is to participate in this collective endeavor and to outline how notions about gender and sexuality, that is, about women, formed a part of the new political arrangement that we now call the Revolution of 1789.

I hope therefore to bring together "love and patriotism," again with the help of the gentleman whose amorous and patriotic transports I just cited—

Jean-Baptiste Louvet de Couvrai. The name is probably not familiar; Louvet has received little attention from literary critics and less from historians. To the latter, he is the author of a set of memoirs that shed light upon the fate of the Girondin deputies after their proscription by Robespierre and the Mountain. Because of his connections with the ill-fated Girondins, Louvet occupies a couple of lines or a footnote in most histories of the Terror.[5] For literary critics, Louvet is author of the bestseller of 1787, *Une année de la vie du chevalier de Faublas*, and its sequels *Six semaines de la vie du chevalier de Faublas*, (1788) and *La fin des amours du chevalier de Faublas* (1789). In 1789, Louvet was among the most popular authors of his day, but literary analyses, even those dealing with licentious and libertine novels, accord him scarce space.[6]

Given the obscurity to which history has condemned him, Louvet might seem an odd choice, but it is his tendency to mix love and politics, fiction and political action, that make him interesting to students of the connection between gender and politics. Unlike other political personalities of his day, Louvet wrote fiction—and a great deal of it—that deals specifically with women and their relationship to civil society. Thanks to his novels, we know more about Louvet's feelings concerning sexuality and women than we do about almost any other political figure of the period, with the exception of Mirabeau.[7] Moreover, his novels were widely read and extremely popular: *Une année de la vie du chevalier de Faublas* went through at least six French editions and more in German and English. Although we have scarce indication of just how the men and women of 1787 read *Une année de la vie du chevalier de Faublas*, it is likely they found sentiments in the text that if not mirroring their own, at least were not overtly contradicting them.

Louvet occupied not only the literary mainstream, but also the political center. Unlike other authors, such as Laclos, the chevalier de Nerciat, or de Sade, he engaged in political action, and far from viewing the political scene from the wings as an exile or prisoner, he occupied the center of the stage as a pamphleteer, Jacobin official, and finally, elected deputy.[8] Thanks to his memoirs and political pamphlets, we can identify Louvet's politics—fervently republican and vehemently anti-Robespierrists—and situate them vis-à-vis other currents (royalist, reactionary) of the day. Thanks to his political writings, we can also see just how gender and politics mixed in the "real" struggles of the revolution. I do not claim for Louvet any exceptional insight or any literary genius; nor do I view him as absolutely typical or representative of the period. I would argue that he *is* neither marginal nor aberrant and, therefore, provides insight into republican, liberal politics, which emerged during the French Revolution. I would also defend him as a subject for analysis because the role of gender is particularly clear and its relationship to politics (or as he would say "patriotism") particularly salient in his writing.

My procedure will be to scrutinize Louvet's work, both fiction and nonfiction, and outline his notions about politics, women's public role, sexuality (male and female, aristocratic and republican), marriage and patriarchy. Louvet's novels, principally the Faublas series, will provide most of the material, but I will also rely upon his memoirs. I see no reason to distinguish between Louvet's novels and his political pamphlets, between fact and fiction. Both constitute texts; both reflect Louvet's values and beliefs. Eighteenth-century readers did not make such clear distinctions and preferred to muddle the "real life" of authors and pure fiction.[9] Louvet was not an exception: When he first appeared at the tribune of the Legislative Assembly, many were disappointed, Madame Roland reports, that he was not a youth, not Faublas, the hero of his novels.[10] Louvet himself contributed to or at least suffered from this confusion. He called his second wife "Lodoiska," after a character in *Une année de la vie du chevalier de Faublas*, and when curiosity seekers visited his book shop in the quiet years after Thermidor, he introduced Madame Louvet as Lodoiska and claimed that she *was* the heroine of his novel.[11]

Because Louvet has always occupied such a small place in the history of the revolution, a few words about his life are probably in order.[12] He was born in Paris on June 12, 1760, in the rue St. Denis, the son of a papermaker. While still an adolescent, he fell in love but his sweetheart's father forced her to marry a wealthy jeweler of the Palais-Royal. Louvet would be a lifelong opponent of arranged marriage and a fervent supporter of divorce. Louvet then spent sometime in Strasbourg as the secretary to the famous mineralogist, de Dietrich. Thereafter he returned to Paris where he found employment at the Prault library as a clerk with special responsibility for licentious books. A steady diet of such works led in 1787 to the publication of *Une année de la vie du chevalier Faublas*. In this novel of a sentimental education, the twenty-year-old Faublas comes to Paris and encounters Madame de B*** an "older" (twenty-six-year-old) woman who initiates him into love and the "world." At the same time, Faublas meets the love of his life, the innocent Sophie, whose father is a Polish nobleman fleeing the political turmoil in his homeland. Just why this mixture of Rousseauist sentiment, libertine sexuality, and republican politics had such appeal is not clear, but a number of editions quickly appeared in England, Germany, and America, as well as France. Two years later, Louvet wrote a sequel, *Six semaines dans la vie du chevalier de Faublas*, and in 1788 yet another addition, *La fin des amours du chevalier de Faublas*.[13] In these works, Faublas continues his quest for Sophie just as he continues to wrestle with his own inability to forsake the charming but devious Madame de B***. A new character, a sixteen-year-old countess, also attracts Faublas's affections and further embroils him in rivalry with a host of wronged husbands. Finally, after numerous close calls, Louvet and Madame de B*** are discovered *in flagrante* by her husband and she is murdered. The countess also meets a sad end, throwing herself into the Seine when she learns that Faublas still loves Sophie. Faublas then goes mad but is finally "saved" by Sophie and settles down to domestic bliss in Poland, her homeland.

Louvet was in the midst of writing *La fin des amours* when the revolution broke out. He had taken refuge in Nemours with the woman whom he refers to as Lodoiska and whom he would eventually marry after the legalization of divorce. Louvet first emerged as a political figure in October of 1790 when he wrote a pamphlet ("Paris justifié") defending the actions of the Parisian mob in the march on Paris.[14] In 1791, Louvet published *Emilie de Varmont ou le divorce nécessaire*, an epistolary novel, which tells the story of a young woman driven into a loveless marriage by her greedy and debauched brother. A series of misadventures lead Emilie to seek refuge with a country priest, the curé Sévin, who resents the vows that keep him from marrying. The brother tries unsuccessfully to murder Emilie, she falls in love with her best friend's brother, and the priest falls in love with her. At the close of the novel, none of these relationships is resolved though an afterward announces a sequel once divorce is legalized and priestly vows abolished.[15]

The promised sequel never appeared though *Emilie* was quite successful, for Louvet, to use his own words, now "mounted the political stage."[16] He became active in the Parisian section of the Lombards and on December 25, 1791, spoke for the first time before the Legislative Assembly. Thereafter, he became tied to the party of the Rolands, Pétion and Brissot, the so-called Girondin faction of the Jacobin club. In 1791, he was appointed to the club's corresponding committee and met his archrival Robespierre. At the same time, Louvet used his Girondin connections to launch a journalistic career as the publisher and author of *La Sentinelle*, a newspaper-poster (*affiches*) that served as a vehicle for his intensely republican and anti-Robespierrist feelings. In September 1792, Louvet was elected deputy from the department of the Loiret and took a seat in the National Convention. There he distinguished himself by opposing the execution of the king (he insisted on a national plebiscite) and by publishing two bitter pamphlets accusing Robespierre of tyranny.[17]

With the expulsion of the Girondine in 1793, Louvet fled from Paris to Normandy where, along with his fellow Girondins, he tried to foment a rebellion. When this plan failed, he fled again to the Jura, where he hid with his beloved Lodoiska, writing his memoirs and biding his time, until the fall of Robespierre. In the period after Thermidor, Louvet returned to Paris with Lodoiska to open a bookshop in the Palais Royal. The decree of 18 Ventose Year III (March 8, 1795), which allowed the Girondin deputies to resume their seats in the Convention, brought Louvet back to the political arena. He forcefully argued for the rehabilitation of the Girondin deputies and against the growing spirit of reaction and royalism. In the years after Thermidor he represented, in the words of Alphonse Aulard, "the thermidorean spirit, not in its royalist guise, not in its hypocrisy (*tartufferie*) but in what was most honorable," and most republican.[18] Indeed, in the midst of reaction, Louvet remained a staunch defender of the republic and the Parisian masses. In 1797, he was elected to the Conseil des Cinq-Cents and appointed to the Institut. Despite his new stature as a statesman, he was still the target of attacks and harassment. On the 8 Fructidor Year V (August 25, 1797), a crowd made up of the Parisian *jeunesse doré* gathered outside his shop and hurled insults at Louvet and his beloved Lodoiska. Louvet responded by condemning the crowd as "vile slaves," but the shock was too much and he died the same day. Lodoiska tried to commit suicide but failed.

Throughout his career, Louvet's politics remained consistent. He abhorred royalism (his vote on the king's death penalty notwithstanding) and believed fervently in the sovereignty of the people. He supported the direct action of the Parisian masses but condemned the tyranny of its self-appointed representatives, Marat and Robespierre. Even after Thermidor, Louvet remained a republican and used that adjective frequently when describing his life and values. His novels, even the Faublas series written before 1789, reflect many of the values celebrated after 1789. As Louvet himself argued in 1793, "As for these little books, I hope that any impartial men will do me the justice of admitting that in the midst of many frivolities, one finds here serious passages where the author shows a great love of philosophy and especially the principles of republicanism which at the time I wrote them were still very rare."[19]

As for his "great love of philosophy," there is no doubt that Louvet displayed a deep affinity with the works of the philosophes, most particularly Rousseau. He advocated free thinking, though he was personally a Deist, and asserts approvingly in a humorous passage of *Six semaines* that a valet who reads the *Discourse on the Origins of Inequality* will "corrupt his comrades and steal from his master."[20] Louvet also shares Rousseau's disdain for the "artificial," "unnatural" world of the Parisian aristocracy. In all his novels, Louvet portrays the aristocrats who people Faublas's world as artificial, frivolous, devious, and downright predatory. After 1789, the anti-aristocratic theme becomes more pronounced. In *Emilie de Varmont*, written in 1791, Emilie's brother, Varmont, is the ultimate aristocrat, obsessed with his pedigree, and openly disdainful of "those of lower station." At the same time, he is Louvet's most sinister creation, for he hides his evil under a veneer of charm and secretly works against his sister, having recourse to sabotage and finally ambush. Like the "aristocratic plot" that Louvet and his fellow revolutionaries never tired of denouncing, Varmont is superficially harmless, but secretly "monstrous" (*dénaturé*) and deceitful.

Only after 1789 did Louvet engage in such a clear critique of the aristocracy, but his position vis-à-vis king and court was clear from the first pages of *Une année de la vie du chevalier de Faublas*. The court, he says, is debauched, a bordello where favors of all sorts are traded for political preferment.[21] Kings receive no better treatment. In *Une année*, Louvet describes the Polish monarch as no better than a traitor and a rogue. He praises Pulaski, who proposes to do nothing less than "seek change in the constitution of this state."[22] And he has Lovinsky kidnap the king and deprive him of his throne! Such treatment of royalty in 1787 could only be described as bold; hence it is not surprising that Louvet had some trouble with the censors.[23]

If Louvet criticizes the political and social arrangements of his day, he also holds out an alternative, albeit a rather vague, romantic one. Sophie, the distant heroine of the Faublas stories, represents the alternative, ideal realm of Nature, simplicity and transparency.[24] But Sophie is one of the tale's least defined characters: she spends the whole Faublas series either imprisoned in a convent or confined by her father. Closer, I think, to Louvet's notion of an earthly paradise is the Poland of *Une année de la vie du chevalier de Faublas*. Here the domestic virtues symbolized by Sophie are replaced by civic virtues, by heroic deeds and the republican struggle for liberty. The hero of this section,

Pulaski, is a "true republican"; an enemy of monarchy and a friend of liberty. He is also "known for the austerity of his rigid morals, the inflexibility of his truly republican virtues."[25] His "intentions are pure," and his patriotism is above question: the "proud republican" tells Faublas that "if love of country has its fanaticism and superstitions then I am guilty."[26] Unable to effect the "regeneration of Poland," Pulaski decides to serve Washington's army and falls at the siege of Savannah, "a martyr to American liberty." On his deathbed, he recounts a vision

> of a happier future; I see one of the first nations of the world stir after a long
> sleep and demand of its oppressors its antique liberties, and the sacred, rights
> of humanity. I see a capital, long downtrodden, and dishonored by all kinds
> of slavery, a crowd of soldiers become citizens and thousands of citizens
> become soldiers. Under their blows, the Bastille crumbles and the signal is
> given from one end of the empire to the other: the reign of tyrants is
> over. . . .[27]

Small wonder that the Jacobins of 1791 who promoted Louvet to their corresponding committee found the Faublas novels sufficient to attest to his revolutionary integrity.[28]

Louvet shared with most French liberals a belief in the nobility of civic life and imminence of national "regeneration" and "liberty." What role, one might ask, were women to play in Louvet's "revolution?" A very circumscribed one it appears. In his memoirs, Louvet has nothing to say about agitation for women's rights during the revolution, but we do know that he moved on February 10, 1792, to have women who were "disrupting" the proceedings excluded from the Jacobin club.[29] Of the women active in the revolution only one—Charlotte Corday—finds her way into Louvet's memoirs. He describes her as "decent," "modest," "a mixture of sweetness and pride," with a "fiery gaze tempered by humility," and a "profound sentiment of republican delicacy." He then praises her beauty, which her enemies have denigrated and contrasts her loveliness to the deformities of Marat.[30] Even when describing an independent woman, active in the public domain, Louvet falls back on the lexicon of "modesty" and "simplicity" and reduces her to her feminine, "beautiful" body.[31]

Which is not to say that he gives women no role in public life, just a very circumscribed one determined by their affiliations with men. For Louvet, it is as sisters and wives, as witnesses to their men's heroic political acts that women participate in civic life. Like the women of classical literature or the figures of David's paintings, the two Lodoiskas do little more than bemoan their husband's fate.[32] When Pulaski and Lovinski threaten to march into battle without her, the formerly mute Lodoiska suddenly finds her voice and shouts, "My father and Lovinski listen to me! I will live or die with my father and my husband! Unhappy woman, what would I be if you left me!"[33] Her role thereafter is to endure, stoically and without complaint, the loss of her children, starvation, and death while following her husband. The real Lodoiska did little more. At critical moments in Louvet's *Mémoires*, she curses Louvet's enemies and bemoans the fate that will deprive her of his company and perhaps his life. She has "moments of irresolution" when she "foresees the ills that will befall the country and her husband," moments when she regrets the "price" that the revolution will exact, but she never objects to Louvet's political activities. "Her great heart could not reject such glorious sacrifices; she wept over (Louvet's) plans and ordered (him) to follow them."[34] Once Louvet is prescribed, Lodoiska runs real risks and accompanies her husband into hiding.[35] Such a gesture is more or less expected of patriotic women and Louvet reserves for the self-sacrificing Girondin wives those few pages of his *Memoirs* in which women appear. Following her husband's suicide, Madame de Clavière takes her own life; the same is true of Madame Cabanis and Madame Rabaut de St. Etienne.[36] "They had worthy companions, whom they rendered happy and by whom they were adored, all these republicans," remarks Louvet about his fellow Girondins. "And that," he goes on, "is my response to those libelists who not content to slander their public lives, dare to denigrate their private lives."[37]

Women can only participate in public life through their husbands and then only by self-sacrifice. The division between private and public runs throughout Louvet's work and any woman who crossed those barriers posed a serious threat. Such dangers were personified in the seductive and destructive Madame de B***. Certainly, Louvet's most compelling creation, Madame de B*** crossed all boundaries and muddled distinctions. The Faublas series was best known among contemporaries for the travesty that opens the novels and allows Faublas, dressed as a woman, to get close to Madame de B***. But Faublas never loses his virility; indeed, it is only enhanced as he beds married women and thwarts wronged husbands and eventually Louvet dispenses with it altogether. The real travesty is Madame de B*** who frequently appears as a young man, the comte de St. Florentin. In this guise, she roams freely around Paris, carries pistols, fights a duel, and successfully dispatches her male rival. Her husband may finally murder her, but not before Madame de B*** has wielded her pistols and wounded a bystander. In manipulation as in warfare, Madame de B*** is any man's equal—a "lion" one of her lovers calls her. By a series of ruses—anonymous letters, false messages, and assorted deceits—she manipulates the hapless Faublas, cultivating his worst instincts and depriving him of his beloved Sophie. She contrives to have him locked up a number of times but then frees him from the Bastille thanks to her "influence" at court, that is, her "prostitution" as Louvet puts it more bluntly. Madame de B*** is thus little better than a whore, but she is also Louvet's most intriguing character, and he is at pains to "save" her, to invest her with "ennobling" characteristics. On her deathbed, she does repent. She tells Faublas that she has only conserved the appearances of those "virtues which one assigns to my sex, modesty and wisdom." Born by "chance into the highest ranks and possessed of a restless spirit and an ardent soul," Madame de B*** greatest crime, she concedes, was "the crime of ambition."[38]

When women dare to wander into the public sphere, only disaster results. Female energies, especially libidinal energies, must be harnessed and repressed, not just because they are inappropriate in the public realm, but because they are extremely dangerous. Women pose a danger to society because of their sexuality, because of their ability to divide men and set one against the other. Throughout the three novels, Faublas finds himself embroiled in one triangle after another and faced with angry husbands and fathers. On two occasions, he has to fight duels but his victories leave him with a bitter taste in his mouth. He cannot savor these triumphs; he describes them as "punishments." At one point, his friend Rosambert even lectures him on the stupidity of duels and makes him concede that nothing is more absurd than men killing one another because of a woman, especially a woman like Madame de B***.[39]

Female sexuality poses another danger, a more serious one that threatens to undermine civil society as a whole. For Louvet, sexual passion risks distracting men from "virtue." Faublas, for example, consistently ignores virtue in favor of sexual pleasure, and the novels are as much the story of his struggle to master his instincts as the chronicle of his quest for the pure Sophie. Even the ideal Lodoiska sometimes threatens to assert her claims and draw Lovinski away from politics, and Pulaski advises him to leave without consulting her. "I know," he says, "that Lodoiska has more courage than any other woman, but she is also a tender and sad mother; her tears will soften you, in her embrace you will lose your strength, your resolve which you need now more than ever."[40] "Go!" he tells Lovinski, "leave; father, wife, children you must sacrifice everything when the homeland is at issue!" Luckily, Lodoiska arrives on the scene only to abjure her claims and urge her husband on to greater deeds, which will eventually lead to her own death.

Femininity, either in the form of sexuality or domesticity, must be contained because it risks drawing men away from political life. Moreover, for Louvet and many of his contemporaries, female sexuality and libertinism bore a distinctly aristocratic mark. Madame de B*** the most sexually voracious of his characters is, as he is wont to tell, "high born" and "well placed in the high ranks." The count de Rosambert, a genuine if affable libertine, is also an aristocrat who cynically seduces women and doubts that any really virtuous women exist.[41] With *Emilie de Varmont*, Faublas's last novel, sexual libertinage becomes a badge of class, a trait associated only with the nobility and "aristocratic pretention." Varmont, Emilie's sinister brother, is nothing if not a *roué* and his friend Murville recognizes him as such. Murville is more of a neophyte, much subject to Varmont's influence, but he still scoffs when his brother tells him that he has fallen in love with a woman of the lower orders. "You are wrong to accuse us (the libertines)," he writes cynically, "of disdaining humble creatures; we do not disdain them at all if they are pretty."[42] He goes on to suggest just how his brother might seduce this creature, and make of her "an amusement."[43]

For Louvet, predatory sex is a metaphor for political domination, and he never hesitates to identify sexual license with "unpatriotic behavior." In his *Mémoires*, Louvet, like many of his contemporaries, delights in accusing his enemies of licentious behavior, of "frequenting the Palais Royal," of being corrupted by prostitutes and debauchery. Sexual excess and treason sometimes seem to go hand in hand, and it is surprising the degree to which Louvet reaches into the private sphere to besmirch his enemies. He ascribes Parisians' loyalty to the Mountain to "their effeminate habits, fostered by comfort and luxury and the pleasures of gallantry which they call love. . . ." Small wonder, he remarks, that such a people is enslaved.[44] As for the Mountain itself, "From its core to its top, it was presumptious ignorance claiming the honors of fame, avid greed aspiring to riches, the dregs hoping for long debauches." "One steals," he adds, "the other prefers to kill; another likes to torture his enemies; still another to requisition their wives; yet another (why mince words) decides to rape his daughter. . . ."[45]

It is hard to take such inflammatory remarks seriously, but they stem from a deeply felt if poorly articulated critique of the social arrangements of the Old Regime. Previously, I noted that Louvet feared the divisive potential of women, their ability to set one man against another and create deadly rivalries. Women can erode male solidarity, but they can also create it. As Gayle Rubin points out in a justly famous article, men exchange women and thereby create (masculine) civil society.[46] By "traffiking" in females, males create alliances, usually family alliances, which allow for political life and its peaceful development. In a seigneurial, paternalistic society like Old Regime France, which was based upon family and not individual affinities, this mechanism operated with particular clarity. Men "gave" their daughters in marriage to other men thereby creating alliances or patronage relationships that would lead to preferment in the state and the church, in other words, to power.

In Old Regime society, power passed through women and Louvet first accepted this "social fact," indeed gloried in it, and then rejected it. In the Faublas stories, Louvet places his hero in a series of triangles, in most of which the rival quickly becomes more important than the loved one. Faublas's on-again, off-again affair with Madame de B*** constitutes the ostensible center of the plot. But the reader quickly realizes that Faublas's relationship with his rival for Madame de B***'s affections, Rosambert, is equally important, for it drives the plot of *Une année* forward and occupies a good third of the book. At the same time, Faublas's affair with Madame de B*** allows him to establish dominance over her feckless husband. Eve Kofsky Sedgewick has related cuckoldry—the centerpiece of much seventeenth- and eighteenth-century literature—to the exchange of women and explained why it exercised such power over the eighteenth-century imagination. Cuckoldry, she demonstrates, allows the hero to manipulate the gender system, to "use" women to get at their husbands and pollute what is theirs, their women.[47] This certainly describes Faublas's behavior and his transvestism is nothing more than a new, creative strategy to manipulate the old system. But Faublas and Louvet's other hero, Loviniski, show signs of adopting a more traditional strategy: both spend most of their time thinking about, wondering about their prospective fathers-in-law. Faublas's quest for Sophie is really a concerted effort to outwit and manipulate her father. In the Polish episode, the relationship between Lovinski and Pulaski is much closer, much warmer and more intimate that between Lovinski and his "love," the virtually invisible Lodoiska.

Here we have a hierarchal, father-son, patron-client relationship most typical of the Old Regime, a relationship both created and cemented by women. But Louvet is not entirely happy with the old state of affairs. Though the Polish episode may turn on an arranged match (that of Lovinski-Lodoiska), Louvet generally has only scorn for such traditional ways. For Louvet, the *mariage de convenance* produces only the worst consequences. Faublas's penultimate love, the teenage countess de Lignecourt, is the victim of a marriage to a much older, virtually impotent husband. She seduces Faublas (or allows him to seduce her) out of boredom, spite, and lust.[48] The real threat of such marriages is demonstrated by the evil Madame de B***. Louvet explains her outrageous behavior by citing her arranged marriage to a foolish husband. From this flows her sexual misconduct, her political shenanigans, in short the eruption of feminine sexuality into the public sphere.

For Louvet, such marriages were the special province of the aristocracy. In the case of Madame de B***, her misconduct is clearly the product of her social situation, that of a woman of the nobility. Why, she asks, is it so hard for women "of her rank" to fulfill their connubial duties? Because, she responds they are married as ignorant children to men they learn to detest. "Their parents tell them birth, station and gold make for happiness; you cannot fail to be happy because you will still be noble; your husband must be a man of merit because he is a man of birth."[49] Louvet clearly identifies arranged marriages— "tyranny" in marriage he would say—with the aristocracy, even though such marriages were common in all ranks of Old Regime. He is not entirely wrong because the ties established by marriage cemented the old, familial order and stood at the root of traditional, hierarchical society.

A new political order meant a new social order, a restructuring of the private domain, which included a revision in the "traffic" in women. Historians have been wont to dismiss the "private" side of Jacobin ideology as a marginal, inconsequential, and trivial.[50] Like their republican subjects, they respect the division between private and public and, with only a few exceptions, fail to see that a new social contract necessitates a new sexual contract. Louvet for one had no doubts about the importance of restructuring "private" life along what he would call "republican" lines. In his work, the new social order is evidenced in two domains: first, in a victory of fraternal over paternal power; second, in a reevaluation of marriage along individual and egalitarian lines.

In the Faublas novels, paternal order is first asserted and then undermined. Faublas's father, the Baron, initially poses problems. He will not allow the young Faublas to marry Sophie because he intends Faublas for a friend's daughter. Here is a fairly clear-cut example of traditional paternal power. But Louvet's attitude is ambivalent if not condemnatory. In such struggles, he knows whose side he is on. Like Justine, Madame de B***'s enterprising servant, "in households divided between fathers and children, (he) has always been on the side of the children."[51] But Faublas's father ceases to be an obstacle once it is discovered that Sophie *is* the friend's daughter. Indeed, the Baron de Faublas recedes altogether as a character in the novel. Faublas learns that his father is debauched, that he maintains an opera dancer as a mistress. The baron also becomes the dupe of an unscrupulous, sexually voracious woman and succumbs to feminine power. Faublas takes to calling the baron not "father" but rather "friend." Before our eyes, patriarchal authority dwindles until it almost disappears.

In *Emilie de Varmont*, fathers are literally absent. Emilie's own father is conveniently killed in a shipwreck before the story even begins. Here there is no conflict between father and son because Louvet creates a world devoid of parental authority, indeed of any fathers, a work made up solely of brothers and sisters. Everyone in the novel is the brother or the sister of another character, and where blood relations do not exist, fraternity is suggested by having the characters address one another as "brothers" and "sister." In this fraternal order, women are still exchanged but among brothers, and Emilie and the other female characters serve to link males of equal age and status. Several romantic triads run through the book: Murville loves the sister of his best friend, Emilie, who loves Dolerval; the curé Sévin also loves Emilie, who loves his best friend, Dolerval; Bovile loves Eleonore, who is unhappily married to an abusive husband. In none of the instances, however, is it a question of a love between brother and sister or sibling incest. Brothers and sisters do not fall in love (as would be fairly common in the Romantic novel).[52] Rather, brothers, be they blood brothers or "spiritual" siblings, share their love for a particular woman. And their common love simply reaffirms, indeed creates or cements, their fraternal bond. This is particularly true in the case of the Sévin-Emilie-Dolerval triad for the two men spend much of the novel praising the common object of their affections. Throughout the novel, Louvet uses women to create not hierarchal bonds between families or fathers but fraternal ties between equal males or brothers. Women are used to generate "fraternité," which is, of course, created both through women and against them.

In the new order as conceived by Louvet, paternal power over women may be vanquished but it is quickly superseded by fraternal authority. The brother (or husband, for Louvet often confuses them) takes control of his sister and usually for the best. It is Dolerval who deftly engineers his sister's widowhood and then remarriage to her lover, Bovile. But brothers are not always a beneficent force. Emilie's brother, Varmont, persecutes her, trying to confine her in a convent, then forcing her to marry, then trying to kill her in order to collect her dowry, until he is finally shot in yet another attempt to murder her. Sinister, devious, cruel, and "denatured," this brother seeks to control, indeed to annihilate his sister. He does not succeed in murdering her, as does Restif's Edmond in *Le Paysan perverti*, and he certainly does not sleep with her, which would be too flagrant an abuse of fraternal guardianship. But the authority that Varmont exercises over the passive, simple Emilie is virtually total.[53] But before the reader concludes that fraternal power is as bad as paternal authority, a *deus ex machina* saves brotherly love. Varmont we learn in the last pages of the novel is the fruit of an adulterous union. He is no more than Emilie's half brother and fraternal power over women comes out almost unscathed.

Now that brothers control women and women are used to create not hierarchical but horizontal bonds between men, one fundamental social institution, marriage, has to be rethought. Louvet is keenly aware of the problem and *Emilie de Varmont* is in many ways one Jacobin's attempt to do just that.

He condemns in unequivocal terms the old-fashioned marriage arranged by fathers to promote ties between lineages and suggests that a new "republican" type of union be substituted. This relationship will be based upon republican principles of consent and solidified by divorce. Louvet's personal conundrum, his inability to marry the real Lodoiska because she married to another, cropped up early in the Faublas series. In *Six semaines de la vie du chevalier de Faublas*, Louvet calls for divorce as a means of bringing to an end forced marriages. "Institute divorce," he claims, "and barbarous parents will no longer sacrifice their daughters; the parent will fear that the daughters will break the chains the next day."[54] Divorce constitutes for Louvet the salvation of marriage, the institution that will encourage domestic life and assure its continuation. When divorce is instituted, "one will see men who were horrified by the spectacle of current marriages, who were afraid to take on a woman for eternity, turn away from seduction." Divorce will operate nothing less than "the regeneration of morals" and the multiplication of the human species.

Divorce is so important to Louvet because it renders an ancient, traditional institution—marriage—modern and republican. Like all Jacobins, Louvet argued that man is not bound by his past, that he cannot alienate his own freedom by a promise or a vow. Consequently he draws parallels between priestly vows and the marriage contract. He argues throughout *Emilie de Varmont* that the curé Sévin, who was forced to become a priest, be freed from his promises as Emilie will be freed from those she made to her husband of convenience, Bovile, Dorothée, Emilie's sister will also be freed from her monastic vows (she has been confined in a convent by the Varmont family), and all the characters will be liberated from the arrangements made for them by their parents. In private as in political life, men will no longer be bound by the past or by their forebearers.

For Louvet, marriage will now become a compact entered into freely by equal individuals. Families no longer play a role and all vows are more or less reversible. In this regard, his views differed little from those of the revolutionaries who undertook the reformulation of marriage law. Usually this story is told as a part of the religious history of the revolution and the expulsion of the Church is presumed to be its principal though not sole motivating factor.[55] But the redrawing of the "sexual" contract stemmed not just from the anti-clericalism of the revolution but from its whole political outlook. A new, individualistic society, based upon ties between equal males, required a rethinking of the ties between male and female. "Republican" marriage as conceived by Louvet provided the answer to the old-fashioned paternalistic marriage and reflected in many ways broader political and social arrangements.

It also revealed the contradictions at the heart of republican liberal ideology. Louvet claimed as did his contemporaries that the new sexual contract brought together consenting, equal adults in a union that could be dissolved at any time. Like the universalizing doctrine from which it sprang, Louvet's sexual politics carefully veiled the inequities between male and female both in and out of marriage. Like his fellow Jacobins, Louvet never considered the social and historical circumstances that made women's choice illusory and considerably less than free. Few eighteenth-century women could afford to say "no" to marriage; lower wages froced them to say "yes" to the marraige contract. Nor could women necessarily use the new divorce law freely. Few women of the laboring classes could hope to support themselves and several children.[56] Given the dependence of women, "consent" was an ambiguous term. Nor were women equal to men in this "new" marriage contract so praised by Louvet and others. Women retained many of the legal disabilities ascribed to them under the Old Regime and their exclusion from civil society doomed them to a perpetual minority, equated with children.[57]

There was no doubt in anyone's mind, including Louvet's, that marriage meant the subordination of women and the containment of their dangerous sexuality. Divorce, he believed, would compel women to abide by their marriage vows, that is, their promise to obey. Because of the threat of divorce, both partners (but especially the wife) would be careful to observe the contract lest it be revoked.[58]

In the new social order, the civil society envisioned by Louvet and so many of his contemporaries, the social contract would be founded upon a sexual contract that promised equality and freedom but delivered subjection and dependence to over half of the French population. Women's sexuality would be chained to marriage, and marriage itself would constitute a respectable, republican form of subjection. Men equal in their rights and prerogatives—that is brothers—would control women and create a regime that promised (but did not deliver) equality and liberty. "Love and patriotism" are joined in Louvet's Jacobin republic but in a marriage that would leave women dependent upon and subordinate to men.

Notes

1. Jean-Baptiste Louvet de Couvrai, *Memoires de Louvet de Couvrai sur le révolution française*, ed. A. Aulard (Paris, 1939), 6–7.

2. A particularly convincing and provocative exploration of this relationship appears in Joan Wallach Scott, "Gender: A Useful Category of Historical Analysis," in *Gender and the Politics of History* (New York, 1989), 41–50.

3. Carole Pateman, *The Sexual Contract* (Stanford, 1988).

4. Darline Gay Levy, Harriet Branson Applewhite, Mary Durham Johnson, eds., *Women in Revolutionary Paris, 1789–1795* (Chicago, 1979); Joan B. Landes, *Women and the Public Sphere in the Age of the French Revolution* (Ithaca, 1988); Lynn Hunt, *Politics, Culture, and Class in the French Revolution* (Berkeley, 1984); Sara Maza, unpublished papers on the Kornmann Affair and the Diamond Necklace Affair.

5. Studies of the Girondin deputies provide some information on Louvet. See Alphonse de Lamartine, *Histoire des Girondins* (Paris, 1865; reedited 1984, Plon); Gary Kates, *The Cercle Social, the Girondins and the French Revolution* (Princeton, 1985).

6. For some analysis of the Faublas cycle, see Philippe Laroch, *Petits-maitres et roués, évolution de la notion de libertinage dans le roman français du XVIIIe siècle*

(Québec, 1979); Georges May, *The Dilemma of the Eighteenth-Century French Novel* (New Haven, 1963); Jacques Rustin, *Le vice à la mode, étude sur le roman français de la première molitié du XVIIIe siècle* (Strasbourg, 1979).

7. Mirabeau's erotic novels have recently been collected and re-edited under the title *Oeuvres érotique de Mirabeau*, Charles Hirsch, ed. (Editions Fayard, Paris, 1979). To my knowledge, no one has undertaken a study of Mirabeau's "sexual politics" though the material is ripe for just such an approach. Although I will refer to Mirabeau's work in this paper, I decided not to focus upon him for two reasons: (1) all his works predate the revolution and he died in 1790; (2) I think that one can safely argue that Mirabeau's political views were not those of the liberal mainstream. He was a royalist, less of a liberal than Louvet who more closely mirrored the "new" politics that emerged after 1789 and especially after 1792. On Mirabeau's politics see an excellent biography by Guy Chaussinand-Nogaret, *Mirabeau* (Paris, 1982).

8. Louvet was one of the few Old Régime novelists who made a relatively successful political career during the revolution. Laclos became embroiled in the Orleanist faction and dissipated his energies promoting a royalist coup. The chevalier de Nerciat, author of the very popular *Felicia ou mes fredaines*, had a more checkered career. He joined the counterrevolution and fought in Brunswick armies but later found employment in Napoleon's secret police, ironically ending his days in an Italian prison. As for de Sade, he spent the revolution in a prison cell with only a brief period of freedom during the Jacobin dictatorship. Emile Henriot, *Les livres du second rayon, irréguliers et libertins* (Paris, 1948), 279–99, 313–39.

9. On the new kind of "reading" that emerged in the late eighteenth century, see Robert Darnton, "Readers Respond to Rousseau: The Fabrication of Romantic Sensitivity," in *The Great Cat Massacre and Other Episodes in French Cultural History* (New York, 1984).

10. Madame Roland cited in Alphones Aulard, "Préface," in Louvet, *Mémoires*, v.

11. This incident is recounted in John Rivers, *Louvet: Revolutionist and Romance Writer* (London, 1910), p. 326.

12. There is only one biography of Louvet, Rivers, *Louvet*. It is poor and relies a great deal on Louvet's *Memoires*; it is also almost solely concerned with Louvet's political career. Better sources are, of course, the *Memoires* and the preface by Aulard to his edition of the same, Aulard, "Preface," 1–xxxviii.

13. All references to the Faublas novels refer to the Pleiade volume, *Romanciers du XVIIIe siècle*, Etienne Etiemble, ed. (Paris, 1965), in which the novels are included.

14. Aulard, "Préface," iii.

15. Louvet de Louvrai, *Emilie de Varmont ou le divorce nécessaire et les amours du curé Sévin* (Londres, 1794).

16. Louvet, *Mémoires* 1:28.

17. See *Mémoires* 1:67–198.

18. Alphonse Aulard, "Préface," xxi–xxii.

19. Louvet cited in Etiemble, *Romanciers du XVIIIe siècle*, 1980, ff 3.

20. Louvet, *Six semaines de la vie du chevalier de Faublas*, p. 820.

21. See Louvet, *La fin des amours du chevalier de Faublas*, 1067.

22. Louvet, *Une année de la vie du chevalier de Faublas*, 577.

23. Just what this trouble amounted to is unclear. To my knowledge, the Faublas novels were never banned. But Louvet in his memoirs complains about the persecution of the Old Régime censors and celebrates the freedom of the press effected by the Revolution. Louvet, *Mémoires* 1:32.

24. Readers will, of course, recognize the influence of Rousseau here. For a fuller development of these themes in Rousseau's work, see Jean Starobinski, *Jean-Jacques Rousseau: La transparence et l'obstacle, suivi de sept essais sur Rousseau* (Paris, 1973).

25. Louvet, *Une année de la vie du chevalier de Faublas*, 482.

26. Louvet, *Une année de la vie du chevalier de Faublas*, 576–77.

27. Louvet, *Une année de la vie du chevalier de Faublas*, 588.

28. "They (the Jacobins) asked if this Louvet was the author of the Faublas novels and on the affirmative they appointed me (to the corresponding committee)." Louvet, *Mémoires* 1:30.

29. Aulard, "Préface," viii.

30. Louvet, *Mémoires* 1:114–15.

31. Obviously, Louvet embraces the distinction between private and public, which has become such a familiar part of modern political discourse. On the history of this division, see Jean Bethke Elshtain, *Public Man, Private Woman: Women in Social and Political Thought* (Princeton, 1981).

32. Here I am thinking, of course, of David's *Oath of the Horatii*. An excellent analysis of this painting from a feminist perspective appears in Joan B. Landes, *Women and the Public Sphere*, 152–68. Louvet also clearly shares the obsession with stoic self-sacrifice in the service of the *patrie* described by Dorinda Outram, *The Body and the French Revolution: Sex, Class and Political Culture* (New Haven, 1989), 90–106.

33. Louvet, *Une année de la vie du chevalier de Faublas*, 589.

34. Louvet, *Mémoires* 1:27.

35. Though Louvet is content to portray his wife as helpless and anxious that was clearly not the case. Inadvertently, he reveals her as resourceful and clever: she engineers their escape on more than one occasion and takes up hammer and nails to build Louvet a "hiding place" when he is incapable of doing so. Louvet, *Mémoire*, vol. 2, 40.

36. Here Louvet appears to be describing a female variant on the "heroic suicide" favored by revolutionaries and described by Dorinda Outram, *The Body and the French Revolution*, 90–105. The wife's suicide is clearly dependent upon and peripheral to the husband's suicide; it reinforces her solidarity with him, not with a broader group as, Outram argues, is the case with the male heroic suicides, Outram, *The Body and the French Revolution*, 104–5.

37. Louvet, *Mémoires* 2:46.

38. Louvet, *La fin des amours du chevalier de Faublas*, 1185.

39. Louvet, *Une année de la vie du chevalier de Faublas*, 479, 703.

40. Louvet, *Une année de la vie du chevalier de Faublas*, 472–73.

41. Faublas produces Sophie to disabuse Rosambert of his cynicism, Louvet, *Une année de la vie du chevalier de Faublas*, 477.

42. Louvet, *Emilie de Varmont*, vol. 2, 122.

43. Louvet, *Emilie de Varmont*, vol. 3, 117.

44. Louvet, *Mémoires*, vol. 1, 121.

45. Louvet, *Mémoires* 1:122.

46. Gayle Rubin, "The Traffic in Women: Notes Toward a Political Economy of Sex," in *Toward an Anthropology of Women*, ed. Rayna Reiter (New York, 1975), 157–210.

47. Eve Kofsky Sedgwick, *Between Men: English Literature and Male Homosocial Desire* (New York, 1985).

48. See Louvet, *La fin des amours du chevalier de Faublas*, 859–1123.

49. Louvet, *Six semaines de la vie du chevalier de Faublas*, 747.

50. See Crane Brinton, *The Jacobins* (New York, 1952).

51. Louvet, *Une année de la vie du chevalier de Faublas*, 33.

52. On incest in the early Romantic novel, see Peter L. Thorslev Jr., "Incest as Romantic Symbol," *Comparative Literature Studies* 2 (1965):41–58; Alan Richardson, "The Dangers of Sympathy: Sibling Incest in English Romantic Poetry," *Studies in English Literature 1500–1900* 25 (1985):738–54.

53. See Restif de la Bretonne, *Le paysan parverti*, ed. François Jost, 2 vols. (Paris, 1977).

54. Louvet, *Six semaines dans la vie du chevalier de Faublas*, 747.

55. The best account of revolutionary legislation on marriage and related matters appears in James F. Traer, *Marriage and the Family in Eighteenth-Century France* (Ithaca, 1980).

56. For a good treatment of the material condition of women in eighteenth-century France, see Dominique Godineau, *Citoyennes tricoteuses, les femmes du peuple à Paris pendant la Révolution* (Paris, 1989).

57. Though his treatment of revolutionary reforms tends to be celebratory, Traer still gives an excellent account of both the new and the old elements in divorce legislation in the years between 1789 and 1799.

58. Louvet, *Emilie de Varmont*, vol. 3, 164.

4

Incorruptible Milk: Breast-feeding and the French Revolution

MARY JACOBUS

In 1791, the women citizens of Clermont-Ferrand wrote to the French National Assembly: "Nous faisons sucer à nos enfants un lait incorruptible et que nous clarifions à cet effet avec l'esprit naturel et agréable de la liberté (*Applaudissements*)."[1] From the vantage point of the bicentennial of the French Revolution, we might ponder the politicization of what has come to seem so private a matter. But to place maternal nurture—that is, breast-feeding—unequivocally in the personal domain is to forget that, for the eighteenth century at least, wet-nursing was both a social institution and a state-regulated industry. My concern, however, is not so much with changing definitions of public and private that coincided with the French Revolution, nor with the ideological situating of women vis-à-vis either domain, as with what might be called the semiotics of maternal breast-feeding. The history that interests me is the history of revolutionary signs, and the sign that interests me here is the figure of the breast-feeding mother.

What light does this patriotic communiqué from the women of Clermont-Ferrand shed on the meaning of mother's milk during the French Revolution? And if liberty's milk is incorruptible, what does that make the milk of the ancien régime? In enlightenment writing about maternal breast-feeding, the imaginary source of spoiled or adulterated milk is invariably the wet-nurse. Serving as the figure for a generalized maternal alienation and neglect associated with the ancien régime, the wet-nurse is often paired with her opposite, the woman of society who refuses to nurse her own child—although we should remember that, in reality, the institution of wet-nursing had as much to do with the economics of a hard-pressed urban artisan class, who could not afford to keep their infants at home when both parents had to work for the family to survive at all.[2] Enlightenment advocacy of maternal breast-feeding in France should therefore be read as at least as much an expression of changing cultural attitudes towards mother-infant relations and the family as an informed social critique; significantly, enlightened women of the middle- and upper-classes (who could afford to do so) rather than of the lower classes (who couldn't) typically responded to the call to nurse their own children in the decades leading up to the French Revolution.[3] But the advocacy of maternal breast-

54

feeding represented, for instance, by Rousseau can also be read as extending into the symbolic realm where the dominant allegories of the French Revolution were themselves played out. In this realm, questions about the relations of specific historical practices and cultural formations to seemingly transhistorical psychic mechanisms are likely to arise in their most perplexing form. I want to address at least some of these questions in what follows, particularly as they relate to the symbolic ordering of gender during the French Revolution.

As a start, I will begin by asking the meaning of mother's milk in enlightenment writing about maternal breast-feeding, and go on to argue that the Rousseauian sexual ideology associated with it leads to unresolved problems in revolutionary thinking about women. In addition, I will sketch a semiotic reading of the representations of the Republic as a nursing mother that figure in the festivals and allegories of the revolution, where anxieties about controlling women intersect with anxieties about purifying—about revolutionizing—signs themselves. Finally, I will argue that questions involving breast-feeding that present themselves in the body of psychoanalytic writing represented by Freudian theory may also be interestingly related to quite another set of questions—questions, however, that bear on the relationship between history and psychoanalysis. What, for instance, is the relation between any instinctual satisfaction actually experienced by the baby at the breast, and the psychic satisfaction hallucinated by the baby in relation to a symbolic breast? Just as the infant's fantasy of satisfaction is only ever "propped" on the instinctual experience, to use Jean Laplanche's term (*étayage*—itself a translation of Freud's term, *Anlehnung*, or "anaclisis"), so the powerful symbolic domain of public spectacle—one might equally claim—may only ever be propped metonymically on the material practices from which it derives its representations.[4] The relation between the two is neither referential nor causal. That is to say, the deployment of a psychoanalytic reading in the context of the French Revolution does not amount to transferring explanatory power or motivating force from material practices to unconscious fantasy. Rather, the temptation to make this transfer—to view symbolic representations as a reflection of social realities (or more wishfully, to attribute transformative power to symbolic representations)—may in itself be what a psychoanalytic reading of revolutionary sign-systems most tellingly reveals.

I'll be contending, therefore, not only that the discourses of history and psychoanalysis meet, so to speak, at the breast—at once provoking the wish that they should mean each other, and resisting any simple reduction of one to the other; but also that in both enlightenment writing about maternal breast-feeding and in the festivals of the revolution, women are simultaneously viewed as the guarantors of the family and of an incorruptible sign-system. My chief examples will be, first, the most widely influential enlightenment case for maternal breast-feeding, Rousseau's *Émile* (1762), along with Marie Anel Le Rebours's popular and much-reprinted handbook, *Avis aux mères qui veulent nourir leurs enfants* (1767), which raises some of the same issues; and, secondly, the debates surrounding women's participation in the French Revolution during the late summer and autumn of 1793, along with the allegory of the

Republic as breast-feeding mother, or "Nature," that figures prominently in the closely contemporary festival of August 10, 1793. I will be considering both the enlightment case for maternal breast-feeding and the historical instance of women's political and symbolic role during the French Revolution in the light of their contradictory and ambivalent deployment of the symbolic figure of the breast-feeding mother; finally, I'll return to the question of the relationship between "history" and "psychoanalysis," and to the possibility that the psychic formations and subjectivity associated with Freudian psychoanalysis are themselves the product of changes in late eighteenth-century attitudes to the family—or rather, as some critics and theorists of the family would claim, the product of the specific form of the modern family known as "bourgeois" whose emergence arguably coincides with the French Revolution.[5]

"L'homme de la nature"; or, Let Them Eat Grass

A popular eighteenth-century engraving depicts Rousseau as *l'homme de la nature* presenting a nosegay to a mother as she nurses her child outside a rustic cottage; nearby, a ewe obligingly suckles her lamb (the caption reads: *"Il rendit les mères à leurs devoirs et les enfants au bonheur"*) (Figure 4.1).[6] In another famous engraving of 1784, Voysard's "L'alaitement maternel encouragé,' Rousseau figures as "Un Philosophe Sensible" who indicates to charity where she should bestow her bounty, while Comedy, in the guise of Figaro, spills his sack at the feet of breast-feeding mothers (the allusion is to Beaumarchais's offer to contribute the profits from *The Marriage of Figaro* to a charity that would enable poor mothers to nurse their own children—an offer taken up by the city of Lyon (Figure 4.2).[7] Rousseau's call for a return to breast-feeding in *Émile* is famous for indicting the socialite mother of the upper classes for her irresponsibility and lack of maternal feeling; erasing the economic conditions that actually sustained the institution of wet-nursing in eighteenth-century France as a necessity for the urban artisanal classes. *Émile* replaces the unnatural mother by the figure of a maternal nurse—a figure who stands for an imaginary natural family immune to social forces, and cemented by the bonds of mutual love. The case for maternal breast-feeding in Rousseau's writing, however, is complicated by the fact that his own life notoriously embodied a contradiction undermining both his self-representation as man of nature and his ideal of the natural family: his (self-confessed) abandonment at their birth of his five children by Thérèse to the *Enfants trouvés*, or Foundling Hospital.[8]

Rousseau's account in the *Confessions* initiates an argument for the Republic as parent; thus he can claim that he idealistically surrendered his children to the classless parental state embodied by the *Enfants trouvés* and the rural wet-nurse: "by destining them to become workers and peasants instead of adventurers and fortunehunters, I thought I was acting as a citizen and a father, and looked upon myself as a member of Plato's republic."[9] When the Republic is imagined as Platonic parent, both the *enfant trouvé* and the culpable father disappear from the record (and so, incidentally, does the mother). But Rous-

Figure 4.1 Augustin le Grand, *Jean-Jacques Rousseau or l'homme de la Nature: "Il rendit le mères à leurs devoirs et les enfants au bonheur." Source*: Fanny Fay-Salloïs, *Les Nourrices à Paris au XIXe Siècle* (Paris: Payot, 1980), p. 137; credited to "Photo Claude Caroly."

seau's apology contains an unspeakable subtext. Consigning one's children to the *Enfants trouvés* was a solution to which poor parents often resorted in eighteenth-century Paris, especially during the economic crises that preceded the revolution.[10] As Rousseau himself must have known, the exceptionally high incidence of infant mortality among children thus abandoned (as well as the infant mortality rate associated with wet-nursing generally) was an acknowl-

Figure 4.2 Voysard, after Borel, *L'alaitement maternelle encouragé*, 1784. "Un Philosophe Sensible indique à la bienfaisance les objets sur lesquels elle doit verser ses dons. La Comédie, sous la figure de Figaro, teins des gros Sacs. Elle en repand un aux pieds de plusiers mères qui donnent le sein à leurs enfans. Au dessus du Philosophe est la Statue de l'humanité, portant ces mots: 'Secours pour les Méres nourices.'" *Source*: Wellcome Institute, London.

edged scandal at the time and led to repeated attempts to bring the institution of wet-nursing under state surveillance. Leaving one's children at the *Enfant trouvés* therefore meant not just consigning them to oblivion (still less to imagined rural innocence); it was a form of socially condoned infanticide.[11] In unburdening himself of his children, Rousseau at a stroke ensured a repetition of his own abandonment by the mother who had died at his birth, and put a stop to it. When, therefore, he writes in *Émile* that "women have stopped being mothers," he was complaining about a stoppage that intimately concerned himself.[12] His solution was to get rid of the mother as well as the *enfant trouvé*, leaving the educator in charge.

Rousseau's account of the wretched infant, in *Émile*, "unhappier than a criminal in irons," reads like a dark parody of Wordsworth's blessed babe in *The Prelude* ("*No* outcast he, bewildered and depressed," *Prel*. ii. 261; my italics). Deprived of freedom at the outset by his swaddling bands, the anti-Rousseauian infant grows up without affect or morality. Pain and suffering are its first sentiments, crying its only means of protest, bondage its legacy—"The first gifts they receive from you are chains."[13] Rousseau attributes the infant's wretched psychic state directly to the connected practices of peasant swaddling and peasant wet-nursing. He blames the wet-nursing system not only for consigning infants to neglect and increased risk of death at the hands of ignorant, unsupervised, and uncaring country wet-nurses, but for preventing maternal attachment ("There is no substitute," he insists, "for maternal solicitude"). As a mother-substitute, the wet-nurse is already by definition suspect for Rousseau, since, "She who nurses another's child in place of her own is a bad mother. How will she be a good nurse?"[14] And if attachment should develop between wet-nurse and child (as it must often have done in practice, when the infant survived), then the natural mother must either abdicate her own claim, or else teach her child to look down on and reject the peasant nurse to whom it has become tenderly attached. In Rousseau's account, class division provides the symbolic nexus for institutionalized alienation between mother and child.[15]

Riven by contradictions (the child forms an attachment to a despised mother-substitute, yet can only despise the mother who has failed to nurture it herself), the mother-child bond inscribes for Rousseau an unhealable division traversing both the social and the psychic. To resolve this impasse, the model child of *Émile* is rendered conveniently motherless; a wet-nurse replaces the mother, under the supervision of a Rousseauian "governor."[16] In his exhaustive detailing of the enlightenment infant-rearing and childcare practices that became associated with him (although, of course, they did not originate with him), Rousseau establishes the nursery as the first site of rational surveillance. In doing so, he anticipates not only the regulatory surveillance actually exercised by the state and the police over the wet-nursing business in an attempt to remedy its haphazard, entrepreneurial workings and high rate of infant mortality, but also, ironically, the later nineteenth-century move to bring the wet-nurse herself under the direct supervision of her employer represented by the employment of a *nourrice-sur-lieu* within the bourgeois home itself.[17] Émile's wet-nurse is reduced to the sum of her milk, viewed as the product of a carefully regulated system of biological, temperamental, moral, and dietary components. Rousseau's recipe for purifying both milk and morals is pastoralization. Ideally, he says, the wet-nurse should be a healthy peasant woman of good character, living in the country, and (this is important) eating a largely vegetarian diet: "The milk of herbivorous females is sweeter and healthier than that of carnivors. Formed of a substance homogeneous with its own, it preserves its nature better and becomes less subject to putrefaction."[18] Meat-eating on the part of the wet-nurse leads to bad morals as well as (so Rousseau believes) intestinal parasites in infants. Since corruption begins at the breast, the only safeguard against moral infection or infestation by worms is to put women out to grass.

In Rousseau's regime, the herbivorous nurse not only comes to occupy the place of any other lactating herbivorous female—that is, the fields—but is also excluded from the realm of reason. "Do not reason with nurses. Give orders."[19] Reason is the necessary dietary supplement supplied by the governor. One might ask what constitutes a natural mother for Rousseau since mothers no longer want to be mothers and wet-nurses, however carefully selected, rank scarcely above sheep; by his own admission, the natural order has long since been abandoned ("as soon as one leaves the natural order, to do anything well has its complications").[20] There are two obvious implications of Rousseau's argument, the first ideological, the other harder to categorize. On one hand, the effect of *Émile* is less to validate a mother-child bond than to reestablish the status quo along traditional gender lines; the family becomes the place where women nurse and men teach. Even the mother who nurses her own child only does so until it can enter the care of the father ("Let the child pass from the hands of the one into those of the other").[21] Gender hierarchy replaces social division, healing the split at the site of the mother-child relationship, but doing so at the price of relegating the mother to a secondary role, that of nurturer. The other implication is more troubling. *Émile* suggests that every mother is unnatural—either refusing to nurture her own child, like the woman of society, or choosing to nurture someone else's for money in place of her own, like the peasant wet-nurse. No mother can ever be (in Winnicott's phrase) good enough, no milk impervious to corruption. The parasite is endemic to the system.

Émile suggests how enlightenment advocacy of breast-feeding such as Rousseau's can coincide with conservative views of the family and with a consolidation of women's traditional role within it; bringing up baby—a prelude to educating the natural man—means disciplining the mother. Le Rebours's popular *Avis aux mères*, which was endorsed by Samuel Tissot, the enlightened Swiss doctor, as well as by the Faculty of Medicine of Paris, represents a practical guide to infant care and nursing written by a midwife for women themselves. Consulted by, among others, Madame Roland, it reads at times like a proto-feminist exhortation to women to oppose not only their traditional birth-attendants but their husbands in choosing to breast-feed their babies. But Le Rebours also, inadvertently, throws light on a problem that arises once more in the place occupied by the mother, and it is this aspect of her manual I want briefly to explore before moving on to the revolution itself. For Le Rebours, the problem involves the corruption of man's natural, natal nobility by what Le Rebours calls "bastard" milk: "Quel étrange abus est-ce donc de pervertir cette noblesse naturelle de l'homme qui nous vient de nature, de corrompre son corps et son esprit . . . en lui faisant prendre *la nouriture degenerée d'un lait étranger et bâtard*."[22] The "strange abuse" isn't simply that of perverting nature, but of corrupting body and spirit with milk defined as both alien and illegitimate. As well as being bad, ugly, libertine, or drunken, the wet-nurse, according to Le Rebours, might infect the infant with her very blood (a popular belief, this): "Comment souffrons-nous que notre enfant soit infecté d'un sang impur et contagieux."[23] A body-fluid credited with almost supernaturally pervasive powers, bastard milk—milk, that is, from outside the family circle—becomes associated with the fear that the child's love for its parents ("ce ciment . . . qui [forme] l'union naturelle des infants et des pères et mères") will be replaced by a love tagged as merely political and calculating; or, as we might gloss this concern, "nature" risks exposure as "culture."[24] That blood alone could cease to be an effective guarantor or glue (*ciment*) of family relationships is the unuttered anxiety that gives advocacy of maternal breast-feeding its special urgency at a time when, arguably, the family was increasingly under siege, whether for economic reasons or as an institution viewed as politically continuous with the ancien régime.

Le Rebours reveals the "natural" family as a structure always dependent on the repression or casting out of a debased other—actually the mother, whose blood is necessarily foreign to that of the father, given the laws of exogamy. Once more, the place of this symbolically debased other is occupied by the wet-nurse, who serves as a fantasized conduit for all that is illegitimate or arbitrary in the social order.[25] According to this scheme of things, maternal milk not only gives the family its imaginary natural identity; it also provides the means by which social relations may be filtered of their impurities. In addition, maternal breast-feeding leads to permanent attachment to the mother, giving milk a single, unproblematic referent: "Ceux que ne changent point de mères, conservent leur attachment pour elles toute leur vie."[26] The mother comes to stand for conservation as well as for attachment, providing the ground for signification itself. One might speculate, too, that in the face of the defamiliarizing threats by which the family was assailed during a period of revolutionary upheaval, she becomes the guarantor of the social order—preserving the inheritance of property by ensuring the legitimacy of the infant's blood. Some historians, indeed, have argued that the principal achievement of the French Revolution was not only to consolidate the emerging bourgeois family as the norm, but to install it in place of the monarchy. Interestingly enough, the fifth edition of *Avis aux Mères* (published in Year VII of the revolution) ends with a verse tribute by a teen-age son, specified as being "en âge de raison," to the mother who nursed him with "le nectar le plus doux" ("c'est sur ses genoux/ Que j'ai pu savourer le nectar le plus doux").[27] Breast-milk becomes the nectar of the Age of Reason. The role of the republican mother, one might reasonably predict, will be at once to purify the ancien régime and to sweeten or clarify the very disorders (of blood and property) signified by the revolution itself.

"*La France Républicaine*"; or, Let Them Eat Signs

I want to turn now to the sign of the breast-feeding mother in revolutionary iconography and to the figure she cuts both in debates about the political role of women during the revolution, and in revolutionary festivals, such as David's, where the issues raised by Rousseau and Le Rebours surface as a concern with the purification of signs. Saint-Just (himself an orphan), whose revolutionary blueprint for the first five years of the revolution, *Sur les institutions républicaines*, places maternal breast-feeding at the foundation of the educational system, writes that "the mother who has not nursed her baby ceases to be a mother in the eyes of the fatherland."[28] The breast-feeding mother provides

Figure 4.3 Clément, after Boizot, *La France Républicaine. Ouvrant son Sein à tous les Francais. Source*: Michel Vovelle, *La Révolution Française: Images et Récit 1789–1799* (5 vols.; Paris: Éditions Messidor/Livre Club Diderot, 1986), iii.220; Musée Carnavalet, credited to "photo Édimédia."

the revolution with one of its most powerful images of the Republic; in one engraving, "*La France Républicaine*"—described as "*Ouvrant son Sein à tous les Français*" (Figure 4.3)—wears a level to indicate equality of access to the republican breast. In 1793, the need to consolidate attachment to the Republic at a time when Jacobin centralization had recently been threatened by Girondin federalism coincided with legislation specifically designed to encourage maternal nursing; the Convention's decree of June 28, 1793, stipulated, for instance, that only mothers who nursed their own children would be eligible for state aid, unless certified as unable to do so by the officer of health.[29] In another engraving apparently dating from around the same time, a young mother nurses a baby (presumably a boy, as we shall see) wearing the red, white, and blue republican cockade (Figure 4.4). As it happens, the cockade that tags maternal nursing with patriotic and nationalist significance came to hold particular meaning for women during 1793, when a contest about the extent to which they might occupy roles other than that of republican nurse was played out with the cockade as its symbolic stake. This struggle over women's participation in the public political arena came to a head during the summer and autumn of 1793 and ended in the dissolution of the Society of

Figure 4.4. Anonymous, *Republican mother and child*, c. 1793. *Source*: Fanny Fay-Salloïs, *Les Nourrices à Paris au XIXe Siècle* (Paris: Payot, 1980), p. 120; credited to "photos Bibliothèque nationale."

Revolutionary Republican Women in October after a series of public disturbances, focusing on the wearing of the republican cockade by women, which have come to be known as the "war of the cockades."[30]

The Society of Revolutionary Republican Women defined themselves from the start in terms of their refusal to remain in "the confined sphere of their households."[31] The subsequent exclusion of women from politics has usually been read as the inevitable product of constructing revolutionary gender-ideology on the basis of Rousseauian theory—most recently, for instance, by Joan Landes, who argues that the bourgeois redefiniton of the public sphere as essentially masculine led to women's relegation to the home, in contrast to their relative political influence under the ancien régime.[32] But one could also see the confinement of women to their domestic and nurturing function as a punitive response to revolutionary violence that became associated with the body of the woman, onto which all the turbulence of revolution was conveniently projected and then disciplined.[33] In this revolutionary backlash against women, a sexual order equated with gender-hierarchy was substituted for a generalized disorder laid at the mother's door. Two motifs stand out in the campaign against revolutionary women's groups, which led to the dissolution of the Society of Revolutionary Republican Women: first, the tendency to view women's political participation as inherently dangerous; second, the tendency to locate the threat of disorder posed by revolution generally in the confrontation between warring groups of women. In contemporary documents recording the debates about women's participation in revolutionary politics, the spectre of women's association with public disorder goes hand in hand with the fear that the Revolutionary Republican Women were disordering stable distinctions between the sexes.

The Society of Revolutionary Republican Women had become an embarrassment for the Montagnards (whose May 1793 coup against the Girondins they initially supported) when they pressed for implementation of a radical Jacobin program of political terror and strict economic controls on the price of necessities.[34] This legislation, which they successfully pushed through in September, included a particularly troublesome decree of September 21, 1793, involving the compulsory wearing of the republican cockade by all women, and bringing the Revolutionary Republican Women into open conflict with the market women, or women of Les Halles (always a symbolic and actual force to be reckoned with, and—not surprisingly—committed to the notion of a free market economy). The struggles between the Society and the market women over the wearing of the cockade gave credibility to the idea that women were responsible for the public disorder that must always have been close to the surface in the streets of Paris at this time. At a Meeting of the Jacobin Society on September 16, a citizen attributed to women "all the disorders which have occurred in Paris."[35] A police report of September 21 called the wearing of the cockade "a new apple of discord which the evildoers have thrown among us; they inspire in women the desire to share the political rights of men."[36] The struggle extended to the wearing of the *bonnet rouge*, which the Society of Revolutionary Republican Women began to adopt but which some women objected to as "only for men to wear."[37] Cockades were snatched, bonnets thrown in the mud; in one dispute, male bystanders joined in, asserting that "it's only men who should wear *bonnets de police* [*bonnets rouges*]." The official police *procès-verbal* concluded that "this recent habit of women wearing *bonnets de police* can be regarded as a rallying sign or as an occasion for disorder."[38]

The "war of the cockades" underlines the gap between the feminized allegories of the revolution and the gender-ideology actually being played out within revolutionary organizations and in the marketplace.[39] In other words, the liberty cap became sexually as well as politically transgressive when it moved from the head of "Marianne," the popular embodiment of Liberty, to the heads of actual militant women in the streets. When Amar, on behalf of the Committee of General Security, reported on efforts to deal with "the consequences of disorders" that had broken out at a meeting of the Society shortly before, his account of the immediate issues (which could be summed up as cross-dressing and public disorder) was overshadowed by a general consideration of women's case for involvement in the political sphere. He ruled decisively against women, claiming that since they are disposed to "an over-excitation which would be deadly in public affairs . . . interests of state would soon be sacrificed to everything which ardor in passions can generate in the way of error and disorder."[40] Chaumette, President of the Paris Commune, responded similarly to a women's deputation wearing *bonnets rouges* by calling for the uproar to be recorded in the *procès-verbal* ("It is horrible, it is contrary to all the laws of nature for a woman to want to make herself a man"). In an escalating sequence of rhetorical questions, he demanded: "Since when is it permitted to give up one's sex? . . . Is it to men that nature confided domestic cares? *Has she given us breasts to breast-feed our children*? . . ."[41] The threat to public order is swiftly redefined as a breakdown of sexual roles; Chaumette's hysterical demand reveals what is at stake for him when women wear the cockade or *bonnet rouge*: the unmanning of revolutionary men. If bare-breasted Liberty erupts into marketplace or commune, conversely, men may have to stay home and play the nurse.

The great festivals of the revolution attempt to channel the spectacle of public disorder into public displays of a different kind. Rational exercises in instant history and mass pedagogy, the official festivals were designed to install the participants in a specular, imaginary relation to the symbolic authority of the Republic; this aim necessarily included the symbolic ordering of gender-roles, which, as we can see from the reactions of Amar and Chaumette, were never far from the surface. David's carefully orchestrated Festival of August 10, 1793, the Festival of the Unity and Indivisibility of the Republic, made the image of maternal nature its point of origin by erecting the Fountain of Regeneration on the site of the Bastille (we might note in passing the irony that an opera house is the modern bicentennial tribute to popular and national public spectacle). The festival's other "stations" included a monumental figure of Hercules representing the people crushing federalism, a reference to the unsuccessful Girondin revolt in the summer of 1793. Lynn Hunt has argued that the edging out of Liberty, or "Marianne," by this decisively masculine figure of popular strength during the latter part of 1793 was in part a response to the threat of women's increasing political participation.[42] The commemorative coin struck for the "Festival of the Unity and Indivisibility of the Republic" (Figure 4.5) depicts the first station, where the president of the Convention, followed by the representatives, drank the regenerative waters springing from the breasts of an Egyptian deity representing Nature (seen also in close-up, in an anonymous contemporary engraving) (Figure 4.6). As one bemused onlooker complained, with a touch of xenophobic chauvinism, "I would like to know why her hair was dressed in that way. We are French, and under the pretext that we have been corrupted in our morals and in our monuments, they want to turn us into Egyptians, Greeks, Etruscans."[43] The president's gesture was accompanied by a speech explaining how nature had made all men free and equal (presumably in their access to the breast), and the fountain bore the inscription "Nous sommes tous ses enfants."[44] But where, one might ask, were women positioned (interpellated, in Althuserian terms) in David's elaborately staged tableau of revolutionary ideology?

As the president of the Convention explained to the people when they halted in front of the Hercules, "that giant is you!"[45] But not all of you. In this carefully scripted and choreographed festival, only men drank from the Fountain of Regeneration; the role of the republican mother was to offer (or to be—

Figure 4.5 Medal, *Régenération française*. 10 août 1793. *Source*: Michel Vovelle, *La Révolution Française: Images et Récit 1789–1799* (5 vols.; Paris: Éditions Messidor/ Livre Club Diderot, 1986), iv.142; Bibliothèque Nationale, Paris.

to symbolize) the breast. Prominently displayed in the center-foreground of Monnet's engraving of the scene is a republican mother breast-feeding her infant; with her free hand she points to the representatives drinking from the fountain (Figure 4.7). The meaning of the station (the meaning we, too, as onlookers, are supposed to swallow) lies in that deflection of the gaze from the exemplary republican mother to the allegory into which she is subsumed—not that of an all-providing Nature, but rather the visually dominant, ideologically charged, abstract image of the State as Mother Republic.[46] Behind the figure of the breast-feeding mother we glimpse the great, failed, enlightenment project of the revolution, the proposed abolition of the poor altogether by way of a system of legislated poor relief, which would have done away with the *enfant trouvé* and the wet-nurse alike.[47] If one iconographic source for revolutionary images of the Republic as breast-feeding mother is the figure of Nature the many-breasted, the other is the allegorical figure of the wet-nurse or nursing mother who traditionally represents *Charité*, as she does, for instance, in Gravelot's and Cochin's source book for revolutionary iconography, *Iconologie par Figures* (1791) (Figure 4.8).[48] Subsumed into an all-encompassing program, state-regulated "Charity" becomes synonymous with the state apparatus that replaces an absolute monarchy. From this angle, Louis XIV's motto, "L'État, c'est moi" is the hidden subtext of the motto inscribed on the Fountain of Regeneration ("Nous sommes tous ses enfants").

It could be argued that one motive for official attempts to identify the Republic with an all-nurturing mother was to mystify social relations and mask contemporary political and economic disarray; both republican unity and

Fontaine de la Régénération elevée sur les Ruine de la Bastille .

Figure 4.6 Anonymous, *Fontaine de la Régénération elevée sur les Ruine de la Bastille.* *Source*: Michel Vovelle, *La Révolution Française: Images et Récit 1789–1799* (5 vols.; Paris: Éditions Messidor/Livre Club Diderot, 1986), iv.143; Bibliothèque Nationale, Paris.

basic food supplies were matters of intense political anxiety for the Montagnards during the summer of 1793. But I want instead to consider the very notion of "unity and indivisibility" as it bears both on production (market production, for instance—the matter of supplies) and reproduction (the reproduction of signs and children).[49] For both Rousseau and Le Rebours, maternal breast-feeding supposedly creates a family unit immune to corruption; in Rousseau's imaginary pastoral economy, a pure equivalence of production can be maintained (good diet plus good morals equals good milk), while for Le Rebours, the mother who nurses her own child protects the family from the taint of bastard blood. As the symbol of a closed circulatory system (a system that keeps the transfer of bodily fluids and property within the family), the breast-feeding mother preserves not only the legitimate bloodline, but also, more generally, a fantasy of incorruptible signs—of meanings "unified and indivisible," the meanings that David's elaborate interpretive devices and commentaries sought, prophylactically, to guard against corruption.[50] The Foun-

Figure 4.7 Helman, after Monnet, *La Fontaine de la Régénération. Source*: Michel Vovelle, *La Révolution Française: Images et Récit 1789–1799* (5 vols.; Paris: Éditions Messidor/Livre Club Diderot, 1986), iv.143; Bibliothèque Nationale, Paris, credited to "photo Tristant."

tain of Regeneration can be read as allegorizing not only the unity of the centralized Jacobin state, but the power of the state to control meanings themselves during the time of state-regulated suspicion and legalized terror that has come to be associated with Robespierre's regime. Not for nothing did Madame Roland nickname Robespierre "the Incorruptible"; what David claimed, on Robespierre's behalf, was nothing short of control over the production of an incorruptible sign-system. David's festival thus attempts to "restore"—to purge—the symbolic system itself. The breast-feeding mother figures the purification of Liberty's signs. (Swallow that one.)

David's fantasy of a revolution in signs takes us back to the very basis of wish-fulfillment as Freud describes it in *The Interpretation of Dreams*, where his example of its infantile origins are the perceptions of the hungry baby. Freud emphasizes not so much the wish as the imaginary nature of its fulfillment. When the hungry baby screams, he explains in a complicated passage, only the "experience of satisfaction" can effect a change; but this experience of satisfaction has as a central component a perception, or "mnemic" image, associated

Figure 4.8 H.-F. Gravelot and C.-N. Cochin, *"Charité," Iconologie par figures, ou Traité complet des Allégories, Emblèmes, etc. A L'Usage des Artistes* (4 vols.; Paris, Lattré, n.d. [1791]), i. 55: "Amour du prochain, vertu bienfaisante qui seule comprend toutes les autres. On la représent sous la figure d'une femme offrant le sein à un enfant, & tenant dans sa main un coeur enflammé. Près de la Charité sont plusiers autres enfans auxquels elle donne ses soins." *Source*: H.-F. Gravelot and C.-N. Cochin, *Iconologie par figures, ou Traité complet des Allégories, Emblèmes, etc. A L'Usage des Artistes* (4 vols.; Paris, Latrré, n.d. [1791]; repr. Geneva: Minkoff Reprinte, 1972).

with the original experience. The reevoking of the perception amounts to a wish, and the hallucinated reappearance of the perception corresponds to— even brings about—its fulfillment. "Nothing," Freud writes in a startlingly radical speculation, "prevents us from assuming that there was a primitive state of the psychical apparatus in which this path was actually traversed, that is, in which wishing ended in hallucinating."[51] The baby's wish, then, may lead to the hallucination of a satisfaction that involves, not milk, but an image of the absent breast that we might call the "symbolic" breast.[52] The distinction here (between breast as signifier and milk as signified) repeats, on another level, the crucial distinction to which I alluded at the outset, between the representations of the revolution and the material conditions or social practices of the time. What Freud calls "perceptual identity"—the hallucinated oneness and indivisibility of what is seen (the breast as signifier) and the experience of satisfaction (the appeasement of hunger signified by the breast, or rather, by breast-milk)—approximates to the wish embodied in David's festival; that is, the wish that the revolution might be effected on the level of signs. Representations of revolution, in David's book, amount to the hallucination of material trnsformation, or at any rate, are guaranteed to bring with them their own satisfaction.

The same hallucination attends any reading of history that treats its discourses and representations as a merely mystified or displaced expression of (for instance) institutionalized wet-nursing or actual hunger—treats them as ultimately referential (as distinct from material in their effects, as such discourses and representations on some level certainly were). If psychoanalysis and social history neither signify nor explain each other, a psychoanalytic reading of the meaning of breast-feeding during French Revolution, such as the one I have sketched here, would be one that draws attention to the persistence of *our* wish to take the shortcut from hunger to hallucinating the breast; or from material conditions and social practices to the revolutionary allegories and symbolic systems propped on them at a crucial remove. Indeed, in the current phase of French Revolution studies, the breast-feeding mother may even mark the site of a yet more obstinate, and startlingly contrary wish: the wish, not so much that the discourses land representations of the revolution might be rendered transparent to (rather than permeable by) what we are in the habit of calling "history," but rather that we might be allowed to rest content on the symbolic breast of a hallucinatory or "mnemic" image—on rhetoricity, representations, signs; on the analysis of discourses and symbolic systems as if they were the end of the story, just because they constitute a history of and in themselves. But that is another argument altogether.

*   *   *

As a footnote to this history of (among other things) the *enfants trouvés* of the French Revolution, I want to invoke a touching piece of propagandist theatre involving none other than Chaumette, as recounted in Michelet's *History of the French Revolution*. When a veteran corporal came before Chaumette in the autumn of 1793, wanting to be reassured that in adopting the orphaned baby daughter of a man who had been executed he was not acting against the national interests,

> Chaumette took the little girl in his arms and sat down next to the corporal. "On the contrary," he replied, "What a splendid example of republican virtue you are giving! . . . this is reason snatching innocence from the jaws of vile prejudice. Citizens, join with this noble old warrior! By your embraces, show

this child that she who is an orphan in law is herewith adopted by the Nation."[53]

As a result of this session, Michelet goes on, "the Convention founded an asylum for the 'Children of the Nation,' as the offspring of the condemned were called." As Rousseau himself had fantasized, the Rousseauian revolution sought to wipe out inherited guilt by substituting a new parent, the Republic, who played the part of both mother and father. In this instant allegory of innocence rescued from vile prejudice by republican reason, every parentless infant became the Child of the Nation; every orphan, however aristocratic or politically suspect its parents, could be rehabilitated by popular adoption. Autumn 1793 was also the moment that saw the adoption of the new republican calendar, with its symbolic attempt to wipe out the inscriptions of prerevolutionary history. The same utopian narrative of fresh beginnings underpins both the image of the breast-feeding mother whose apotheosis is David's Fountain of Regeneration and the inverted family romance of popular origins that haunts Rousseau's apology for abandoning his children to the *Enfants trouvés*. In the revolutionary imaginary, the revolutionary subject—the masculine subject of the French Revolution—finds himself in the bosom of the State, just as he finds inscribed in his own bosom the psychic structures that bind the Freudian unconscious to the emerging bourgeois family; the motto borne by every cockade-bearing man is not "L'état, c'est moi," but some variant on it that might be glossed as "I am in-stated." For the revolutionary woman, by contrast, given a political agenda involving compulsory maternal nurture, the motto may read a little differently: "Le tit, c'est moi"—a phrase it seems scarcely necessary to translate.

Notes

1. *Adresse des citoyens de Clermont Ferrand à l'Assemblée Législative*, December 7, 1791; quoted in Marc de Villiers, *Histoire des Clubs de femmes et des Légions d'Amazones 1793-1848-1871* (Paris: Plon-Nourrit et Cie, 1910), 97; see also Pierre Trahard, *La Sensibilité Révolutionnaire* (1789-1794) (Paris: Boivin & Cie., 1936), 201-2. For other patriotic uses of milk, see also Olwen Hufton, "Women in Revolution 1789-1796," *Past and Present* 53 (1971):100.

2. See George D. Sussman, *Selling Mother's Milk: The Wet-Nursing Business in France 1715-1914* (Urbana: University of Illinois Press, 1982), 22, for an eloquent breakdown of the figures: "of approximately 20,000 babies born each year in Paris at the end of the Ancien Régime, nearly one-half were placed in the country with rural wet-nurses procured through the Bureau of Wet Nurses, 20 to 25 percent from the wealthiest classes were placed directly by their parents with more highly paid wet nurses closer to Paris, 20 to 25 percent were abandoned with the foundling administration to die early or be nursed far from Paris by a poorly paid woman, and a small remainder (a few thousand at most) were nursed in their own homes either by their mothers or by live-in wet nurses." Cf. also ibid., 110-11, for the changing trend; by Year X of the revolution (1801-1802), about half of all Parisian babies were nursed by their own mothers, although the persistence of a state-regulated wet-nursing business right through the

nineteenth century makes this the most tenacious of the institutions associated with the ancien régime.

3. See ibid., 19–35, for a brief history of wet-nursing and the Enlightenment. For a specimen history of maternal breast-feeding, Mme. Roland's nursing of her baby daughter, see ibid., 79–86. Valerie Fildes, *Wet Nursing: A History from Antiquity to the Present* (Oxford: Blackwell, 1988), 111–26, also briefly surveys eighteenth-century theory and practice in England and France.

4. See the discussion of "propping," with reference to the infantile origins of sexuality, in Jean Laplanche, *Life and Death in Psychoanalysis*, trans. Jeffrey Mehlman (Baltimore: Johns Hopkins University Press, 1976), 15–18. Laplanche returns to the subject in *New Foundations for Psychoanalysis*, trans. David Macey (Oxford: Blackwell, 1989), 77–78.

5. For this argument, and for an anti-psychoanalytic critique of Freud's concept of the family for assuming the "bourgeois" family as its ahistorical norm, see Mark Poster, *Critical Theory of the Family* (New York: Seabury Press, 1978), 1–41, 166–205.

6. I am grateful to Adela Pinch for drawing my attention to this engraving, reproduced here from Fanny Fay-Sallois, *Les Nourrices à Paris au XIXe Siècle* (Paris: Payot, 1980), facing p. 136.

7. See Sussman, *Selling Mother's Milk*, 30; the charity aided nearly 500 Lyonnais mothers between 1785 and 1786. In the background of the Voysard engraving is the prison where, in the popular imagination, the many parents who could not afford to pay the rural wet-nurses to whom they had entrusted their babies were imprisoned for debt. In 1791, when the National Assembly pardoned all nursing debts, there were found to be only three such prisoners in Paris, but altogether over 5,000 had judgments outstanding against them, 75 percent of which dated from the economic upheavals of the first three years of the revolution; see Sussman, *Selling Mother's Milk*, 61–62.

8. See Carol Blum, *Rousseau and the Republic of Virtue: The Language of Politics in the French Revolution* (Ithaca: Cornell University Press, 1986), 74–92, for the debate surrounding Rousseau's abandonment of his children and a reading of Rousseau's defense; Blum reproduces the Voysard engraving (ibid., 76) in connection with her discussion of Rousseauian virtue and pity.

9. *The Confessions of Jean-Jacques Rousseau*, trans. J. M. Cohen (Harmondsworth: Penguin, 1953), 333. Or, as he put it elsewhere, "Plato wanted all children raised in the Republic; let each one remain unknown to his father and let all be children of the State"; Jean-Jacques Rousseau, *Oeuvres complètes*, ed. Bernard Gagnebin and Marcel Raymond, 4 vols. (Paris: Pléiade, 1959), 1:1431; quoted and trans. by Carol Blum, *Rousseau and the Republic of Virtue*, 81.

10. See Sussman, *Selling Mother's Milk*, 22, 62–64, as well as Fildes, *Wet Nursing*, 144–58, for a general account of infant abandonment. For the abandonment of legitimate children by the poor, see O. H. Hufton, *The Poor of Eighteenth-Century France 1750–1789* (Oxford: Oxford University Press, 1974), 329–49; Hufton estimates that in the last decade of the ancien régime, 40,000 children each year were abandoned (see ibid., 318). Although at an earlier period poor parents often (as Rousseau did with his first child) enclosed some form of identification so that the child might later be reclaimed, the habit was discouraged by the authorities and died out in the immediately prerevolutionary decades (see ibid., 333).

11. In 1751, apparently a good year, only 68.5 percent of the children admitted to the Paris Foundling Hospital died under the age of one; but in the second half of 1781, 85.7 percent of newborns died before they were a year old. Infant mortality (lowest for infants nursed by their own mothers) meant that whereas 25–40 percent of infants put

out to wet nurses, by their parents died, anything from 65–90 percent of abandoned newborns did not survive their first year; see Sussman, *Selling Mother's Milk*, 66–67. The incidence of infant mortality associated with the Foundling Hospital was accentuated by the scarcity of wet-nurses, delays in placement, and the rigors of the journeys to wet-nurses in the provinces (babies were often suckled several to each nurse, increasing the likelihood of cross-infection); see ibid., 22.

12. Jean-Jacques Rousseau, *Émile, or On Education*, trans. Allan Bloom (New York: Basic Books, 1979), 46.

13. Ibid., 43.

14. Ibid., 44–45.

15. Pierre Roussel, in his *Système Physique et Moral de la Femme* (1777), saw the argument as going the other way; one benefit of wet-nursing, he claims, may be to teach the nursling not to look down on the class to which he owes his nurture; see *Système Physique et Moral de la Femme*, 6th ed. (Paris: Caille et Ravier, 1813), 210. For the social background of the rural wet-nurse, see Sussman, *Selling Mother's Milk*, 50–56; a substantial body of material—both written and pictorial—attests to the sentimental attachment that must often have existed between nursling and nurse.

16. Rousseau's model in his overseeing of nurse and child is Cato the Censor, a man of rustic origins associated in Roman history with policies of moral, social, and economic reconstruction, who "himself raised his son from the cradle and with such care that he left everything to be present when the nurse—that is to say, the mother—changed and bathed him," *Émile*, 61, 49 n.

17. See Sussman, *Selling Mother's Milk*, 37–44, for successive prerevolutionary attempts to bring the wet-nursing bureaus under state control, culminating in the king's declaration of July 24, 1769; and see Fay-Sallois, *Les Nourrices à Paris*, 193–239, for the combined privileging and surveillance of the *nourrice-sur-lieu* in the late-nineteenth-century bourgeois family, as well as Sussman, *Selling Mother's Milk*, 153–55.

18. *Émile*, 57–58. For debates about the merits of city versus country for the welfare of the nursing infant, see Marie-France Morel, "City and Country in Eighteenth-Century Medical Discussions about Early Childhood," *Medicine and Society in France: Selections from the Annales*, vol. 6, ed. Robert Foster and Orest Ranum, trans. Elborg Forster and Patracia M. Ranum (Baltimore: Johns Hopkins University Press, 1980), 48–65.

19. *Émile*, 61.

20. Ibid., 57; Rousseau's comment occurs in the context of his insistence that the nurse's milk should be new—that is, she should recently have given birth to a child.

21. Ibid., 48.

22. Le Rebours, *Avis aux mères qui veulent nourir leurs enfants*, 5th ed. (Paris: Th. Barrois père, 1799), 66–67; my italics. See also Sussman, *Selling Mother's Milk*, 28, 89–90.

23. Ibid., 66. In fact, although a syphilitic nurse might in theory infect her nursling, infection usually traveled the other way—from syphilitic city baby to rural nurse; for syphilis as an occupational disease of wet-nurses, see Fildes, *Wet Nursing*, 238–40.

24. *Avis aux mères*, 68.

25. See "Below Stairs: The Maid and the Family Romance," in Peter Stallybrass and Allon White, *The Politics and Poetics of Transgression* (Ithaca: Cornell University Press, 1986), 149–70.

26. *Avis aux mères*, 105.

27. Ibid., 281.

28. See Saint Juste, *Oeuvres complètes*, ed. Charles Vellay, 2 vols. (Paris: Charpent-

ier and Fasquelle, 1908), ii:516–17; quoted and trans. by Carol Blum, *Rousseau and the Republic of Virtue*, 190. Children were to belong to their mothers until five, and thereafter to the fatherland.

29. Title 1, article 27; See Fay-Sallois, *Les Nourrices à Paris*, [120].

30. I am indebted to the invaluable documentary account of the women of the revolution provided by *Women in Revolutionary Paris 1789–1795*, ed. Darline Gay Levy, Harriet Branson Applewhite, and Mary Dunham Johnson (Urbana: University of Illinois Press, 1979). For a succinct account of responses to women's activism during the revolution, see also Harriet B. Applewhite and Darline Gay Levy, "Responses to the Political Activism of the Women of the People in Revolutionary Paris," in *Women and the Structure of Society*, ed. Barbara J. Harris and JoAnn K. McNamara (Durham, N.C.: Duke University Press, 1984), 215–31. For the history of the Society of Revolutionary Republican Women, see Marie Cerati, *Le Club des Citoyennes Républicaines Révolutionaires* (Paris: Éditions Sociales, 1966); and Paule-Marie Duhet, *Les Femmes et la Révolution 1789–1794* (Paris: Julliard, 1971), 135–60; and de Villiers, *Histoire des Clubs de femmes*, 223–74. For the story of Olympe de Gouges, see also Joan Scott's essay in this volume, "'A Woman Who Has Only Paradoxes to Offer', Olympe de Gouges Claims Rights for Women."

31. See Levy, Applewhite, and Johnson, *Women in Revolutionary Paris*, 176.

32. See Joan B. Landes, *Women and the Public Sphere in the Age of the French Revolution* (Ithaca: Cornell University Press, 1988), passim. For this particular chapter of the history of women during the revolution, as well as for revolutionary motherhood in general, see ibid., 93–151, esp. 139–46; and cf. also the account given by Blum, *Rousseau and the Republic of Virtue*, 204–15.

33. In the contemporary representations of revolutionary anticlericism, what Michel Vovelle calls "la caricature incendiaire" occupies a special place—caricatures incendiary not only in their politics, but as a form of pornography that involves disciplining women's bodies. "La Discipline patriotique or le fanatisme corrigé," for instance, represents a sequence of salacious pictures based on an incident during Passion Week 1791, in which the women of les Halles took it on themselves to chastise nuns for their religious fanaticism—a visual encounter with what might be called the bottom line of revolutionary satire; see Michel Vovelle, *La Révolution Française: Images et Récit 1789–1799*, 5 vols. (Paris: Messidor/Diderot, 1986), ii:268, fig. 4.

34. See Levy, Applewhite, and Johnson, *Women in Revolutionary Paris*, 145–47; the program included legalized terror, the creation of an *armée populaire*, the notorious Law of Suspects, and strict controls on the price of necessities (a woman's issue throughout the revolutionary period).

35. Ibid., 183.

36. Ibid., 199–200.

37. See ibid., 205–7.

38. Ibid., 207–8.

39. For the feminized allegories of the revolution and their permutations, see Maurice Agulhon, *Marianne into Battle: Republican Imagery and Symbolism in France, 1789–1880*, trans. Janet Lloyd (Cambridge: Cambridge University Press, 1981), esp. 11–37, and Lynn Hunt, *Politics, Culture, and Class in the French Revolution* (Berkeley: University of California Press, 1984), 87–119.

40. Levy, Applewhite, and Johnson, *Women in Revolutionary Paris*, 215–16.

41. Ibid., 219; my italics.

42. See Hunt, *Politics, Culture, and Class*, 94–117, esp. 94–98 for the dominance of Hercules as opposed to Marianne, and his emergence in the context of the festival of

August 10, 1793: "The masculinity of Hercules," she writes, "reflected indirectly on the deputies themselves . . . [and] served to distance the deputies from the growing mobilization of women into active politics" (ibid., 104). For a critique of the same festival, see also Mona Ozouf, *Festivals and the French Revolution*, trans. Alan Sheridan (Cambridge: Harvard University Press, 1988), 154–57.

43. Quoted in Ozouf, *Festivals*, 314.

44. See Judith Schlanger, "Le Peuple au front gravé," *L'Enjeu et le débat: les Passés Intellectuels* (Paris: Denoel/Gontier, 1979), 160.

45. See Hunt, *Politics, Culture, and Class*, 104–10, quote on 107; and see also Schlanger, *L'Enjeu et le débat*, 155–68, for an account of David's plan to inscribe allegorical ideas in the form of words on the figure of Hercules itself.

46. See Marina Warner, *Monuments and Maidens: The Allegory of the Female Form* (New York: Atheneum, 1985), 281–82, for a suggestive formulation of the ways in which Liberty's exposed breast might mutate into the breast of Tyche, matron and nurturer, as a type of the care-giving state.

47. For the difficulties in implementing this project—chiefly, the numbers of poor involved and the inadequate financial resources for dealing with them, especially once the war began to take its full toll—see Hufton, "Women in Revolution 1789–1796," in *Past and Present* 53 (1971), 90–108, esp. 97–89. As Hufton points out, women (and, of course, children) were those most directly affected by the economic dislocations of the French Revolution.

48. See Agulhon, *Marianne into Battle*, 11–13.

49. For an interesting account of related issues in connection with representations of revolution, see Neil Hertz, "Medusa's Head: Male Hysteria under Political Pressure," in *The End of the Line: Essays on Psychoanalysis and the Sublime* (New York: Columbia University Press, 1985), 161–91, esp. 173–75, and see also the response by Catherine Gallagher, ibid., 194–96.

50. See Ozouf, *Festivals:* "Images seem to be so threatened by ambiguity that they need the reassurance of commentary. . . . It was the task of this commentary to provide a fixed translation, capable of restraining the uncontrolled movement of meaning and of limiting severely the room for interpretation" (214).

51. *The Standard Edition of the Complete Psychological Works of Sigmund Freud*, ed. and trans. James Strachey, 24 vols. (London: Hogarth Press, 1953–74), v. 567, 565–66.

52. As Laplanche and Pontalis comment apropos of this passage, "How . . . can an infant *feed itself* on wind alone? The Freudian model is incomprehensible unless one understands that it is not the real object, but the lost object; not the milk, but the breast as a signifier, which is the object of the primal hallucination"; see Jean Laplanche and J.-B. Pontalis, "Fantasy and the Origins of Sexuality," *International Journal of Psychoanalysis* 49 (1968), 15 n.; see also Laplanche, *New Foundations for Psychoanalysis*, 77–78: "in the prototypical example, the almost fictive model of suckling, breast and milk do not coincide; there is a displacement from breast to milk. The 'hallucination' does not substitute an imaginary real for the real, or one form of food for another."

53. Michelet, *History of the French Revolution*, trans. Keith Botsford (7 vols.; Wynnewood, Pa.: Livingston Publishing Co., 1973), vii, 31.

II

The *Other* Revolution: Women as Actors in the Revolutionary Period

5

Women and Militant Citizenship in Revolutionary Paris

DARLINE GAY LEVY and HARRIET B. APPLEWHITE

In revolutionary Paris, the political identity of women as *citoyennes* was made problematic not only by constitutional definitions but more generally by an exclusive, gendered political language. Notwithstanding legal, linguistic, and ideological limits and exclusions, women of the popular classes and smaller numbers of middle-class women claimed citizenship. Their practice of citizenship was shaped and limited by prevailing cultural values; but it also is true that their *citoyenneté* challenged and episodically recast or subverted these values.

The problem of women and citizenship—not only in revolutionary France but throughout the western world in an age of democratic revolutions—is the subject of a large and growing literature.[1] In the conclusion of her *Citoyennes Tricoteuses*, Dominique Godineau formulates that problem as a paradox: "When one studies the women's revolutionary movement, isn't one asking . . . : How is it possible to be a *citoyenne*? How is it possible to participate in political life without possessing citizenship in its entirety? How is it possible to be part of the Sovereign without enjoying any of the attributes [of sovereignty]?"[2]

The Declaration of the Rights of Man and of the Citizen held out the promise of a political coming of age for all humanity. However, the Declaration left indeterminate the question of whether universal rights of man were rights of woman and whether, or in what sense, woman was a *citoyenne*. The constitutions of 1791 and 1793 and the debates surrounding their acceptance presumably resolved the issue. Women were denied political rights of "active citizenship" (1791) and democratic citizenship (1793).

This constitutional exclusion can be related to neo-classical and Rousseauian formulations and representations of citizenship and civic virtue that pervaded revolutionary political culture—for example, the *langage mâle de la vertu* recently analyzed by Dorinda Outram. In this language of virtue, the citizen was defined as a public man imbued with *"un vertu mâle et répub-*

This paper forms part of our collaborative research toward a book on gender and citizenship in Revolutionary Paris. An earlier version from which it is adapted was authored by Darline Gay Levy and presented as a Florence Gould Distinguished Lecture at New York University in March 1989.

licain," which prepared him for a life of service to the *patrie*. Women, the wives, sisters, mothers of citizens were depicted enclosed in domestic spheres and at best confined to roles as educators of future citizens. By the terms of these definitions, public man was a self-sacrificing hero, while women who assumed political roles in public arenas were "public women," courtisans and prostitutes.[3]

Neo-classical imagery is replete with these gendered representations of citizenship and civic virtue. In Jacques-Louis David's painting, "The Oath of the Horatii," two spaces are delineated. On one side of the canvas, we see a politicized space in which male citizens, three sons and their father, in an act of patriotic oathtaking, demonstrate physical fortitude and moral and political resolve—civic virtue, in short. On the other side, a private space is depicted. Here, daughters and wives, with their children, collapse in grief; they conspicuously display their physical incapacity along with their moral limitations— their inability to extend their allegiances beyond the home, the sphere in which their characteristic virtue, a narrowly circumscribed, private virtue, is expressed exclusively in loyalty and devotion to family members.[4]

Revolutionary power struggles between 1789 and 1793 created and multiplied opportunities for eluding or challenging and reworking these gendered formulations of revolutionary citizenship and civic virtue. Much of the time, revolutionary authorities were uncertain about how to react. They hesitated, they veered between co-opting, directing, and exploiting women's claim to a political identity and political power; they ridiculed it, symbolically recast it in order to defuse it, and repressed it.

In the spaces opened up by ambivalence and vacillation, women assumed political identities as *citoyennes*. Clearly, under the old regime, complex combinations of needs, customs, and opportunities brought women of all classes into the public sphere and facilitated their interactions with authorities at all levels as they organized and presided over salons, functioned as intermediaries at court, plied their trades, participated in or witnessed royal, municipal, or neighborhood ceremonies, or became involved in acts of *taxation populaire* and riots and other collective protests. Official strategies for controlling women's presence and involvement in public and political events were immensely complex. What can be said with certainty is that the repertory of responses did not include general policies of clean repression. Such policies simply would have been unthinkable, given the number, breadth, and scope of roles that women already were playing out in the public and political arenas.

Beginning with the royal decision of May 1788 to convoke the Estates-General, new political questions about elections, representation, constitutional rights, and political legitimacy urgently engaged the attention of all residents of the capital, women as well as men—and not only men with the properties that entitled them to attend electoral assemblies, but also the unenfranchised "Fourth Estate." Elections in Paris in April 1789 opened a revolutionary period of rapid institutional and ideological change, including the dislocation, collapse, abolition, and reconstitution of systems of justice, lawmaking, and administration. The proliferation of revolutionary journals, the establishment of Paris districts, and later, sections, the formation of the National Guard, and the opening of political clubs and popular societies all created new opportunities for political involvement, for women as well as for men. Many women joined popular societies and clubs where they received a political education and established bases for political communication with local, municipal, and national authorities. They formed deputations to deliberative bodies to present petitions and demands for legislation, or intervened from the galleries, applying collective pressure upon constituted authorities. Women swore oaths of loyalty to nation, law, king,and later, the Republic, solemn declarations of patriotic allegiance, affirmations of the political responsibilities of citizenship, which later supported some of their most audacious claims to political rights. Women participated in this ceremonial dimension of citizenship in other ways, through roles in festivals and in patriotic gift giving. In revolutionary *journées*, women repeatedly applied insurrectionary force to test the legitimacy of executive and legislative power under successive regimes. In formally stated demands for equal political and civil rights, Etta Palm d'Aelders, Condorcet, and Olympe de Gouges in *Les Droits de la Femme* with its ringing declaration— "The law must be the expression of the general will; all female and male citizens must contribute either personally or through their representatives to its formation . . ."—all forced radical expansions in the conceptualization of citizenship to realize the promise of universality encoded in the Declaration of the Rights of Man.

The de facto participation of women in the political life of the revolutionary nation through all these activities is what we are calling their practice of citizenship.[5]

We focus here on militant citizenship, practices of citizenship linked to the use of force. We are using the term to include women's claim to a right to bear arms, either in self-defense, or for purposes of offensive action against the nation's enemies—in its most radical formulation, a claim for membership in the sovereign nation. We also mean by militant citizenship women's threats to use force and their actual application of armed force in collective demonstrations of sovereign will and power.

Women's episodic empowerment through the use of armed force, their threats to use arms, and their claims to the right to bear arms, in conjunction with the confused, ambiguous reactions of revolutionary leaders, tended to blur or eclipse prevailing gendered definitions of citizenship and civic virtue, or to multiply competing and conflicting definitions and norms. By the fall of 1793, women's escalating claims and practices literally invited either a total reconceptualization of citizenship, or a radical repression of militant *citoyennes* as a threat to the political hegemony (and even the potency) of the Jacobin leadership and to the gendered vision of nature, society, polity, and ideology which that leadership finally fixed upon as the foundation of the new order.

Here, we present three instances of women's practice of militant citizenship in revolutionary Paris: the women's march to Versailles in October 1789; women's participaion in armed processions and their demands for the right to

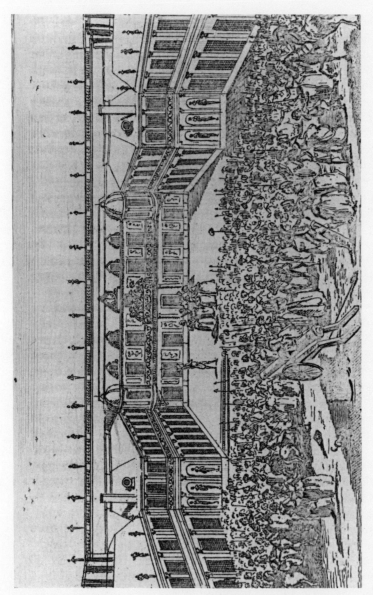

Figure 5.1 Anonymous, Depiction of events during the *journée* of October 6, 1789. Engraving from *Révolutions de Paris* (Vol. 1, no. 13, 3–10 October 1789). This engraving appeared with the following caption: "The National Guard of Paris and Versailles, numbering more than 20,000, not counting the more than 12,000 men and women, armed with various weapons, who complained to the King about the lack of bread in the capital, pressing the King to establish his residence in Paris." Note that the artist has depicted women in large numbers, carrying pikes, as well as a group of women in the courtyard of the chateau, addressing members of the royal family who stand on the balcony above.

bear arms during the spring and summer of 1792; and the organized insurgency
of women in the Society of Revolutionary Republican Women between the
spring and fall of 1793.

On October 5, 1789, 7,000 women from the districts and faubourgs of
Paris—fishwives, housewives, shopkeepers, peddlars—the *menu peuple*—rose
in insurrection against the municipal government, the king and the National
Assembly. According to a newspaper account, trouble started when a young
market woman began beating a drum in the streets and crying out about the
scarcity of bread.[6] According to Loustalot, an editor of the *Révolutions de
Paris*, "Women of the people, principally merchants from the central markets
and workers from the Faubourg Saint-Antoine, took upon themselves the
'*salut de la patrie*.'" They rounded up in the streets all the women they
encountered there; they even went into houses to lead off all those who could
add to the numbers in the procession; they went to the square in front of the
Hôtel de Ville."[7] An eyewitness recounted how the women invaded the Hôtel
de Ville, denounced the Mayor, Bailly, and the Commander-General of the
National Guard, Lafayette; snatched up papers and threatened to burn them;
and mockingly, scornfully declared, as one observer put it, that "men didn't
have enough strength to avenge themselves and that they [the women] would
demonstrate that they were better than men." Having located and seized
weapons, the women stated their intention of going directly to the National
Assembly "to find out everything that had been done and decreed until this
day, the fifth of October."[8]
   An extraordinarily acute observer, the Parisian bookseller Siméon-Prosper
Hardy, noted in the entry to his journal for October 5 that the armed marchers,
women and men, left for Versailles "allegedly with the design of . . . asking the
king, whom they intended to bring back to Paris, as well as the National
Assembly, for bread and for closure on the Constitution."[9]
   The women set off on the fourteen kilometer march to Versailles in a
driving rain, armed with pikes, clubs, knives, swords, muskets, and other
weapons; dragging cannon; led by one of the conquerors of the Bastille, and
followed hours later by somewhere between eighteen and twenty-four thousand civilians in arms, and twenty thousand guardsmen with their Commander-General, Lafayette.
   At Versailles, one detachment of this women's armed force, backed by men
with heavy artillery, including cannon, headed toward the chateau. There, the
women threatened to open fire on royal troops; they insulted the king, and
made scathing references to his failure to sign the Declaration of Rights; they
demanded an interview. After a delegation of women was received and brought
the king's verbal promises of wheat supplies for Paris, the women waiting at the
gate demanded the king's commitment in writing—a clear indication that, for
them, the image of the king as protector and provider was dissolving into the
picture of an unreliable executive agent whose authority was limited at best,
and who must be pinned down to signed contractual agreements.[10]

A second prong of marchers took over the national legislature, demanded a guaranteed supply of affordable bread, passed mock legislation, and also pressed the deputies into issuing decrees on subsistence. The following day, the marchers invaded the chateau; tens of thousands, women and men, military and civilians—many of them armed—crowded into the palace courtyard and forced the king to return with them to Paris, a captive monarch (see Figure 5.1). Eyewitness accounts and visual documentation of the procession depict women seated astride cannon—the world turned upside down, a *tableau vivant* of feminine empowerment; women marching with swords in hand, women waving the branches of trees, women threatening the captured royal body-guards and fraternizing with the National Guardsmen who carried loaves of bread on the tips of their pikes; women shouting and chanting as they marched: "Courage my friends, we won't lack bread any longer, we are bringing you the baker, the baker's wife, and the baker's boy"[11]—dramatic demonstrations of the crowd's demotion of the king from sacrosanct absolute authority, a patriar-chal provider and protector, to a mere provisioner, a fundamentally untrust-worthy baker who, like other suspected hoarders and profiteers, must be subjected to continual popular surveillance, backed by armed force.[12]

We narrow our focus to one episode of the October days, the women's invasion of the National Assembly on the evening of the fifth. Initially, only a deputation was admitted to the bar; shortly afterward, crowds of women rushed in; some were armed with hunting knives or half-swords that hung from their skirts.[13] They took over the hall of the legislature, milled about the floor, filled all the galleries, interrupted debate, pressured and intimidated the depu-ties, and demanded that they discuss subsistence problems in Paris.[14] One journalist reported that two or three thousand women voted with the deputies on motions and amendments relating to legislation on the circulation and distribution of grains. "Thus, on this incomparable day, they exercised the functions of legislative and executive powers."[15]

Observers noted the carnavalesque behavior of the "legislators" of the night of October 5: like role reversals—sitting in the president's chair, voting on motions; impromptu farce—shouting, singing, declaiming; and personifica-tions of the objects of their ridicule—chiding the deputy Mounier for his support of *Monsieur le Véto, ce vilain véto*.[16] However, on this rainy Monday, which clearly was not a carnival day, and in the middle of the National Assembly, this burlesque behavior merged into revolutionary dramaturgy—the marchers' collective exploitation of a subsistence crisis inextricably bound up with a crisis of political legitimacy, a crisis over the locus of sovereign authority in the new political order.

"Do what you are asked," an insurgent ordered a deputy who had referred the Parisians back to their city government for decrees relating to price ceilings on meat and bread: "don't fancy we are children you can play with; we have our arms raised." Later, a group of women seized this deputy by the coat when he tried to leave the meeting hall. He repeated that the Assembly did not have the authority to grant their demands; at precisely that moment, a woman was occupying the president's chair.[17] Such role reversals can be read as the women's symbolic seizure of power from deputies whom they perceived to be either incapable of representing them, or unwilling to do so.

The women who marched to Versailles from their neighborhood bases in the districts and faubourgs of Paris did not formally state concepts of revolutionary sovereignty, entailing the people's right to express and impose its will through collective applications of armed force. Rather, in deeds, they shattered the traditional authority and sovereignty of absolute kingship. They demonstrated how the people itself functioned as sovereign legislator. They enacted what the deputies and the radical publicists were calling popular sovereignty. They placed an armed force behind these acts. They forged links between the traditional priorities and values of their communities—especially guaranteed subsistence and the expectation of paternal benevolence from the king—and the revolutionary nation—its emblems, symbols, military force, and nascent ideology. In the context of revolutionary developments between the spring and fall of 1789, these acts mark a transitional moment in the transformation of subjects into a militant citizenry identifying itself as the sovereign nation.

For the *menu peuple* of Paris, especially for women, militant citizenship would continue to mean at least a politics of intimidation, unrelenting surveillance and control, practiced sometimes through legal means (like petitioning or forming delegations within popular societies), but also in insurrection. The power of insurrection is necessarily episodic and ephemeral, but it also is real. Perhaps most important, from the beginning of the revolution, radical publicists and polemicists appropriated and reworked this traditional popular politics of subsistence and surveillance, with its underlying assumption that the application of force is justified where it enforces the collective moral will of the community. They recast it in a Rousseauian language, legitimating insurrection as the arm of the sovereign nation, the most authentic embodiment and expression of the general will. In calculating the power of that general will, the revolutionary leadership continued, reluctantly, episodically, to include women; and women persisted in including themselves.

Some contemporaries who lived through the October days gave accounts of the events that carried radical, even feminist messages. One middle-class woman, a writer for the *Étrennes nationales des Dames*, cited women's courage and enterprise during the *journées d'octobre* to support her case for women's complete liberation from a state of "inferiority" and "slavery" to men.[18] The author of a provocative brochure, *Requête des dames à l'Assemblée nationale*, appealed both to universal rights embodied in the Declaration of August 1789 and to the example of women's militancy, their "martial courage" during the insurrectionary events of the summer and fall of 1789, to support demands for absolutely equal rights and an equal share of power for women as legislators, magistrates, ecclesiastic officers, and military officers.[19] Under the old regime, such texts might have been passed off as deprecatory parody; in the context of the great hopes of 1789, the message could be read as ambiguous, at least, and positively radical, at most. In both documents, strong links were forged between women's militancy on October 5 and 6 and remarkably broad demands for the political and military status and rights of female citizenship.

The meanings and impacts of women's militant citizenship emerge most clearly during the critically important period of revolutionary radicalization between the bloody repression of petitioners by National Guardsmen on the Champ de Mars in July 1791 and the legal exclusion of women from organized political activity in October 1793.

During these two years, women publicists, petitioners, demonstrators, and insurrectionaries claimed rights of militant citizenship and enacted them. When it suited their purposes, male revolutionary leaders enlisted or co-opted women for demonstrations of popular power. At the same time, they struggled to rein in behavior that threatened to blur definitions of appropriate gender roles. They invoked a political lexicon—nature, virtue, civic virtue—derived largely from Rousseauian and classical philosophy and gendered to define public and political roles for male citizens and exclusively domestic roles for women. As we noted at the outset, a body of recent scholarship interprets revolutionary political opportunities and outcomes for women as largely predetermined by this gendered political discourse and by the male-dominated hegemonies it supported and reflected. Our documentation of women's involvement in ceremonial, institutional, and insurrectionary politics suggests the need for a more complexly nuanced reading than these cultural determinisms encourage. Our interpretation of women's practice of militant citizenship cautions against reading back into the ever-shifting ideological constellations and power struggles in which women were caught up between 1789 and 1793 a repressive linguistic-political-military hegemony that the Jacobins established only in the fall of 1793, and even then, only incompletely.

The period between the autumn of 1791 and the overthrow of the monarchy on August 10, 1792, saw the radicalization of politics in Paris, that is, the accelerated mobilization of the "passive citizenry" in the sections and faubourgs and the intensification of constitutional crises pitting the king against the legislature and both against the organized masses. Radicalization accelerated a temporary but critically important empowerment of women and that power in turn contributed to the paralysis of repressive armed force and the triumph of republicanism.[20]

On July 17, 1791, less than a month after the king's aborted attempt to flee France, National Guardsmen under the command of Lafayette fired on a crowd of thousands of men and women with their families, principally "passive" citizens who had gathered on the Champ de Mars in Paris to sign a petition asking for a national referendum on the future of the monarchy. The massacre of some fifty petitioners led not only to a general repression of pro-republican individuals and organizations but also to calls on the left for revenge and eventually to a reconstruction of the broken alliance between the people and the armed forces, particularly the National Guard.

Radical journalists reacted to the massacre with expressions of horror and sympathy for the victims that were calculated to provoke a powerful political response. Jean-Paul Marat, in his *Ami du peuple*, described the events on the Champ de Mars as a slaughter of innocents, a massacre of helpless victims, "poor old men, pregnant women, with infants at their breast."[21] "The blood of old men, women, children, massacred around the altar of the *patrie*, is still warm, it cries out for vengeance."[22] This radical rhetoric became part of a political campaign developed by members of the Jacobin Club and other radicals to reunify a fragmented National Guard, rally the populace behind the Guard and other segments of the armed forces, and thereby reconsolidate the shattered alliance between the military and the people.

The campaign began toward the end of 1791 with plans to rehabilitate forty soldiers from the Swiss regiment of Châteauvieux who had been condemned to the galleys off Brest as punishment for a rebellion against their commanding officer and then amnestied by the Legislative Assembly in December. In the spring of 1792, these soldiers were honored as revolutionary heroes in armed processions and fêtes organized to celebrate their release. Women played principal roles in these dramatic demonstrations of liberty, unity, and strength.

On April 9, 1792, women, children, and men from the sections and faubourgs of Paris—a "passive" citizenry—accompanied by battalions of National Guardsmen, participated in an armed march through the national legislature to escort and honor the forty soldiers from the Châteauvieux regiment. These marchers, bearing arms and displaying a liberty cap on a pike and other revolutionary emblems and symbols, were arranged to give the appearance of a united family, which was at the same time a reunited militant citizenry, ready and able to resist oppression. The effect of the whole was to replace the publicists' calculated, provocative characterization of the people as *victim* with a moving picture of the people as *the nation in arms*. This demonstration suspended and, momentarily at least, superseded all other business. As they took over the Assembly, filling it with their shouts, their drumbeat to martial rhythms, their symbols, their weaponry, and the strength of their numbers, the marchers practiced popular sovereignty as a direct unmediated intervention in the legislative process.[23] Their acts forged links between popular sovereignty and militant citizenship which accelerated the consolidation of a section-based, democratically controlled armed force—a critically important phase of revolutionary radicalization.

On the fifteenth, in a Festival of Liberty organized by commissioners from the Jacobin Club and paid for by the Paris municipal government, the sections celebrated the liberation of the Châteauvieux soldiers. Observers noted that the breach between the National Guard and the people, which had been opened in July 1791 when the Guard fired on the Champ de Mars petitioners, was closed by the formation of the 1792 march, in which citizens and *citoyennes* were interspersed among the Guardsmen. ". . . the field of the massacre has become the field of fraternity and the scaffold of patriots has been renamed the altar of the patrie."[24] The helpless victims depicted by Marat nine months earlier were avenged here by a mighty populace embodying the nation, with the National Guard as its army.

Citoyennes were central to the organizers' work of reclaiming the National Guard for the people; observers noted their placement in the line of march and their prominent roles in symbolic representations of liberty.[25] A published plan described the first group of marchers as "citizens and *citoyennes* marching eight in a row; in their midst the Declaration of the Rights of Man will be carried."[26]

In these two ceremonies, women bearing arms as they marched with the national armed forces, but also carrying their children (April 9), or unarmed, dressed in white, and marching arm-in-arm with national guardsmen and Châteauvieux soldiers (April 15) created a picture of the sovereign people as a national family whose rights and liberty were linked inextricably to its armed force and whose strength was further augmented by the ceremonial transformations of rebel soldiers into victims of tyranny, champions of liberty, the people's kin, their protectors and defenders, their comrades in arms.

Clearly, revolutionary leaders responsible for the events deliberately programmed or included women in roles as pike-bearing *citoyennes*, patriot mothers, daughters, and wives. However, in so doing, and with or without full awareness of the subversive implications, they transposed the family into the political arena and imparted new symbolic and political significance and legitimacy to women as political actors, family members in arms, emblems of civic virtue, national unity, and sovereign power. Women armed with pikes, carrying "tricolor flags and other emblems of liberty," and marching through the Legislative Assembly, or parading arm in arm with the national armed forces, obliterated the gendered divide between the private virtue of women and the civic virtue of men. At least in ceremony, these women and men empowered a "powerless" and "passive" citizenry, publicly dramatized their militant citizenship—their sovereignty. These acts were symbolically charged. No matter how the organizers might struggle to control and direct them, they retained their subversive potential to blur or invert gender roles and beyond that, to link women's political identities as militant citizens to the life and fate of the sovereign nation.

Not all women who participated in these ceremonies were content to limit themselves to enacting roles officially prescribed for them as militant *citoyennes*. On March 6, 1792, Pauline Léon, an outspoken revolutionary activist, led a deputation of women to the Legislative Assembly and presented a petition with more than three hundred signatures demanding women's right to bear arms. Léon claimed for women the universal natural rights to self-protection and resistance to oppression guaranteed in the Declaration of Rights of 1789. "We want only to defend ourselves as you do," she told the legislators. "You cannot refuse, and society cannot deny, the right nature gives us, unless you pretend that the Declaration of Rights does not apply to women and that they should let their throats be cut, without the right to defend themselves." Léon also claimed for women the political and moral attributes of revolutionary citizenship, including civic virtue, and she based that claim partly on the evidence of recent revolutionary history. She represented the women's march to Versailles and their return with a king in tow as an event that fixed women's political identity, not least of all in the minds of the enemy. "For can you believe the tyrants would spare us? No! No!—they remember October fifth and sixth"—all the more reason to provide women with the means of self-defense. "We are *citoyennes*," Léon proclaimed; women's citizenship, their capacity for practicing civic virtue, now made it impossible for them to remain "indifferent to the fate of the *patrie*."

On behalf of the petitioners, Léon asked permission for women to arm themselves with pikes, pistols, sabres, and rifles; to assemble periodically on the Champ de la Fédération, or in other places; and to drill under the command of the former French Guards.[27]

The response of the Legislative Assembly was ambiguous. The president invited the delegation to attend the session. One deputy voiced his concern that if the petition were honored, "the order of nature would be inverted." The delicate hands of women "were not made for manipulating iron or brandishing homicidal pikes." As serious motions crossed with parody—the petition should be sent to the Military Committee, no! to the Committee of Liquidation!—the Assembly decreed a printing of the petition and honorable mention in its *procès-verbal* and promptly passed to the order of the day.[28]

One conservative journalist, Montjoie, was uneasy about the inconclusiveness of the Assembly's action and the precedents it might establish: "Perhaps in interpreting this decree, women will arm themselves nonetheless"; to avoid a dangerous confusion, he observed, the Assembly ought to have declared that there was no cause to deliberate on the matter in the first place.[29]

Pauline Léon's address is a remarkably bold attempt to capture the discourse on militant citizenship and redefine and expand its parameters to include the military and political rights and responsibilities of women. Immediately, that discourse was challenged with a counter-definition of feminine nature in terms of women's fateful difference, an innate weakness and incapacity that made it unnecessary, and more, impossible, for revolutionary leaders to recognize their claims to universal rights of self-defense and a share of civic responsibility. The delicate hands of women "were not made for manipulating iron or brandishing homicidal pikes." The remark would seem to reflect a vision of a political culture structured by clear gender divides and narrowly defined roles for women. However, what is most telling is the Assembly's indecisiveness at this juncture, and more generally, the unwillingness of leaders either to sanction officially or deny categorically the claims of women to the right to bear arms, a right of militant citizenship. In the interstices that opened up in the midst of confusion and public debate over how to encourage the political, indeed, military mobilization of women without provoking their emergence as autonomous political actors, women persisted in discourses and deeds of militancy that proved progressively more unsettling and threatening to male revolutionaries.

Women's repeated demands for the right to bear arms through the spring and summer of 1792 strongly suggest that at a critical juncture in the revolution, as the nation mobilized for war, an emerging concept and practice of female citizenship was dissolving distinctions between active/passive citizens, male/female citizens, and public/private roles—without however, provoking the legal and constitutional revisions that would fix and guarantee their real, if precarious, de facto political standing. Arguments for women's natural and constitutional rights of self-defense buttressed the claim that political-moral imperatives, their civic virtue, an aspect of their identity, impelled them to protect and defend the *patrie*. In at least one image dating from this period, an anonymous engraving (see Figure 5.2), the artist inscribes the emblem and acts

Francoises devenues Libres.

Figure 5.2 Anonymous engraving, probably issued during the summer of 1792. The engraving bears the caption "French women [who] have become free," and depicts a woman who boldly faces the viewer, conspicuously displaying on her hat the tricolor cockade, symbol of French liberty. She bears a pike inscribed with the motto: Liberty or Death. A medal attached by a tricolor band to her waist, is inscribed with the motto: "Libertas Hastata Victrix! 14 Juillet" ("Liberty [when she is] armed with her pike [is] victorious!" 14 July.). Contemporaries may have associated this figure either with Pauline Leon who had publicly expressed her determination to fight, pike in hand, during the *journée* of August 10, or with her equally militant friend, Claire Lacombe, whom the fédérés decorated with a tricolor sash for her role during this *journée*. *Source*: Bibliothèque nationale, Cabinet des estampes, B 1503.

of Liberty onto the costume of his female subject; imprints her weapon with the watchword of a militant, virtuous citizenry: "Liberté ou La Mort"; and by means of the title "Françoises devenues Libres" links female militancy to women's revolutionary emancipation. In the light of these radical formulations, the women, armed and unarmed, who marched on April 9 and 15, not only symbolized a united national family in arms; they also dramatized principles of women's militant citizenship. This massive mobilization of a "passive" citizenry, strengthened by myths of a united and mighty national family, inverted Marat's images of families martyred on the Champ de Mars and contributed to consolidating the popular force that brought down the monarchy.

Women enacted principles of militant citizenship once again on June 20, 1792, two months after the declaration of war against Austria and during a constitutional crisis, which erupted when the king dismissed his Girondin ministry and vetoed decrees that radical deputies considered vital for the safety of the nation.

During the *journée* of June 20, impressive numbers of armed women marched in a procession involving tens of thousands of people, most of them from the working class faubourgs of Saint-Antoine and Saint-Marcel (see Figure 5.3). This armed force passed through the halls of the Legislative Assembly, into the Tuileries Gardens, and then through the king's residence in the Tuileries palace, symbolically reclaiming and reconsecrating these spaces for the work of executing what their spokesmen were calling the general will of the sovereign people.

In earlier work, we closely documented women's involvement in the insurrectionary dramaturgy of this *journée*.[30] Here, we limit ourselves to brief comments on the failure of authorities to repress a frontal challenge to executive and legislative powers, which presaged and prepared the collapse of the constitutional monarchy and the proclamation of a republic. Our documentation suggests that the massive involvement of women in some measure was responsible for the paralysis on the twentieth of authorities of all sympathies who had been charged with controlling or preventing insurrections.[31] Their hesitation, and in the end, their failure to fire on crowds filled with armed women and children, especially after events on the Champ de Mars in July 1791 and the campaign by radicals to represent those events as a massacre of innocent families, fueled the myth that the sovereign people was irrepressible and gave further impetus to radicalization. During a summer of intense political power struggles, the insurrectionary involvement of women in arms made a historically significant difference for the outcome of events.

Furthermore, the enlistment of women by revolutionary leaders, coinciding with women's escalating claims to the rights of militant, democratic citizenship, especially the right to bear arms, tended at least at that juncture, to blur and even subvert classical and Rousseauian models of appropriate gender roles and to superimpose a language of women's rights and responsibilities upon the *langage mâle de la vertu*, enlarging fields of political discourse and multiplying available repertories of political-military action.

Eventually, a victorious republican leadership encoded legal and constitu-

Figure 5.3 Anonymous, "Celebrated Journée of 20 June 1792." Engraving from
Révolutions de Paris (Vol. 12, No. 154, 6–23 June 1792). The accompanying caption
reads: "Reunion of Citizens from the Faubourgs St. Antoine and St. Marceau en route
to the National Assembly to present a petition, followed by another [petition] to the
king." Women armed with swords and pikes are shown marching with their families and
neighbors in arms and accompanied by National Guardsmen.

tional definitions of citizenship that democratized and "universalized" political
rights of citizenship for men—access to political office, the suffrage, the right
to bear arms in the National Guard and other armed forces—while underscor-
ing women's political "passivity" and further validating the gendered models of
nature, citizenship, and virtue that rationalized it. In 1792 and for more than
another year, these exclusive definitions coexisted with behaviors that occa-
sionally all but cancelled them out; in any case, this discourse did not have a
decisive impact on women's escalating militancy.

The militant citizenship we have traced through women's acts and words in
revolutionary Paris between 1789 and 1792 was institutionalized most fully and
practiced in its most radical form in the Society of Revolutionary Republican
Women, a political club exclusively for women. The society was founded by
Pauline Léon and Claire Lacombe in May 1793, at a time when the nation was
wracked by internal war, international war, economic dislocation and crisis, and
intense factional division between Jacobin and Girondin deputies and other rival

political groups. No complete memberships lists survive, but several members of the society whom we have been able to identify were socially marginal, actresses and workers in the luxury trades, for example, rather than market women.

On May 12, two days after registering with the Municipality of Paris, several members of the new society appeared at the Jacobin Club where they stated that their principal intention was to form an armed body of women to combat "internal enemies." "We have resolved to guard the interior while our brothers guard the frontiers."[32] The women embedded in this language a determination to expand the scope of their activities beyond the domestic sphere of their homes to embrace "the interior" of the nation, its welfare and its safety.

Principles of militant citizenship were encoded in the society's printed regulations of July 9, 1793. The preface stated that the recognition of "one's social duties" was the necessary condition for "fulfill[ing] one's domestic duties adequately"; and that the society had been formed to provide *citoyennes* with every opportunity to master and practice their civic responsibilities. Article I read: "The Society's purpose is to be armed to rush to the defense of the patrie: *citoyennes* are free nonetheless to arm themselves or not." And Article XV stipulated that all "newly received *citoyennes*" swear an oath to defend the *patrie*: "I swear to live for the Republic or die for it."[33] The society's regulations emphatically formulated the members' rights and responsibilities as citizens of a republic. Women's right to bear arms and their civic responsibility "to live for the Republic or to die for it" were inextricably linked in this understanding of militant citizenship and placed at the center of women's political self-definition. This recasting of political identities carried the Revolutionary Republican Women far beyond certain earlier revolutionary behaviors (for example, marching and petitioning—acts that, although transformed by revolutionary circumstances and ideology, nonetheless may have been more readily tolerated by revolutionary leaders because they replayed roles deeply rooted in the popular culture of the ancien régime). By the summer of 1793, the Revolutionary Republican Women were laying full claim to wartime rights and responsibilities of citizenship; in fact, they proclaimed that the performance of a patriotic duty was a precondition for fulfilling one's domestic duty as wife and mother.

In the aftermath of the insurrection of May 31 to June 2, 1793, (the ouster of Girondin moderates from the National Convention, which the *républicaines révolutionnaires* had done so much to engineer),[34] Jacobin leaders as well as sans-culotte section officials lauded the members of the society—for the proofs they had given of "the purest civic mindedness"; for their propagation of good principles," which had contributed to "the holy insurrection of the thirty-first of May and the second of June"; for their powers of patriotic persuasion and their effectiveness as keepers of law and order and agents of an unremitting surveillance.[35] At this point, it was not the Jacobins, but Girondin leaders, the deputy and journalist A.-J. Gorsas, for example, who experienced the armed militancy of the society as an overwhelming threat: "Some women meet, undoubtedly excited by the furies; they are armed with pistols and daggers; they make public declarations and rush to all the public places of the city, bearing before them the standard of license. . . . These drunken bacchanalians . . . what do they want? What do they demand? They want to 'put an end to it'; they want to purge the Convention, to make heads roll, and to get themselves drunk with blood."[36]

By the end of the summer, another tone and a real ambivalence toward militant women permeated Jacobin speech. At the Festival of Reunion on August 10, marking the first anniversary of the downfall of the monarchy, Jacobin organizers acknowledged, celebrated, but also conspicuously reworked and defused the revolutionary antecedents of women's militant citizenship under the republic. In this *fête*, imagery, dramaturgy, and discourse functioned to integrate militant women into the united ranks of the sovereign. At the same time, the organizers subsumed, if they did not quite bury, women's militant acts under a rigid conceptualization of appropriate gender roles in a republic.

At the second of five stages in the procession, Hérault de Séchelles, President of the National Convention, addressed a group of women selected to represent the "heroines of the fifth and sixth of October 1789." As programmed by Jacques-Louis David, the architect of this *fête*, these "heroines" were seated on their cannons, under a commemorative triumphal arch, which bore the inscription "they chased the tyrant before them, like a vile prey." The orator began by mythologizing an historical event, the march to Versailles and the women's return with a captive king. "*Quel specatacle! La faiblesse du sexe et l'héroisme du courage.*" He attributed to the miraculous interventions of an abstract "Liberty" the deeds of seven thousand women backed by thousands of National Guardsmen and armed civilians. Liberty had ignited "in the heart of several women this courage which caused the satellites of tyrants to flee or fall before them." Making use of the "delicate hands" of women, Liberty had caused the cannons to roll—these "mouths of fire" whose "thunder" forced the king to capitulate to the people. Only after this rhetorical reconstruction, complete with a *dea ex machina*, "Liberty," were the "heroines of October" authorized to "reunited themselves with the sovereign"—but not before having been instructed by Hérault to play their true part in an ongoing revolutionary drama, the people's conquest of tyrants. They should confine themselves to giving birth to "a people of heros" and nourishing them with breast milk to develop their martial virtue.[37]

In the late summer and fall of 1793, in alliance with the *enragés*, a group of radical democrats, the Society of Revolutionary Republican Women began calling for systematic terror against hoarders and aristocrats, maximum prices for subsistence commodities, and related legislation—what Albert Soboul called a "popular program of public safety."[38] The *républicaines révolutionnaires* moved among political institutions at all levels—popular societies, section assemblies, the Cordeliers Club, the Jacobin Club, the city government, the National Convention—practicing a politics of confrontation, intimidation, and abuse, which Jacobin leaders experienced as an intolerable political, social, psychological, and physical threat to the new revolutionary republican order.

The final defeat of the society was provoked in September and October by clashes between Society women and hostile market women over women's obligation to war the tricolor cockade and the liberty cap—emblems of republican citizenship. On 8 Brumaire, the market women brought the dispute before the National Convention. They were concerned, for one thing, about the society's policing of markets to enforce price ceilings on foodstuffs; the surveillance was destroying their trade. But they had a more basic concern. They demanded a decree abolishing the Society of Revolutionary Republican Women. Their spokeswoman, referring directly to a point made in their petition, stated that a woman had caused the misfortunes of France and had just atoned for her heinous crimes. The market women's thinly veiled reference to Marie-Antoinette linked a treasonous queen to a treacherously radical women's political club and hinted at the appropriateness of an identical fate for both. The deputies, after further discussion, decided to postpone a vote on the future of the society until after they had heard the report of an investigation conducted by the Committee of General Security. The market women, however, would brook no delay. Their spokeswomen returned to the bar to demand once again the abolition of all *"sociétés particulières de femmes."*[39]

The Jacobins, now firmly in control of the National Convention, seized the opportunity created by this clash between market women, concerned for the stability of their trade, and the Revolutionary Republican Women, determined to escalate surveillance and enforce the terror. Taking up the attack on the society, the Jacobin deputy Fabre d'Eglantine focused attention on links between society members' early demands for the right to wear cockades, their recent demands for the right to wear the liberty cap, and their predictable escalation of demands to display emblems of citizenship into calls for laws authorizing them to wear military accoutrements: ". . . soon they will demand belts, complete with pistols . . ."; soon you would see armed women marching in military formation to get bread "the way one marches to the trenches." Fabre found this image so intolerably explosive that he had to defuse it with the unintentionally revealing observation that men probably were behind women's demands for arms; *men* would use the arms in which women decked themselves out; women did not even know how to fire them! Fabre proceeded to instate models of public and private spheres and rigidly defined gender roles directly at the center of the Jacobin vision of the revolutionary order—a vision that finally had become perfectly clear. Fabre characterized members of women's societies as "species of adventurous women, errant cavaliers, emancipated girls, female grenadiers." He distinguished them from mothers of families, young girls at home, sisters caring for younger siblings. He relegated militant *citoyennes*—precisely the *républicaines révolutionnaires* whose acts the Jacobins had just recently validated and exploited—to the rank of aberrant political, moral, and sexual beings.[40]

The following day, 9 Brumaire, André Amar, speaking for the Committee of General Security of the Convention, reported on his committee's investigation of the market brawls. He also raised two more general questions: "(1) Can women exercise political rights and take an active part in the affairs of government? (2) Can they deliberate together in political associations or popular societies?" Amar's answers were negative in both cases.

Women lacked the requisite moral qualities and physical strength to participate in politics—that is, to govern, debate, legislate in the public interest, and resist oppression. Nor could there be any question of women's meeting in political associations, like clubs, the purpose of which was to unveil enemy maneuvers, to exercise surveillance over authorities, to provide examples of republican virtue, and to enlighten through "in-depth discussion." Women were "destined by their very nature," in all its expressions—biological, psychological, intellectual, moral—to engage in "private functions" (like caring for their households, supervising their children's education, counseling their husbands). "Each sex," Amar explained, "is called to the kind of occupation which is fitting for it; its action is circumscribed within this circle which it cannot break through because nature, which has imposed these limits on mankind, commands imperiously and receives no law." In a detailed comparison of the two sexes, Amar depicted the strength, energy, audacity, robust constitution, and courage of man, and above all, his aptitude for "profound and serious thinking which calls for great intellectual effort and long studies." In contrast, he brought into relief "women's softness and moderation." And he exposed their overall fragility. "Women are disposed by their constitution to an over-excitation which would be deadly in public affairs"; women "are ill-suited for elevated thoughts and serious meditations."

On the basis of Amar's report, the Convention decreed the prohibition of clubs and popular societies of women. This proscription was followed on 27 Brumaire by legislation prohibiting deputations of women to the Paris Commune.[41]

The Jacobin repression of 9 Brumaire is an extreme political response to the militant citizenship that women had been practicing since 1789. The Jacobins rationalized this repression with a full-blown gendered interpretation of nature and its laws that read women out of the polity: women's "nature" and revolutionary citizenship were defined as mutually exclusive. Strength, reason, endurance, and an aptitude for civic virtue—the qualities of man's nature, prepared him for citizenship. Timidity, modesty, weakness, susceptibility to over-excitation, ineptitude for elevated thoughts and serious meditations, determined women's natural incapacity for political life.

The repression of October 1793 is overdetermined. Here we expose three strands of thinking that fed into it. First, the Jacobins, compelled to rein in a popular, grass-roots regulationist *économie politique* as they struggled to mediate among conflicting economic interests in a period of an international war, had come to perceive the *républicaines révolutionnaires* as absolutely ungovernable—Fabre's "adventurous women, errant cavaliers, emancipated girls, female grenadiers"—ungovernable perhaps in part because their organized and relentless practice of a politics of subsistence and surveillance, unlike the politics of sans-culotte men, could not be regulated through the usual mechanisms of political coercions, co-optations, and controls. Women were not part of the political system—they did not hold office, they did not vote, they did not sit in assemblies or on committees. Second, the Jacobin leadership perceived the society's institutionalized practice of militant citizenship as threatening to the stability of the family, and above all, to the formative roles within the family of mothers—producers and reproducers of values and virtues capable of softening and moderating the necessarily hard, cold, and inflexible civic virtue of male citizens.[42] Third, women exercising politico-military powers and grounding their claims to these powers in declarations of natural rights were women who, in point of fact, had broken through both classical and Rousseauian definitions of femininity as weakness, lack, and incapacity. In the most fundamental sense, the threat the *républicaines révolutionnaires* posed to the Jacobins may have been a threat of castration or impotence—hence the fixation of Fabre d'Eglantine on women with pistols; and hence the obsession of the Jacobin deputy Chaumette with getting male and female physiology absolutely straight once and for all. Chaumette's sorting out of anatomies and political destinies in the body politic took place at a meeting of the Paris Commune on 27 Brumaire Year II at which a deputation of women wearing red caps of liberty—presumably the prohibited *républicaines révolutionnaires*—made an appearance. "It is horrible, it is contrary to all the laws of nature for a woman to want to make herself a man . . . Well! since when is it permitted to give up one's sex? . . . Is it to men that nature confided domestic cares? Has she given us breasts to breast-feed our children?" [A crying question remained unasked by the speaker: Has nature given women penises?] "No," Chaumette exclaimed, "she has said to man: Be a man: hunting, farming, political concerns, . . . that is your appanage. She has said to woman: Be a woman. The tender cares owing to infancy . . . the sweet anxieties of maternity, these are your labors . . ."[43]

Most interpretations of women's citizenship in revolutionary Paris have centered on the historical significance of the repression of the fall of 1793. As the Jacobins wrested political power from their antagonists and tightened their control over revolutionary discourse, they also consolidated a republican regime based upon deeply gendered definitions of revolutionary principles like civic virtue, liberty, equality, and citizenship. These definitions were perpetuated in the patriarchal institutions, laws, and language of later regimes.

However, we also see that in a relatively fluid and malleable situation between 1789 and 1793, even where gendered definitions of citizenship were encoded in constitutional law and in cultural representations, women nonetheless practiced militant citizenship as they integrated themselves into the political nation, participated in grass-roots democratic institutions, marched armed in ceremonies as members of a united military force, a national family in arms, led or participated in revolutionary *journées*, and in the case of the Society of Revolutionary Republican Women, policed markets, mobilized support among radicals within section organizations, and exercised surveillance over the National Convention. Through all these activities, they identified themselves as members of the sovereign body politic—*citoyennes* notwithstanding their exclusion from codified political rights of citizenship. In strident discourse, spokeswomen like Pauline Léon self-consciously linked women's practices of militant citizenship to principles. As they demanded the right to bear arms, they invoked universal laws of human nature (like the capacity for rational thought) and universal rights of nature codified in the Declaration of the Rights of Man (the right of self-preservation and self-defense, the right to resist oppression). They also insisted on women's innate capacity for acting on moral/political imperatives—for practicing civic virtue—and, in short, for assuming precisely the full responsibilities and the rights of citizenship that the Jacobins were recasting as "universal" political prerogatives—of male citizens exclusively. During this period, gender roles became one focus of political power struggles, including struggles for control of the revolutionary vocabulary, with its definitions of virtue, vice, and the parameters of citizenship. As part of that struggle, women repeatedly challenged, eluded, or subverted cultural constructs that dictated rigidly defined gender roles and limits (including those based on a presumption of women's innate or socially determined incapacity for assuming political identities). In discourse and act, they forced real, if short-lived and incomplete, transformations and expansions of the meaning and practice of citizenship and sovereignty.

Notes

1. See, for example, Harriet B. Applewhite, Darline G. Levy, eds., *Women and Politics in the Age of the Democratic Revolution* (Ann Arbor, 1990); Joan Wallach Scott, *Gender and the Politics of History* (New York, 1988), 46–50.

2. Dominique Godineau, *Citoyennes tricoteuses. Les femmes du peuple à Paris pendant la Révolution française* (Aix-en-Provence, 1988), 352.

3. Dorinda Outram, *"Le langage mâle de la vertu:* Women and the Discourse of the French Revolution," in Peter Burke, Roy Porter, eds., *The Social History of Language* (Cambridge, Eng., 1987), 120–35.

4. For one analysis in this vein, see Joan Landes, *Women and the Public Sphere in the Age of the French Revolution* (Ithaca, 1988), esp. chap. 5.

5. For our earlier documentation and interpretation of women's political participation in revolutionary Paris, see Darline Gay Levy, Harriet Branson Applewhite, Mary Durham Johnson, eds., *Women in Revolutionary Paris, 1789-1795)* (Urbana, Chicago, London, 1979, 1980); Levy and Applewhite, "Women and Politics in Revolutionary Paris," in Renata Bridenthal, Claudia Koonz, Susan Stuard, eds., *Becoming Visible. Women in European History*, 2nd ed. (Boston, 1986), 278–306; Levy and Applewhite, "Responses to the Political Activism of Women of the People in Revolutionary Paris, 1789-1793," in *Women and the Structure of Society. Selected Research from the Fifth Berkshire Conference on the History of Women*, ed. Barbara Harris JoAnn McNamara (Durham, N.C., 1984); Levy and Applewhite, "Women of the Popular Classes in Revolutionary Paris," in Carol Berkin, Clara Lovett, eds., *Women, War, and Revolution* (New York: 1980), 9–35; Applewhite and Levy, "Ceremonial Dimensions of Citizenship: Women and Oathtaking in Revolutionary Paris," in *Proceedings of the Fifth George Rudé Seminar*, Department of History, Victoria University of Wellington, New Zealand, August 26-29, 1986). We are presently preparing an expansion and synthesis of our previous work, tentatively titled *Gender and Citizenship in Revolutionary Paris, 1789-1793* (forthcoming, Duke University Press). For the citation from Olympe de Gouges, *Les Droits de la Femme*, see Levy, Applewhite, Johnson, *Women in Revolutionary Paris*, 90.

6. *Réimpression de l'Ancien Moniteur* 2, no. 70 (October 10, 1789):25.

7. *Révolutions de Paris* 1, no. 13 (October 3–10, 1789):9.

8. *Extraits de la procédure criminelle instruite au Châtelet de Paris sur la Dénonciation des faits arrivés à Versailles dans la journée du 6 octobre 1789 . . .*, witness no. 81, reproduced in *Réimpression de l'Ancien Moniteur* 2:538.

9. Siméon-Prosper Hardy, "Mes Loisirs," October 5, 1789, in Bibliothèque nationale, MSS fr., no. 6687, fol. 502. Unquestionably, the idea of returning the king to Paris was in the air. Only a fortnight before the march to Versailles, an individual who had made that very suggestion had been indicted for treason. See J. M. Thompson, *The French Revolution* (New York, 1966), 101.

10. This discussion of the October days is drawn from our unpublished paper, "Gender and the Politicization of Space in Revolutionary Paris: Beyond the Public/ Private Dichotomy," Seventh Berkshire Conference of Women Historians, Wellesley College, June 1987. Testimony by the king's bodyguards concerning confrontations with armed women marchers in front of the chateau at Versailles can be found in Archives Nationales, C.222, 160[157]. For instances of testimony on demands for an interview with the king, see letter of M. d'Albignac, lieutenant of the king's bodyguard, January 10, 1790, ibid; De Maleden, *Par Qui, comment, et pourquoi les gardes du corps ont été assassinés à Versailles le 5 octobre 1789* (n.p., n.d.), ibid. Re the women's demands for written commitments from the king concerning his promises of bread supplies for Paris, see report of M. de Huiller, Lodge Marshall, Scottish Company, n.d., ibid.; letter from the Colonel de l'Artigue, March 7, 1780, ibid.

11. For descriptions of the procession from Versailles to Paris on October 6, see, for example, testimony of Noël-Joseph Madier de Montjau, in "Extraits de la Procédure criminelle," in *Réimpression de l'Ancien Moniteur*, no. 170:568–69; *Chronique de Paris* no. 45 (October 7, 1789):178; *Révolutions de Paris*, no. 13 (October 3–10, 1789), p. 22. For the quote, "Courage my friends, we won't lack bread any longer . . . ," see *Réimpression de l'Ancien Moniteur* 2, no. 72 (October 12, 1789):44.

12. This interpretation owes much to Steven Kaplan's pioneering study, "The Famine Plot Persuasion in Eighteenth Century France," *Transactions of the American Philosophical Society*, vol. 72, part 3 (Philadelphia, 1982). Kaplan, however, does not argue, as we do here, that the crowd's designation of the king as a baker is indicative in itself of a shattering of popular trust in his ability to function as royal father-provider. See ibid., 66–67.

13. *Journal de Paris*, no. 281 (October 8, 1789).

14. *Journal de Paris*, no. 281 (October 8, 1789). See also Jean-Félix Faydel's testimony in "Extraits de la Procédure criminelle," in *Réimpression de l'Ancien Moniteur* 2:560 ff.

15. *Révolutions de Versailles et de Paris, Dédiées aux dames françoises*, no. 1 "du samedi 3 octobre au 7" (Paris, 1789), 1.

16. *Journal de Paris*, no. 281 (October 8, 1789). Jean-Joseph Mounier, *Exposé de la conduite de M. Mounier dans l'Assemblée nationale et des motifs de son retour en Dauphiné* (Paris, 1789), 75.

17. Testimony of Jean-Félix Faydel, in *Procédure criminelle, instruite au Châtelet de Paris, sur la Dénonciation des faits arrivés à Versailles dans la journée du 6 octobre 1789* (Paris, 1790), witness no. 148.

18. *Etrennes nationales des Dames*, no. 1 (November 3, 1789), 1.

19. *Requête des dames à l'Assemblée nationale* (n.p., n.d. [end of 1789, following the October days]), in *Les Femmes dans la Révolution française* [ed. Albert Soboul], 2 vols. (Paris, 1982), I, no. 19.

20. For our detailed analysis of women's participation in ceremonial and insurrectionary politics during the period between July 1791 and August 1792, see Darline G. Levy, Harriet B. Applewhite, "Women, Radicalization and the Fall of the French Monarchy," in Applewhite and Levy, eds., *Women and Politics in the Age of the Democratic Revolution* (Ann Arbor, 1990). See also Levy and Applewhite, "Women and Politics in Revolutionary Paris," *Becoming Visible*, 293–98. We wish to thank the University of Michigan Press and Houghton Mifflin Company for permission to cite and paraphrase material from these chapters.

21. Jean-Paul Marat, *Ami du peuple*, no. 529, Wednesday, August 10, 1791, 1–2.

22. Jean-Paul Marat, *Ami du peuple*, no. 524, July 20, 1791, 2.

23. For a complete description of the armed march of April 9, see Levy and Applewhite, "Women, Radicalization and the Fall of the French Monarchy," in Applewhite and Levy, *Women and Politics in the Age of the Democratic Revolution*. See also *Archives parlementaires*, First Series, vol. 41, April 9, 1792, 387–91.

24. For a general description of the fête of April fifteenth: *Archives parlementaires*, First Series, vol. 42, April 15, 1792, pp. 682–97. See also *Révolutions de Paris*, no. 145, April 14–21, 1792, p. 100. The quote is from this issue of the *Révolution de Paris*. For another account [Mme. Rosalie Jullien], see *Journal d'une bourgeoise pendant la Révolution, 1791–1793*, ed. Edouard Lockroy (Paris, 1881), 65–68.

25. See for example, Mme. Jullien, *Journal d'une bourgeoise pendant la Révolution*, 65.

26. *Courier français*, no. 97, April 6, 1792.

27. *Archives parlementaires*, First Series, vol. 39, March 6, 1792:423–424.

28. Ibid.

29. Montjoie, *Ami du Roi*, no. 58, Thursday, March 8, 1792, 270, reporting on a session of the Legislative Assembly on Tuesday evening, March 6, 1792.

30. Levy and Applewhite, "Women, Radicalization, and the Fall of the French Monarchy."

31. For the position of the mayor of Paris, who was sympathetic to the marchers and their leaders, see Jérome Pétion, "Conduite tenue par M. le maire de Paris à l'occasion des événements du 20 juin," in *Revue retrospective*, 2me série, I, 221–34. For discussion by hostile officials in the Department of Paris, see *Extrait des registres des délibérations du Conseil du Département de Paris, 6 juillet 1792* (Paris, 1792).

32. Cited in Godineau, "Les Femmes des milieux popularies parisiens pendant la Révolution française (1793–Messidor An III)," 3 vols., doctoral dissertation, University of Paris I, 1986), vol. 2, 455. Aulard refers to this deputation in *La Société des Jacobins*, vol. V, 186. In the published version of her dissertation, *Citoyennes tricoteuses*, 395, no. 2, Godineau indicates her source for citations from the Society members' address to the Jacobins as *Journal des débats et de la correspondance des Jacobins*, no. 412.

33. *Règlement de la Société des citoyennes républicaines révolutionnaires de Paris* (n.p., n.d.), trans. in Levy, Applewhite, Johnson, *Women in Revolutionary Paris*, 161–65.

34. For further discussion, see Marie Cerati, *Le Club des citoyennes républicaines révolutionnaires* (Paris, 1966), chap. VII.

35. "Extrait du procès-verbal de l'Assemblée générale des commissaires des autorités constitués du Département et des sections de Paris, tenue en la Salle de l'Evêché, le dimanche 30 juin 1793, l'an seconde de la République française une et indivisible,' signed Dupin, secrétaire. This extract appears along with an address by L. P. Duforny, President of the Assemblée générale, on a poster titled *Département de Paris. Les Autorités constitués du Département de Paris & les commissaires des sections, aux*

Républicaines Révolutionnaires (Paris, n.d. [1793]. The document is included in a packet of posters published with *Les Femmes dans la Révolution française* [ed. Albert Soboul].

36. A. J. Gorsas, *Précis rapide des événements qui ont eu lieu à Paris dans les journées des 30 et 31 mai, premier et 2 juin 1793* (n.p., n.d.), trans. in Levy, Applewhite, Johnson, *Women in Revolutionary Paris*, 154–55.

37. "Discours prononcé par Hérault, Président de la Convention nationale lors de la cérémonie qui a eu lieu pour l'acceptation de la Constitution," in *Réimpression de l'Ancien Moniteur* 17:367. Godineau, "Les femmes des milieux populaires parisiens" II:517; Jacques-Louis David's report to the National Convention on July 12, 1793, on plans for the fête of August 10, 1793, in *Réimpression de l'Ancien Moniteur*, vol. 17, 119–21, reproduced in Marie-Louise Biver, *Fêtes révolutionnaires à Paris* (Paris, 1979), 183–87.

38. Albert Soboul, *Les Sans-culottes parisiens en l'an II. Mouvement populaire et gouvernement révolutionnaire, 2 juin 1792–thermidor an II* (Paris, 1958), 150.

39. *Archives parlementaires*, Series I, vol. 78 (October 29, 1793), 20, 21; *Réimpression de l'Ancien Moniteur*, vol. 18, 290.

40. Paule Marie Duhet, *Les Femmes et la Révolution, 1789–1794* (Paris, 1971), 149–50. See also *Archives parlementaires*, Series I, vol. 78, 22; *Réimpression de l'Ancien Moniteur* 18:290.

41. Session of the National Convention, 9 Brumaire Year II, in *Réimpression de l'Ancien Moniteur* 18:298–300, trans. in Levy, Applewhite, Johnson, *Women in Revolutionary Paris*, 213–17. Session of the General Council of the Paris Commune, 27 Brumaire Year II, in *Réimpression de l'Ancien Moniteur* 18:450–51, trans. in Levy, Applewhite, Johnson, 219–20.

42. For discussion of this theme, see William H. Sewell, Jr., "Le citoyen/la citoyenne. Activity, Passivity, and the Revolutionary Concept of Citizenship," in Colin Lucas, ed., *The Political Culture of the French Revolution* (Oxford, 1989), 105–23.

43. Session of the General Council of the Paris Commune, 27 Brumaire Year II, in *Réimpression de l'Ancien Moniteur* 18:450–51, trans. in Levy, Applewhite, Johnson, *Women in Revolutionary Paris*, 219–20.

6

"A Woman Who Has Only Paradoxes to Offer": Olympe de Gouges Claims Rights for Women

JOAN WALLACH SCOTT

Si j'allais plus avant sur cette matière, je pourrais m'étendre trop loin, et m'attirer l'inimitié des hommes parvenus, qui, sans réfléchir sur mes bonnes vues, ni approfondir mes bonnes intentions, me condamneraient impitoyablement comme une femme qui n'a que des paradoxes à offrir, et non des problemes faciles à résoudre.

Olympe de Gouges, 1789

For women, the legacy of the French Revolution was contradictory. On the one hand, the unit of national sovereignty was declared to be a universal, abstract, rights-bearing individual; on the other hand, this human subject was almost immediately given particularized embodiment as a man. The abstraction of a genderless individual endowed with natural rights made it possible for women to claim the political rights of active citizens and, when denied them in practice, to protest against exclusion as unjust, a violation of the founding principles of the republic. There is no question, from this perspective, of the powerful impetus such universal theory gave (and continues to give) to democratic movements. But there is also no question that the equally abstract gesture of embodiment—the attribution of citizenship to (white) male subjects—complicated enormously the project of claiming equal rights, for it suggested either that rights themselves, or at least how and where they were exercised, depended on the physical characteristics of human bodies. This particularization of the human in the name of universality introduced into discussions of equality the problem of difference: How could those who were

I wish to thank Sara Melzer and Leslie Rabine for helpful editorial readings and Judith Butler, Jacquelyn Dowd Hall, Ruth Leys, Denise Riley, Donald Scott, and Elizabeth Weed for their invaluable critical suggestions. A somewhat different version of this essay appeared as "French Feminists and the Rights of 'Man': Olympe de Gouge's Declarations," in *History Workshop*, 28 (Autumn 1989), pp. 1–21.

not white men—blacks, mulattoes, and women—claim for themselves the rights of 'Man'?

The general answer is: with difficulty. There was no simple way either to expand the category of Man to take in all his Others or to disembody the abstract individual so that literally anyone could represent him. Specific contests about the rights of excluded groups did not resolve this paradox, but exposed it; the terms of debate and the strategies of the contenders show equality to be a more elusive ideal in both its formulation and achievement than was ever acknowledged by the revolution's most visionary architects or, for that matter, by many of its historians.

There is no denying the presence of differently marked bodies—of the physical traits of sex and skin color—in the political debates of the French Revolution. Whether we take the conflicting opinions expressed during the writing of constitutions; the arguments about slave, mulatto, or women's civic rights propounded by Barnave, Brissot, Condorcet, or Robespierre; the contrasting reflections of Edmund Burke and Mary Wollstonecraft; or the minutes of section meetings in Paris, we find interpretations that assume that bodies and rights alike could be thought of as "natural" and that this "naturalness" provided a connection between them. Rights were often referred to as being inscribed on bodies, inalienably attached to them, indelibly imprinted on human minds or hearts.[1] But the connection between "natural" bodies and "natural" rights was neither transparent nor straightforward. The meanings of nature, rights, and bodies, as well as the relationships among them, were at issue in the revolutionary debates and these contests about meanings were contests about power. One sees this clearly in the debates occasioned by femininsts' demands for rights in the course of the revolution.

I

From the outset of the Revolution, there were scattered demands for women's rights. These were most often rejected by revolutionary legislators, the vast majority of whom insisted firmly that women were by nature unfit to exercise political rights. During discussion of the Constitution of 1793, for example, the deputy for île-et-Vilaine, Jean Denis Lanjuinais, reported to the Convention that though it had received several protests against the exclusion of women from active citizenship, his committee would uphold the exclusion. Even in the future under the best circumstances, he argued, when institutions were more just and more in conformity with nature, "it is difficult to believe that women ought to be called to exercise political rights. It is beyond me to think that, taking all into account, men and women would gain anything good from it."[2]

Attention to women seems to have increased in 1793 in association first with the drafting of the new constitution and then with the execution of Marie Antoinette on October 16.[3] Several days after the queen's execution, the question of citizenship was rephrased as a more general question of women's political role. Using the occasion of a street disturbance between market women and members of the Society of Revolutionary Republican Women, the Convention outlawed all women's clubs and popular societies, invoking Rousseauist themes to deny women the exercise of political rights and to end, some hoped definitively, persistent feminist agitation.[4] "Should women exercise political rights and meddle in the affairs of government?" asked André Amar, the representative of the Committee of General Security. "In general, we can answer, no." He went on to consider whether women could even meet in political associations and again answered negatively:

> because they would be obliged to sacrifice the more important cares to which nature calls them. The private functions for which women are destined by their very nature are related to the general order of society; this social order results from the differences between man and woman. Each sex is called to the kind of occupation which is fitting for it; its action is circumscribed within this circle which it cannot break through, because nature, which has imposed these limits on man, commands imperiously and receives no law.[5]

An even more explicit articulation of these so-called natural facts came from Pierre-Gaspard Chaumette, a radical hébertist and member of the Paris Commune. On behalf of the Commune he indignantly rejected an appeal for support from female petitioners protesting the Convention's decree:

> Since when is it permitted to give up one's sex? Since when is it decent to see women abandoning the pious cares of their households, the cribs of their children, to come to public places, to harangues in the galleries, at the bar of the senate? Is it to men that nature confided domestic cares? Has she given us breasts to feed our children?[6]

Less brilliantly than Rousseau, but no less clearly, the Jacobin politicians set forth the terms of their new social order. Their invocation of nature as the origin of both liberty and sexual difference drew on certain prominent (but by no means uncontested) views of political theory and medicine. These views treated nature and the body as synonymous; in the body one could discern the truths upon which social and political organization ought to rest. Constantin Volney, representative for the Third Estate of Anjou at the meetings of the Estates General from 1788 to 1789, argued firmly in his catechism of 1793 that virtue and vice "are always ultimately referable to . . . the destruction or preservation of the body."[7] For Volney, questions of health were questions of state; "civic responsibility [was] health-seeking behavior."[8] Individual illness signified social deterioration; the failure of a mother to breast-feed her infant constituted a refusal of nature's corporeal design, hence a profoundly antisocial act.[9] The misuse of the body incurred not only individual costs, but social consequences since the body politic was, for Volney, not a metaphor but a literal description.

The body, of course, was not considered in these writings a single phenomenon; sexual difference was taken as a founding principle of the natural, hence the social and political order. Tom Laqueur has shown that ideas of sexual difference are not fixed; their long and variable history demonstrates that sexual meanings are not transparently attached to or immanent in sexed bodies. Laqueur argues that by the eighteenth century biological theory emphasized incommensurable differences between the bodies of women and men.[10] Indeed, genital difference made all the difference; masculinity or femininity constituted the entire identity of biological males or females. One of the differences between them, in fact, had to do with how completely sex defined their beings. A Dr. Moreau offered as his own Rousseau's explanation for the commonly accepted notion that women were (in Denise Riley's words) "thoroughly saturated with their sex."[11] He maintained that the location of the genital organs, inside in women, outside in men, determined the extent of their influence: "the internal influence continually recalls women to their sex . . . the male is male only at certain moments, but the female is female throughout her life."[12]

In the intersecting discourses of biology and politics, theories of complementarity resolved the potentially disruptive effects of sexual difference. Species reproduction and social order were said to depend on the union of the opposite elements, male and female, on a functional division of labor that granted nature her due. Although it was logically possible to present complementarity as an egalitarian doctrine, in fact it served in the predominant political rhetoric of this period to justify an asymmetrical relationship between men and women. The goals of the revolution, after all, were liberty, sovereignty, moral choice informed by reason, and active involvement in the formation of just laws. All of these were firmly designated male prerogatives, defined in contrast to the female. The contrasting elements were:

active	passive
liberty	duty
individual sovereignty	dependency
public	private
political	domestic
reason	modesty
speech	silence
education	maternal nurture
universal	particular
male	female[13]

The second column served not only to define the first, but provided the possibility for its existence. "Natural" sexual difference permitted a resolution of some of the knotty and persistent problems of inequalities of power in political theory by locating individual freedom in male subjects and associating social cohesion with females. Maternal nurture awakened or instilled human empathy (pity) and love of virtue, the qualities that tempered selfish individualism; modesty at once equipped women to perform their roles and served as a corrective to their inability otherwise to restrain (sexual) desire. Women's modesty was, furthermore, a precondition for the successful exercise of male reason in restraint of desire.[14] The containment of voracious female sexuality was, in this Enlightenment theory, a prerequisite for the achievement of public virtue. And it required the restriction of women to the domestic realm, their exclusion from politics.[15] The dependency of the domestic sphere elicited from men the fulfillment of their social duty; indeed duty denoted here not women's obligations but their position as the objects of male obligation.

The active/passive distinction, in fact, resting as it did on contrasting theories of natural rights, summed up the differences: those who enjoyed active rights were individual agents, making moral choices, exercising liberty, acting (speaking) on their own behalf. They were, by definition, political subjects. Those who enjoyed passive rights had the "right to be given or allowed something by someone else."[16] Their status as political subjects was ambiguous, if not wholly in doubt. This was the view of women's rights expressed by the exasperated Chaumette in October 1793: "Impudent women who want to become men," (I imagine) he shouted, "aren't you well enough provided for? What else do you need?"[17]

II

The logical answer to Chaumette involved a reassertion of the demand for rights and a rejection of the so-called natural grounds on which they had been denied. But, as the work of Olympe de Gouges will show us, the answer did not come easily. Confronting the paradox of an embodied equality created paradoxes for feminist thought and these were not "problems easy to resolve."[18]

By looking at how feminists articulated their demands we can explore the effects of the paradox of embodied equality and perhaps answer some of the thoughtful and provocative questions raised by the British historian Barbara Taylor. She asks:

> What does it mean when [feminists] engage with a theory of the subject in which the reasoning speaker—that is the person who displays possession of natural rights and a place in the civic sphere *through* . . . speech—is actually constituted on the male side of the sexual axis? And where does that take us with egalitarianism?[19]

Taylor's questions assume that asymmetrical representations of rights are not easily corrected by universalist or pluralist arguments and that such arguments can never be formulated entirely outside the discourses they challenge. Cora Kaplan puts it this way: "There is no feminism that can stand wholly outside femininity as it is posed in a given historical moment. All feminisms give some ideological hostage to femininities and are constructed through the gender sexuality of their day as well as standing in opposition to them."[20]

This means that feminism's inherently political aspect comes from its critical engagement with prevailing theories and practices; it does not stand as an independent philosophical movement with an autonomous content and a independent legacy of its own.[21] It must be read, therefore, in its concrete manifestations, and then not only for its programmatic recommendations.

Tests of logical consistency of philosophical purity, like categorizations of feminist "schools" of equality or difference, entirely miss the point. The historical and theoretical interest of modern feminism (which I take to date from the seventeenth century) lies in its exposure of the ambiguities and repressions, the contradictions and silences in liberal political systems that present themselves as coherent, comprehensive, rational, or just because they rest on "natural", "scientific," or "universal" principles. This suggests that feminism must not only be read in its historical contexts, but also that it cannot be detached from those contexts as evidence either for some transcendent Woman's identity or for the teleology of women's emancipation. The meaning of any feminism instead lies in the historical specificity of a recurring critical operation.

My interest in this essay is in the ways feminists addressed the issue of equality during the French Revolution. How did they formulate their claims for political rights? How did they create the political subject they claimed already to represent? How did they demand citizenship when such public status for women was taken as a contradiction of nature's functional design for social order? How did they attempt to refute or confound what was assumed to be the indisputable evidence of the body? How did they understand the influence of nature on the definition of their rights?

A full-scale study of all the manifestations of feminism in the French Revolution is beyond the scope of this chapter. I will instead concentrate on one figure—Olympe de Gouges (1748–93). I take de Gouges neither as a typical feminist nor an exemplary heroine, but because she provides a site where cultural contests and political contradictions can be examined in some detail. Her writings (the most famous of which is the *Declaration of the Rights of Woman and Citizen*, written in 1791 as the first constitution was being debated) are full of ambiguities and paradoxes that expose the operations of particularity and exclusion in the abstract concept of universal Man.

Olympe de Gouges! This name always calls forth smiles from those who hear it for the first time, bemused recognition from veterans of women's history courses. Its pretention and inauthenticity seem to produce a comic effect, comic because satirical or transgressive. The name Olympe de Gouges was not, indeed, the one recognized in law for this woman; rather it was one she crafted for herself. Born Marie Gouzes, daughter of a butcher and former servant in Montauban, she was married at age 16 to a man much older than herself. Shortly after the birth of their son, her husband, Louis Yves Aubry died, but Marie refused to use the customary designation, Veuve Aubry. Instead she took her mother's middle name, Olympe, added a "de" and changed her father's surname to Gouges. She vowed never again to marry, although she had at least one long-standing heterosexual liaison. At the same time, she suggested that the butcher hadn't been her father at all, but that she was the illegitimate offspring of a romance between her mother and a local notable, the marquis Le Franc de Pompignan.[22] This lineage added intrigue and status to her life and (since the marquis had won a reputation as a man of letters) provided a genealogy for her own literary aspirations. It also, of course, made a mockery of the rules of patrilineal origin and naming. (The theme of naming and renaming the father reappears, albeit with inconsistent and varied usage, throughout de Gouges's life and work.)[23] De Gouges never managed to prove the story of her birth, but that is less important than her repeated assertions of its veracity. These assertions, like her self-renaming, constituted her identity: tentative, ambiguous, and never fully secured.[24]

De Gouges was always involved in a process of self-construction. She fought valiantly, for example, for recognition as a playwright and exaggerated her standing when she did succeed in having several of her plays accepted (and even performed) by the Comédie Française. Writing was an important, indeed primary, aspect of her self-representation, although she apparently wrote with great difficulty, dictating most of her texts. Speaking came more easily; she was apparently eloquent and inspired in her verbal displays; but these she considered an insufficient measure of her talents.[25] When the revolution came, she demonstrated her capacities as an active citizen by rushing into the fray, writing and speaking on behalf of a number of causes: freedom from bondage for slaves, the creation of a national theater and also of a theater for women playwrights, clean streets, provision of maternity hospitals, divorce, and the recognition of the rights of illegitimate children and unmarried mothers. In order more fully to follow the deliberations of the various political assemblies, de Gouges rented lodgings adjacent to their headquarters, in this way literally attaching herself to these august bodies. She was a familiar figure in the galleries and at the podium and her proclamations often covered the walls of the city of Paris. It was as if only her continuing physical presence could assert her status as a political subject; and even then, of course, this was a tentative, contested identity at best, one whose terms she could never fully control.

Along with her proposals usually came a sometimes playful, sometimes disturbing reminder of the fact that a woman was speaking. De Gouges at once stressed her identity with the universal human individual and her difference. Indeed, her formulations demonstrate the difficulty for a woman in unambivalently securing status as an abstract individual in the face of its masculine embodiment. In order to claim the general status of "human" for women, she insisted on their particular qualifications; in the process of insisting on equality, she constantly pointed out and acknowledged difference. "It is a woman who dares to show herself so strong and so courageous for her King and her country. . . ."[26] "They can exclude women from all National Assemblies, but my beneficient genius brings me to the center of this assembly."[27] "Oh people, unhappy citizens, listen to the voice of a just and feeling woman."[28] The title of one of her brochures was "Le Cri du Sage: par une femme."[29] When she put herself forward to defend Louis XVI during his trial she suggested both that sex ought not to be a consideration ("leave aside my sex") and that it should be ("heroism and generosity are also women's portion and the revolution offers more than one example of it.")[30]

De Gouges never escaped the ambiguity of feminine identity, the simultaneous appeal to and critique of established notions of femininity, and she often exploited it. On the one hand, she attacked women as they were—indulgent, frivolous, seductive, intriguing, and duplicitous[31]—insisting they could choose to act otherwise (like men); on the other hand, she appealed to women to unite to defend their special interests, and to the legislature to recognize its duty to protect mothers. If she asserted that their worst characteristics had been constructed for women by unjust social organization, she nonetheless appealed to her sex to unite (around her leadership) regardless of rank, in order to exert political power in the common interest.[32] And, while she maintained that equality, and not special privilege, was the only ground on which woman could stand, she nonetheless (unsuccessfully) sought special advantage by claiming that she was pregnant in order to avoid, or at least postpone, the death sentence conferred on her by the Jacobins in 1793.

The *Declaration of the Rights of Woman and Citizen* contains these ambiguous invocations of stereotypes of femininity and of claims to equality that deny those stereotypes. For the most part, its articles parallel those of the *Declaration of the Rights of Man and Citizen* of 1789, extending to women the rights of 'Man.' Woman and Man are usually both invoked, for in her effort to produce the complete declaration de Gouges most often simply pluralized the concept of citizenship. But she also addressed her declaration to Marie Antoinette, first woman of the realm, with the coy remark that if the queen were "less educated . . . I would fear that your special interests would prevail over those of your sex."[33] And her preamble to the document, after echoing phrases about how ignorance, forgetfulness, or contempt of (women's) rights had been "the sole causes of public unhappiness and the corruption of governments," concluded with the stunning assertion that "the sex superior in beauty as in courage during childbirth, recognizes and declares, in the presence and under the auspices of the Supreme Being, the following rights of woman and citizen."[34] The very difference of women, this formulation suggests, as well as their exclusion, requires a separate discussion of their rights.[35]

Article XI of the *Declaration* on the right of free speech stands out for the attention it draws to the distinctive needs of women:

> The free communication of ideas and opinions is one of the most precious rights of woman, since this liberty guarantees that fathers will recognize their children. Any citizen (citoyenne) can thus say freely: I am the mother of your child, without being forced by barbarous prejudice to hide the truth. . . .[36]

What is striking about this statement is the particularity of its interpretation—a particularity that rests on physical difference. De Gouges could not stay with the abstract universal language she used in most of the other articles of her proclamation; simply adding Woman to the *Declaration of the Rights of Man* did not suffice at this point. Why? Clearly the right to speech was, for her, *the* expression of liberty and so most important to discuss at length. In article X, in fact, (which dealt with freedom of opinion) de Gouges added a phrase that belonged more properly in article XI: "woman has the right to mount the scaffold, she ought equally to have the right to mount to the rostrum."[37] (De Gouges here plays with the notion of "right." She turns being subject to the coercive power of the state into a recognition of individual rights, insisting on the literal terms of the social contract.) In this phrase and in article XI, the right to speech is at issue. But in both places, representing women as speaking subjects seems to have required more than expanding or pluralizing the category of citizen. It called for refuting sexuality and maternity as grounds for silencing women in the public/political realm.

In de Gouges's article XI, the unstated grounds of exclusion became the explicit reasons for inclusion. The sexual contract that established the social contract was here (and in the appendix to the *Declaration*) made visible.[38] De Gouges contradicted, with a concrete example, the revolutionaries' endorsement of oppositions between active and passive, liberty and duty, individual and social. Naming the father acknowledged the power of law and exposed the transgressions of the powerful. Without the right to speak, she insisted, women were powerless to enforce paternal duty, to call men back to their obligations, the obligations on which social cohesion and individual liberty depended. Naming the father was both a claim on paternal obligation and an exposure of the abuses of patriarchal power; it also arrogated to women a masculine prerogative.

From one perspective de Gouges's article XI was an argument for equality that gained force and persuasive power from its use of specific detail. At the same time, however, its very specificity weakened its objective. The abstract clauses of the *Declaration of the Rights of Man* never indulge in this level of specific and particularized detail, and so de Gouges's declaration seems by contrast to lack seriousness and generalizability. At the most crucial point in the argument—the demand for liberty to speak—the specificity of Woman marks her difference from the universality of Man. But the addition of Woman is also disruptive because it implies the need to think differently about the whole question of rights.[39]

There is another even more troubling ambiguity in de Gouges's argument. For it is precisely in the area of pregnancy that a woman's speech is simultaneously most authoritative and most open to doubt. Only a woman is in a position to know the truth and so designate paternity (only she can say, "I am the mother of your child" or "you are the father of my child"). But precisely because that is the case—because a man can't know the truth—he must take the woman's word and she may be lying. The terms by which de Gouges claims the rights of speech for women, then, raise the spectre of the unreliable feminine, the devious and calculating opponent of rational, truth-speaking man, and so they are literally fraught with uncertainty.[40]

If de Gouges unwittingly evoked prevailing views of women, she also sought explicitly to counter them. Her analysis of women's artifice and unreliability stressed their lack of education and power. She particularly attacked marriage, "the tomb of trust and love," for its institutionalization of inequality. Through it men imposed "perpetual tyranny" on women, in contradistinction to the harmonious cooperation evident, she insisted, in nature.[41] The prevailing inequality had important personal effects for it forced women to resort to manipulative ploys in their dealings with men and it had negative political effects as well, since a just social order depended on granting all parties to the social contract the same interest in its preservation. For this reason de Gouges recommended replacing the marriage contract with a social contract. She appended to the *Declaration of the Rights of Woman* a "social contract for Man and Woman" and she defined the Nation as "the union of Woman and Man." By this she meant to equate marriage and society, both voluntary unions, entered either for life or "for the duration of our mutual inclinations" by rights-bearing individuals. These were unions, moreover, in which neither partner had any legal advantage. Property was to be held in common and divided according to parental discretion among children "from whatever bed they come." Moreover, the children "have the right to bear the name of the fathers and mothers who have acknowledged them;" the father's name having no special status in the family.[42]

De Gouges used examples about marriage to counter notions of fixed social hierarchies, pointing out, as the Estates General debated the question of how to represent the three orders of the nation, that fixed divisions between these groups did not exist and hence were absurd to maintain since marriage had already mingled the blood of members of the nobility and the Third Estate.[43] The very last line of her *Declaration of the Rights of Woman* improbably took up the question of the separation of powers under the new constitution. There de Gouges argued for a reconciliation of the executive and legislative powers (aligning herself with the supporters of constitutional monarchy): "I consider these two powers to be like a man and a woman, who ought to be united, but equal in power and virtue, in order to establish a good household."[44] In these discussions, many of which read like non sequitors, women's rights were not separable from, but integral to all considerations of politics. The union of man and woman replaced the single figure of the universal individual, in an attempt at resolving the difficulty of arguing about rights in univocal terms. But de Gouges's notion of this union was ambiguous. It could be read as an endorsement of functional complementarity based on sex, but also as an attempt to dissolve or transcend the categories of sexual difference. De Gouges tried to deny the possibility of any meaningful opposition between public and private, political and domestic, while at the same time working with a notion of marital or sexual union conceived in terms of those very oppositions.

In the past, de Gouges reminded her readers, the exclusion of women from politics had led to the corruption associated with "the nocturnal administration of women," when seduction displaced reason and crime prevailed over virtue.[45] These ruses of the weak would disappear in the future, when women were granted full political rights, equal access to property and public employment. Here de Gouges seemed to acknowledge implicitly an often expressed fear of female sexuality, but she attributed it to faulty institutions. Inherently, desire was polyvalent; social usage gave it its meaning and value. For this reason de Gouges urged, in another context, that women be mobilized to "incit[e] young men to fly to the defense of the Fatherland," promising the "hand of your mistress" for those who were brave, rejection for cowards. "The art we possess to move the souls of men would produce the salutary effect of enflaming all spirits. Nothing can resist our seductive organ."[46] Deployed in defense of the nation, as an exercise in active citizenship, female sexuality might secure, not destabilize, the social order. Yet the appeal to this kind of femininity also carried the risk of unleashing a desire already defined as antithetical to rational politics. The ambiguity of woman seems always to haunt de Gouges's most creative arguments.

De Gouges's statements about sexuality, rights, and the possibilities for men and women referred for legitimation, like the arguments she criticized, to "Nature." This reference was at once ingenious and limiting; it allowed her to reinterpret the meaning of the ground for arguments about rights, but not ultimately to contest the usefulness of "natural" justifications for human political arrangements.

De Gouges refused the differentiation of bodies into fixed binary categories, insisting instead on multiplicity, variety, ranges of difference, spectra of colors and functions, confusion of roles—the ultimate undecidability and indeterminacy of the social significance of physical bodies. Running through many of her writings are examples and observations meant to elucidate (what was for her) a primary truth: (she didn't put it this way, but she might have) Nature abhors binary categorization. Appealing to the prevailing rules of science, de Gouges reported her observations and what she saw, she said, confirmed her own experience, her perception of the distance between her "self" and the social category of woman. "In my writings, I am a student of nature; I might be (je dois être), like her, irregular, bizarre even, yet also always true, always simple."[47] In one of her autobiographical pieces, de Gouges explained that the sexes were differentiated only for the purposes of reproduction; otherwise "nature" had endowed all members of a species with similar, but not necessarily identical, faculties.[48] Physical difference, however, was not the key to other differences; for there was no system to nature's variations. De Gouges accepted the prevailing belief in the originary status of nature, and then she redescribed it, drawing new implications for human social organization. Systems, she argued, were man-made, and she implied that all systems interfered with natural anarchic confusions. The *Declaration of the Rights of Woman* began by contrasting men's tyrannical oppression of women with the harmonious confusions of the natural world:

> look, search, and then distinguish if you can, the sexes in the administration
> of nature. Everywhere you will find them mixed up (confondus), everywhere
> they cooperate harmoniously together in this immortal masterpiece.[49]

Like distinctions of sex, distinctions of color defied clear categorization. Only the cupidity and greed of white men could explain for de Gouges the enslavement of blacks; only blind prejudice could lead to commerce in human beings and to the denial of a common humanity between black and white. This was the theme of a brochure she issued (as well as a play she wrote) that contained her "Reflections on Black Men." In it she insisted that "nature had no part" in the "commerce d'hommes." "The unjust and powerful interests of the whites did it all," she maintained, suggesting that here particular interests, masquerading as universal, had usurped human rights. She then pondered the question of color, asking where the lines could be drawn absolutely to differentiate whites, mulattoes, blacks, and whether any hierarchy could be established on the basis of these differences:

> Man's color is nuanced, like all the animals that nature has produced, as well as the plants and minerals. Why doesn't the night rival the day, the sun the moon, and the stars the firmament? All is varied and that is the beauty of nature. Why then destroy her work?[50]

Underneath the visible variety of nature, de Gouges detected a fundamental physical identity. Distinctions of color were not only interdeterminate, but superficial, she insisted, for the same blood flowed in the veins of masters and slaves. They were, in fact, "fathers and brothers," but "deaf to the cries of blood, they stifle all its charms."[51] This comment, placed as it was near the end of the *Declaration of Rights of Woman*, raises the issue of how de Gouges understood the relationship between the situation of women and blacks. There was more than an analogy between two groups deprived of liberty. Rather they partook of the same question: the status in nature, and so in politics, of observable physical difference. If undecidability was the answer in nature, decisions became human actions for which people could be held accountable; they were necessarily relative and open to reasonable debate and interpretation. The legitimation for laws could lie only in "common utility" (article I of both declarations stated that "social distinctions could only be based on common utility"), and that was inevitably decided through political processes. Justice, not nature, required the participation in these processes by everyone affected. The body—or more precisely, structural physical difference—was an irrelevant factor in one sense, for the meaning of these differences were the products not the prerequisites of politics. In another sense, bodies provided the universal ground of human identity, in the identical blood that animated them all and as the site of natural rights. For de Gouges, at least, rights were embodied and universal at the same time, and this conception required not denying the existence of physical differences, but recognizing them as at once essential and irrelevant to the meaning of equality.

De Gouges's invocations of nature were always ambiguous. On the one hand, she insisted (in opposition to her Jacobin adversaries) on undecidability and thus on human responsibility for the imposition of categories; on the other, she accepted the originary "truth" of nature and so left in place the notion that social arrangements could be referred to natural truths. This, in turn, could focus the argument on what *was* in nature rather than on what should be in politics. And de Gouges could always be open to the charge that, untutored in scientific observation, she had simply misread the facts of the physical world. Nonetheless, the destabilizing implications of her redefinition of nature were undeniable; if nature was "irregular, bizarre even," it could not provide, in her terms (it might in ours), a reliable guide for politics. Rather than being a matter of science, justice had to be understood as a mediation of power.

III

It is possible to read Olympe de Gouges and other feminists, male and female, during the French Revolution, in the context solely of established categories of political debate. Implicit in her critique was an interpretation of liberal political theory that countered the authoritarianism of Rousseauian doctrines of the general will with more conflictual notions of politics. Her alliances with the Gironde faction in the Convention bear this out; indeed she was finally sent to the guillotine in 1793 not for her feminism, but for plastering the walls of Paris with posters urging that a federalist system replace Jacobin centralized rule. Indeed, the moment of Jacobin centralization was accompanied by ruthlessly masculine political assertions and by the expulsion of prominent women from the Jacobin club. The association between bourgeois democracy and feminism in France goes beyond de Gouges; it is Condorcet, after all, also a Girondist, who is usually cited as the preeminent feminist of the revolution.[52]

This kind of reading, while acceptable, would be insufficient, I think, on both empirical and philosophical grounds. First, Girondist politicians were not unanimous on the issue of women's rights; most accepted the "natural" version of the sexual division of labor, and these included prominent women such as Madame Roland.[53] Long after the revolution, the antiauthoritarian current of French liberalism shared with other political tendencies an aversion to feminism; sexual difference, as explained by science and medicine, seemed to offer a nonpolitical (hence natural) justification for the assignment to women of passive, not active rights. Moreover, in succeeding generations, feminism was as often associated with socialism as with liberalism; indeed it is frequently argued that the real start of a feminist tradition in France began not with the revolution, but with the utopians—the St. Simonian and Fourierist movements of the 1830s and 1840s.[54]

Second, to treat feminism within the received categories of revolutionary politics ignores the most powerful aspects of its critique and leaves apart many questions, among them the question of how references to the "natural" legitimated political theory and practice and complicated any critique of them. It forsakes the opportunity to examine the interconnections among discourses as well as the contradictions within any one of them; it accepts at face value the terms within which most revolutionaries viewed politics rather than subjecting those terms (as well as the specific programs advocated) to critical scrutiny. The dichotomies that defined those politics are then perpetuated in our histories as so many natural or functional "realities," thus obscuring not only their relative meanings but all contests about them. Indeed the most fundamental contests, those about first premises, become most marginal for these histories because they are categorized as concerning nonpolitical matters. The protests of feminists are heard as cries from the sidelines about the exclusion of particular interests, as superfluous utterances rather than as fundamental (and central) critiques of the notion of different categories of rights based on physical difference. The existence of particularized critiques of universality then becomes a way of confirming rather than questioning the very notion of the universal. Its embodiment as a white male is explained as a temporary historical contingency with no overtones of power, for to associate the concept of the universal with relationships of power—of domination, subordination, and exclusion—would be to contradict the meaning of the universal, at least as it was offered in liberal theories of political rights. It is precisely that contradiction that the feminine already embodied in those theories and that feminists pointed out again and again, though with different arguments and in different terms.

The recurrence of feminist critiques raises the question of their success or failure, and thus of their depth and significance for political movements. If feminism cannot be subsumed into politics as we have known it (as the conflict of parties and interests in the public realm: Gironde versus Jacobin, republican versus socialist), can it be given a political status of its own?

Certainly Olympe de Gouges (like her feminist contemporaries) cannot be considered successful in the usual terms of political evaluation. She did not win acceptance of her proposals for women's rights; her refiguration of marriage, women, and nature was generally dismissed by those in power (in the government and in various political groupings) as outrageous rather than taken seriously. Within a few days of her death (in November 1793) Chaumette set the terms of her historical reputation. He warned republican women who dared to question their roles of the fate of others who had broken the rules: "Remember that virago, that woman-man [*cette femme-homme*], the impudent Olympe de Gouges, who abandoned all the cares of her household because she wanted to engage in politics and commit crimes. . . . This forgetfulness of the virtues of her sex led her to the scaffold."[55]

Although her *Declaration of the Rights of Woman* inspired feminist challenges to successive governments throughout the nineteenth and the first half of the twentieth centuries, formal histories either excluded her entirely or classed her with the "furies" of the revolution, those women who caused and expressed the excesses of unrestrained passion.[56] In 1904, a Dr. Guillois analyzed de Gouges as a case of revolutionary hysteria. Her abnormal sexuality (caused by excessive menstrual flow), her narcissism (evinced by a predeliction for daily baths), and her entire lack of moral sense (proven by her repeated refusal to remarry) constituted the definitive signs of her mental pathology. A defective femininity, in short, had led to her unfortunate interest in politics.[57] The implications of this diagnosis for Guillois's contemporaries was unmistakable: demands for women's rights (as well as all reforming zeal) could not be taken seriously as politics, but must be treated as illness.

These references to de Gouges are misleading, however, for they exaggerate the attention paid to her by historians. The most characteristic treatment of her (as of feminists generally) has been silence. I do not in any way want to argue for her rehabilitation as a heroine, although there are some historians who would insist that that is the only way to grant her agency, the only justification for attending to her. Rather, I want to suggest that de Gouges's practice—her writings and speeches—offers a useful perspective for reading the history of politics and political theory in the French Revolution and for considering questions about contemporary feminist politics. What was the legacy of the French Revolution for women? What did feminism reveal about that legacy? What was/is the status of feminism as a politics?

In a way I've already answered most of these questions but I will restate what I've said: If by political we mean a contest about power, feminism was a political movement poised in critical opposition to liberal political theory, constructed within and yet subsumed or repressed by the terms of that theory. By those terms, political was synonymous with rational, public, and universal, with the free agency of autonomous subjects. Woman, by a set of definitions attributed to nature, was construed as having antithetical traits, hence being outside politics. In order to formulate a critique of this theory, feminists like de Gouges contested its definitions, and sometimes also its legitimating premises. But this produced an ambiguous discourse, which both confirmed and challenged prevailing views, and which exposes to us a fundamental paradox of the political theory of the revolution: the relative and highly particularized aspect, the undeniable embodiment, of its claim to universality.

The ambiguity of de Gouges's feminism is not a measure of its inadequacy as philosophy and politics; rather it is an effect of the exclusions and contradictions of the political theory within and against which it was articulated. The same can be said of subsequent feminisms in the nineteenth and twentieth centuries. Indeed, the recurrence since the revolution of feminist critiques reminds us not only that the democratic promise of liberal (or republican or socialist) political theory is as yet unfulfilled, but also that it may be impossible of fulfillment in the terms in which it has so far been conceived.

Notes

1. Thus Robespierre's evocation of "the reign of that eternal justice, the laws of which are graven, not on marble or stone, but in the hearts of men, even in the heart of the slave who has forgotten them, and in that of the tyrant who disowns them." Maximilien Robespierre, *Report upon the Principles of Political Morality which are to Form the Basis of the Administration of the Interior Concerns of the Republic* (Philadelphia, 1794), reprinted in *History of Western Civilization: Selected Readings* Topic VIII (Chicago: The University of Chicago Press, 1964), 73–74.

2. *Archives Parlementaires* (Convention Nationale), vol. 63, session of April 29, 1793, (Paris 1903), 561–64. See also the statements submitted in favor of women's voting rights by an Englishman, David Williams, and by Pierre Guyomar, deputy from the Côtes-du-Nord, 583–99.

3. On the representations of Marie Antoinette, see Chantal Thomas, *La Reine Scelerate: Marie Antoinette dans les pamphlets* (Paris: Seuil, 1989) and Lynn Hunt, "The Many Bodies of Marie Antoinette: Political Pornography and the Problem of the Feminine in the French Revolution" (unpublished paper, 1989).

4. On the history of women and feminism (two different topics) in the French Revolution see Maité Albistur and Daniel Armogathe, *Histoire du féminisme français*, vol. I (Paris: Des Femmes, 1977); Paule-Marie Duhet, *Les Femmes et la Révolution 1789–1794* (Paris: Julliard, 1971); Jane Abray, "Feminism in the French Revolution,"

American Historical Review 80 (1975):43–62; Jeanne Bouvier, *Les Femmes pendant la Révolution* (Paris: E. Figuière, 1931); Olwen Hufton, "Women in the French Revolution," *Past and Present* 53 (1971):90–108; Hufton, "The Reconstruction of a Church, 1796–1801," in Gwynne Lewis and Colin Lucas, eds., *Beyond the Terror: Essays in French Regional and Social History, 1794–1815* (Cambridge: Cambridge University Press, 1983), 21–52; Scott Lytle, "The Second Sex" (September 1793), *Journal of Modern History* 26 (1955):14–26; Jules Michelet, *Les Femmes de la Révolution* (Paris, 1854); R. B. Rose, "Women and the French Revolution: The Political Activity of Parisian Women, 1789–94," University of Tasmania Occasional Paper 5 (1976); David Williams, "The Politics of Feminism in the French Enlightenment," in P. Hughes and D. Williams, eds., *The Varied Pattern: Studies in the Eighteenth Century* (Toronto: A. M. Hakkert, 1971); Darline Gay Levy, Harriet Branson Applewhite, and Mary Durham Johnson, eds., *Women in Revolutionary Paris, 1789–1795* (Urbana: University of Illinois Press, 1979). See also Dorinda Outram, "Le langage mâle de la Vertu: Women and the discourse of the French Revolution," in Peter Burke and Roy Porter, eds., *The Social History of Language* (Cambridge: Cambridge University Press, 1987), 120–35.

5. Levy, Applewhite, and Johnson, *Women in Revolutionary Paris*, 215.

6. Levy, Applewhite, and Johnson, 219.

7. Ludmilla J. Jordanova, "Guarding the Body Politic: Volney's Catechism of 1793," in Francis Barker et al., eds., *1789: Reading, Writing Revolution* (University of Essex, Proceedings of the Essex Conference on the Sociology of Literature, July 1981, 1982), 15.

8. Jordanova, "Guarding the Body Politic," 15.

9. Ludmilla J. Jordanova, "Naturalizing the Family: Literature and the Bio-Medical Sciences in the Late Eighteenth Century," in Jordanova, ed., *Languages of Nature* (London: Free Association Books, 1986), 115.

10. Thomas Laqueur, "Orgasm, Generation, and the Politics of Reproductive Biology," *Representations* 14 (1986):3.

11. Denise Riley, "Does a Sex Have a History? 'Women' and Feminism," *New Formations* 1 (Spring 1987):39–40.

12. Yvonne Knibiehler, "Les Médecins et la 'Nature Féminine' au temps du Code Civil, *Annales, E.S.C.* 31 (1976):835. The original version can be found in J.-J. Rousseau's *Émile* and is cited in Denise Riley, *"Am I That Name?" Feminism and the Category of 'Women' in History* (London: Macmillan, and Minneapolis: University of Minnesota Press, 1988), 37, n. 57. See also, D. G. Charlton, *New Images of the Natural in France* (Cambridge: Cambridge University Press, 1984); Jean Borie, "Une gynécologie passionnée," in J.-P. Aron, ed., *Misérable et Glorieuse: La Femme du XIXᵉ siècle* (Paris: Fayard, 1980), 153–89; and M. Le Doeuff, "Pierre Roussel's Chiasmas: From Imaginary Knowledge to the Learned Imagination," *Ideology and Consciousness* 9 (1981–82):39–70.

13. On education and maternal nurture, see Mona Ozouf, "La Révolution Française et l'idée de l'homme nouveau," unpublished paper, 1987, 15. For a critique of binary constructions of liberal politics, especially the antimony between reason and desire, see Roberto Mangabeira Unger, *Knowledge and Politics* (New York: Free Press, 1975).

14. My discussion here draws on Jacques Derrida, *Of Grammatology* (translated by Gayatri Chakravorty Spivak) (Baltimore: Johns Hopkins University Press, 1974), part II, chap. 3, 165–95.

15. On this point see Cora Kaplan's discussion of Mary Wollstonecraft, "Wild Nights: Pleasure/Sexuality/Feminism," in her *Sea Changes: Culture and Feminism*

(London: Verso, 1986), chap. 2, esp. 33 and 166–67. On women and republican politics, see Joan Landes, *Women and the Public Sphere in the Age of the French Revolution* (Ithaca: Cornell University Press, 1988).

16. Richard Tuck, *Natural Rights Theories: Their Origin and Development* (Cambridge: Cambridge University Press, 1979), 5–6.

17. Levy, Applewhite, and Johnson, *Women in Revolutionary Paris*, 220.

18. Olympe de Gouges, *Le Bonheur Primitif de l'Homme, ou les Reveries Patriotiques* (Amsterdam, 1789), 23.

19. Barbara Taylor, commenting on Geneviève Fraisse, "The Forms of Historical Feminism," *m/f* 10 (1985):17.

20. Kaplan, "Wild Nights," 49. See also Riley, *"Am I That Name?"* 68: "Feminism never has the option of putting forward its own uncontaminated, self-generated understandings of 'women': its 'women,' too, is always thoroughly implicated in the discursive world."

21. On these questions see the following articles by Fraisse, "Historical Feminism," 4–19; "Natural Law and the Origins of Nineteenth-century Feminist Thought in France," in Judith Friedlander et al., *Women in Culture and Politics* (Bloomington: Indiana University Press, 1986), 318–29; "Singularité féministe: Historiographie critique de l'histoire du féminisme en France," in Michelle Perrot, ed., *Une Histoire des Femmes est-elle possible?* (Paris: Rivages, 1984), 189–204; "Du bon usage de l'individu féministe," *Vingtième Siècle* 14 (avril–juin 1987):45–54, and *Muse de la Raison: La démocratie exclusive et la différence des sexes* (Paris: Alinea, 1989). See also Kaplan, *Sea Changes*, 49, 166–67, 226.

22. For biographical treatment, see Olivier Blanc, *Olympe de Gouges* (Paris: Syros, 1981); and "Introduction" to *Olympe de Gouges: Oeuvres* by Benoite Groult (Paris: Mercure de France, 1986). See also, Léopold Lacour, *Les origines du féminisme contemporain. Trois Femmes de la Révolution: Olympe de Gouges, Théroigne de Méricourt, Rose Lacombe* (Paris, 1900).

23. I am grateful to Judith Butler for calling my attention to this point.

24. De Gouges's actions were not unique or specific to women in this period. In the eighteenth century the article "de" was often added to the names of aspiring young men; during the revolution "new men" displayed their regeneration or rebirth by rebaptising themselves often with heroic classical names. De Gouges's self is, in this sense, revealing of a process not confined to one gender and can be taken as emblematic of the process of self-construction more generally.

25. Chantal Thomas, "Féminisme et Révolution: les causes perdue d'Olympe de Gouges," in *La Carmagnole des Muses: L'homme de lettres et l'artiste dans la Révolution* (Paris: Armand Colin, 1988), 309.

26. De Gouges, "Remarques Patriotiques: par la citoyenne, Auteur de la lettre au Peuple, 1788" in Groult, *de Gouges: Oeuvres*, 73.

27. "Le cri du sage: par une femme, 1789," in *de Gouges: Oeuvres*, 91.

28. "Lettre au peuple ou projet d'une caisse patriotique par une citoyenne, 1788," in *de Gouges: Oeuvres*, 69.

29. In *de Gouges: Oeuvres*, 88–92.

30. Groult, "Introduction," *de Gouges: Oeuvres*, p. 47.

31. "Introduction," 28; and de Gouges, "Lettre au peuple ou projet d'une caisse patriotique," in *de Gouges: Oeuvres*, 72.

32. "Preface pour les dames, ou le portrait des femmes, 1791," in *de Gouges: Oeuvres*, 115–19.

33. "Déclaration des droits de la Femme, dédiée à la reine, 1791," in *de Gouges: Oeuvres*, 100.

34. "Déclaration," in *de Gouges: Oeuvres*, 102.

35. Like much of de Gouges's writing, the *Declaration of the Rights of Woman* has an excessive quality. It strains within its chosen format. Surrounding the seventeen articles that list women's rights, there is first a long dedication to Marie Antoinette, then a preamble more than twice the length of the one for the *Declaration of the Rights of Man*. At the end there is a postamble, followed by a model "marriage" contract, followed by a rambling discussion that touches on ancient marriage customs, the rights of men of color in the colonies, and the role of the legislative and executive power in the French nation. It is as if the statement of women's rights cannot stand without explanations. It must correct all upon which the *Declaration of the Rights of Man* rests in order to make its point. This sense of strain, the excessive quality of the writing, is an attempt to deal, I would argue, with contradiction, with the paradoxical problem of claiming equality in the name of, or without glossing over, difference.

36. De Gouges, "Déclaration," in *de Gouges: Oeuvres*, 104.

37. "Déclaration," 104.

38. Carole Pateman, *The Sexual Contract* (Stanford: Stanford University Press, 1988).

39. In this sense, article XI, as the entire *Déclaration*, operates according to the contradictory logic of the supplement, as discussed by Jacques Derrida. It provides additional material, above and beyond what is necessary, and it points out a lack or absence in the original declaration of rights. It is both excessive and absolutely necessary, hence ambiguous and destabilizing. See Derrida, *Of Grammatology*, 141–64; and *Positions*, trans. Alan Bass (Chicago: University of Chicago Press, 1981).

40. I am grateful to Ruth Leys for suggesting this point.

41. Here we find her playing with versions of Rousseau's distinctions between artifice and nature, between man in civilization and man in nature. See Maurizio Viroli, *Jean-Jacques Rousseau and the 'Well-Ordered Society'* (Cambridge: Cambridge University Press, 1988), chap. 2. See also the discussion of the ways republican thinkers linked artifice with the feminine and with aristocracy in Landes, *Women and the Public Sphere*. One of de Gouges's strategies here is to attempt to disentangle the feminine from its prevalent association with artifice and aristocracy and to identify it instead with the public virtues of a republic.

42. Levy, Applewhite, and Johnson, *Women in Revolutionary Paris*, 94–95.

43. De Gouges, "Le cri du sage," in *de Gouges: Oeuvres*, 91.

44. De Gouges, "Déclaration," in *de Gouges: Oeuvres*, 112.

45. "Déclaration," 109–11.

46. Levy, Applewhite, and Johnson, *Women in Revolutionary Paris*, 170.

47. De Gouges, "Départ de M. Necker et de Madame de Gouges, ou, Les Adieux de Madame de Gouges aux Français et à M. Necker (avril 1790)" in *de Gouges: Oeuvres*, 96.

48. De Gouges, "Autobiographie," in *de Gouges: Oeuvres*, 226.

49. De Gouges, "Déclaration," in *de Gouges: Oeuvres*, 101.

50. De Gouges, "Réflexions sur les hommes nègres, février 1788," in *de Gouges: Oeuvres*, 85.

51. De Gouges, "Déclaration," in *de Gouges: Oeuvres*, 112.

52. Condorcet, "On the Admission of Women to the Rights of Citizenship (1790)," in *Selected Writings*, K. M. Baker (Indianapolis: Bobbs-Merrill, 1976).

53. Gita May, *Madame Roland and the Age of Revolution* (New York: Columbia University Press, 1970).

54. On this history, see Claire Goldberg Moses, *French Feminism in the Nineteenth Century* (Albany: SUNY Press, 1984).

55. Cited in Groult, "Introduction," *de Gouges: Oeuvres*, 59.

56. "Introduction," 60–62. See also Neil Hertz, "Medusa's Head: Male Hysteria Under Political Pressure," *Representations* 4 (Fall 1983):27–54.

57. Cited in Groult, "Introduction," *de Gouges: Oeuvres*, 61–62.

7

Outspoken Women and the Rightful Daughter of the Revolution: Madame de Staël's *Considérations sur la Révolution Française*

LINDA ORR

In the *Considérations sur la Révolution française*, Madame de Staël refuses to separate out her own family romance from her analytic reflections on history and politics. Her family romance and political or historical theory not only complement, but mutually constitute each other. This strange dialectic may make Staël's history less than legitimate in the context of historiographical tradition, but it also engenders a different kind of history, less restricted in its self-definitions, in its ways of knowing and expression.

Her father, Jacques Necker, the popular Finance Minister on the eve of the revolution, embodies within him the key connection between the modern state and its new reference, public opinion. Her mother, Madame Necker, shows her daughter a space where this public opinion is formed in the presence of women, the salon. Daughter Germaine does not just synthesize these influences, for they are both inadequate to the full realization of the revolution Staël would like to articulate herself. But she has a rival: Napoleon.

Father/Trust

As Louis XVI's Director General of Finances, Necker understood the way public borrowing would change the political situation. Staël recounts her father's analysis of the historical conjuncture that produced the interdependence of fiscal planning and people: "for no country can nor should wage war with its revenue alone: credit is therefore the true modern discovery which has linked governments with peoples."[1] Modern warfare made old resources of tax collecting inadequate; like the first investment companies (proto-trusts in which Necker participated), the monarchy needed the promise of future funds. Thus, it had to instill confidence in its people. Necker knew that the original trust between king and subjects derived from those long-forgotten medieval pacts or charters. Moreover, his daughter, Madame de Staël, became one of the first and most articulate political thinkers to remind the French of their basic liberal heritage: "It is liberty that is old [*ancienne*], and despotism that is modern" (70). Necker added the modern twist of money, which should have given the king more impetus to cooperate.

According to Necker (as read by his daughter), public opinion was a kind of national credit rating. If the population supported the state, the state could raise money. By the second half of the eighteenth century, the relationship between opinion and credit was like two sides of the same coin: "Opinion and credit, which is only opinion applied to financial affairs, became more essential each day" (79). Etymologically both public opinion and credit have to do with belief, with the trust between participants that creates the integrity of the nation. The credibility of a government depends upon the people's belief in itself, and this confidence establishes the state's credit line.

Necker, not Mirabeau or Robespierre, incarnated, in Staël's view, the true principles of the new society. The Finance Minister warned the king that he should make the national budget public. In these times of upheaval, Necker never lost sight of the true political north, the direction of the future, what he and his daughter called *l'esprit public* or *l'opinion publique*: "M. Necker constantly studied the *esprit public* like a compass" (134). Necker was a member of that esteemed group, first among equals, whom Staël names the "true friends of liberty" (386). And *in principle* this group never erred in its judgments and never misread the compass of opinion: "The true friends of liberty are enlightened in this regard by an instinct which does not deceive them" (386).

As the revolution progressed, however, that public *esprit* became harder to read, so the "cause" of freedom became obscure: "The fear of counterrevolution had unfortunately disorganized the *esprit public*: one didn't know where to grasp the cause of liberty between those who dishonored it and others accused of hating it" (332). Are the "true friends of liberty" unaffected by this eclipse of liberty in a present confusion where neither opposing attitude corresponds to the freedom it is supposed to represent? In the face of this crisis, Staël needed to keep some (symbolic) figure uncontaminated, someone she could trust to read opinion—why not her father? These political beliefs of father and daughter did not prevent them from being accused of occupying the false alternative of the political right: "those who hate liberty." The walks with daddy "under the tall trees of Coppet" (258) provide the calm in the storm. Necker, the model of exile in Switzerland, would always appear to his daughter as "this large shadow that is there on the summit of the mountain, and that points a finger to the life of the future" (389). That finger was Staël's compass. All this gives Necker more legitimacy as the real father of the French Revolution. Even Napoleon said so: "Bonaparte indicated M. Necker as the principle author of the revolution" (378).

Necker is so closely linked with the revolution in Staël's story that his second exile seems to trigger the march to the Bastille. "As soon as the news of M. Necker's departure spread around Paris, they barricaded the streets" (161,

July 11, 1789). A few days later, on his return to Paris after the king recalls him, women kneel all along the road at the carriage's passage. By the time Necker arrives at the Hôtel de Ville on July 30, he is given a rousing hero's welcome. The extraordinary scene parallels that other scene of apotheosis, equally ambiguous in the later histories of Cabet, Michelet, and Blanc: Marat's triumph after his acquittal (April 24, 1793). The scene also anticipates Lamartine's illusory victory in the exact same spot, February 1848. Staël's history pivots around these scenes, familial or more often self-dramatic. They cannot be extracted from the analysis;[2] indeed, they are integral to the analysis, despite or because of their excess and melodrama.

After pleading inside the Hôtel de Ville for amnesty (reminiscent of the old Swiss tradition of the fourteenth century *confédérés du Rutli*), Necker appears on that famous balcony amid the cheers and hysteria of the crowd. The phantasmic joy of the crowd brings about a complete political union, also sexual in its connotations, which expresses the daughter's desire. Or rather, the daughter represents in one intense figure the symbolic total adherence of the crowd's gaze. "M. Necker then came out onto the balcony and proclaimed in a loud voice the saintly words of peace among the French of all parties; the entire multitude responded to this with emotion. I saw nothing more after that moment, because I lost consciousness from so much joy" (168). The moment of communal and personal ecstasy blends into a universal swoon. But the gaze in Staël is not simple, as Nancy Miller and Naomi Schor have demonstrated in their respective essays.[3] The protagonist loses consciousness in both climax and prohibition. No reader can look on this most public of private moments, or this most private of public moments.

Almost every history of the revolution has its apogee, the celebration of society's union, if only fleeting and symbolic: the Tennis Court Oaths, the *Fêtes des Fédérations, L'Être Suprème*. And this moment often has sexual overtones, even if virgins present the bouquets. Unlike Michelet whose hero is *le peuple* of the *fêtes*, more like Cabet who places hopes on Robespierre, Staël preserves an individual leader in the midst of this scene. And this leader merges not only with the crowd but with an individual in the crowd, his own daughter, who also doubles as the ideal (female) reader. The high point of the new society would be like this intimacy of father and daughter, that kind of unspoken understanding. *Foule* would be no different from *fille*. This is an astounding metaphor for a goal of social, or revolutionary, communication. In *Corinne*, Staël reverses the fantasy, putting the woman in the center of the people-lover.

Staël's Terror keeps that reversal of the woman—Staël herself—in the middle, but the fantasy has turned into nightmare. In the same square of the Hôtel de Ville, the daughter is almost the sacrificial victim of the radicalized revolution. Is that the punishment for the illusion of harmony the father tried to enforce—or for dreaming of putting him and so herself in the center, for usurping that sacred, paradoxical space of the popular democratic leader?

The rumors of the September massacres spread. On September 2, 1792, a pregnant Madame de Staël takes off in her biggest Berlin carriage with horsemen in their finest livery. She thought the spectacular effect would help, not condemn her. But did she also want to intensify the risk? Or do I suggest that she "asked for it"? Her carriage is stopped by the old harpies of the people and dragged slowly to that fateful square where the new Commune under Robespierre will verify her passport. There Madame de Staël emerges into "an armed multitude": "I advanced under a vault of pikes." A man lifts his pike that a gendarme blocks with his sabre: "It is in the people's nature to respect what is still standing; but when the victim has already been struck, they finish it (her?) off" (285). Staël is like a doe being charged by hunters. Once inside the Hôtel de Ville, Manuel, a friend still in good graces, hides her and her maidservant in his office. Another man in trouble, a knight of Malta, very unchivalrously insists at the hearing that his case has nothing to do with that lady's. He shamelessly abandons her. Such an experience inspires her vow to herself: "to be useful to myself" (285). This scene in which the female protagonist is given (reads) the lesson of vulnerability and betrayal is as troubling and suggestive as the apogee of her father.

Staël does a short analysis of the Terror as a throwback to the familiar tactics of the Old Regime. Michelet and Quinet take up this same interpretation and elaborate on it.[4] The modern reader, however, does not share a horror for the Terror, especially when the Terror is rendered in overly dramatic—so almost comical—scenes like the one above. Already in her day, the fact that Madame de Staël linked the Terror up with the past started the process of assimilating it into the history of France, as Thiers and nineteenth-century historians after him also did without always meaning to. In the *Considérations*, the Terror occupies only two chapters in Part Three of a book divided between Necker (Parts One and Two) and Napoleon (Parts Four and Five). These proportions confirm that Napoleon instigates a more lasting terror for Staël than 1793.

Mother/Talk

A subhistory of the salon parallels the history of the revolution, if not the history of France; or rather, the salon represents a condensed version of that history, its essence. At first in the *Considérations*, the salon appears to be the private in opposition to public space, the living room as opposed to the Place de l'Hôtel de Ville. But when it works, the salon fuses private and public, personal and political domains, just as Staël's *Considérations* fuses memoir and history, family and nation, anecdote and analysis. The year 1791 marks the height of the salon, the revolution, and French culture in general. But the salon, like public opinion—even like that symbol of public opinion, the father—could not keep up its reputation as the place of the "true" revolution. The brilliant conversation that inspired constitutions could turn into petty bickering over etiquette. Public opinion could become bitchy.

Madame de Staël got her training and aspirations from her mother's prestigious prerevolutionary salon in Paris. At that time, artistocratic women held considerable social and political status that was, nonetheless, susceptible to being undermined—by none other than the father. "Women of a certain rank were involved in everything before the revolution. Their husbands or brothers always used them to go see the ministers; they could insist without violating decorum, go too far even, without anyone's having reason to complain; all the insinuations that they knew how to make while talking, gave them a lot of influence [*empire*] on most of the men around. M. Necker listened to them very politely; but he was too smart not to unravel these ruses of conversation which produced no effect on enlightened and natural intelligence" (101). In this disturbing, almost schizoid passage, Staël begins by extolling women like her mother and ends by appearing to take on, hook, line, and sinker, the opposite judgment of her father. The women could go farther than the men in expressing their opinions. At the end of Staël's long, impressive sentence, the metaphor of "*empire*" describes women's power. But then comes the flip of interpretation: from female to male? All that talk, superficial complicity, really went nowhere, because the naturally smart men did not listen.

The parents' culture taught the daughter this double standard. Women appeared to have power when they actually had none. One time Necker was upset because his wife went to plead at court in his behalf without his knowing. Was she more effective than he was? Was there a *scène de ménage* when she got home that the daughter remembered? The daughter was smart, like her mother, and even more ambitious—was the daughter jealous that her mother could argue beyond the measure of decorum while she herself was constantly, rebuked? The men whom Madame de Staël wanted to impress humored her by pretending to listen: Necker and Napoleon.

In the early years of the revolution, the salon managed, however, to achieve its full, utopian potential. By then Madame de Staël had left her parents in Switzerland and set up her own coterie. Brilliant language, both talk and speech, characterized the period: "In no other country or time has the art of talking in all its forms been so remarkable as in the first years of the revolution" (228). Parliamentary speeches could spill over into the talk of the salon, and vice versa. If men ruled the Assemblée, women led the salon conversation even when the subject turned to politics. French women had an advantage over their British sisters: "Women in England are accustomed to being quiet in front of men, when it is a question of politics, the women in France direct almost all the conversations in their houses" (228). In her salon, Madame de Staël rivaled Mirabeau.

The revolutionary salon stood as the privileged place (the place of privilege) where public opinion shaped itself to the maximum satisfaction of all potentially hostile parties, left and right (male and female).[5] In this hybrid public/private space, public disputes could soften and blend: "Talk [*la parole*] was still an acceptable mediator between the two parties. . . . It is the last time and in many ways also the first, that Parisian society could give the idea of this communication of superior minds among themselves, the noblest pleasure of which human nature is capable" (229). Staël makes strong claims for this time and place as the one instance of true social communication. Whereas she participated in the *jouissance* that the communication of her father with the people generated in 1789, this pleasure, restricted but no less symbolic, is all hers. The utopian suggestion plays on a magic cord (Athenian?) in Madame de Staël's work that returns at regular intervals: the communion of great minds together, in talk or, at the very least, in books. This social vision lacks modern class-consciousness, and I suspect that the "great minds" Staël has in mind are male. But she, the author, chips away at her own image of the ideal society as her history progresses. Even so, she needs that utopian reminder just as she needs the principles of liberty and true public opinion while her critique expands to ever-broader social forms.

If the *fêtes* of 1790 and 1791 are Michelet's revolutionary high points and everything after is decline, or Robespierre's social program is Blanc's, then the salon of 1791 is Staël's revolution. Before Madame Roland's prominence and unlike the people's hero Théroigne de Méricourt, Madame de Staël was a power-broker of her time. The Constitution of 1791 was supposedly composed in part at her house. She and her lover Narbonne (the baron de Staël has long ago been left behind) seemed to command politics, foreign policy, and society from their room. Michelet titles a chapter of his history: "Madame de Staël and Narbonne in Power (December 1791–March 1792)."[6] But the power does not stay forever, nor does the lover Narbonne.

In the same *Considérations*, the 1791 salon-society can also contradict that utopian space. The critique is clearer in *Corinne* where the salon is seen through the eyes of Oswald, influenced by D'Erfeuil. The Parisian revolutionary salon does not enhance public opinion, but degrades and deforms it. Critics Gengembre and Goldzink remark that "D'Erfeuil expresses how impoverishing it was for opinion to be assimilated into manners and decorum (*convenances*, *bienséances*)."[7] High-minded talk of liberty slips into picky disagreements about social behavior. The salon is less a place of uplifting negotiation as one of social repression. Had that always been one of its functions, even in Madame Necker's day? Did the mother try to give the daughter manners in her salon?

Staël does not clarify from where the reverse and negative judgment comes: "In the first years of the revolution, you could suffer somewhat from the terrorism of society" (481). The word "terrorism," even if flattened into a catechresis, is too close to the Terror in this context not to take on some of its power. The place that situated the true revolution, the salon, is here closely related to its other, the Terror. In the context of the passage, *société* is a euphemism for salon culture, although it can also suggest that this particular society, the "aristocracy" of the revolution, serves as a synecdoche for the entire social body. In any case, are the people left out? *On* is either someone excluded from what might have then appeared to be even more brilliant and powerful because of the exclusion, or someone finally admitted into the salons without being able to keep up with the scintillating conversation: "The influence of women, the ascendency of the right company, what one vulgarly called the *salons dorés*, appeared formidable to those who were not admitted" (317). As these men, Jacobins, gained in political power, the women needed to flatter them as much as Old Regime ministers before. How can Madame de Staël separate herself and her own salon from this contaminated figure of the utopian space? Was the "terrorism" snide, ostracizing play or a serious political threat to those who did not respect salon values? Was the salon allied with a superficial, dying aristocracy, a seventeenth- and eighteenth-century custom, or was it the place where liberty traveled up from the ancient charters to modern liberal society?

The Directory proved to be as suspicious of salon conversation as the Jacobins were.[8] In 1795 Madame de Staël managed to divert her order of exile, but in 1796 the police were supposed to arrest her if she returned to France.

Step-brother/Police

In the *Considérations*, the salon—its "terrorism"—was the only place of resistance left for the "friends of freedom," led by outspoken women, when Napoleon consolidated his power. "The political personality most in contrast with the principles we just outlined" (394), Napoleon inverts Necker and all he stands for. In place of the sincere light of public budgets and common trust stands the dark slimy secrets of arbitrary decision: "In fact, if the friends of liberty respect opinion, want public information [*publicité*], look everywhere for the sincere and free support of the national wishes, it is because they know that only the dregs of souls show themselves in the secrets and intrigues of arbitrary power" (434). Whereas Necker respects, even reveres "divine" public opinion, Napoleon, figure of "the arbitrary without boundaries" (412), shows a total "indifference toward fate and disdain for men" (367). But, paradoxically, suspicion and an excessive system of security attest to the vulnerability of this indifference.

It is easy to criticize Staël's analysis of Napoleon as being subjective, personal, and even based on that most irrational informant, the body. Jacques Godechot gives Napoleon's response to Madame de Staël in the notes to his edition ("That woman is crazy"). The note makes it look as if Staël complained about Napoleon's indifference because of the indifference he showed to her overzealous advances: "The general answered only with an indifference which is never forgiven by women" (*Mémoires de Sainte Hélène*, in *Considérations*, 651). Napoleon destroyed Madame de Staël's letters so we cannot judge for ourselves.

In the *Considérations*, Staël recalls that every time she was in Napoleon's presence, she had trouble breathing. She generalizes her physiological or psychological reaction to Napoleon as the effect he had on the society at large: "a difficulty in breathing which has since become, I believe, the sickness of everyone who has lived under Bonaparte's authority" (358). Staël theorizes or transforms into social critique what could be read as a hysterical response to the all-powerful general. In the process, Staël renders the French body politic in a most concrete manner. Everything slowly suffocated around Napoleon:

good writing, interesting conversation, and independent thought. Staël describes the desolation of any country under foreign occupation fairly early in her book, but that description begins to fit retrospectively more closely Napoleon's regime, whether in an occupied country like Staël's Switzerland or in Paris itself. People's homes, their heads and hearts, are (as in World War II Paris) dominated by an inside/outsider. The only response possible is silence; "As in prison where silence placates the jailors more than complaint, you have to be quiet as long as locks have closed down both feeling and thought" (190). All of Europe became a prison under the Occupation.

This was personally intolerable to Staël because Napoleon, the foreign usurper, literally "grafted" himself onto the tree of revolution. A kind of Tartuffe, he tried to slip inside the holy family and presented himself as rightful and natural heir to the revolution. The true daughter of the revolution—Swiss but more Parisian than the Corsican . . . —could not believe people were so blind to the hypocrisy of the false son. Staël was the chosen daughter of the revolution both literally and figuratively. She could see through Napoleon and accuse him: "Many said: he is the child of the revolution. Yes, doubtless, but a patricidal child" (420). Whereas patricide usually referred to the crime of killing Louis XVI, Napoleon killed the revolution that fathered him. If Necker's exile prompted the fall of the Bastille, his death signals the end of liberty: "His life ended the same year as Bonaparte was going to make himself emperor" (391). The scandal of the Empire kills the old man on the Swiss mountaintop. Napoleon is not only Creon dealing with all the vengeful daughters rolled into one—Electra, Antigone, Cordelia—but a sibling rival. This rivalry between brother and sister, man and woman, gives a different twist to the tragedies.

A crucial passage in Staël's chapter "De l'exil" (Part Four) analyzes the female resistance to Napoleon. Whereas at first she had effaced herself in front of her father's work, here Staël finally brags. But hers is a strange claim to fame:

> I was the first woman Bonaparte exiled; but soon after, he banished many others with the same opposing opinions. One especially interesting person, among others, the Duchess of Chevreuse, died from the heartache her exile caused. . . . And since, on the one hand, women could not further in any way his political plans, and on the other, (these women) were less accessible than men to fears and hopes which power dispenses, (the women) annoyed him like rebels, and he got pleasure from saying hurtful and vulgar things to them. . . . He retained his old behavior from during the revolution, a certain Jacobin antipathy against brilliant Parisian society, where women exercised great ascendency; he feared in them the art of banter (*plaisanterie*), which, we have to agree, belongs especially to French women. If Bonaparte had wanted to keep to his superb role of a great general and first magistrate of the republic, he would have soared with the elevation of a genius over the petty, sniping aspects (*petits traits acérés*) of salon mentality. But when he had designs on becoming an upstart king, bourgeois gentilhomme on the throne,

he exposed himself precisely to the high-toned mockery, and he couldn't restrain it except as he did, through spies and terror. (386–87)

The women, whom Napoleon disdained and didn't listen to, had nothing to gain from him, so they formed the only possible enclave of independence. They were "like rebels": the word *rebelle*, usually an adjective, is made for feminist politics. Their conscious, un-Freudian weapon was wit. The use of wit makes literal meaning hard to pin down in the tribunal. This witty, mocking passage itself is one of the best examples of what Staël means.

Bonaparte begins as the socially ill-at-ease, envious Jacobin. He tries to compete where he has no business competing and ends up looking foolish. In the salon of sharp-tongued, articulate women, the outflanked general resembles Molière's *bougeois gentilhomme*. Because there is a tiny place on earth where he does not excel and dominate, which humiliates him, he must stamp it out. But the salon is still an ambiguous place. Do the banter, snipping and mocking *ton* compose an organizable opposition or only aggravation? Whether mere distraction or rebellion, the salons elicit the response from Napoleon with which he is most at home: police terror.

Staël mentions in particular the Duchess of Chevreuse. In a note, Godechot tells us that the *Bulletins* of Napoleon's secret police listed her in 1808 as "*une des plus mauvaises langues*" (658)—translated as "bad mouth" or "evil tongue"? How much worse a tongue did Madame de Staël have, whose salon bred conspiracy? In both 1802 and 1813, Madame de Staël tried to put her man, Bernadotte, on the throne, in place of Napoleon. Staël's traveling salon (Germany, England, Sweden) could have helped crystallize the opposition that did eventually bring him down.

So exile defined Madame de Staël during the last years of her life (*Dix années d'exil*, published posthumously). Add the exile of being a woman and the internalized exile of being a passionate, committed, smart, and powerful woman surrounded by silence. Daughter of the revolution, daughter of liberty, Madame de Staël was, like the "true" revolution, exiled wherever she went. She fills in the gap of exiles in the Swiss mountains between Voltaire and Quinet. She joins the grand tradition of exiles dating back to Dante and the Biblical Ruth. She stands beside the self-created giant exiles of her century, Chateaubriand and Hugo. Hugo's poetic model of exile went back to Satan (*La fin de Satan*), echo of the *révolte* created by Milton whose work Staël also particularly admired. Rebuffed by each regime in turn, the endlessly exiled Madame de Staël settled on this aphorism: "Resist, keep resisting, and find the center of your support in yourself" (245). Not only the regimes, but the men she depended on—father, Manuel, Narbonne, Constant, Barante—were so many knights of Malta that (luckily) could not defend her. She is finally useful to herself. Staël held onto her Revolution through the perverse forms of the false revolutions: Terror, seedy Directory, stifling Empire, cynical Restoration. She was the revolution's last activist and the first "intellectual dissident" (Pierre Barbéris's term)[9] of postrevolutionary, modern society. She could very well have written her own version of Hugo's line: "S'il n'en reste qu'une, je serai celle-là." (If only one is left, it will be me).

Daughter/Writer

The *Considérations* are Staël's revenge on Napoleon, her way of competing with the little general, the illegitimate son, for the true heritage of the French Revolution. Napoleon and Staël were engaged in a duel not only for the memory of the revolution but for the future of France. Whichever side prevailed, Staël and the friends of liberty, or the partisans of the arbitrary, would decide the kind of society to come. They were engaged in an old duel, as proverbial as the game of paper, stone, scissors, to see who wins: pen, monument, or sword. In this ongoing struggle, conditions seem to favor the historian. The historical actor cannot defend his glory when he is dead. Chateaubriand delighted in calling himself Tacitus to Napoleon's Nero. In the *Mémoires d'outre-tombe*, more like the *Considérations* than any other book, Chateaubriand sees his mission in metaphorical, political terms: "When everything trembles before the tyrant . . . the historian appears, charged with the vengeance of peoples."[10] Here the historian assumes the same role in historiography as the hero in history (Charlotte Corday, Brutus). Along with her modesty, Staël, too, sees herself in no lesser light. But the joke is then on them, the historians, for the mortal combat of words and historical or literary tradition can never stop with any one. Chateaubriand and Staël become subject to interpretation and the projection of others' desires and political agendas.[11] Each in turn enters into the open cultural space of discursive competition.

Exiled from orality, Staël, like Corinne, turned to writing. Her writing, as Joan DeJean observes, retains the "openness" of the salon tradition from which it comes.[12] But this displacement from orality to writing elicits even more repression. (During her life was she "exiled" as well into fiction, while Constant and Barante wrote political philosophy and history?) In 1802 *Delphine* may have incited Napoleon's ire as much as had Necker's *Dernières vues de politique et de finances*. The 1803 order of exile demanding that she stay at least "40 leagues outside of Paris" was, in an approximate count, her fourth or fifth exile not counting Necker's three in which she too participated. In 1810, Minister of Police Rovigo both exiles her from France and orders the destruction of any trace of *De l'Allemagne*. Then Napoleon extends his police to Geneva, and Staël is essentially exiled from her exile. At that point the only place left to go is England, by way of Moscow, Petersburg, and Stockholm. She begins the manuscript of the *Considérations* in Stockholm on the run. It will be published after her death (1818).[13]

It is hard to gauge what caused Madame de Staël the most suffering: interminable political exiles or attacks and ridicule heaped upon her work by the "literary police" (419). A sniveling host of little scribblers thrived in the wake of Napoleon's power. Their newspapers, Staël laments, "harassed you with their state-ordered banter" (419). Is this barbed persecution the inverse of the bantering Parisian women perfected? The same weapon is put to the service of opposite values, on the one hand servility, on the other, independent thinking.

A fleeting but uncanny image of Madame de Staël in her own history haunts me as much as the one of Michelet brooding over the empty Champ de Mars or Hugo talking to the seawinds from his Guernsey promontory. On August 1, 1812, Madame de Staël arrives in Moscow just ahead of Napoleon's continental forces. The text is uncanny because it superimposes one upon the other a double consciousness, that of Madame de Staël the character and that of Staël the narrator. They are different, in fact, extreme opposites. Like Carla Petersen's reading of *Corinne*, the narrator achieves a victory the character cannot envisage.[14]

> I was in Moscow a month, day for day, before Napoleon's army entered, and I did not dare stop but a few moments, already fearing its approach. Walking on top of the Kremlin, palace of the ancient czars which looks out over the immense capital of Russia, and over eighteen hundred churches, I thought that Bonaparte would surely see empires at his feet, as when Satan offered them to our Savior. But precisely when nothing was left for him to conquer in Europe, destiny grabbed him up to hurl him down just as quickly as he rose. (430)

Madame de Staël, the literary character, is a breathless, terrified woman tearing across Europe like Frankenstein's monster pursued by the master. She is also a little girl transgressing on the promenade of ancient czars and modern dictator. She imagines Bonaparte arriving at the Kremlin after her own flight; he is now conqueror of the world, like Christ to whom all the earth has been offered. But Christ resisted the temptation. Not Napoleon. And the little woman who rushes before him also comes after him as narrator and historian and (pre)knows his defeat there where she most trembled at his imminent victory. Now the writer can take pleasure at the certainty of her enemy's downfall (at the time of her writing, Napoleon is at Saint-Hélène). The vulnerable female character turns into the victor of the victor. She did not flee Napoleon as much as lead him on to his demise. She becomes herself the ultimate Romantic epic figure of exile: a female Satan. In imaginary retrospect from her literary heights, she looks over the wide world of her readership from the Kremlin.

The unfinished *Considérations* ends in a situation of profound ambiguity. The concluding section, which I'll call *De l'Angleterre* (counterpiece to *De l'Allemagne*), should have functioned as the synthesis French history was not able to achieve. English liberal democracy should have brought together both the legitimacy of public opinion and salon social space. But the implicit disregard for women's opinion in the French prerevolutionary salon reappears explicitly confirmed in the British parlor. The reader is left, then, with Staël's bitterness and rage—which other Romantic historians, too, express—when all the inspiration, promises, and efforts toward liberty end up in a post-Napoleonic society of complete political indifference, or worse: a total complicity with a naturalized repression.

Staël first attributes the reticence of English women to "custom," but later she goes on to say that men who get their free speech back "naturally" reclaim their position of dominance over women: "(English) women are, in this case, extremely timid; because, in a free state, when men assume again their natural dignity, women feel subordinate" (556). Does this tricky sentence imply, first, that women are better off in societies without freedom (like Rosie the Riveter in a time of war) and, second, that men are "naturally" more dignified than women who are naturally subordinate?[15] Again, is there irony here? Whether Staël accepts the ideology of "natural" oppression, she shows that gender roles are no mere quirk but fundamental to the system. The silence of women allows British society to function, is inseparable from its public political life, religious and moral supports.[16] Liberalism, like the French Republic, depends upon the repression of women's speech and political activity. In England, Corinne can no longer perform her stunning improvisations, and eventually her writing is stifled. This kind of liberalism is a kind of social, not just political, terrorism integrated so thoroughly into everyday practices that it is taken for granted.

The last chapter of the *Considérations*, "De l'amour de la liberté," lyrically evokes liberty, still latent like public opinion and the "true" revolution but lost in the superficial, indifferent post-Napoleon French *société*. A sixteen-line sentence recalls in its rhetorical sweep all the time spent, sacrifices made, and even progress of the last twenty-seven years (1789–1816), if not centuries, which then funnel down to a shrug, the *grande fatuité* (Constant's favorite theme, too)[17] that so disgusted Staël about this new modern society: "When for so many centuries all generous souls have loved freedom; when the greatest actions have been inspired by it; when (etc.) . . . what can we say about these petty, extremely fatuous men who declare in a dull and affected accent like their whole being . . . that after all the horrors we've witnessed, no one cares anymore about freedom" (602). Staël recognizes like her other romantic colleagues that the revolution will not logically unfold as hoped for according to a public opinion that turns out to be much harder to read than originally suspected. Instead, the revolution is either deformed inside or remains radically outside a nonlinear history, in which essence and accident can switch places brutally or almost imperceptibly. In such a history, the revolution is not lost or discredited. On the contrary, it is what gives history momentum, if not meaning. This illusive quality of revolution and of democracy makes the history book all that much more important for nineteenth-century writers. For Staël, as for Michelet or Tocqueville, liberty lives, if nowhere else, at least in their writing.

Staël, like her nineteenth-century descendents, was obsessed with what it meant to be a postrevolutionary writer.[18] She knew it meant praxis, something subtler and more influential than education, that ultimate nineteenth-century republican value. She wrote in *Des circonstances actuelles qui peuvent terminer la Révolution et des principes qui doivent fonder la république en France* that "writers advance public spirit quicker and farther than national education."[19] Writing has a special relationship, perhaps the closest one, with *opinion*, which, it turns out, is feminine or at least androgynous: "It/she [*Elle*] possesses both finesse and force at the same time" (115). That all-important figure of *opinion*, moving through the entire *Considérations*, is also the self-reflection of the author.

The postrevolutionary writer had to keep renewing the preconditions for liberty upon which rests the capacity of public opinion to read and express herself. Democratic values cannot by definition be forced. A whole new kind of technique is needed: "You have to arouse [*faire naître*] desire instead of commanding obedience and even when the government with reason wants particular institutions to be established, it has to treat public opinion carefully enough [*ménager*] to give the impression of according what it [public opinion] desires. Only what is well-written can in the long run direct and modify certain national habits."[20] Instilling one's desire in the other—the *faire désirer* of seduction or, using Staël's maternal metaphor, the *faire naître*—replaces both teaching and military or police methods of compliance. But already the defects and reversals show up: obligation and necessity return, *il faut* [you have to] and *il doit* [it has to]. Then comes hypocrisy, "*to give the impression.*" How far away is crime? But trust me, implies Staël, because only the best writing of the friends of liberty succeeds in blending so closely with the popular psyche and "national habits." The whole point of the revolution is to make the new "nation" appear as old, customary, and friendly as "habit." Literature is on the side of liberty, but it, too, employs invisible strategies similar to the dark intrigue of arbitrary states.

Staël's *Considérations* participates in the founding of both modern liberal political thought and modern historiography (its touchstone: the French Revolution). She should be there in the historical canon with Thiers and Michelet, and in the canon of political philosophy with Mill, Constant, and Tocqueville. Moreover, the ambiguities of her work do not allow for an easy definition of liberal democratic society, revolution, or historical knowledge.[21] If these ambiguities are preserved, readings of Staël could help change the political and historiographical traditions as we now know them.

Just as the French Revolution evolved a hegemony that nonetheless twisted and ignored many essential differences (gender, regions, religion, race), the historiography of the revolution continues the constant process of social and political reorganization, if not repression. The "brothers,"[22] from Payne and Burke to Vovelle and Furet, have dominated that history and the modern practice of history in general. The competition still goes on to see who is the real "son" of the revolution (witness the Bicentennial) with more disruptions from the "daughters" and other dissatisfied siblings.

Changing the historiographical canon like the literary canon is, therefore, a political act. But such a program, which calls for all strategies possible (revisions of the canon, analyses of how the canon and canonic writers function and dominate, an overabundance of studies on the same and different noncanonical writers), also demands rethinking as it goes along. How much critical self-consciousness is possible and even desirable; is it compatible with retaining as much passion in our studies as possible? How do we critics and historians want to set up parallel canons? If canons require hegemony as societies and histories do, that is, some consensus, can the intellectual community radically redefine how the canon or tradition works, what status it holds?

Where Staël is most subversive to me is her form. Her *Considérations sur la Révolution française* is a book of many books: My Life with Father, The Story of My Life, The History of the Revolution and of Modern France, On England, On Liberty, ... It practices almost every genre imaginable: lyricism, autobiography, satire, travelogue, political philosophy, aphorism, journalism, the study of comparative governments and societies, fiction, with, as ensemble and interruption, history. This diversity pushes the limits of history, even the "omnigenre" of Romantic history, which Madame de Staël inaugurates,[23] beyond fiction to one of the most innovative forms of writing available then, and now.

Notes

1. Madame de Staël, *Considérations sur la Révolution française*, ed. Jacques Godechot (Paris: Tallandier, 1983), 90. All subsequent references will be cited parenthetically in the text. Translations from the French are mine.

2. The disquieting narrator(s) of Staël's history, who vary from omniscience to polemics to self-dramatization, recall the impossible unity of Staël's fictional narrators. See Marie-Claire Vallois, *Fictions féminines: Mme de Staël et les voix de la Sibylle*, Stanford French and Italian Studies, no. 49 (Saratoga, Calif: Anma Libri, 1987).

3. Nancy K. Miller, "Performances of the Gaze: Staël's *Corinne, or Italy*," in *Subject to Change: Reading Feminist Writing* (New York: Columbia University Press, 1988), 162–203; Naomi Schor, "The Portrait of a Gentleman: Representing Men in (French) Women's Writing," *Representations* 20 (Fall 1987):113–33.

4. See Michel Delon, "La Saint-Barthélémy et la Terreur chez Mme de Staël et les historiens de la Révolution au XIXème siècle," *Romantisme* 11, no. 31 (1981):49–62.

5. Recent studies of the Enlightenment salon make a case for its central importance in the invention of public opinion, if not the modern republican polity. Daniel Gordon, "'Public Opinion' and the Civilizing Process in France: The Example of Morellet," *Eighteenth-Century Studies* 22, no. 3 (Spring 1989):302–28. Dena Goodman, "Enlightenment Salons: The Convergence of Female and Philosophic Ambitions," *Eighteenth-Century Studies* 22, no. 3 (Spring 1989):329–50. This same salon was associated with the frivolity of the Old Regime by revolutionaries eager to discourage women's participation in politics. See Joan B. Landes, *Women and the Public Sphere in the Age of the French Revolution* (Ithaca: Cornell University Press, 1988).

6. Jules Michelet, *Histoire de la Révolution française* (Paris: Gallimard, 1952) 1:1529 (Table of Contents, Book VI, chap. V).

7. Gérard Gengembre and Jean Goldzink, "L'opinion dans *Corinne*," *Europe* issues 693–94 (January–February 1987):51.

8. Prosper de Barante, historian and statesman, one of Madame de Staël's protégés and her lover during the rebirth of her salon at Coppet in 1805, looks back at 1795 and explains hostility against her. Is there mockery in his tone? He ironically chose that key word associated with Necker, "credit," to discredit her: "She really did not have any credit. However liberal and republican her opinions were, she could not be acceptable to (*convenir à*) such a government. Her aristocratic habits and inclinations, her

eagerness to mix in affairs and treat them indiscretely in conversation; her theoretical and ideal manner of judging things, the affection she kept for friends strongly opposed to the regime, made her annoying (*fâcheuse*) to the Directory, so much so that she even ended up being more or less exiled." *Souvenirs*, quoted in Simone Balayé, *Madame de Staël: Lumières et Liberté* (Paris: Klincksieck, 1979), 66–67. Again, she is accused of being a busybody, instead of a smart participant; abstract, instead of intellectual; partisan, instead of loyal to any friend.

9. Pierre Barbéris, "Mme de Staël: Du Romantisme, De la Littérature et de la France nouvelle," *Europe* issues 693–94 (January–February 1987):11.

10. François-René de Chateaubriand, *Mémoires d'outre-tombe*, ed. Maurice Levaillant (Paris: Flammarion, 1982), 2:178 (part 2, book 4, chap. 11).

11. For an example of political agendas, see Françoise Escoffier's review of Godechot's edition of the *Considérations*, "Mme de Staël: Une *politologue* intemporelle," *Revue des deux mondes* (March–April, 1984):95–100. "In short, excellent preface: I only reproach M. Godechot for having blamed Mme. de Staël for not understanding and approving of the Terror: Praise God, she had a horror of it!" (96).

12. See Joan DeJean, "Staël's *Corinne*, The Novel's Other Dilemma," *Stanford French Review* 11, no. 1 (1987):77–87. "The only creative avenue seemingly still open to them (literary women) would require them to take possession of their production in the male script, thereby silencing the conversational voice, a lesson borne out by the future of women's writing in nineteenth-century France" (87).

13. The *Considérations* were put together and edited by Staël's son-in-law, the Duc de Broglie, and her son, the Baron de Staël. On the dangers of such editing, see Mary Ann Caws, "The Conception of Engendering, The Erotics of Editing," *The Poetics of Gender*, ed. Nancy K. Miller (New York: Columbia University Press, 1986), 42–61.

14. Carla Petersen, *The Determined Reader: Gender and Culture in the Novel from Napoleon to Victoria* (New Brunswick: Rutgers University Press, 1986): Corinne falls into decline because oral improvisations are not available to her in England as in Italy, but "the narrator emerges as the truly superior female Romantic genius" (61).

15. See Madelyn Gutwirth's discussion of this sentence from Staël's *Concerning the Influence of the Passions upon the Happiness of Individuals and of Nations*: "men are the masters of public opinion, men have the power over their lives; men will overthrow your existence for the sake of a few moments in their own." "Forging a Vocation: Germaine de Staël on Fiction, Power, and Passion," *Bulletin of Research in the Humanities* 86, no. 3 (1983/85):242–54.

16. Gengembre and Goldzink, "L'opinion dans *Corinne*," 58.

17. Benjamin Constant, *Adolphe* (Paris: Garnier-Flammarion, 1965): "A doctrine of fatuousness, fatal tradition, which bequeaths to the vanity of the coming generation the corruption of the generation that has grown old" (39).

18. See Henri Coulet, "Révolution et roman selon Mme de Staël," *Revue d'histoire littéraire de la France* 87, no. 4 (1987):638–60.

19. Madame de Staël, *Des Circonstances actuelles qui peuvent terminer la Révolution et des principes qui doivent fonder la république en France*, ed. Lucia Omacini (Geneve: Droz, 1979), 276.

20. Madame de Staël, *De la littérature considérée dans ses rapports avec les institutions sociales*, ed. Paul Van Tieghem (Geneva: Droz, 1959), 1:31–32.

21. It is not unusual for Staël to question historical knowledge in general: "If one wanted to bear down on the past in order to get from it the immutable law of the present, even though this past has been founded itself on the alteration of another past; if one wanted to, I repeat, one would get lost in endless discussions. Let's return

therefore to what cannot be denied: circumstances where we have been the witnesses" (133). After such a thorough deconstruction of the historical process, what is the status of this last-ditch subjectivity in Staël?

22. Lynn Hunt has recently been drawing out the implications of the symbolic family romance in the representation of the French Revolution. Awaiting her forthcoming book, see "The political psychology of revolutionary caricatures," catalogue for the exhibit *French Caricature and the French Revolution 1789–1799* (Los Angeles: University of California Press, 1988), 33–40.

23. So that the papers from the conference "Women and the French Revolution" could appear together in a collection, we were asked not to publish our essays elsewhere. I, therefore, left this essay out of my book, *Headless History: Nineteenth-Century French Historiography of the Revolution* (Ithaca, Cornell University Press, 1990). For me, the essay on Staël is incomplete without the context of nineteenth-century historiography (and my book), and my book is incomplete without this essay, a kind of origin. I decry the fact that Jacques Godechot left Staël out of his *Un jury pour la Révolution* (Paris: Laffont, 1974) and the way he justifies the exclusion: "The *Considérations* have more in common with personal testimony and pamphlet than history. That is the reason why I eliminated this book from my *Jury pour la Révolution*, in which I wanted only the works of historians who used authentic sources" (26). Unfortunately, my book may well have the same effect as his, exclusion from the canon. The predicament is common in the practice of feminist studies: when we cannot have it both ways—do we want it both ways?—should women writers be collected together or assimilated into the canon?

Godechot limits Staël's liberal thought to a particular historical period, the July Monarchy, and, more specifically, to the rise to power of her son-in-law, the Duc de Broglie: "Germaine de Staël's liberalism is, in fact, that of the Restoration and July Monarchy liberals, that of her son-in-law, the Duc de Broglie" (31). Staël's historical context is important, but the comment suggests that her thought goes no further than that moment and that masculine derivation. Godechot also criticizes Staël for ignoring social structures (Russian peasants, English working class), which impunes her liberalism even more. Attempts to show Staël's social conscience (Béatrice Jassinski) are "in vain," warns Godechot (Introduction, notes, 31, 32, 41). Godechot's notes and comments are very useful, but they do not hesitate to correct Staël's own ideas as if the present-day historian can judge her work from a more privileged position (that includes my ability to judge Godechot). Some of his notes are distracting, if not bordering on the tactics of "literary police":

"We will note yet again the naive and worshipful admiration of Mme. de Staël for her father" (631).

"We see how Mme. de Staël treats the 'populace'" (635).

"Total error" (642), "Mme. de Staël's completely subjective judgement" (642).

"We confirm that Mme. de Staël takes on the tone of a pamphlet" (655).

"This thought shows to what extent Mme. de Staël represented the ideas of the rich bourgeoisie" (655).

Another more modest, even humorous, example of literary police, comes up in Henri Coulet's note 53: "Madelyn Gutwirth, in the first general study on Mme. de Staël as novelist (*Madame de Staël Novelist: The Emergence of the Artist as Woman*, Urbana: University of Illinois Press, 1978), where the feminism attributed to Mme. de Staël appears to us a little too radical." In "Révolution et roman selon Mme de Staël," and significantly the journal that best represents the official French literary tradition, *Revue d'histoire littéraire de la France* 87, no. 4 (1987):638–60.

III

Constructing the New Gender System in Postrevolutionary Culture

Plate I Anne-Louis Girodet-Trioson, *The Funeral of Atala*

8

Triste Amérique: Atala and the Postrevolutionary Construction of Woman

NAOMI SCHOR

Historians and art historians have in recent years begun to recognize the extraordinary significance of the prevalence of feminine civic allegory in the iconography produced by the French Revolution. As Lynn Hunt writes: "The appearance of feminine allegorization was momentous for it became associated with the Republic ever after."[1] Though, as Hunt beautifully documents, the figure of Marianne, emblem of Liberty and of the French Republic, did not immediately impose itself as the unique, consensual icon of national sovereignty, from the time of its first appearance in 1792 it became an increasingly powerful visual source of legitimation for the successive revolutionary regimes that ruled France and eventually, after periods of eclipse and contestation, the official symbol of the state.[2]

Curiously, however, literary critics and historians—myself included—have been slow to draw the consequences of this important iconographic shift for the representation of women in nineteenth-century French fiction. And yet arguably the most lasting effect of the French Revolution on nineteenth-century French representations of women from Chateaubriand's virginal Atala to Zola's courtesan, Nana, may well have been the powerful revolutionary conflation of the feminine and the state, the tendency for representations of woman in post-absolutist France to be collapsed with the stabilization and destabilization of the new social order instituted by 1789.

So heavily politicized and so insistently genderized is representation in the wake of the revolution that the feminine subject in postrevolutionary French fiction from early romanticism through naturalism becomes fully intelligible only when viewed in light of the historical circumstances that presided over its construction. Because of the widespread feminization of republican iconography in France, the nineteenth-century heroine, in contradistinction to her eighteenth-century predecessor, is always inhabited by the uncanny shadow of the state whose very laws serve to silence and oppress her. This allegorical specter, sometimes muted, sometimes boldly foregrounded, encumbers the female protagonist in the nineteenth-century French novel with an ideological charge that neither prerevolutionary female protagonists in French novels nor female protagonists in other nineteenth-century European literatures carry to quite the same degree, though of course feminine civic allegory is both an ancient and a pervasive phenomenon. Throughout the century the representation of woman in France will be trapped between two excesses, which stem from the matrix from which it emerges: the disembodiment inherent in allegorism and the hyper-embodiment characteristic of naturalism, which are in fact two sides of the same representational coin, as demonstrated by the synchronous putrefaction of Nana's corpse and the decline and fall of the Second Empire in the final chapter of *Nana*.[3] Bearing in mind that the relationship between woman and representation is always saturated with history I want in what follows to consider through a specific example the modalities of that relationship in the immediate aftermath of the French Revolution.

I

Two fictional scenes delimit the space in which I want to inscribe my reflections on the relationship between women, representation, and the French Revolution in nineteenth-century French fiction. The first scene is drawn from the opening pages of one of the major feminocentric narratives of the eighteenth century, *Manon Lescaut* (1731). The first person narrator is the Marquis de Renoncour, the man of quality within whose memoirs *Manon Lescaut* is embedded. By way of framing Des Grieux's first-person narrative of his love for Manon, Renoncour recounts his first sighting of the tragic pair in the town of Pacy. Manon, condemned to exile in America, is part of a group of twelve women being transported under guard to Le Havre:

> Parmi les douze filles qui étaient enchaînées six à six par le milieu du corps, il y en avait une dont l'air et la figure étaient si peu conformes à sa condition, qu'en tout autre état je l'eusse prise pour une personne du premier rang. Sa tristesse et la saleté de son linge et de ses habits l'enlaidissaient si peu, que sa vue m'inspira du respect et de la pitié. Elle tâchait néanmoins de se tourner, autant que sa chaîne pouvait le permettre, pour dérober son visage aux yeux des spectateurs.

> amongst the twelve women who were chained together by the waist in two rows of six was one whose face and bearing were so out of keeping with her present situation that in any other setting I would have taken her for a lady of the gentler birth. She was in abject misery and her clothes were filthy, but all that had so little effect on her beauty that I felt nothing but pity and respect for her. She was trying to turn away as much as the chains would allow, so as to hide her face from us onlookers, and this effort at concealment was so natural that it seemed to come from feelings of modesty.[4]

Suspending for a moment any commentary on this remarkable tableau I want to turn now to my second scene, this one drawn from Chateaubriand's *Atala*, whose publication date of 1801 makes it the most immediately postrevolutionary fiction published in France and still retained, however grudgingly, in the canon. We are now in the new world, indeed among its native inhabitants. The speaker is Chactas, an aged and blind Natchez Indian; the story, his youthful love for Atala, a fair young Indian maiden. Taken prisoner by the tribe to which Atala belongs, Chactas has been tied down Gulliver-like prior to his being put to death. In his sleep he dreams he is being freed. Upon awakening he finds he is not dreaming:

> A la clarté de la lune . . . j'entrevois une grande figure blanche penchée sur moi et occupée à dénouer silencieusement mes liens. . . . Une seule corde restait, mais il paraissait impossible de la couper sans toucher un guerrier qui la couvrait tout entière de son corps. Atala y porte la main, le guerrier s'éveille à demi et se dresse sur son séant. Atala reste immobile et le regarde. L'Indien croit voir l'Esprit des ruines; il se recouche en fermant les yeux et en invoquant son Manitou. Le lien est brisé. Je me lève; je suis ma libératrice . . .

> By the light of a moonbeam filtering between two clouds, I made out a large white figure leaning over me, silently untying my bonds. . . . A single rope still remained, but it seemed impossible to cut it without touching a warrior who was covering its whole length with his body. Atala placed her hand on it. The warrior half awakened and sat up. Atala remained motionless, watching him. The Indian thought he was looking at the Spirit of the Ruins and lay down again, closing his eyes and invoking his Manitou. The bond was broken. I stood up and followed my deliverer . . .[5]

Suffused with eroticism each of these tableaus enacts a different fantasmatic scenario of bondage. Permeated by an erotics of female vulnerability, the eighteenth-century text represents the titillating pathos of a woman in chains. The emphasis here is on the marks of class and the redemptive virtues of modesty. Soiled, exposed, bound, Manon is a woman in distress. Entirely bound over to the exchange system that makes of her a mere commodity, Manon's chains can be lightened only by bribing her jailers. A radical paradigm shift marks the scene from *Atala*. Grandiose, ghostly, garbed in white, Atala is represented as a near-mythic figure of power and cunning. In Chactas's captivity narrative, the captive is male and his liberator, a liberatrix. In what appears to be a striking instance of role reversal, in this enactment of the bondage fantasy, the male protagonist is reduced to the passivity of an object, the helplessness of an infant. Disempowered by the multiple bonds pinning him to the ground, Chactas, the brave Indian warrior, awaits deliverance from the hands of an all-powerful female. Furthermore, in this beyond of the European market economy, money is uncoupled from liberation and class differences wither away.

The paired readings of the bondage scenes from *Manon* and *Atala* I have just performed are, of course, tendentious, informed by the assumption that in some manner still to be determined the reslotting of the female protagonist as liberatrix is, so to speak, bound up with the events of the French Revolution.

Bracketing for the moment the endlessly vexed question of the relationship between Text and Event—which is precisely what is at stake in this paper—a couple of thorny methodological questions present themselves: first, the juxta-position I have just staged is rigged. An entirely different intertextual relation-ship between these same two texts might be constructed to entail a less optimistic conclusion regarding the effect of the revolution on the representa-tion of women. Indeed if we were to read jointly the death scenes of Manon and Atala—and we will—we would have to conclude that the syntax of the female literary text continues undisturbed from the Age of Enlightenment to the Age of Napoleon. The presumption of progress, of some sort of liberation of and for women fostered by the macro-narrative of the revolution is denied by the seemingly ritualistic sacrifice of the eternal female protagonist, as well of course as by the historical record. And then there is the second problem: granting the heuristic value of my admittedly selective double reading, the question arises: why *Manon Lescaut*, why *Atala*? The question, I hasten to note, is not: Is this comparison legitimate? For at least ever since Sainte-Beuve the intertextual relationship of *Manon* and *Atala* has been a critical common-place of the writing, meager as it is, on *Atala*.[6] The question I am raising is somewhat different: What grounds are there for attributing to these two fictional works representative status? In short, one of the main issues this comparison raises is the issue of canonicity. At this point a distinction must be introduced between the cases of *Manon Lescaut* and *Atala*, for whereas *Manon* has long occupied a secure position in the canon, which is, of course, subject to change, *Atala* has not.

II

A brief recall of some of the circumstances surrounding the genesis, publica-tion, and critical reception of *Atala* is necessary in order to understand the uniquely liminal position it occupies in standard histories of French literature. Begun in 1792, during or shortly after Chateaubriand's voyage to America, *Atala* was originally conceived of as part of a work on the Natchez Indian tribe, the *Natchez*. However, for reasons that remain obscure, in 1801 Chateaubriand decided to publish *Atala* separately, as a sort of prepublication "teaser" for his coming magnum opus, *The Genius of Christianity*, which appeared in 1802. The publication of *Atala* was by all accounts (and not just Chateaubriand's, that master of self-promotion) a major literary event. The exotic tale of doomed love between a Europeanized noble savage and a Christianized Indian maiden made Chateaubriand a celebrity and gave rise to a veritable industry of popular iconography and artifacts. But, for all its spectacular success and popularity, *Atala* was not to be Chateaubriand's main claim to fame as a novelist. That claim rests on *René*, yet another spin-off from Chateaubriand's apologetic work.

Written virtually in tandem with *Atala, René* was first published as part of *The Genius*. It was only in 1805 that *Atala* and *René*, presumably in response to popular demand, assumed their definitive literary existences as autonomous yet linked works of fiction. Connected by a double synecdoche via the same master text, actantially conjoined through the character of René, who is Chactas's interlocutor in *Atala* as well as the narrator of the text that bears his name, the literary fates of *Atala* and *René* have been radically different. Whereas *Atala* is generally characterized as having "aged," which is to say having aged badly—and in many ways it has, but that is hardly the point— *René* has been preserved in the literary histories that constitute the French canon as eternally youthful, the embodiment of literary adolescence. Because of its prestigious posterity—*René* is *the* founding text of French Romanticism—the androcentric novel has completely eclipsed the feminocentric, now relegated to the nebulous limbo of the transitional work. Viewed as the dying fall of neo-classicism or, at best, pre-Romanticism, *Atala* is never viewed as inaugural, foundational. Primogeniture and contiguity have to date assured its place in the canon, but that place is that of a quaint curio rather than that of a work of major cultural significance. Reproducing the same fratricidal scenario as that played out in both *René* and *Atala*, *René*, the brother-text, has killed *Atala*, its incestuous female Other.

I use the vocabulary of the nuclear family structure and sibling rivalry advisedly, for it is intrinsic to Chateaubriand's metaphorics of literary paternity. Thus, for example, in his *Mémoires*, Chateaubriand casts *Atala* in the role of daughter, indeed devoted, self-sacrificing daughter; like the proverbial Bible, during a military engagement the daughterly manuscript of *Atala* acts to shield her father from enemy bullets: "A l'affaire de la Plaine, deux balles avaient frappé mon havresac pendant un mouvement de conversion. Atala, en fille dévouée, se plaça entre son père et le plomb ennemi" [At the business of the plain two bullets had struck my knapsack during a change of front. Atala, acting as a devoted daughter, placed herself between her father and the enemy shot].[7] Elsewhere in the *Mémoires* Chateaubriand describes the perplexity generated among the academicians by *Atala*'s "birth" in these revealing terms: "On ne savait si l'on devait la classer parmi les monstruosités ou parmi les beautés; était-elle Gorgone ou Vénus? Les académiciens assemblés dissertèrent doctement sur son sexe et sa nature" [They didn't know whether to class her among the *monstrosities* or the *beauties*; was she a Gorgon or Venus? The assembled academicians learnedly held forth on her sex and her nature].[8] The taxonomic undecidability provoked by the text is doubly coded as sexual: in the first instance there seems to be no doubt about the text's sex, rather about its precise inscription within the mythic paradigm of femininity. In the second, it is the text's very sex that is at issue: the alternative is no longer between Venus and Medusa but between maleness and femaleness, or Atala as Hermaphrodite. The figure of Medusa mediates these two apparently mutually exclusive statements; for if the text is in fact monstrous, *more* Medusa, then its very sex is thrown into doubt.

Now I will want to argue that it is precisely that doubt, that sexual indeterminacy that *Atala* functions to check. And I will want to argue further that the "sexual fix" (Heath) of *Atala* is inseparable from what I take to be one of the text's major ideological effects: the putting into place of a cultural construction of femininity adequate to the reactionary sexual regime brought into being by the French Revolution. There is, in other words, a sense in which *Atala* helped pave the way for the Napoleonic Code first promulgated in 1804, and which all historians of women and feminism in nineteenth-century France agree was a disaster for women, tightening the loopholes in the Old Regime legal system so as to subject all women to the same inequitable laws regarding marriage and property rights, depriving women of the fragile gains they had made during the revolution, setting back women's rights in France by at least a century.[9] At the same time, it should be noted that feminist historians of the French Revolution have argued that the very betrayal of women by the revolution and the repressive regimes that followed it is perversely largely responsible for the coming into being of modern French feminism.

What *Atala* participates in is the prevalence of allegorism in nineteenth-century French figurations of the revolution; what *Atala* founds is the tradition of representing woman in nineteenth-century French fiction as sexually stigmatized. Let me develop each of these points in turn. Considering the magnitude and the significance of the French Revolution in ushering in the modern era in France it is a striking fact of nineteenth-century French cultural production that the revolution, especially in its mythic form of 1789, is significantly underrepresented in mimetic high art, with the emphasis on the word mimetic.[10] Scenes from the revolution are, of course, abundantly documented in popular iconography and the bloody battles of the Chouan resistance, memorably depicted in the works of Hugo, Balzac, and Barbey d'Aurevilly, among others. Better yet, French Romanticism, Realism, and Naturalism all draw their impetus from the revolution: nineteenth-century literature in France is a protracted and therapeutic working through of the trauma of regicide and the shock of democraticization. But the French Revolution—at least in France, the situation in England is quite different—in some very real sense escapes representation, except in the displaced mode of allegory. This tendency to depict the revolution by displacement is perhaps most famously apparent in the neoclassical history paintings of David. The recourse to a preexisting Greek, but especially Roman, repertory of images and stories can be explained by what Ronald Paulson has called the "central aesthetic challenge" posed by the French Revolution, "how to represent the unprecedented."[11] As Marx was the first to note in the celebrated opening pages of *The Eighteenth Brumaire of Louis Bonaparte*, from 1789 to 1814 that challenge was met in large part by reappropriating earlier, notably Roman modes of representation, and as historians such as Maurice Agulhon have recently demonstrated, these earlier modes included the predominantly female allegorical figures that have since antiquity served to represent civic virtues.[12]

Atala, whose writing spans the revolutionary decade, is, to borrow a phrase from Jane Tompkins, "social criticism written in an allegorical mode,"[13] and that explains in large part why it appears to have "aged" so badly. The aging effect is produced by the misguided application to an allegorical work of the aesthetic standards and readerly expectations grounded in high realism; it is only when one reads *Atala* through the appropriate allegorical lens that its youthful beauty is restored and one can begin to grasp the reasons for its immense popular success. Written largely in exile by an aristocratic French emigré, *Atala* enlists the ready-made generic conventions of travel literature and stereotypical schemata of exotic romance to the ends of consolidating the reaction to the revolution. And that consolidation takes the form of a spectacular binding or rebinding of female energy, a containment that only makes sense as a response to an equally spectacular explosion of female energy: the active participation of women in the revolution. Indeed, so terrifying to the male leaders of the French Revolution was the invasion of the public sphere by women and especially lower-class women, that the binding of female energy and the resulting silencing of women follow immediately upon their increasingly threatening attempts to represent themselves in the arena of public debate. As early as 1793, "women were," according to Joan B. Landes, "banned from active *and* passive participation in the political sphere."[14]

The "crisis in representation" (Hunt) of the 1790s was, as Mona Ozouf, Lynn Hunt, and Marie-Hélène Huet have persuasively argued, bound up with a struggle by such figures as Robespierre and David to reclaim the sphere of symbolic representation from the hordes of unruly women unleashed by the revolution and to realign representation with the male principle from which it had been severed after the beheading of the king: thus David actively promoted the virile effigy of Hercules over the feminine figure of Liberty as a candidate for the seal of the Republic, while Robespierre, with David's expert help, choreographed the Festival of the Supreme Being to stamp out the female-centered cult of Reason in favor of a sublime, suprasensorial ceremony.[15] This last contest for an appropriate secular celebration of the revolution is of particular pertinence to our reading of *Atala*, for what was at stake in Robespierre's iconoclastic superproduction was the wish not so much to hasten the dechristianization of France, a purpose already served by the Festival of Reason, rather, as Huet argues, to avert the perceived threat posed by the triumphant female embodiment of Reason, a fully corporeal female allegory: "La femme et l'image seront de fait inextricablement liées dans la stratégie des partisans du culte de l'Etre suprême, et l'on pourrait voir, dans la détermination dont ils feront preuve pour instaurer un culte 'sublime,' le rejet conjugué de l'idole et du féminin" (Woman and the image are in fact inextricably linked in the strategy of the partisans of the cult of the Supreme Being, and one might see in the determination they will display in order to institute a "sublime" cult, the conjoined rejection of the idol and the feminine).[16] The highly successful festival of Reason held in the Cathedral of Notre-Dame on November 10, 1793, (20 Brumaire Year II) featured, let us recall, an allegory of Reason fully and sensually embodied by an actress, and this was only the most spectacular instance of such a live personification of a civic virtue and moreover one generally held to be incompatible with femininity.

Chateaubriand's *Atala* is deeply implicated in the struggle to recontain the female energy briefly unchained by the revolution and to ward off the dangers

represented by a too palpably embodied female cult figure. That Chateaubri-
and was aware of the active participation of women in the revolution and that
he deplored it is indicated in *Atala* through the depiction of a blood-thirsty
chorus-like group of Indian women who call for Chactas's condemnation to
death, as well of course as by the Dickensian passage in his *Mémoires* describing the women of la Halle [*sic*], knitting in the galleries of the National
Assembly, banging their clogs and foaming at the mouth as they called for the
death of the members of the royalist opposition.[17] That Chateaubriand
grasped that the most effective way to counter the threat posed by women to
the symbolic order involved the decorporealization of feminine allegory is
clearly evident from his treatment of the figure of Atala. Which brings me to
my second point.

Nineteenth-century French fiction, especially in its hegemonic realist-natu-
ralist modality, relies heavily, as I have argued elsewhere, on the containment
of female sexual energy to propel its narratives forward.[18] Chained, hysteri-
cized, maimed, women's disciplined bodies provide an essential motor for the
smooth running of the nineteenth-century textual machine. Atala, whose access to sexuality is barred by the vow her mother made at her birth committing
her to virginity, is but the first of a long line of nineteenth-century French
heroines denied jouissance. This is not to say that the eighteenth-century novel
represents a pre-Lapsarian paradise for the female protagonist, nor for that
matter that the nineteenth is in Jane Gallop's words "beyond the jouissance
principle"[19]: Manon, as we have seen, makes her debut on the scene of
representation in chains and the Marquise de Merteuil in *Dangerous Liaisons*
exits the same scene hideously disfigured for her sins. But whereas Sade's
heroines are subjected to multiple bodily wounds and suturings for the greater
delight of their male lovers, the earth does move for Emma Bovary.

Even if we were able to demonstrate persuasively that the sexual economies
of key eighteenth-century texts differ in significant and predictable ways from
their nineteenth-century equivalents, say *Atala*, *Les Diaboliques*, and *Nana*, we
would still be confronted by the enormous difficulty of specifying those reified
entities, the eighteenth- and nineteenth-century novels. Historicizing the representations of women (but also of men, crowds, etc.) is an infinitely complex
task, certainly far more so than I allowed in *Breaking the Chain*. Periodization,
then, as well as canonicity—can the two ever really be separated—is here at
issue. Earlier I asked what grounds there were for according, indeed claiming
for *Atala* representative status. The question now becomes: wherein lies *Atala*'s
historical specificity, what an earlier generation of critics called its "original-
ity"? What are the markers of *Atala*'s post-revolutionary production?

III

To begin to answer these questions requires bringing into play a third novel,
the text that serves by all accounts as *Atala*'s privileged intertext. I am referring
to Bernardin de Saint-Pierre's hugely popular *Paul et Virginie* (1778). For

Chateaubriand's contemporaries there was little doubt but that *Atala* was (nothing more than) a rewriting of this now little known text that was to mark the imaginary of nineteenth-century French novelists in a way few other eighteenth-century novels did, a text Chateaubriand explicitly and significantly comments on in a chapter of *The Genius of Christianity*.[20] Set in the Ile de France (Mauritius), *Paul et Virginie* is the story of two children who are raised together by their mothers, who have sought refuge on this tropical island to escape the injustices of patriarchal society: misogyny, slavery, violence. In time, however, Virginie leaves this matriarchal paradise to go off to Paris to be educated. Upon her return there is a terrible storm and the ship that is carrying her home is wrecked. Faced with the choice of taking her clothes off to swim to safety or preserving her modesty and drowning, Virginie does not hesitate: she drowns, her modesty intact.

Two aspects of the novel have garnered the most readerly attention: the bliss of the children's dyadic fraternal relationship—rarely in modern European fiction has the mirror stage been portrayed in more lyrical terms—and the implausibility of the ending. The incest motif is, of course, present in *Atala*, since Chactas's adoptive father, the Spaniard Lopez is, as is slowly revealed in the course of the narrative, also Atala's biological father. Hence Chactas's somewhat melodramatic exclamation on burying Atala: "Lopez, m'écriai-je alors, vois ton fils inhumer ta fille!" ["Lopez," I cried out, "behold your son interring your daughter" (122/74)]. But in *Atala* sexual difference precedes and precipitates desire; we are from the outset plunged into a degraded world beyond the supposedly idyllic pre-Oedipus. When Chactas first appears in the frame-"Prologue," he *is* (at least by analogy) Oedipus: "Une jeune fille l'accompagnait sur les coteaux du Meschacebé, comme Antigone guidait les pas d'Oedipe sur le Cythéron . . ." [A young girl accompanied him over the slopes along the Mescacebe, just as Antigone once guided the steps of Oedipus over Mount Cytheron (43–44/20)]. What is more for the white, European male, Chateaubriand's new world is like Lévi-Strauss's irremediably *triste*: despite the signifiers of exoticism flaunted in the landscape descriptions, the forests of the Louisiana territory are in *Atala* the site of a lost French empire, reciprocal violence, and ontological homelessness. Fleeing the unspecified "passions et [des] malheurs" ["passion and sorrow" (44/20)] that had driven him from Europe (compare *René*), René finds in America only more of the same, of sameness itself. Dystopia turns out to be a prison house of mirroring, where René cannot escape his specular image. An extended chiasmus figures this negative mirror-stage: "Je vois en toi," says Chactas to René, "l'homme civilisé qui s'est fait sauvage; tu vois en moi l'homme sauvage, que le grand Esprit . . . a voulu civiliser. Entrés l'un et l'autre dans la carrière de la vie par les deux bouts opposés, tu es venu te reposer à ma place, et j'ai été m'asseoir à la tienne . . ." ["I see in you the civilized man who has become a savage; you see in me the savage whom the Great spirit has . . . chosen to civilize. Having entered life's path from opposite ends, you have now come to rest in my place while I have gone to sit in yours . . ." (47/22)].

Clearly then if *Atala* is in the words of one disgruntled nineteenth-century literary critic, "l'exagération, je n'ose pas dire la charge de *Paul et Virginie*" ("the exaggeration, dare I say the caricature of *Paul et Virginie*"] what *Atala* mimes in the earlier text is not the joy of fraternal fusion, rather the implausibility of the virtuous ending.[21] Here I want to be quite explicit about the connection between the pre- and the postrevolutionary texts: in both instances, the mother-daughter dyad precludes the daughter's consummation of her sexual desire, indeed her sexuality *tout court*. The princess of Clèves, the founding victim of the reproduction of mothering in the French novelistic canon, does at least marry and presumably lose her virginity. But in *Atala*, as in *Paul et Virginie*, the intensity of the mother-daughter relationship results in a veritable taboo on the daughter's virginity. Atala's secret, the fatal enigma of her femininity—Chactas describes her as "un être incompréhensible" ["an incomprehensible being" (75/41)]—is her mother's vow: feeling herself on the verge of succumbing to Chactas's impetuous desire, Atala commits suicide rather than break the promise extracted from her by her dying mother, that she respect the vow her mother made at her birth in exchange for her life.

There is then no radical discontinuity between the sexual politics of the two novels: in both cases the daughter is suicided by the author to serve a double imperative: the maternal critique of patriarchy—better dead than seduced and abandoned—and, at the same time, patriarchy's censure of female sexual activity—better dead than troubling the homosocial order. And yet, there is to my mind a crucial difference between *Atala* and *Paul et Virginie*, which can best be grasped by considering the mother's deathbed speech to her daughter, which surely deserves to be set besides Mme. de Chartres's famous last words to the princess of Clèves:

> "Ma fille, me dit-elle," en présence d'un missionaire qui consolait ces derniers instants; ma fille, tu sais le voeu que j'ai fait pour toi. Voudrais-tu démentir ta mère? O mon Atala! je te laisse dans un monde qui n'est pas digne de posséder une chrétienne, au milieu d'idolâtres qui persécutent le Dieu de ton père et le mien, le Dieu qui, après t'avoir donné le jour, te l'a conservé par un miracle. Eh! ma chère enfant, en acceptant le voile des vierges, tu ne fais que renoncer aux soucis de la cabane et aux funestes passions qui ont troublé le sein de ta mère! Viens donc, ma bien aimée, viens; jure sur cette image de la mère du Sauveur, entre les mains de ce saint prêtre et de ta mère expirante, que tu ne me trahiras point à la face du ciel. Songe que je me suis engagée pour toi, afin de te sauver la vie, et que si tu ne tiens ma promesse tu plongeras l'âme de ta mère dans des tourments éternels.

> "My daughter," she said, "you know about the vow I once made for you. Would you have your mother speak falsely? O my Atala! I leave you in a world unworthy of having a Christian woman in the midst of heathens who persecute your father's God and mine, the God who first gave you life and then preserved it by a miracle. Ah, my dear child, when you accept the virgin's veil, you give up only the cares of the cabin and the mortal passions which distressed your mother's bosom. Come, then, beloved daughter, swear upon this image of the Savior's mother, under the hands of the holy priest and before your dying mother, that you will not betray me in the face of

Heaven. Remember that I gave my word for you in order to save your life, and if you do not keep my promise, you will plunge your mother's soul in everlasting woe" (100/58–59).

Maternal discourse in *Atala* does not emanate from the depths of some timeless, transhistorical unconscious, nor does it draw its affective power from the matrix of the pre-Oedipus. The language of the mother is coextensive with that of the Christian apologist; the key words in her vocabulary are persecution, salvation, and damnation. This then is what I will not hesitate to call Chateaubriand's brilliant innovation in *Atala*: in the guise of rehabilitating Christianity in the wake of the secularizing trends of eighteenth-century philosophy and the dechristianization promoted by the revolution, Chateaubriand fuses to stunning effect the categories of gender with those of religion. The coupling of the two is mutually beneficent and reinforcing: a threatened Christianity draws renewed strength from being mapped onto sexual difference while a threatening breakdown of sexual hierarchies is averted by sanctifying the cultural construction of femininity. In *Atala*, a work written in the white-heat of a historically unprecedented revolution, we catch a stunningly rare glimpse of anaclisis doing the work of ideology over the body of a woman. To say this is neither to deny nor to paper over the ideological fissures in *Atala*—prominent traces of Chateaubriand's original *roman à thèse* condemning the excesses of Christian dogma do persist in the irony of Atala's unnecessary suicide; the knowledge that she might have been relieved of her vow by higher Church authorities comes too late to save her from death. But, however unorthodox Chateaubriand's apologetic discourse, however much the powerful eroticism of the doomed love story strains against the exigencies of denial—Atala does come vertiginously close to succumbing to temptation—it performs its double ideological function with remarkable efficacy.

The same potent linkage of Christianity and femininity—as well one might add as the same dogmatic lapses—are at work in the larger apologetic design of the *Genius*. For, as Stéphane Michaud has pointed out in his study of Mariolatry in nineteenth-century France, Chateaubriand's case for Christianity is grounded in an inherited discourse of naturalized feminine inferiority. The weakness inherent in woman's sex, especially in regard to pleasure, necessitates her faith, while at the same time the goodness and compassion inherent in woman's maternal nature make of her a quasi-religious figure on the order of the Virgin Mary: "la religion est en effet un aussi indispensable soutien à sa fragilité qu'une alliée naturelle de sa pudeur et son ignorance" [Religion is in effect as much an indispensable support for her frailty as a natural ally for her modesty and her ignorance].[22]

Let us return now as promised to the death or rather burial scenes in *Manon Lescaut* and *Atala*. First *Manon*:

Je rompis mon épée pour m'en servir à creuser, mais j'en tirais moins de secours que de mes mains. J'ouvris une large fosse, j'y plaçai l'idole de mon coeur, après avoir pris soin de l'envelopper de tous mes habits pour empêcher le sable de la toucher. Je ne la mis dans cet état qu'après l'avoir embrassé mille fois avec toute l'ardeur du plus parfait amour. Je m'assis encore auprès d'elle. Je la considérais longtemps. Je ne pouvais me résoudre à fermer sa fosse.

I broke my sword so as to use it for digging, but it was not as useful as my hands. I opened a wide trench and into it I committed the idol of my heart, having first wrapped her in all my clothes lest the sand should touch her. But first I kissed her a thousand times with all the tenderness of perfect love. I could not bring myself to close her grave, but still sat for a long time contemplating her (213/188).

Because the section of *Atala* entitled "The Funeral" is more protracted than the shockingly brief section of *Manon* devoted to Manon's sudden death and unceremonious burial, I want to compare the scene of Manon's burial with an icon indelibly engraved on every French child's conscience, the painting invariably reproduced in literary manuals to illustrate the excerpt from *Atala* describing the dead Atala, Girodet's 1808 painting, "Atala carried to the grave" (see Plate I).[23]

This scene does not in fact correspond to any single passage in the text, but rather synoptically and idiosyncratically interprets the entire section; for in this complex representation Girodet is, it should be noted, promoting his own homoeroticism even as he lends striking visual immediacy to Chateaubriand's more homosocially inflected apologetic design.[24] In the strikingly immediate foreground there are not two but three figures: to the left a prostrate and highly idealized Chactas embraces Atala's legs, in the center the highlighted, virginally white body of Atala hangs suspended over the dark gaping hole of the freshly dug grave, and to the right, holding up Atala's upper body stands the bent, hooded, and patriarchally bearded père Aubry. Corresponding to the three figures three crosses are arrayed in full view: in the foreground on the horizontal plane and ostentatiously placed near the grave, a curiously cross-shaped shovel is bled over the edge of the painting; just over Atala's right breast a fragment of the cross she holds in her demurely folded hands can be made out; and finally, in the background, a cross rises vertically in the gash of open sky glimpsed through the woodsy grotto opening.[25]

Whether read from right to left or from top to bottom the painting tells the same story: in sharp contrast with Manon's remarkably secular burial, Atala's is a pieta. The ritualistic death of the female protagonist is here powerfully reconfigured through the ostentatious display of the full panoply of Christian symbolism: in death, Atala syncretizes the attributes of both the Virgin and Christ. Here again the comparison with *Paul et Virginie* serves to confirm the thesis I am putting forward, for if Manon is denied a decent Christian burial, and Atala virtually canonized in death—"nous passerions la nuit en prières auprès du corps de cette sainte" [we resolved to spend the night in prayer beside the body of the saintly maid (119/72)]—Virginie, whom Chateaubriand not surprisingly insists on describing as a "*Christian* virgin," is given a ceremonial burial, but the ceremony is, *pace* Chateaubriand, resolutely and exotically pagan:

Lorsqu'elle fut arrivée au lieu de sa sépulture, des négresses de Madagascar et des Cafres de Mozambique déposèrent autour d'elle des paniers de fruits, et suspendirent des pièces d'étoffes aux arbres voisins, suivant l'usage de leur pays; des Indiennes du Bengale et de la cote Malabre apportèrent des cages pleines d'oiseaux, auxquelles elles donnèrent la liberté sur son corps: tant la perte d'un object aimable intéresse toutes les nations, et tant est grand le pouvoir de la vertu malheureuse, puisqu'elle réunit *toutes les religions* autour de son tombeau.

When she had reached her burial-place, black women from Madagascar and Kafirs from Mozambique laid baskets of fruits around her and hung rolls of cloth on neighboring trees in keeping with the customs of their countries; Indian women from Bengal and the coast of Malabar brought cages full of birds which they set free over her body. So affecting is the loss of a fair object to all nations and so great is the power of unhappy virtue, since it brings together all religions around its grave.[26]

Though both Virginie and Atala die for virtue, the contrast between the two virgins' burials could not be greater: Virginie's burial is a colorful, life-affirming, and above all ecumenical affair officiated at by an ethnically diverse group of women, whereas Atala's is, as we have already seen, a gloomy rite presided over by two men whose very real cultural differences are overridden by the homogenizing and allegorizing discourse of Christian apologetics: "Quiconque eût ignoré que cette jeune fille avait joui de la lumière, aurait pu la prendre pour la statue de la Virginité endormie" [Whoever was unaware that this maid had once enjoyed the light of day might have taken her for a statue of sleeping virginity (120/72)].

By making of the lifeless corpse of the young Indian maiden an allegory of Virginity, Chateaubriand successfully manages to capitalize on the legitimating power of feminine allegory, while voiding the feminine form of female corporeality and desire and erasing from it the marks of racial difference. The allegorization of woman, a sort of degree zero of female representation, can only be brought about through a violent act of suppression of all particularities, not to mention of life. And, once again, Zola's hyperembodied Nana confirms the rule: during her last appearance on stage before disappearing from Paris and returning there only to die, Nana is cast in an entirely silent role, effectively silenced the better to be allegorized.[27]

IV

Recently I saw a fascinating video documentary, *Mother Ireland*, produced by the Derry Film and Video Collective, which explores the various uses to which the allegorization of Ireland as Woman or Mother has been put and the effects that this allegorization have had on "real Irish women" in their nationalist and/or feminist political struggles and activities. As Annie Goldson, the documentary's editor, points out in her commentary on the video:

> On the one hand, it can be said that allegory is oppressive for women, denying them power. Feminists cogently argue that the representation of gender within culture contributes to the process of aligning an object, woman, with an image, Woman, and bringing her under social control. . . . On the other hand, as is apparent in *Mother Ireland*, many women admire and derive strength from allegorical representations. These symbolized female images can affirm women in their choices and political struggles, not only as role models, but also as a symbol of the general good in which they, as half of humanity, are deeply implicated.[28]

Though it is difficult to evaluate the effects of the allegorical representations of women produced by the French Revolution on the lives of the "real women" of nineteenth-century France,[29] we can at least raise the question: How did postrevolutionary women writers in France cope with the allegorical imperative? Were female allegories disempowering or empowering for them? Not surprisingly for nineteenth-century women and more especially feminist authors[30]—I am thinking chiefly of Staël and Sand—this representational constraint posed special difficulties, while at the same time offering unsuspected if limited opportunities for subversion. Staël's *Corinne, or Italy* (1807) poignantly testifies to the complexities of postrevolutionary feminine allegorization for the feminist writer: the relationship between Corinne and Italy, so enigmatically foregrounded in the novel's title, can quite properly be described as allegorical and, as Madelyn Gutwirth has shown, in portraying Corinne as a modern-day goddess, Staël knowingly appropriates the iconographic attributes of the Nike figure so popular during the first Empire to her own ends.[31] But Corinne's triumph is short-lived and the feminine allegory is soon recoded in a dysphoric mode: as Corinne's love affair with the Scottish peer, Lord Nelvil, precipitates her from her divine pinnacle to an all too human end, her erotic victimage at Lord Nelvil's hands comes to allegorize in a feminine form the political fate of Italy under Napoleon's regime.

What we might call the *secondary feminine allegory* in *Corinne* suggests why the first cannot hold, cannot be sustained: it is because primary feminine allegory is grounded in the idealization of woman, which is to say in the denial of the contingencies of her body and its history, the erasure of her lived experienced under bourgeois and imperialist patriarchy. If feminine allegorization served in the dominant male culture to consolidate the power of the state and the newly enfranchised middle class, for postrevolutionary French women writers such as Staël but also Sand (see *Lélia*) allegory could never be but a failed form of representation, a representation of a revolution that failed them.[32]

Notes

1. Lynn Hunt, "Engraving the French Republic: Prints and Propaganda in the French Revolution," *History Today* (October 1980) 30:14.

2. For further details on the gradual emergence of Marianne as the emblem of the Republic, see Lynn Hunt, *Politics, Culture, and Class in the French Revolution* (Berke-

ley: University of California Press, 1984), esp. 87–119. Hunt's account should be read in conjunction with the now classical work by Maurice Agulhon, *Marianne au Combat: L'Imagerie et la Symbolique Républicaine de 1789 à 1880* (Paris: Flammarion, 1979).

3. In an article brought to my attention after I had written this paper, Kaja Silverman in some sense confirms my conflation of disembodied and hyperembodied female figures, by emphasizing the political uses to which images of female nudity were put in France from Delacroix's *Liberty Guiding the People* to Courbet's *Origin of the World*. The diaphanously veiled Nana is the literary equivalent to this recurrent figure of the revolutionary prostitute. See Kaja Silverman, "Liberty, Maternity, Commodification," *New Formations* 5 (Summer 1988):69–89.

4. Abbé Prevost, *Manon Lescaut* (Paris: folio, 1972), 48; *Manon Lescaut*, trans. Leonard Tancock (Harmondsworth: Penguin, 1949), 26.

5. René de Chateaubriand, *Atala. René. Le Dernier Abencerage* (Paris: folio, 1971), 69–70; *Atala/René*, trans. Irving Putter (Berkeley: University of California Press, 1967), 37–38.

6. Jules Lemaitre puts the matter this way: "If the two lovers did not meet the old missionary, if Atala succumbed during the storm, and if she later died in the woods . . . the story of Atala could end the same way Manon Lescaut's does," *Chateaubriand* (Paris: Calmann-Lévy, n.d.), 92. All translations mine except where otherwise noted.

7. François René Chateaubriand, *Mémoires d'outre-tombe* 1–2 (Paris: Flammarion, 1949), 414.

8. Chateaubriand, *Mémoires* 1–2:20. It is interesting to note that in his eyewitness accounts of the revolution, Chateaubriand refers to Marat's hideous friends as a "series of Medusa's heads" (*Mémoires*, 1–2:376), and on the very next page describes Danton's companions as "male furies" (377), further confirming the sexual indeterminacy of these figures in his imaginary. Chateaubriand's sexual panic in the face of the Revolution of 1792 also confirms Neil Hertz's argument regarding the troping of the threat of political violence as the fear of castration in, "Medusa's Head: Male Hysteria under Political Pressure," *Representations* (Fall 1983) 4:27–54.

9. On women and the French Revolution my main sources of information are Claire Moses, *French Feminism in the 19th Century* (Albany: SUNY Press, 1984); Darlene Gay Levy, Harriet Branson Applewhite, Mary Durham Johnson, eds., *Women in Revolutionary Paris, 1789–1795* (Urbana: University of Illinois Press, 1979); Paule-Marie Duhet, ed., *Cahiers de Doléances des femmes en 1789 et autres textes* (Paris: des femmes, 1981); Maïte Albistur and Daniel Armogathe, *Histoire du féminisme français*, 2 vols. (Paris: des femmes, 1977); and Joan B. Landes, *Women and the Public Sphere in the Age of the French Revolution* (Ithaca: Cornell University Press, 1988).

Concerning the convergence of Napoleon's politics of religious restoration and Chateaubriand's Christian apologetics, one need perhaps only recall that the second edition of the *Genius* published in 1803 was dedicated to "the first Consul, general Bonaparte," and that coincidentally during that same year Chateaubriand received the diplomatic posting in Rome he had ardently coveted. In the words of Victor Giraud, the author of a two-volume study on *Le Christianisme de Chateaubriand* (Paris: Hachette, 1928): "The book and the author squared perfectly with the designs of his [Napoleon's] policy: he asked only to use the one and the other" (2:154).

10. Because of the extravagant and sweeping nature of this assertion, I was particularly gratified to find confirmation of my analysis in my colleague and fellow conference participant Linda Orr's important new book, *Headless History: Nineteenth-Century French Historiography of the French Revolution* (Ithaca: Cornell University Press, 1990). Noting that, "The Revolution is a 'black hole' in French Literature" (17), Orr goes

on to say: "So nineteenth-century French histories threw themselves where other writers feared to tread directly" (17). Directly is the key word here, because as Orr remarks in a footnote to this sentence, "Yet almost every nineteenth-century novel and many poems approach *indirectly* the traumatic space of the French Revolution" (17, n25). Another name for this indirect approach is allegory. "*Le rouge et le noir*," writes Orr, "is the allegorical repetition of Revolutionary history in Restoration terms." For those French writers who would somehow engage with the French Revolution, there were then two possible narrative modes: the displacements of allegory or the abyss of history.

11. Ronald Paulson, *Representations of Revolution (1789–1820)* (New Haven: Yale University Press, 1983), 26.

12. See Paulson, *Representations of Revolution*; Karl Marx, *The Eighteenth Brumaire of Louis Bonaparte* (New York: International Publishers, 1972); Agulhon, *Marianne au Combat*; and Lynn Hunt, "Engraving the Republic."

13. Jane Tompkins, *Sensational Designs: The Cultural Work of American Fiction 1790–1860* (New York: Oxford University Press, 1985), 103.

14. Landes, *Women and the Public Sphere*, 147.

15. See Hunt, *Politics, Culture and Class*; Mona Ozouf, *La Fête révolutionnaire, 1789–1799* (Paris: Gallimard, 1976); Marie-Hélène Huet, "Le Sacre du Printemps: Essai sur le sublime et la Terreur," *Modern Language Notes* 103 (1988):781–99.

16. Huet, "Le Sacre du Printemps," 789.

17. See Chateaubriand, *Mémoires* 1–2:230.

18. Naomi Schor, *Breaking the Chain: Women, Theory, and French Realist Fiction* (New York: Columbia University Press, 1985).

19. Jane Gallop, "Beyond the jouissance principle," *Representations* (1984) 7:110–15.

20. See François René de Chateaubriand, *The Genius of Christianity* (New York: Howard Fertig, 1976), 287–90. What is striking about Chateaubriand's reading of *Paul et Virginie* is his insistence on its Christian dimension: "We may even go still farther and assert that it is religion, in fact, which determines the catastrophe. Virginie dies for the preservation of one of the principal virtues enjoined by Christianity. It would have been absurd to make a Grecian woman die for refusing to expose her person; but the lover of Paul is a *Christian* virgin, and what would be ridiculous according to an impure notion of heathenism becomes in this instance sublime" (290).

21. On this point I disagree with Naomi Segal when she insists in *Narcissus and Echo* (Manchester: Manchester University Press, 1988) on reading (and quickly and smartly dispatching) *Atala* as merely a less domesticated, hence less successful incest *récit* than *René* (54–57). While the presence of the incest motif in *Atala* is anything but hidden, it strikes me as a trivializing gesture to reduce *Atala* to just another variation on Chateaubriand's incestuous eros, thereby confirming what one had set out to prove: namely that the canon is always right and that *Atala* has no other claim to our attention but as René's "mirror-piece" (54), a singularly (in)apt choice of words in a book devoted to unmasking the workings of male narcissism in the classic French *récit*.

22. Stéphane Michaud, *Muse et madone: Visages de la femme de la Révolution française aux apparitions de Lourdes* (Paris: Seuil, 1985), 31. Michaud's remarks are especially valuable for the continuum they reestablish between the eighteenth-century medical discourse of female debility and the postrevolutionary misogynistic discourse of Christian apologetics.

23. Interestingly, Girodet, the author of a striking portrait of Chateaubriand, produced yet another prominent icon, the painting of the sleeping Endymion featured in Barthes's *S/Z*, and which Chateaubriand acknowledged was a source for his description in *Les Martyrs* of the *sommeil d'Eudore*. On Chateaubriand and Girodet, see

George Levitine, "Some unexplored aspects of the illustrations of *Atala*: the *surenchères visuelles* of Girodet and Hersent," in *Chateaubriand Today*, ed. Richard Switzer (Madison: The University of Wisconsin Press, 1970), 139–45.

24. I owe this important qualification to Carol Ockman who during the discussion following my presentation of this material at Williams College pointed out that the most eroticized figure in Girodet's painting is the muscular backlit Chactas.

25. Following my presentation of this paper at the "Women and Representation" conference held at Rhode Island College (May 1989), Elizabeth Anne Wolf was kind enough to provide me with an image that presents striking and suggestive similarities with the scene depicted by Girodet. Drawn from the de Bausset's, *Mémoires du Palais Intérieur* (1827), the engraving by Chasselat portrays the scene of Josephine and Napoleon's last supper at the Tuileries: as Napoleon stands by the door with his hand on the knob, the prostrate body of Josephine, who has fainted upon hearing of the Emperor's decision to divorce her, is held up by the kneeling Count de Bausset. Though Josephine is no Atala and Napoleon, no Chactas, the homologous positioning of the male figures on either side of the lifeless central figure of the woman in both images produces a telling visual analogue of the joint Chateaubriand-Napoleon ideological venture.

26. Bernardin de Saint-Pierre, *Paul et Virginie* (Paris: Garnier-Flammarion, 1966), 162; *Paul and Virginia*, trans. Andrew Lang (New York: Howard Fertig, 1987), 115.

To complete my argument I would need to bring into play here yet another, perhaps the most famous, episode of male necrophilia in eighteenth-century French fiction: the dilated and endlessly deferred death of Julie in Rousseau's *La Nouvelle Héloïse*. While it is true that Julie, like Atala, dies a Christian (Protestant) death, indeed engages in extended theological discussions with her local minister while on her deathbed, Julie who dies for having saved her small son from drowning, is in the minister's words: "a martyr to motherly love." This remark points up a crucial aspect of *Atala* and its ideology of gender which I do not want to neglect: marking a hiatus between the maternalist politics of Rousseau and those of the many nineteenth-century figures who, following Rousseau, promoted in Barthes's words a "sticky ideology of familialism" centered on the mother-woman and grounded in Christian values, in *Atala* there is a blight on maternity, a rejection of domestic values, and a curse on the genealogical imperative. Though *Atala* founds the nineteenth-century French construction of femininity, that construction is not yet here fully in place.

For more on the textual misogyny of the *Natchez* as symptomatized by a denial of maternal attributes to its female protagonists, see Pierre Barbéris, *Chateaubriand: une réaction au monde moderne* (Paris: Larousse, 1976), esp. 75–84. Regrettably Barbéris has to date never produced the study on *Atala* announced in *Chateaubriand*, perhaps because like so many readers he reads *Atala* entirely through the thematic grid (incest, love, and prohibition) of *René*.

27. Chateaubriand not only practiced allegory, he theorized it, notably in the chapter of *The Genius of Christianity*, entitled "Of Allegory" (303–5). Arguing that allegory is not incompatible with Christianity, Chateaubriand distinguishes between two types of allegory, what he calls the moral and the physical. About moral allegory, which he approves of, he has little to say; most of this brief chapter is taken up with physical allegory, which he disapproves of. Physical allegory consists in the personification of natural entities, such as the air, water, and most disturbingly for Chateaubriand, "mute and motionless objects" such as stones. Chateaubriand's devalorization of this lesser form of allegory is curious: according to him physical allegory is incompatible with the development of mimetic art; only Christianity favors the truthful description of

nature. So long as nature is viewed as inhabited by Nymphs and Naiads there can never be a properly descriptive poetry.

28. Annie Goldson, "Other Speech," *Afterimage* 16 (May 1989).

29. There is in Dominique Godineau's *Citoyennes Tricoteuses* (Paris: Alinea, 1988) a tantalizing allusion to women of the people's passage through Paris streets decorated with "allegories of Liberty" (30), but no information about the role of these urban wall-paintings in inspiring their revolutionary activities.

30. In *Subject to Change: Reading Feminist Writing* (New York: Columbia University Press, 1988), Nancy Miller makes an important and necessary distinction between women and feminist writers, see in particular 8–10.

31. Madelyn Gutwirth, *Madame de Staël, Novelist: The Emergence of the Artist as Woman* (Urbana: University of Illinois Press, 1978), 176–81.

32. Cf. My "*Lélia* and the failures of allegory," *L'Esprit Créateur* 29 (1989):76–83.

9

Being René, Buying Atala:
Alienated Subjects and Decorative
Objects in Postrevolutionary France

MARGARET WALLER

The canon of nineteenth-century French literature begins with a strange coupling. At the turn of the century, François-René de Chateaubriand published his first two novels separately, only to pair them a few years later. Together, the two works form a diptych in which men exchange stories about the dead women who had loved them. In *Atala*, a half-civilized American Indian, Chactas, tells how his lover, Atala, died to save her virginity. In *René*, the half-savage European René reveals his sister's incestuous love for him. Despite their obvious symmetry, the two works make a study in contrasts. While *Atala* harks back to its Enlightenment predecessors, *René* points the way toward Romanticism. Whereas *Atala* focuses on a virtuous, virginal heroine of the New World, *René* features an alienated, aristocratic antihero of the Old World.

Recent feminist work suggests, however, that this odd couple is also a paradigmatic pair. In *Breaking the Chain*, Naomi Schor argues that *Atala* emblematizes the "enchaining of the female protagonist" that is crucial to nineteenth-century French fiction.[1] I have proposed reading *René*, on the other hand, as the *urtext* for an insidious empowerment of men characteristic of the Romantic novel.[2] Whereas *Atala* reveals that the free-roaming heroine is in fact morally and then physically bound, *René* shows that the constraints on the hero are the basis of a new kind of male power. Together, then, the founding texts of the nineteenth-century canon signal the ever more pronounced imbalance of power between the sexes that came to characterize gender relations in postrevolutionary France.[3]

Atala and *René* did more than just mirror or herald these changes in French culture and society, however. The publication of *Atala* in 1801 inspired

I would like to thank Barbara Cooper and Julia Przybos for sharing their expertise on popular culture and, particularly, Kate Jensen, Sara Melzer, Cris Miller, and Leslie Rabine for their invaluable comments on an earlier version of this chapter. I am grateful to Pomona College for the grant that made this research possible.

All translations are my own.

countless imitations, from theatrical parodies to sentimental elegies, from official salon paintings to cheap wax figurines. For decades the story was a cultural totem for a wide spectrum of French society.[4] *René*, on the other hand, helped shape the ethos and literature of a new generation: readers identified with Chateaubriand's Romantic hero; writers imitated the work's subject and style. Inasmuch as the two novels updated time-honored assumptions about the hierarchy of the sexes for modern consumption, their reproductions during Napoleon's Consulate, the Empire, and the Bourbon Restoration helped dash the hope for greater equality between the sexes that had been glimpsed during the French Revolution. While *Atala* popularized an image of woman as an exotic, idealized object that made her a highly marketable commodity, *René* reinvented modern man as an alienated yet elevated subject.

Although examples of the two novels' influence have been amply and carefully documented by literary and cultural historians,[5] the imitations of *Atala* and *René* have not yet been studied as symptomatic moments of a crucial turning point in the construction of femininity and masculinity. The historical circumstances of *Atala*'s and *René*'s publication, the nature of their reception, and the myriad forms of their cultural reproductions offer specific and concrete examples of the redefinition of the rights of man—and the place of women—that took place in the wake of the French Revolution.

Back to the Future

Eight years after fighting a losing battle with his fellow émigrés against the French revolutionary army and seven years after leaving France to live in exile in England, a young, impoverished French aristocrat returned to his fatherland under a passport issued in someone else's name. Despite the ignominy of Chateaubriand's return, this royalist sympathizer's luck was about to change. With him Chateaubriand carried the manuscript of *Génie du Christianisme*, a defense of Christianity on aesthetic and sentimental grounds that would sound the death knell for what remained of French revolutionary culture. Convinced that the time was ripe for restoring Catholicism to France, Chateaubriand's friends encouraged him to publish the story of Atala, which was one of the two illustrative fictions in *Génie du Christianisme*, as part of a prepublication publicity campaign for that weightier, analytical tome. Excerpted from *Génie du Christianisme* and published in 1801, *Atala* was an instant hit. The first literary bestseller of the postrevolutionary era galvanized a large and influential segment of the population eager for a return to old-time values and Old Regime religion.

The two works' extraordinary success played into the designs of the ambitious young consul, Napoleon. In a marked reversal of the anticlerical policies of his revolutionary predecessors, Napoleon was eager to make the Catholic Church's time-honored hold over the French population buttress rather than undermine state power. He therefore gave Chateaubriand's two-volume apology for Christianity unofficial state sanction and used its publication in 1802 to orchestrate public opinion in favor of the Concordat he was about to sign with the Catholic Church. Thus, Chateaubriand, royalist émigré and persona non grata, and Napoleon, his former political adversary, formed an alliance that consolidated public opinion in Napoleon's favor, established Chateaubriand as a spokesperson of stature, and set the tone for the new reactionary era. While *Génie* made religion intellectually defensible, *Atala* made it fashionable.

Within only a few years of its publication, Chateaubriand's tale of the virtuous heroine who committed suicide rather than break her vow of chastity appeared in six editions and at least sixteen translations. The novel's countless imitations included numerous pantomime adaptations and parodic theatrical takeoffs. During the next several decades, more than a dozen salon paintings featured Atala's beatific yet voluptuous corpse. Chateaubriand's story of this nubile Indian maiden in an exotic American wilderness also lent itself to a wide range of consumer items, from costly bronze clocks, porcelain vases, decorated plates, and upholstery fabric to cheap, brightly colored prints. In a word, *Atala* gave rise to a consumer frenzy.

A combination of historical circumstances combined to make Chateaubriand's *Atala* one of the first works of contemporary literature to enjoy this kind of popularization in France.[6] The social upheavals of the revolution, the loss of royal and aristocratic patronage and a rise in discretionary income, opened up a wide and ever-expanding market for nonessential, decorative items during the course of the century.[7] But if the novel's success were solely a matter of timing, then *René*, which was first published as a chapter of *Génie du Christianisme* in 1802 and then as a companion piece to *Atala* beginning in 1805, should have enjoyed the same kind of public attention. Similarly, if Chateaubriand's first two works, *Atala* and *Génie du Christianisme*, owed their popularity, as historians generally argue, to a propitious convergence of public sentiment and state interests favoring a religious revival, then logically, *René* should have enjoyed the same popular success as *Atala* in the early years.

However, *René* did not enjoy this kind of commercial success nor did its heyday come at the same time as *Atala*'s. Instead, this tale of melancholy genius was quietly being devoured in the early years of the century by young readers who would become the proponents of Romanticism. For them, the pleasure of the text hinged on their identification with the despondent yet sublime aristocratic hero. It was not until the 1820s that René was recognized as the paradigm of authorial adolescence and literary genius for the entire generation—a model not only for literature but for life.

Thus, the response to *Atala* and *René* took very different forms. The public paid to *see* or *own* representations of Atala while readers and writers thought they *were* or wanted to *be* René. According to contemporary accounts of these phenomena, the difference between these responses was a matter of gender. Whereas *Atala* and *Génie du Christianisme* were championed primarily by women, *René* was largely taken up by men.

Gendered Readers/Gendered Texts

Fortunée Hamelin, a contemporary of Chateaubriand, writes that the most numerous and ardent defenders of the "young Breton crusader" who singlehandedly gave voice and legitimacy to the reactionary revolt against the revolution were women. She recalls the reaction to the publication of *Génie du Christianisme* as a case of collective female hysteria. "Ce jour-là pas une femme n'a dormi. On s'arrachait, on se volait un exemplaire. Puis, quel réveil! quel babil! quelles palpitations! Quoi! c'est là le Christianisme, disions-nous toutes; mais il est délicieux. Je pris l'avant-garde des jeunes enthousiastes, et lorsque nous rencontrions un académicien, même un très bel esprit, l'escarmouche commençait . . ." ["That day no woman slept. We fought over a single copy, and stole it from each other. Then, what an awakening! What chattering! What palpitations! 'What? This is Christianity?' we said. 'Why, it's delightful!' I was in the vanguard of the young enthusiasts, and when we would come across an academician, even if he were a fine wit, the skirmish would begin . . ."][8] So popular was Chateaubriand and so closely was his first novel tied to a female readership that those who attacked *Atala* found themselves on the defensive.[9] Several prominent male writers of the time banded together "pour barrer la route à l'audacieux qui d'un seul coup, avec un méchant petit livre [*Atala*], leur enlevait leur clientèle" ["to bar the way against the bold man whose second-rate little book robbed them in a single blow of their clientele"].[10] This is not to say that Chateaubriand lacked male supporters. Louis de Fontanes and Joseph Joubert launched his career, and other men, eager for the restoration of the old order, came to Chateaubriand's defense. Nevertheless, when the enthusiasts of *Atala* are described en masse, they are most frequently figured as female. Thus, the first great literary controversy after the revolution, which was played out over *Atala*, is usually portrayed as a battle of male writers over the hearts and minds of women readers. Positing a female readership gives the account of this response a decidedly sexual charge.

In his memoirs, Chateaubriand claims that the publication of *Atala* afforded him a devoted female following: "Alors vinrent se presser autour de moi, avec les jeunes femmes qui pleurent aux romans, la foule des chrétiennes, et ces autres nobles enthousiastes dont une action d'honneur fait palpiter le sein." ["Along with the young women who cry over novels, there came pressing up against me the throng of Christian women and those other noble enthusiasts whose hearts beat faster at the thought of an honorable action."][11] Playing up the sexual innuendos of his transformation from bashful *naïf* to literary lion, he reports that women offered him perfumed love notes and swooned over envelopes written in his hand. For the author, all this attention was a narcissistic fantasy come true: "Je devins à la mode. La tête me tourna," he writes in his memoirs, "j'ignorai les jouissances de l'amour-propre et j'en fus enivré. *J'aimai la gloire comme une femme*, comme un premier amour." ["I became fashionable. My head spun . . . I had not known the ecstasies of pride and I was intoxicated. *I loved fame as I would love a woman*, as I would a first love"] (*MOT*, 1:445; emphasis added). Under the adoring gaze of a female public,

Chateaubriand becomes a man by falling in love with a glorified image of himself—as hero, writer, and ladies' man.

Because of *Atala*'s radical amalgam of traditional genres, academicians of the day, according to Chateaubriand, had trouble deciding the novel's gender.[12] But for the author, there was no doubt. Not only was the readership of *Atala* female, so was his text. He calls the work that made a name for him and even saved his life his "devoted daughter,"[13] and his affection for *Atala* extends even to "her" offspring. Despite his aristocratic disdain for lower-class versions of high culture, Chateaubriand describes the reproductions of Atala—as a figure in the Curtius wax museum, as the heroine of theatrical parodies, and as the subject of garish popular prints and figurines sold on the Paris quays—with a glee only thinly disguised as bashful pride or baffled disdain.

As "Daddy's girl," *Atala*, who made a name for Chateaubriand, cannot be taken seriously even though she can do no wrong. *René*, by contrast, the prodigal son who bears François-René de Chateaubriand's given name and tells his story, can do nothing right. Writing his memoirs in 1837, Chateaubriand, now calling himself François-*Auguste*, disowns *René* and states his death wish for the novel: "Si *René* n'existait pas, je ne l'écrirais plus; s'il m'était possible de le détruire, je le détruirais." ["If *René* did not exist, I would not write it now; if I could destroy it, I would destroy it"] (*MOT*, 1:462).[14] But even this denunciation is not enough; the author also distances himself from his hideous progeny's own "sons." Chateaubriand has nothing but scorn for the Romantics who had adopted his representation of misunderstood genius as their own:

> Une famille de René poètes et de René prosateurs a pullulé: on n'a plus entendu que des phrases lamentables et décousues; il n'a plus été question que de vents et d'orages, que de maux inconnus livrés aux nuages et à la nuit. Il n'y a pas de grimaud sortant du collège qui n'ait rêvé être le plus malheureux des hommes; de bambin qui à seize ans n'ait épuisé la vie, qui ne se soit cru tourmenté par son génie; qui, dans l'abîme de ses pensées, ne se soit livré au *vague de ses passions*; qui n'ait frappé son front pâle et échevelé, et n'ait étonné les hommes stupéfaits d'un malheur dont il ne savait pas le nom, ni eux non plus. [A whole family of René poets and René prose writers proliferated: lamentable and disjointed language was all one ever heard; all they ever discussed were winds and storms, mysterious sorrows delivered up to the clouds and the dark of night. There wasn't a single callow youth just out of school who didn't dream he was the most unfortunate of men; not one lad of sixteen who hadn't exhausted his life, who didn't believe himself tormented by his genius; who, in the depths of his thoughts, didn't give himself over to the *wave of his passions*; who didn't strike his pale brow hidden by his disheveled locks, astounding men who were left speechless by a misfortune neither he nor they could name] (ibid., emphasis in original).

The imitation of *René* produces in its originator an anxiety of influence—and identification—even as he egotistically overstates his case in recounting the novel's effect on the younger generation.

Though he writes, in his memoirs, with the same temporal distance from the publication of both *Atala* and *René*, the author's attitude toward the texts' readers and their cultural reproductions could not be more different. In equating the sex of the novel's main protagonist with the sex of the reader, Chateaubriand plays up the differences gender makes. Whereas the adoring attention of a female readership and the proliferation of images of the female Other in the representations of *Atala* offer the male writer narcissistic gratification, the imitation of the male Self and its adoption by a younger generation of men cause him to revile his rivalrous literary sons.

The author's remarks suggest that *Atala*'s proliferation as an erotic object of the gaze and an exotic object of exchange may be linked to the fact that, unlike *René*, its focus was a woman not a man, the Indians not the French, and thus the Other not the Self. Indeed, it was *Atala*, not *René*, that served France's redefinition of itself as an empire with a sacred duty to civilize the savages and colonize the world, and it was *Atala*, not *René*, that became a household word for a wide spectrum of French society through the proliferation of consumer goods. The medium, message, and price of *Atala*'s imitations underscored the class interests and ideological differences that distinguished and divided the buyers. Nevertheless, whether high culture or popular culture, reverential or parodic, the theatrical, poetic, and artistic reproductions of Atala all feature mutually reinforcing ideologies about gender, race, and class that combine to produce striking and contradictory representations of a woman—dead and alive.

Atala Seen and Sold: Sex, Savages, and Sensibility

From the market women's march on Versailles to the call for a declaration of the rights of women by Olympe de Gouges, the revolutionary period offered numerous and vivid examples of women who made their political demands heard and dared claim equal status with men. Writing from exile in 1797, the young Chateaubriand had decried this attempt to reverse a time-honored and God-given patriarchal hierarchy. For him, the ideal is a state of nature in which "l'enfant se tait et attend; la femme est soumise; le fort et le guerrier commandent; le vieillard s'assied au pied de l'arbre, et meurt" ["the child is silent and waits; the woman submits; the strong man and the warrior command; the old man sits down at the foot of a tree and dies."][15] In the interests of reviving this idyllic arrangement, his later work, *Atala*, is set long before the French Revolution and in the New World.

It is striking, therefore, that at the beginning of the novel, traditional gender hierarchies are reversed. The heroine, who is to provide the religious and literary model for virtuous womanhood, proves herself not only equal to a man, but his rescuer. When we first see Atala, she has come to free the hero, Chactas, who is being held captive by an enemy tribe. In the course of the novel, however, the heroine falls from being the hero's liberator to becoming his would-be lover, a transformation that will lead to her death. Rather than succumb to her sexual desires and thus break the vow her mother made binding her to a life of chastity, Atala commits suicide.

In the novel, the heroine is, as it were, two women—first apparently unfettered, then revealed as bound. For Naomi Schor, *Atala*'s staging of the increasing restrictions on women's freedom in nineteenth-century France gives the novel paradigmatic status in a feminist, revisionist literary history of the representation of women. Whereas Atala's eighteenth-century predecessors enjoyed a certain mobility, "the post-Revolutionary female protagonist," Schor writes, "is consistently deprived of the minimal attribute of subjecthood, which is not, or not merely, the faculty of speech, the capacity to produce signs, but rather the power of locomotion, the right to move about freely."[16]

One of the first theatrical parodies of Chateaubriand's text explicitly makes the freedom and mobility the heroine enjoys in the first part of *Atala* the arrogation of a male privilege. Atala's vow of chastity in Chateaubriand's text becomes in the parody a promise not to wear men's clothes. At the climax of *Encore un ballon* (1801), "Florella [Atala] qui jusqu'alors d'après la défense de sa mère, n'avait pas voulu essayer d'habits d'homme, met ceux que lui a laissés Jactas [Chactas]. . . . Et en revenant [Jactas] . . . la voit ainsi déguisée s'élever tout-à-coup de terre avec le ballon." ["Florella <Atala> who, obeying her mother's injunction, has refused until now to wear men's clothes, dons those that Jactas <Chactas> has left for her . . . And on his return <Jactas> . . . sees her, thus disguised, take off suddenly in the balloon."][17] Florella's cross-dressing (against her mother's wishes) gives her not only freedom of movement but a literal transcendence of earthly constraints. In the parodic comedy, the heroine is forgiven her sartorial (and gender role) transgression and the couple lives happily ever after. In Chateaubriand's text, however, she dies for her illicit desires. As in earlier, eighteenth-century fiction, a woman's sexual misstep is a fatal one.[18]

Whereas the first part of the novel is a tale of adventure, complete with the hero's dramatic liberation and the lovers' harrowing flight into the wilderness, the second part is a moralizing and sentimental story of a virginal heroine's death, which takes place under the watchful eye of a Jesuit missionary. The representation of the story in various media for differing audiences underscores the ideological significance of this split in *Atala*. The exciting first series of episodes lent themselves to decorative renditions of the story on vases, clocks, and fabrics designed for conspicuous consumption by aristocratic and bourgeois buyers. Divorced from its moralizing context, these representations of *Atala* make the novel a tale of love in an exotic American wilderness. Salon paintings, by contrast, focus not on the heroine's initial freedom but on the tale's tragic ending. Following a longstanding beaux-arts tradition accentuated by the sentimentalism that had dominated the previous century, they feature the figure of a woman at her most pathetic and appealing—as she lies dead or dying.[19]

Other media, however, offered the "whole" story. Illustrated dessert plates and popular prints present *Atala* as a series of four to six episodes and thus include both parts of the tale. Popular illustrations carried, in addition, long, explanatory captions that preserve the story as a tale of cause and effect. Although in these series, the heroine's death and/or burial does not come to represent, metonymically, the entire story, these objects of popular culture move toward ideological closure—and reinforce the lesson to be learned. In these versions of *Atala*, as in the novel, Catholic martyrdom and the myth of romantic love have their usual consequences for the woman: silence, immobilization, and ultimately, death.

Unlike many of her eighteenth-century predecessors, however, the heroine of *Atala* does not die, passively, of love. Instead, she is led to kill herself because the temptation to give in to her sexual desires is too strong to be resisted any other way. Her suicide, then, represents an audacious exception to eighteenth-century codes of feminine virtue even as it confirms the fatal consequences of a woman's sexual desire. All but one of the numerous salon representations of *Atala*, however, avoid the question of suicide entirely by simply glossing over the means of her death to concentrate on its ends. In popular engravings, which stress the story's moralizing qualities, on the other hand, the captions teach that "self-preservation can even include suicide, if that is the only way to remain pure."[20] Thus, what is audacious about Chateaubriand's text is almost entirely glossed over in fine art and recuperated in popular art.

Following the novel's logic, the heroine must turn martyr and saint, but first she is shown as a would-be sinner. Although the novel advertizes itself as an exemplary tale of female piety, it flirts with the sensational representation of female desire. Atala's reproductions capitalize on this ideological doubleness in order to have it both ways. Even idealizing imitations of the text ended up replicating the contradictions inherent in attempting to enlist sensuality in the service of Christian abnegation. For example, in his 1806 Salon painting, "Atala s'empoisonnant dans les bras de Chactas, son amant" ["Atala poisoning herself in the arms of Chactas, her lover"]—the only salon work to figure the heroine's suicide—Louis Hersent's classicizing representation locks the two lovers in a tight embrace of billowing draperies and intertwined limbs (Figure 9.1). One commentator on the painting was quick to note Atala's compromising position: "À la sollicitation de sa mère, Attala [sic] fit voeu d'éternelle chasteté; maintenant dans les bras, et pour tout dire, entre les jambes de son amant, elle craint de violer sa promesse, et de damner sa mère par son péché; c'est y songer un peu tard . . ." ["At her mother's urging, Attala <sic> made a vow of eternal chastity; now in the arms, or more precisely, between the legs of her lover, she fears that she might break her promise, damning her mother with this sin; such reflections come a little late . . ."][21] Whether solemn or satiric, the representation of Atala, both in the novel and in its imitations, makes the woman bear the whole weight of sexual guilt and exonerates the man. As in eighteenth-century sentimental fiction, the heroine is subject to the rigors of chastity, which is never even at issue for the hero, and it is her virtue that is put to the ultimate test.

This virtue, which is used to deny desires, also displays them. Despite her ultimate renunciation of sexual pleasure and despite her saintliness, Atala is reproduced as an idealized erotic object. In the salon paintings and sculptured mantel clocks, for example, the heroine appears as a shapely young woman in

Figure 9.1 C. Normand, after Hersent's "Atala s'empoisonnant dans les bras de Chactas" ["Atala poisoning herself in the arms of Chactas"], 1806. Engraving, from C. P. Landon, *Annales du Musée* (Paris, 1806), fig. 43. *Source*: Bibliothèque Nationale.

ideal, neoclassical form. Her clinging, almost transparent sheath leaves little to the imagination. This classicizing representation of Atala makes her part of a timeless, mythologized past even as it serves as an allusion to the newly imperial historical present. In the 1790s and early 1800s, fashion imitated the clothing of antiquity in an implicit reference first to Greek democracy and then to the Roman Empire. During the Directory and Empire, this revealing style with its revolutionary absence of stays and corsets, low-scooped neckline and bared arms also represented a decisive rejection of Robespierrian puritan egalitarianism. The new, decadent look involved a brazen revelation of the body that highlighted and underscored the differences between the sexes. Madame Hamelin, whose reminiscences of women's frenzy over Chateaubriand I cited at the beginning of this essay, was one of the infamous Merveilleuses who paraded naked down the Jardin des Tuileries in a diaphanous robe, not unlike the dress in which Atala appears.[22] Thus, the later salon representations of a virtuous but enticing Atala recall at least some of her female admirers and defenders—and their less than modest comportment.[23]

Each succeeding decade brought the heroine's dress and hairstyle up to date with current fashion, but it would not be until 1864 that Atala would get her "own" hairstyle, which others would copy. The society columnist for the profusely illustrated periodical, *La Vie parisienne*, writes that on a recent visit to high society he had found "une coiffure un peu . . . Atala, les cheveux en touffes au-dessus de la tête et maintenus par trois cercles d'or. Tout cela, porté par des femmes du commun, seraient peut-être à pouffer, mais porté par celles-ci, c'est à nous rendre fous. Et c'est bien ce qu'elles veulent!" ["a coiffure that is somewhat . . . Atala, the hair in tufts above the head and held up by three gold bands. If this style were taken up by common women, it might be laughable, but on these women, it drives us wild. And that is precisely what they intend!"][24] Here, as late as the 1860s and as in earlier representations, Atala becomes a litmus test for class distinction—and the object of an admiring male gaze.

Some popular illustrators, however, used New World exoticism rather than Old World mythologizing in order to underscore the difference between the savage and the civilized. In the process, the bared bodies of the Indian maiden and her lover reveal not only the mark of gender but the signs of race, religion, culture, and class that idealize and/or eroticize the Bon Sauvage in order to validate what is white, Catholic, French, or upper class. Following the eighteenth-century European idea of American Indians, feathers, necklaces, and tattoos adorned the vigorous and well-proportioned bodies of both hero and heroine in popular engravings. More often than not, the hero's chest was bared and a crucifix on a necklace dangled between the heroine's naked breasts, as in the illustrated edition of *Atala* published by Le Normant in 1805 (Figure 9.2). These spectacles of unselfconscious nudity offered the white observer the opportunity for highbrow titillation under the guise of ethnography. Sometimes the exotic was even more obviously a form of the erotic. Chateaubriand recounts that in 1833 on a trip to Austria he found in his room at an inn six engravings of *Atala*: "Elle était bien laide, bien vieillie, bien changée, la pauvre Atala! Sur sa tête de grandes plumes et autour de ses reins un jupon écourté et collant à l'instar de mesdames les sauvagesses du théâtre de la Gaîté." ["She was so ugly, so aged, so altered, poor Atala! On her head there were tall feathers and around her loins a shortened, clinging underskirt, reminiscent of Mesdames the savage ladies of the Gaîté Theatre"] (*MOT*, 2: 843).

Although in the novel Chactas is a pure-blood American Indian (half-civilized by an earlier voyage to the court of Louis XIV), salon works make the hero a Caucasian with darkened complexion. Although Atala is half-Indian (but all Catholic), they, like Chateaubriand, make her white. The most famous and influential of the salon paintings, Anne Louis Girodet's "Funérailles d'Atala" (see Plate I), gives the heroine's Caucasian features a luminous, otherworldly quality that leaves no doubt as to her saintliness—or the color of her skin. What makes the protagonists noble *savages* is their cultural and racial differences from white readers and viewers; what makes the savages *noble*, on the other hand, is their resemblance to the artist's pastoral and mythological models—and his Caucasian public. In popular prints, beginning in 1810,

Figure 9.2 Auguste de Saint-Aubin, "Il y a bien longtemps que je vous cherche" ["I have been looking for you for a long time"], in *Atala, Renè* (Paris, Le Normant, 1805). *Source*: Bibliothèque Nationale.

however, "Chactas will become more 'Indian'; Atala, more French."[25] As a result, he loses his stature and she gains in superiority: "Atala represents European morality and strength, while Chactas symbolizes pagan inferiority" (Delaney, 43). Female beauty and moral purity thus continue to come in only one color—white—and the Indian Other is no match for the European Self. In perhaps the ultimate example of this growing racial and gender demarcation between the protagonists, Chactas changes racial identity. In two of the extant bronze clocks illustrating the theme, the Indian Chactas is not "red" but coal black. Atala, by contrast, is bronze—as is the setting.[26]

The appeal to buyers' or viewers' feelings of superiority to the American Indians was cultural and national as well as racial. In an early theatrical adaptation, *Ima ou les deux mondes* (1802), Cammaille Saint-Aubin transforms Chateaubriand's moralizing novel into a secularized, "allegorical melodrama." In this late-model version of eighteenth-century Enlightenment, the object of attack is not religious ignorance but racial prejudice, and the ideal to be promoted is not virginity but enlightened miscegenation. If, however, at the end of the play, Ima and Oudaïs (Atala and Chactas) can now be married, they do so, writes Léon-François Hoffmann, under the "emblême de l'Europe pacifiant le monde" ["emblem of Europe pacifying the world"] and thanks to Bonaparte, the hero who made this subjugation possible by reestablishing slavery in the colonies in 1802. During the same period, colonial expansion was being justified as a benevolent process of exporting to the "savages" the advantages of Christianity and civilization.[27] Racial harmony was an ideal to the extent that it could justify the new French empire.[28]

As the exotic, erotic, and idealized example of filial duty and virginity, Atala was primarily disseminated as a model for the Other, not the Self. Parents named their daughters after Chateaubriand's heroine,[29] but no large numbers of young women fashioned their looks or behavior after Atala's example or found in her an image of themselves, as was the case with young male readers and René. Instead, the existing evidence suggests that the cultural reproduction of Chateaubriand's first novel was primarily a matter of buying, selling, and seeing an image of woman. It was not, in any case, much of an occasion for hearing her speak.

Unlike René or even Chactas, whose misfortunes incite them to a flood of self-indulgent confession, in the reproductions of *Atala* the heroine does not always live to tell her own tale. Though Chateaubriand had given her a long deathbed speech, and theatrical productions gave Atala a fair share of the stage, the various reincarnations of Atala in prose and poetry followed their gender-marked conventions by memorializing her instead as a woman who did not speak for herself and who was, finally, silenced by death. Others spoke for her, as they had in the novel, where it is Chactas who tells her story and where it is only through his words that we hear hers. In their versified imitations of the novel, contemporary male poets almost invariably gave voice and top billing to the bereft hero so that he might tell the repressive end of the story, not its liberating beginning, in works often entitled "Chactas au tombeau d'Atala." Poetic versions of *Atala* thus make it clear that the death of a woman and her desire for him is precisely what puts the hero at center stage—and gives a male poet voice.[30]

In *René*, Chateaubriand's companion piece to *Atala*, a similar ventriloquism from beyond the grave takes place. In Chateaubriand's second novel, it is the death and desire of the hero's sister that authorize René to tell her tale. Without her, he says, he has no story worth telling. In both *René* and *Atala*, it is the heroes who frame the narratives and tell the stories. In doing so, they become something like writers, something like Chateaubriand himself.[31] But in *René*, there was more to the authorial connection than that. For its readers, René became the portrait not only of his creator but a model for the nineteenth-century writer as an alienated young man, an aristocrat in spirit in an increasingly bourgeois world.

Identifying with René: Aristocracy, Alienation, and Authorship

Chateaubriand's second work of fiction is a tale of failure and a confession of psychological incapacitation. René, the youngest son of a noble family, rejected by his father and turned out of house and home, tells how he roamed the ruins of ancient civilizations and wandered the cities of the modern world. The hero laments his idleness but makes no effort to find for himself a suitable place or appropriate role. Overwhelmed by desires, but devoid of an object in which he might channel them, the hero instead rhapsodizes on the futility of human endeavor. Sensitive and vulnerable, the hero is marked as both feminine and emasculated, unfit to continue the patriarchal line.

On the face of it, then, René was an unlikely candidate for wholesale imitation. Paradoxically, however, the hero's disablement is packaged as empowerment in the novel, and this may account in part for its appeal.[32] First, René's incapacitation makes him the center of a self-indulgent story in which he turns out to be the supreme object of a desire so strong that it defies incest, the most ancient of taboos. René's marginalization from society is linked to his sensitivity, which in turn becomes a sign of his literary promise and the key to his powers of self-expression. The hero thus turns his alienation to advantage by making his malady a form of artistic enablement and aristocratic aloofness.

In the novel, Chateaubriand works a similar kind of empowering transformation on the material of his life. Pierre Barbéris argues that *René* (like *Atala*) may be read as a form of denial through displacement in which the author transposes his postrevolutionary alienation—an experience common to other dispossessed French aristocrats—into a fiction in which the French Revolution has not yet happened, is in fact unimaginable. *René* thus captures the postrevolutionary malaise of this lost generation by creating an anachronistic fiction set during the Regency, almost 100 years in the past.[33] In a similar move, the hero attempts to universalize his predicament as a symptom of Man's metaphysical malaise. "Force de la nature, et faiblesse de l'homme," exclaims René in a characteristic moment, "un brin d'herbe perce souvent le marbre le plus dur de ces tombeaux, que tous ces morts, si puissants, ne soulèveront jamais!" ["O power of nature, weakness of man . . . a blade of grass may pierce through the hardest marble tombstone, which the dead, once so mighty, can never move!"] (152). The father figures to whom he tells his story interpret his withdrawal from the world as a problem of adolescent rebellion expressed as egocentric nonconformity. The moral, baldly stated at the end, appears as an eternal verity: "il n'y a de bonheur que dans les voies communes" ["happiness is found only on the common paths"] (176).

From the very first review of *René*, published in 1802, the byword for the reader's reaction was identification with its "ahistorical" model of alienation—with no mention of its political resonances. The reviewer describes Chateaubriand's novel as a mirror of the past, a reminder of the mature reader's bygone youth: "Ce roman doit surtout plaire aux lecteurs, qui conservent quelques souvenirs de l'âge d'inquiétude et des passions naissantes qu'on a voulu peindre. Ils y verront leur propre coeur, deviné pour ainsi dire, et jusqu'aux nuances de leur existence confuse, fixées dans ces tableaux éloquents." ["This novel will especially please readers who can still remember the restless age of burgeoning passions it portrays. They will see in the work their own hearts, as if their confused existence had been divined in the smallest detail and arranged in eloquent tableaux."][34] The reader's pleasure thus hinges on identification with the adolescent hero who is said to represent a timeless age of man rather than a specific, historical "âge d'inquiétude" ["restless age"].

René, however, unlike *Atala*, did not reach the height of its success until long after its first publication. The novel became a classic in the 1820s, during the Restoration, and its popularity continued through the 1840s and the July Monarchy for a generation that was born too late to have known firsthand the revolution of 1789.[35] Two decades after the publication of *René*, young readers did a repeat performance of the first critics' transhistorical identification with Chateaubriand's "eighteenth-century" hero. If, for the 1802 critic, *René* was a portrait of the "way we were," by the 1820s the seventeenth-century hero had become an uncanny representation of "the way I am." Critical reviews, memoirs, letters, and autobiographies record the shudder of recognition experienced by adolescent readers in the first few decades of the nineteenth century. An 1820 entry in the diary of the 16-year-old Charles Augustin Sainte-Beuve typifies the reaction: "J'ai lu *René* et j'ai frémi. . . . Je m'y suis reconnu tout entier." ["I read *René* and I shuddered. . . . I recognized myself in my entirety."] The note the future doyen of nineteenth-century criticism added ten years later confirms the connection: "Que j'ai deviné juste à seize! Malheureux! Moins d'énergie que jamais!" ["My intuition was so right at the age of 16! O poor wretch! Even less energy than ever!"][36] *René* is the novel of choice because of the tears of recognition it provokes. "Jamais je n'ai pu lire [*René*] sans pleurer . . ." ["I could never read <*René*> without crying . . ."] writes the young Lamartine, who would become one of France's first Romantic poets.[37] The readers of the novel who grew up to become writers claimed both Chateaubriand and René as their own.

Part of the novel's appeal to these primarily bourgeois readers would appear to lie in the hero's class identity. Sainte-Beuve says so explicitly. *René* offered "un modèle plus flatteur pour nous" ["a more flattering model for us"] than Rousseau's and Goethe's works, its bourgeois predecessors.[38] Just as *Atala* updated an old image of woman for the new Empire and Restoration society, with *René* the figure of the aristocrat, outmoded by the revolution, became the model for postrevolutionary man. Through his identification with a disenfranchised upper class, the bourgeois reader allied himself with the margins as a way of denying his connections to a society increasingly organized to promote the interests of his own sex and class.[39] Unlike the aristocratic Chateaubriand, however, these Romantic readers had not been shunted aside by the French Revolution. Instead, it was the subsequent restoration of the monarchy as well as the rise of industrial capitalism that had made them strangers in their own land.[40] When bourgeois male readers of the 1820s looked into the mirror that was *René*, they saw a portrait that transformed their social and economic marginalization into an aesthetic aristocracy of the spirit in the newly Romantic age.

The success of this bourgeois myth of the artist seems to have been due in large part to its "real life" embodiment. Despite Chateaubriand's later denials, the main protagonist of *René* owed much to his aristocratic creator's early biography and gained by his association with the wildly successful author, statesman, and man of action. Thus, despite his own failure and without ever writing a word, the figure of René was associated with would-be artistic greatness. Young imitators of the hero, with or without genius, cultivated, as he had, what were now taken as the outward signs of literary genius: an antisocial solitariness drawn to self-absorption and legitimated through metaphysical abstractions.

If Chateaubriand lent panache to René, *René* served in turn, particularly during the early years, to promote its author's legend. In this mirror game of mutually reinforcing images, the distinction between model and copy became increasingly blurred. Damaze de Raimond, in his ardent defense of the author in 1811, for example, describes Chateaubriand at the age of twenty-one as a copy of René. "Demi-sauvage, sans patrie, sans famille, sans fortune, sans amis, il ne connaissait la société que par les maux dont elle l'avait frappé" ["Half-savage, without a country, family, fortune or friends, he knew society only through the misfortunes it had inflicted upon him"][41]—a veiled allusion to the Revolution of 1789 and to the imprisonment of Chateaubriand's family during the Reign of Terror. Similarly, portraits of the author seem to have drawn their inspiration from his hero. Perhaps the most famous painting of Chateaubriand, and the one most often reproduced, shows him outside, alone, acting out René (Figure 9.3). Behind the well-dressed modern man lie Roman ruins. Though the young man is contemplative and self-contained, his unkempt hair suggests unruly passions and the hand he tucks into his vest jacket perhaps recalls Napoleon's pose—and the Romantic writer's more ethereal but equally grandiose artistic ambitions.[42]

Being René and reading Chateaubriand served writers as a rite of passage to adulthood, to romanticism and to writing itself. For countless nineteenth-century authors, their early attempts at fiction would be their own semi-autobiographical version of René's confession in works such as Senancour's *Oberman* (1804), Constant's *Adolphe* (1816), Sainte-Beuve's *Volupté* (1834), Balzac's *Le Lys dans la vallée* (1835), and Musset's *Confession d'un enfant du siècle* (1836). In them, the hero was a model for the Self both in fact and in fiction. Sainte-Beuve would declare that *René* "est la plus belle production de M. de Chateaubriand, la plus inaltérable et la plus durable; il est son portrait même. Il est *le nôtre*" ["is M. de Chateaubriand's finest production, the most unalterable and the most enduring; it is his own portrait. It is *our* portrait."][43] Though apparently inclusive, the first-person plural pronoun is also exclusive. What is said to be the depiction of an age or of an entire generation in *René* would more appropriately be termed a self-portrait of (some) men.

Figure 9.3 Anne-Louis Girodet, "Un homme méditant sur les ruines de Rome" ["A man meditating on the ruins of Rome"], 1810. *Source*: Musée de Saint-Malo.

Although women writers, such as Germaine de Staël in *Corinne* (1806) and George Sand in *Lélia* (1833) offered their own versions of the impotent nineteenth-century hero, the *mal du siècle* remained almost exclusively a male malady. Sand, perhaps the only author to imagine a heroine—Lélia—who was one of those unhappy but empowered few, was also one of the few women authors who saw herself in and as René. Like her male compatriots, Sand spoke of seeing Chateaubriand's hero as an uncanny reflection: "Il me sembla que René c'était moi." ["It seemed to me that René was me."][44] However, Sand's unusual ability to identify with young male genius went hand in hand with her refusal of woman's conventional role and her audacious adoption of traditionally masculine manners, dress, privileges, and literary ambitions. By contrast, for Daniel Stern, another nineteenth-century woman writer who adopted a male pseudonym, *René* was not a picture of what she was, but instead one of the works that would teach her how to become what she was not yet. She writes that after her convent studies she threw herself "avec une sorte de frénésie dans des lectures romanesques: *Werther, René, Adolphe, Manfred, Faust* qui, en exaltant ma sensibilité m'inoculaient un maladif et poétique dégoût de la vie" ["with a kind of frenzy into the reading of novels: *Werther, René, Adolphe, Manfred, Faust* which, by exciting my sensitivity, infected me with an unhealthy and poetic disgust for life"].[45]

The force of the René example did not have this "contaminating" effect on very many women. As we know, double standards of conduct, education, and expectations inhibited attempts the "weaker sex" might have of acting out an identification with the weak but empowered René and his famous creator. With the rise of the bourgeoisie in mid-nineteenth-century France, an ever growing division between public and private, male and female, further reinforced these gender differences and the hierarchy of the sexes they maintained.[46] Inasmuch as the Romantic myth of the artist as an inveterate loner convinced of his superiority was coded as masculine, it only exacerbated the difficulty would-be women writers might have of "becoming René."

Being Atala Buying *René*

As in early nineteenth-century accounts of the reader response to *Atala* and *René*, I have posited gender as a critical factor in the very different reactions to Chateaubriand's two novels. Although the oppositions I have drawn are overly schematic and valid only at certain levels of abstraction, they disclose and highlight the ideologies about masculinity and femininity that were disseminated in the popularization of these works and that would become the mainstay of a society increasingly dominated by the bourgeoisie. Central to this developing ideology was a notion about "separate spheres" in which women's private domain was distinct from men's public world. Nevertheless, as in the sexual and economic opposition I have posited, the spheres of production and consumption cannot be so easily set apart: the men intent on "being René" were increasingly dependent on women buying *René* and "buying" the idea of woman as Atala.

In her study of nineteenth-century consumer culture, Rachel Bowlby notes that increases in population and literacy as well as advances in technology, distribution, and transportation, made the novel "just another 'novelty' to be devoured or consumed as fast as fashions changed."[47] No longer the beneficiary of aristocratic patronage, novelists in particular were subject to market demands and thus beholden to the sex and class with the leisure time for literary consumption: bourgeois and aristocratic women. Nevertheless, *René* and its Romantic successors offered a myth of Romantic genius that served to figure literature as the production of a solitary man, member of a misunderstood elite. We might say then that this idealized image of the artist served two purposes. On the one hand, it masked art's growing resemblance to industrial production and writers' dependence on its economy. On the other, it served to shore up bourgeois authors' tenuous masculine identity in the face of their dependence on a female reading public and their association with woman's domestic world of leisure and consumption.[48]

Although bourgeois women had effectively been consigned to hearth and home, they were also increasingly impelled to go forth and buy these new forms of culture. By the end of the century they had become the primary consumers in this new market economy. Bowlby argues that what made this growing association of women and consumerism so powerful is that it fit so readily "the available ideological paradigm of a seduction of women by men, in which women would be addressed as yielding objects to the powerful male subject forming, and informing them of, their desires" (20). Furthermore, in the larger society, these female consumers were themselves objects of consumption engaged in "active, commodified self-display" (9) and destined for exchange and circulation between men.

The construction of these kinds of postrevolutionary subjects and their objects for the bourgeois patriarchal order of the later nineteenth century had been adumbrated in the first decades after the French Revolution by the reproductions of *Atala* and *René*. On the one hand, imitations of Chateaubriand's "odd couple" positioned woman as exotic and erotic Other, the object of a male gaze; on the other, they established man as the alienated but empowered Self who packages his own desires as a product for her to buy.

Notes

1. Naomi Schor, *Breaking the Chain: Women, Theory and French Realist Fiction* (New York: Columbia University Press, 1985), 145. For other revisionist readings of *Atala*'s significance, see the chapters by Schor, Marie-Claire Vallois, and Madelyn Gutwirth in this volume.

2. Margaret Waller, "Cherchez la femme: Male Malady and Narrative Politics in the French Romantic Novel," *PMLA* 104 (March 1989):141–51.

3. On the increased restraints on women, see, for example, Joan Landes, *Women and the Public Sphere in the Age of the French Revolution* (Ithaca: Cornell University Press, 1988); and Geneviève Fraisse, *Muse de la raison: La démocratie exclusive et la différence des sexes* (Aix-en-Provence: Alinéa, 1989).

4. My understanding of *Atala* as a multimedia cultural event owes much to Terry Eagleton's analysis of an analogous, earlier phenomenon in England—the public reaction to Samuel Richardson's *Pamela*, *Clarissa*, and *Sir Charles Grandison*—in *The Rape of Clarissa* (Minneapolis: University of Minnesota Press, 1982), esp. 4–17.

5. On *Atala*, see especially the critical introduction by Armand Weil (Paris: Corti, 1950). Susan J. Delaney's invaluable "*Atala* in the Arts" traces the themes of Christian martyrdom, the Noble Savage, and eroticism in representations of *Atala* in fine and popular art, in *The Wolf and the Lamb: Popular Culture in France from the Old Regime to the Twentieth Century* (Saratoga, Calif.: Anma Libri, 1977), 209–31. For the complete account, see her "Representations of Chateaubriand's *Atala* in the Fine Arts and in the Popular Arts," (Ph.D. diss., University of Wisconsin—Madison, 1979). See also Hugh Honour, *The European Vision of America* (Cleveland: Cleveland Museum of Art, 1975), 286–302. On *René*, see the critical introduction by Armand Weil (Paris: Droz, 1935), xl–lxv; and Pierre Barbéris, *À la recherche d'une écriture: Chateaubriand* (Paris: Mame, 1974), esp. 665–92.

6. See Pierre-Louis Duchartre and René Saulnier, *L'imagerie parisienne: L'imagerie de la rue Saint-Jacques* (Paris: Gründ, 1944), 120 and 130.

7. See Rosalind H. Williams, *Dream Worlds: Mass Consumption in Late Nineteenth-Century France* (Berkeley: University of California Press, 1982), 45–57.

8. André Gazot, ed., *Une Ancienne muscadine: Fortunée Hamelin: Lettres inédites, 1839–1851* (Paris: Emile-Paul, 1911), 292–93.

9. In his seventy-two-page brochure on the novel, for example, André Morellet addresses himself to women to insist that his criticism of Chateaubriand's tale of doomed passion does not indicate his own lack of feminine sensitivity. *Observations critiques sur le roman intitulé* Atala (Paris: Denné, 1801), 5.

10. Léon Séché, "Chateaubriand et le centenaire d'*Atala*," *Revue politique et littéraire* 15 (avril 1901):530. See also Louis Hogu, "La Publication d'*Atala* et l'opinion des contemporains," *Revue des facultés catholiques de l'oeust* 22 (avril 1913):450–468.

11. François René de Chateaubriand, *Mémoires d'outre-tombe*, 2 vols. (Paris: Pléiade, 1946), 1:446. Hereafter cited parenthetically as *MOT*.

12. "Les académiciens assemblés dissertèrent doctement sur son sexe et sur sa nature . . ." ["The assembled academicians held forth learnedly on its sex and its nature . . ."] (*MOT*, 1:445).

13. In what is probably an apocryphal recollection, Chateaubriand relates that as a member of the royalist army in 1792, he was hit by two bullets. What saved him was his manuscript: "Atala, *en fille dévouée*, se plaça entre son père et le plomb ennemi" ["Atala, *dutiful daughter* that she was, stood between her father and the enemy bullet"] (*MOT*, 1:333; emphasis added).

14. After the publication of *René*, Chateaubriand took on a modified version of his father's name, René-Auguste, thus erasing "René" twice, once from his given name and once from his father's, symbolically severing the links to the fictional representation of his younger self.

15. Chateaubriand. *Essai sur les révolutions* (Paris: Gallimard, 1978), 438.

16. Schor, *Breaking the Chain*, 135.

17. *Le Courrier des spectacles*, 5 thermidor, an IX–24 juillet 1801.

18. See Nancy K. Miller, *The Heroine's Text: Readings in the French and English Novel, 1722–1782* (New York: Columbia University Press, 1980).

19. Delaney notes that all but one of the paintings before 1827 illustrate the virginal maiden's last rites, her funeral procession or burial. "Representations of Chateaubriand's *Atala*," 166, and "*Atala* in the Arts," 219.

20. Delaney, "Representations of *Atala*," 134–35.

21. *Décade philosophique* 35 (20 vendémiaire an XI–12 octobre 1802), 108. Quoted in Weil, "Introduction," *Atala*, xlv.

22. For further analysis of fashion and the Merveilleuses, see, for example, Richard Sennett, *The Fall of Public Man* (New York: Knopf, 1977), 184–85.

23. Some of the later, popular Atala engravings of the 1820s and 1830s, by contrast, make the Christian Indian maiden an edifying image for French maidenhood. In keeping with their didactic aim, the prints give Père Aubry a prominent place in the scenes, make Atala her buyers' contemporary and keep her dress and pose modest.

24. *La Vie parisienne*, 10 décembre 1864, 703–4.

25. Delaney, "Representations of Chateaubriand's *Atala*," 36.

26. See "Découvertes récentes de pendules Atala," *Bulletin de la Société Chateaubriand* n.s. 27 (1984):57–63, which includes photo reproductions.

27. Léon-François Hoffman, "*Atala* au boulevard: L'*Ima* de Cammaille Saint-Aubin," *Bulletin de la Société Chateaubriand* n.s. 17 (1974):43.

28. The first line of Chateaubriand's text begins by evoking the grandeur of the lost empire that provides the setting for his novel: "La France possédait autrefois, dans

l'Amérique septentrionale, un vaste empire. . . ." ["In bygone days, France possessed in North America a vast empire. . . ."] (71). The Louisiana territory had been claimed by France in 1682 but then ceded in 1763 to Spain, which secretly retroceded the territory to France. However, in 1803, just two years after the first publication of *Atala*, Napoleon would sell this territory to the United States and concentrate his empire building efforts elsewhere.

29. Chateaubriand himself got into the naming game. Francis Gribble writes that Chateaubriand "managed to quarrel even with the priests by insisting that a child to whom he stood as godfather should be christened 'Atala'—which is not, of course the name of a Christian saint though of a heroine who, he said, was 'quite as good as a saint'!" *Chateaubriand and His Court of Women* (New York: Charles Scribner, 1909), 112–13. A nineteenth-century writer observed that "Monsieur de Chateaubriand eut le triste privilège de baptiser du nom d'Atala les filles de portiers." ["Monsieur de Chateaubriand had the sad privilege of baptizing porters' daughters with the name Atala."] Léon Gozlan, "Ce que c'est qu'une Parisienne," in *Le Diable à Paris* (Paris: Michel Lévy, 1857), 6. His remark underscores the perceived class differences between the aristocratic literary original and its lower-class copies. In Flaubert's *Madame Bovary* (1857), "Atala" is one of the many names with Italianate endings that the heroine, besotted with romantic aspirations and aristocratic pretentions, would consider but then reject for her daughter. See Weil, "Introduction," *Atala*, cxxvi.

30. The only two women to have celebrated Chateaubriand's novel in poetry do not engage in male impersonation nor can they make the heroine speak; instead, they tell the story in the third person and from a distance. See Mme Victoire Babois, "Vers sur le tombeau d'Atala, de M. Girodet," *Mercure de France* 24 (3 décembre 1808):435–36; and Mlle Marie-Louise Arnassant, *Atala, poème en six chants, suivi de Pensées poétiques* (Lyon: chez l'auteur, 1810). In the entire corpus of *Atala*-inspired works, there is only one text that makes the heroine the star of her own story. And the only way the novel can do so is, literally, by raising Atala from the dead and keeping Chactas and Father Aubry out of the picture until a final tearful reunion. See the two-volume *Résurrection d'Atala et son voyage à Paris* (Paris: Renard, an X–1802), which is attributed to Raimond.

31. For an example of the close association of Chactas and René with Chateaubriand, see the dense layering of citations from *Atala*, *René*, and *Itinéraire de Paris à Jérusalem* in the parodic *Itinéraire de Pantin au Mont-Calvaire* . . . , published in 1811. If, as Chactas claims in this work, Atala is his ideal addressee, it is perhaps because she does not talk back.

32. I develop this argument at length in "Cherchez la femme."

33. On the uses of this displacement, see Pierre Barbéris's *René de Chateaubriand: Un nouveau roman* (Paris: Larousse, 1973), and his *A la recherche d'une écriture: Chateaubriand*; and Eric Gans, "*René* and the Romantic Model of Self-Centralization," *Studies in Romanticism* 22 (1983):421–35.

34. Article signed "P.M." in *Mercure de France*, Floréal an X: 251. The story of René had not yet been published separately. This review of the piece was designed to serve as an enticement to the reading public to read its source, *Génie du Christianisme*.

35. See Marguerite Iknayan, *The Idea of the Novel in France: The Critical Reaction, 1815–1848* (Geneva: Droz, 1961), 31.

36. Quoted in Marie-Louise Pailleron, "Les Petits Carnets de Sainte-Beuve," *Revue hebdomadaire* (29 juillet 1916):623.

37. Quoted in Weil, "Introduction," *René*, lviii.

38. Sainte-Beuve, *Causeries du lundi*, quoted in Charles Dédéyan, *Chateaubriand et Rousseau* (Paris: Société d'éditions d'enseignement supérieur, 1973).

39. For Roland Barthes, denial and the bourgeoisie are inextricably linked. "La bourgeoisie se définit comme *la classe sociale qui ne veut pas être nommée*" ["The bourgeoise is defined as *the social class that refuses to be named*"], *Mythologies* (Paris: Seuil, 1957), 225, emphasis in original. See also Williams, *Dream Worlds*.

40. See especially Pierre Barbéris, "Mal du siècle, ou d'un romantisme de droite à un romantisme de gauche," in *Romantisme et politique, 1815–1851* (Paris: Armand Colin, 1969), 164–82.

41. Damaze de Raimond, *Réponse aux attaques contre M. de Chateaubriand, accompagnée de pièces justificatives* (Paris: Rosa, 1812), 3.

42. The painting by Girodet was first exhibited in 1810 as "Un homme méditant sur les ruines de Rome" ["A Man Meditating on the Ruins of Rome"]. It served in turn other representations of the author, such as these lines from the adulatory epistle composed in 1820 by Edouard Alletz, "À Chateaubriand, sur le génie poétique de ses ouvrages" (Paris: A. Désanges, 1826): "Seul, tu sembles debout au milieu des ruines,/ Et ce vaste désert, qu'à nos yeux tu domines,/ Semé des vains débris d'un siècle renversé,/ Garde en toi l'héritier des grandeurs du passé! . . . Ton front sublime et fier, ton regard inspiré, . . . / De loin nous présageaient ta puissance nouvelle:/ Le génie est un dieu que son port seul révèle." ["You appear alone amongst the ruins,/ And this vast wilderness,/ o'er which you seem to tower,/ Strewn with the vain debris of an age turned upside down,/ Preserves you as heir to the grandeurs of the past! . . . Your sublime and proud brow, your inspired gaze . . . / Have long foretold your present power:/ Genius is a god revealed only by his bearing."] See also an engraving by Delannoy that places Chateaubriand once again on the ruins of an ancient civilization (perhaps as a figure of the Napoleonic era colonizer as melancholic man), reproduced in *Album Chateaubriand* (Paris: Gallimard, 1988), plate 180.

43. Quoted in Armand Weil, review of Gilbert Chinard, ed., *Atala, René* in *Bulletin de la Société Chateaubriand* 2 (1931):43. Emphasis added.

44. George Sand, *Histoire de ma vie*, vol. 7 (Paris: Michel Lévy Frères, 1856), 223.

45. Quoted in Elyane Dezon-Jones, ed. *Les Écritures féminines* (Paris: Magnard, 1983), 215.

46. See, for example, Renate Bridenthal and Claudia Koonz, eds. *Becoming Visible: Women in European History* (Boston: Houghton Mifflin, 1977); and Claire Goldberg Moses, *French Feminism in the Nineteenth Century* (Albany: State University of New York, 1984).

47. Rachel Bowlby, *Just Looking: Consumer Culture in Dreiser, Gissing and Zola* (New York: Methuen, 1985), 8. Further references cited parenthetically in the text.

48. Marlon B. Ross makes a similar argument about English Romanticism: "Romantic poeticizing is not just what women cannot do because they are not expected to; it is also what some men do in order to reconfirm their capacity to influence the world in ways socio-historically determined as masculine. The categories of gender, both in their lives and in their work, help the Romantics establish rites of passage toward poetic identity and toward masculine empowerment." "Romantic Quest and Conquest: Troping Masculine Power in the Crisis of Poetic Identity," in *Romanticism and Feminism*, ed. Anne K. Mellor (Bloomington: Indiana University Press, 1988), 29.

10

Exotic Femininity and the Rights of Man: *Paul et Virginie* and *Atala*, or the Revolution in Stasis

MARIE-CLAIRE VALLOIS

Historical Preliminaries: Revolution and the Celebration of Mother Nature

On the fifth of October, two months after the public recognition of every man's equality in the eyes of the law by *The Declaration of the Rights of Man and of the Citizen*, the people of Paris marched on Versailles to fetch the king and to bring him back to Paris. It is at this time that, according to most historical accounts but especially Michelet's *History of the Revolution*, women's participation in the events of the revolution became evident.[1] Michelet's claim that "les femmes sont à l'avant-garde de notre Révolution" [women were the avant-garde of our revolution] seems to answer Mirabeau's own dictum: "Tant que les femmes ne s'en mêlent pas il n'y a pas de véritable révolution." [There can be no true revolution until women are engaged in its midst].[2]

In June 1793, the new Jacobin Constitution extended the right to vote to all citizens, regardless of their wealth, women excepted.[3] It is precisely at that moment, in preparation for the festive ceremony of August 10, 1793, that Jacques Louis David had erected, amidst the ruins of the Bastille, a colossal statue of a woman representing Nature.[4] Her arms were crossed and from her breasts flowed streams of pure, regenerating water. Between these two cultural representations of revolutionary women, the image of women as participating in the revolutionary process and "Woman as Mother Nature" as an allegory of the new Republic, a double transformation occurs.[5] First, the lively, feminine crowd is turned into an allegorical statue. This transformation, as it is translated in literary accounts, could be described as a passage from the animate to the inanimate.[6] Second, this transformation marks the passage from the plural to the singular because the crowd, which is a collective of separate persons,

Translated by John Galvin and Joan Gass.

178

becomes an essentialized unity through the abstracted idea of "woman." In other words the very celebration of the concept of womanhood as Mother Nature seems to occur at the same moment that real women are pushed off the stage of the revolution.

In her study, *Rousseau and the Republic of Virtue*, Carol Blum shows how the staging of the kind of celebration mentioned above consecrates, in an emblematic way, that soon-to-be-irremediable split of the body politic along sexual lines.[7] In the newly emergent Republic, according to the very linguistic formulas of the new Constitution of 1793, the word "citizen," is reserved for men only. Citizenship in 1793 has become a masculine virtue following the model of the Roman Republic.

Citizenly virtue, where "citizen" is defined in the positive sense of an active member of the polis, appears, following the Latin etymology of *vir* as the sole attribute of men. Women, once excluded from the ranks of citizens, are thus exempted from the constraints of this virtue. The new republican meaning of the word "virtue" has, nevertheless, as a side-effect the legitimation of the term "virtue" in the private feminine sense, a definition that is the negative replique to the positive political meaning and that will soon be fixed as "modesty," "chastity," and "fidelity." In order for the "Roman" citizen to be resuscitated anew, it was also necessary to recall that other model of femininity, the "Roman" matron, the nurturing, nursing, mother. The "hundred-breasted colossus" that Michelet imagines in the midst of the Bastille's ruins, mythically reproduces this renewed vision of women.

The imposition, at the end of the eighteenth century, of this new ethical order entailing the effacement both of the public woman and the sexually active woman in favor of the figure of the nurturing mother, constitutes a very complex phenomenon that did not occur without resistance and that affected in varying modes the different levels of society. In fact, the new feminine fiction of the woman as Mother Nature was as much the product of an entire culture and literature that was emerging from the preceding age as it was also the result of the new republican law.[8]

It is precisely this problematic question of the cultural and literary staging of the repression (erasure) of one conception of "femininity" in favor of another and the concommitant appearance of the cult of a certain "republican virtue" that will be the focus of my analysis. In order to track this double movement, I have chosen to study two fictive texts, *Paul et Virginie* and *Atala*, texts that at the end of the Enlightenment illustrate, or better, traduce in a symptomatic sense, the work of repression and of the reorganization of this cultural imaginary around the idea of "virtue": of this virtue that becomes the complement of the male citizen's virtue, the "nurturing" virtue of the woman of nature, the natural, "exotic" woman.

One only has to open the first and last pages of these two novels *Paul and Virginie* and *Atala* to see that their proclaimed aim is to narrate, with the aid of exotic accoutrements, a story centered on the virtues of women. The narrator of *Paul et Virginie* begins his story in the following way:

> Mon père . . . racontez-moi, je vous prie, ce que vous savez des anciens habitants de ce désert, . . . du bonheur que donnent la nature et la vertu.
>
> [Father, . . . please tell me, I beg you, what you know about the former inhabitants of this wild land . . . about that happiness that nature and virtue alone can offer] (82).

If the novel relates the story of two children of both sexes, the unfolding of the intrigue and its conclusion is focused on the virtue of the female child, Virginie. This is clearly apparent in the public ceremony of the funerals with which the book ends:

> Huit jeunes demoiselles des plus considérables de l'île, vêtues de blanc, et tenant des palmes à la main, portaient le corps de leur vertueuse compagne, couvert de fleurs. Un choeur de petits enfants le suivait en chantant des hymnes . . . à la suite duquel marchait le gouverneur, suivi de la foule du peuple. Voilà ce que l'administration avait ordonné pour rendre quelques honneurs à la vertu de Virginie.
>
> [Eight young ladies from the most considerable families of the island, dressed in white and carrying palms in their hands, bore the flower-strewn body of their virtuous companions. They were followed by a choir of little children singing hymns. . . . then the governor and last of all a crowd of common people. Such were the arrangements made by the administration to render homage to Virginia's virtue] (161).

The narrator of *Atala* closes his narration with the same scene of the burial of the female body and the same word, virtue:

> Alors versant des flots de larmes, je me séparai de la fille de Lopez, alors je m'arrachai de ces lieux, laissant au pied du monument de la nature, un monument plus auguste: l'humble tombeau de la vertu.
>
> [Then, drowning in a sea of tears, I tore myself away from Lopez' daughter. I dragged myself from that place, leaving behind me next to nature's tomb, an even more august memorial, the humble grave of virtue] (136).

Both novels, *Paul et Virginie* (1787) and *Atala* (1801), two tales of feminine virtue that seem so symmetrically to frame the revolutionary events of 1789, produce however a curious effacement of the problematic history of republican virtue by inviting the reader to efface "history" itself, through the seductive bias of an exotic escapade. The tale of virtue can only be told by following the imaginary protocols of a spatial displacement, a voyage. We recognize here, in the displacement operated through fiction, one of the staples of dream-work in the Freudian "unconscious."[9] Transporting women to the exotic dreamland of the New World, the novels allow all men and all citizens the pleasure of celebrating the new feminine image of virtue in the sensual decor of Mother Nature.

As it is becoming apparent, what is at stake in the following analysis could be formulated by the following question: What, in this revolutionary period, can explain the problematic juncture of these terms "virtue," "exoticism," and "femininity" that, at first glance, seem so totally unrelated?

Exoticism and Femininity: Theoretical Reflections on (A Certain Kind of) Marginality

Bernardin de Saint Pierre's *Paul et Virginie* and Chateaubriand's *Atala* are known and celebrated for having introduced exotic description into the novel. Two brief fictions—more novella than novel—which their authors will present as "fragments" removed from those longer and more ambitious descriptive works: *Les Etudes de la nature* and *Le Voyage en île de France*, in the case of Bernardin de Saint Pierre, *Les Natchez, Le Voyage en Amérique*, in Chateaubriand's. From these travel tales with fictionalized narratives, an original musing is formed whose distinctive quality, "exoticism," can be read against the backdrop of the cultural imaginary in accordance with the trope or figure of the "voyage." This "exoticism" (pre-romantic or romantic), moving from the Virgin islands in the Oceani of Bernardin to the land of Virginia in the America of Chateaubriand partake in a certain mythic view of eternal Nature. It will be no surprise, when we glance at the toponym, "Virginia" to discover that the aim of their journey is to arrive symptomatically on the fascinating and disturbing site of virginity, a peculiar virginity, which, emerging mythically from a time that antidates history, is soon defined, as any encyclopedia will reveal, as the elementary virginity of Mother Nature:

> Exotisme: Le *terme* est introduit proprement dit au 19ème siècle pour désigner les formes d'art et des moeurs des peuples lointains, mais la *chose* exista dès la révélation du nouveau monde. . . . La découverte d'un univers nouveau stimula l'imagination. Le thème de la *nature* bonne et *vertueuse* apparaît alors [my emphasis].

> [Exoticism: the term is introduced in the strict sense in the 19th century to designate the art forms and mores of the faraway peoples, though the matter existed from the moment the new world was revealed. . . . The discovery of a new universe stirred the imagination. It was then that the nature theme appeared, nature good and virtuous].[10]

It is both the marvel and the paradox of the encyclopedic definition that, in its concern to order semantics, it comes to order in utopian fashion the world. This utopian approach recalls the definition of the descriptive genre denounced by Philippe Hamon in his book, *Introduction à l'analyse du descriptif*, in which he shows how in the "referential utopia," the "exotic" thing existed long before any traveler to the New World gave it a name. Language, in this context, is understood as a transparent medium whose function is "to name or designate, term by term, the world/ . . . / A world itself "discrete," cut up into units, once and for all."[11] This notion of language does not account, therefore, for historical changes, or rather denies history altogether. Bernardin's and Chateaubriand's exotic fictions partake, we will see, of the same utopia of a world of nature preexisting its discovery. This utopic and atemporal vision of nature, coming directly from the Enlightenment, and presenting itself as Man's universal truth, produces a specific version/vision of the eternal Woman.[12]

My study, then, is limited to an analysis of those fictional tales written by these male civilized travelers into virgin regions and among wild societies that the ethnologist would term "primitive." The term primitive in this context curiously has, of course, a double referent, the savage and the woman. The kind of voyage envisaged, then, is a voyage through space (a displacement from Europe to America or Africa) and belongs to the perspective of the ethnologist: the European voyager, setting out upon the discovery of another country, another ethnic group, is in pursuit of the Other. But these voyages are similarly found to correspond to an expedition or displacement in time: the civilized man is in search of this other, which he sees as an origin. The voyager and observer of primitives becomes, in this fashion, an anthropologist.[13]

This double gesture of translation, the shift in time and the observation of the distant (the primitive), is the explorer's attempt, while apparently outlining the parameters of the Other, actually to arrive at a definition of the Self/the Same. Ethnic discourse, a discourse of a certain difference, would here be digested, as it were, by anthropological discourse, whose final horizon—the history of humankind—can be effected only with a universal standard of reference: Man.

It is in this way that Chateaubriand, at the outset, in the preface to the first edition of *Atala*, limited his project to the ethnologist's when he says that his purpose is "to portray the mores of the savage" (39). He alters it, though, in the 1805 preface, along the lines of the anthropologist, when he indicates that the ill-fortune of his hero "belongs less to the individual than to the "family of man" (67). This interlocking of ethnology and anthropology is not without considerable consequence for the feminine referent in these two stories, which in exemplary fashion, are centered round the lives and the pathetic deaths of two women: Atala and Virginie. Can we say then, using Michel de Certeau's analysis of the exotic, that feminine exoticism, like the exoticism of the savage, is always, in the end, the story of an execution, of a sacrificial putting to death?[14]

At this point, however, it is necessary to wonder what, in this context, permits the parallel between the primitive and the woman. What could be more different from the intimate vision of the domestic woman than the image of the faraway native of wild lands? Tzvetan Todorov suggests, in his study, *La Conquête de l'Amérique: la découverte de l'autre*, that the implicit similarity between them consists in the fact that for the civilized male they are both positioned as the complete Other. The other may be (1) without or outside, and far away or, (2) within society (as are women for men, and the rich for the poor).[15] In the stories of *Paul et Virginie* and *Atala*, there is a collapsing of these two kinds of difference: the other is both the other without, far away; the savage; *and* the other within: woman, feminine nature.

Paul et Virginie presents, for example, a journey into the wilds of nature that is also described as a return to the intimate site of maternity. In *Atala*, the collapsing of the savage upon the feminine other is more easily done; Atala is the "primitive" Indian woman who presents Chactas, the civilized savage, with the problem of understanding natural desire. Blinded like Oedipus, accompanied by a new Antigone, he is, in the midst of the American savannahs, the incarnation, in Indian guise, of civilized Man.

My initial question could then be rephrased as follows: What in this period of revolution accounts for this collapsing of exoticism and femininity? What would explain this need to present woman not only as Other but also as "without," in the sense of "outside of?" By the authority of what law or what event could this expulsion (this extradition) be made legitimate? A partial answer to this question could be found in the word "revolution." The word revolution is understood here not only in the sense of political change and the setting up of new laws and principles, but also, perhaps in regard to women and, starting in 1793, in the sense of turning, of a turning back, a revolution—a return to the simple life of the primitive family.[16] As far as women are concerned, the revolution sets up two codifying discourses: *The Declaration of the Rights of Man and Citizen* with, as complementary texts, the constitutions of 1791, 1793, 1795 and the Civic Code and Napoleonic Code, partial applications of the constitutions. Two discourses that, while they were quite contradictory in their goals, will have, on the level of their practical application a combined tragic effect: they end up promulgating women's expulsion from the public sphere and from political life, thus signaling the legal impossibility, for women, of becoming citizens of France.

The history of revolutionary women from 1789 to 1793 would have to therefore be told henceforth—and the writings of Michelet in *Les Femmes et la révolution* give, in a peculiar fashion, curious credit to it, but only as a supplement (*supplément*) of history that could be told, in turn, only along the lines of the legendary: a symbolic extradition from the history of men that amounts to an extradition from history plain and simple.[17]

Women and the Revolution: The Supplement of History

The Civil Code and Napoleonic Code (1805), with all their institutional force, mark the end of the revolution for women and finalize the splitting of public space along sexual lines, thus formalizing the dichotomy between masculine public and feminine private space.[18] Women are assigned once and for all, by dint of legal language, their status and place: the wife, forever a minor, can have no other place than the domestic one. This splitting of the space of the polis according to the public/private duality is, for women, first the equivalent of an expulsion, an ousting from public space, and then, secondly, of a confinement.[19] Their confining within the domestic enclosure is quickly translated into the collective imaginary and more specifically in literature, through an interiorization: woman belongs to the interior, to the intimate.

Paul et Virginie and *Atala* are witness-texts both to that imaginary reorganization of social space and to that setting up of the new legislation of domestic law that ensues therefrom. These two novels, pre- and postrevolutionary, frame almost symmetrically the moment of this *supplément* of history of the revolutionary happening, an extraordinary history that will quickly strike as too out of the ordinary, that of the opening of the public place to women—quickly followed by their confinement to the home and their celebration as allegorical divinities (statues).[20]

The history of women under the revolution—such is the third object (*objet supplémentaire*) of this paper. A history swallowed up, repressed, scotomized, which must first of all be written, or rewritten following Michelet's lead, as an historical intermediary or intermezzo. The story of *Paul et Virginie* and *Atala* is therefore the other side of the history, which has been repressed in the process of substitution, of these more or less anonymous bodies of women, gathered into clubs and female revolutionary organizations, "active members" of the revolutionary process from 1789 to 1793.[21]

The year 1793, which first denies women the right of association and then the right to vote, marks, as I have stated, the end of the revolution for women. It soon became clear that any woman who insisted on her rights as political subject was asking for the guillotine. A literal decapitation ironically followed the figural. The newspaper, *Le Moniteur*, reports, for example, an incident occurring on September 16, 1793, in which Chabot casts accusations against *La Société des Républicaines Révolutionnaires* and places them all outside the law. In order to do so, he takes as his target one of the most audacious of them, Claire Lacombe. Claire Lacombe, or "Rose," as she became exotically rebaptized in the legend of the revolution, had become known for, among other things, having defended, in September 1793, the reeducation of prostitutes. Chabot's strategy is precisely to attack Claire Lacombe along with the Society as offenders of "virtue." In fact, the most dangerous activity of Claire Lacombe was probably her eloquence and her insistence in demanding to be considered as a "equal" revolutionary "citizen" by the Jacobins. A more direct attack set forth by another orator present at the meeting unveils the more serious accusation:

> Cette femme se fourre partout . . . s'écria l'orateur, . . . elle demande d'abord la constitution, rien que la constitution, toute la constitution, et finit par calomnier les autorités constituées.
>
> [That woman pokes her nose in everywhere . . . cried the speaker, . . . first she calls for the constitution, the whole constitution, nothing but the constitution, only to finish by slandering the appointed authorities].[22]

On October 30, the Convention dissolves the Society of Revolutionary Republican Women. This extradition from public space will be quickly translated for the accused, Rose Lacombe, into incarceration. Plainly, her crime was to have demanded the full application of the constitution, that is, the indiscriminant application of the rights inscribed in the principles of 1789 in *The Declaration of the Rights of Man and Citizen*. Revolutionary history will move on, in the matter of universal principle, through a syllogistic circumlocution, whose ruse will consist in playing upon the two definitions of the word citizen: the one active and male, the other, passive and female. In the 1793 Constitution the status of citizen is defined in the following way:

> Tout homme né et domicilié en France, âgé de vingt et un ans accomplis;
>
> Tout étranger . . . domicilié en France depuis une année, y vit de son travail, ou acquiert une propriété, ou épouse une Française.
>
> [Any man born and raised in France, having reached twenty-one years of age; Any foreigner . . . who lives in France by his own labor, or who owns property, or has a French wife].[23]

Nowhere can we find in this paragraph of the Constitution a sentence that directly denies women the right to citizenship that they were given in principle by the *Declaration*. The exclusion from this right is, however, implied by default, by the only word that refers here to women, the word "wife." According to constitutional law, woman's status is to be a "wife," not a "citizen." Although one could find this sexual definition in direct opposition to the general principle of the *Declaration*, which states that "tous les hommes sont égaux par la nature et devant la loi" [every man is equal by nature and in front of the law]; one could remark that the word "nature" leaves, in the *Declaration*, room for historical interpretation.[24] It will serve, in fact, as the linguistic alibi that will produce the constitutions and the Napoleonic Code. It is this silent, unconscious reasoning of the law on the different "nature" of each citizen, which is defined according to their sex, that will legitimate women's exclusion from their political rights as well as from their civil rights by both the Civil and the Napoleonic codes. This syllogistic inscription of the law, that is, a reasoning from the general to the particular, comes down to a mere sleight of hand that, as Lyotard concludes in his section on "The Declaration of 1789" in his book, *Le Différend*, consists in interlocking the philosophical discourse of a universal law to the particulars of a historico-political discourse.[25] The abstraction of the first by occulting the power relations implicit in the second, authorizes the passage from the one to the other. In place of the Declaration of principle, which aimed at recognizing in each man and woman "*l'altérité citoyenne*," there will be a declaration of deed of the constitutions and their amendments, established by the revolutionary political practices of the Jacobins and of Napoleon and which will exclude all women from the political sphere.

Olympe de Gouges, because she attempted to lay claim to the writing of legislative discourse by replacing the word "man" with the word "woman," in her proposal for constitutional amendments, will be punished with imprisonment and the ironically egalitarian practice of the guillotine (November, 1793).[26] Another tragic end for a heroine of history who, also, had had the gall, in 1789, to alter Bernardin de Saint Pierre's script, in a drama entitled *Zamor et Mirza ou le malheureux naufrage*. In this first rescripting she links, in a clairvoyant fashion, the destiny of women and the destiny of the exotic savage.

Another semi-legendary silhouette of the revolution, Théroigne de Méricourt, la "belle liégeoise" often described as an amazon in revolutionary accounts, joins symptomatically the gallery of exotic women conjured up by Baudelaire, a poet expert in imaginary voyages, in *Les Fleurs du Mal*:

> Parcourant les forêts ou battant les halliers,
> . . . .
> Avez-vous vu Théroigne, amante du carnage,
> Excitant à l'assaut un peuple sans souliers?
>
> [Riding through the forest, preparing the hunt,
> . . . .
> Have you seen Théroigne, lover of carnage
> Driving on to revolution the ragged mob of the poor?][27]

If the poetic canon charges her with more intimate exploits, revolutionary reality will treat her otherwise. Théroigne is finally locked up in the Salpêtrière, insane and one of the first women whose hysteria will be found fit to figure, as a medical document, among the manuscripts of the physician Esquival.

Before bringing to an end this excursion into the prosaics of history, it is necessary to indicate through what imaginary figure the transition seems secured from those savage revolutionary furies to those flower women of nineteenth-century exoticism. One passage from *Mémoires d'Outre-Tombe*, a voyage in time by that connoisseur of primitivism, Chateaubriand, evokes this terrifying scene of women fanning the fires of the revolutionary hearth: "ces tricoteuses . . . qui se lèvent et crient toutes à la fois, leur chausse à la main, l'écume à la bouche" [These knitters . . . who rise and shriek all at once, their hose in their hands, their mouths foaming].[28] This impassioned dithyramb on those "Gorgon-headed" women seems a reply to the journalist, Gorsas, who, in describing these same women, writes: "Encore si ces dames étaient jolies, mais ce ne sont que des têtes de méduses dont l'aspect pétrifie. [Moreover, if these ladies were at least attractive, but their heads are Medusa-like and their gaze petrifies you . . .][29]

If in history the revolutionary Medusas turned others to stone, literature, pre-romantic and romantic, will take it upon itself to turn *them* to stone in return. As Christine Bucci Glucskman demonstrates in her book, *La Raison baroque: De Baudelaire à Benjamin*, the allegory of romantic beauty speaks like a woman of stone.[30]

If Virginie and Atala figure so spectacularly in the gallery of exotic portraiture, it is because there is at work in these fictions, and in exemplary fashion, the violence of the allegorizing process that transforms the living into the eternal and abstract, a process that appears in direct relation here with the extradition of the women from the public space, as evidenced in the revolutionary festival and iconography by the allegorical statue of the female republic.

It is as witness-texts to this process of allegorization and to this imaginary reorganization of political space that I would consider these two novels. This double process of allegorization and reorganization is not self-evident and its legitimization is, as we have seen, problematic. This problem of legitimization is expressed, moreover, through renewed attempts, on the part of authors and legislators, to tie these tales to discourses already legitimized: to the discourse of the ethnologist, to the discourse of the naturalist, or to that discourse on the way to relegitimization, the discourse of ethics.

From the Discourse of the Naturalist to the Discourse of Nature: The Family Tale of the Universal Discourse

If *Paul et Virginie* and *Atala* made contemporary revolutionary readers and the entire romantic generation quiver with delight, critical works and textbooks cite them only for the beauty and artistry of their descriptive passages. Chateaubriand, who defended his work against its detractors by eliciting the

authority of his sources (the accounts of Caver, Bartram, Imley, and Charle-
vois), concludes by insisting that "la nature américaine y est peinte avec la plus
scrupuleuse exactitude" [The American wildness is there portrayed with the
utmost accuracy] (61). And following scientific protocol, he even offers a cross-
proof: "c'est une justice que lui rendent les voyageurs qui ont visité la Louisiane
et les Florides [All those voyagers who have visited Louisiana and Florida
corroborate the veracity of *Atala*'s descriptions] (61).

Bernardin, in order to vindicate his tale, similarly resorts to this ruse:

> Un jeune homme nouvellement arrivé des Indes . . . raconte qu'il s'est reposé
> sur la vieille racine du cocotier planté à la naissance de Paul. . . . je lui
> recommandai fort d'être toujours exact à dire la vérité.
>
> [A young man recently arrived from the Indies . . . tells of having rested on
> the old root of the coconut palm that was planted the day of Paul's birth. . . .
> I exhorted him to always be exactly factual and to tell the truth] (218).

Observation, verification, cross-verification, all this protocol borrowed from
the discourse of science whose "reality effect" has no longer to be demonstrated, leaves unanswered, however, the question of what in this mixture of
fiction and quasi-scientific discourse is specifically at stake.

We must remember the exoticism of Bernardin and Chateaubriand is first
of all an exoticism of nature. Vegetal nature—one finds no animals in these
texts—the realm of the inanimate, is the chosen object of the naturalist. Now,
naturalist discourse, we know ever since Foucault, is the discourse of a certain
knowledge, of a certain episteme, the clasical episteme in which the fundamental function of language is to "assign a name to things and with this name,
name their essence."[31] We enter into the realm of the eternal, the universal.

In the opening pages of *Paul et Virginie* and *Atala*, the object or thing to be
described is Nature—the primitive and near virgin nature of Chateaubriand,
the tropical, onetime cultivated and now wild again, nature of Bernardin. A
bountiful nature of unlimited resources, the description of which becomes a
stock-taking or inventory:

> Nous mangions des mousses appelées tripes de roches, des écorces sucrées de
> bouleau et des pommes de mai. . . . Le noyer noir, l'érable, le sumach
> fournissait le vin à notre table. . . . Nous bénissions la Providence qui, sur la
> faible tige d'une fleur avait placé cette source limpide au milieu des marais
> corrumpus. . . .
>
> [We ate mosses called "rock tripe," sweet birch bark, and May apples. . . .
> The black walnut, the maple, and the sumac supplied wine for our table. . . .
> Then we would thank Providence which had placed this limpid spring on the
> slender stem of a flower in the midst of foul marshes . . .] (96).

Nature, bountiful and providential, is soon personified: it is Mother Nature.
Naturalist discourse slips into animist discourse. Providential nature is also
nature the refuge, which like a protective mother, offers an island or asylum
not unlike those "mountain gorges" that shelter the families of Paul and
Virginie.

Nature, as the maternal-feminine, is first a *site*. In *Ethique de la différence sexuelle*, Luce Irigaray remarks that this place, "assimilated before any perception of difference," cannot, of course, be constituted as *Other*. This exotic voyage, to the site of Nature, as a return voyage to the maternal-feminine, the voyage toward the other, reveals itself as a voyage toward the Same: "L'amour du même est amour de l'indifférenciation avec la terre-mère, comme la première demeure vivante [The love of the same is a love of the indifferenciation with mother-earth, the first habitus of life].[32]

This return to the Same is carried out in these fictions through a process of appropriation, of colonization, which transforms the discourse of the Other into the discourse of the Same. But this process of appropriation, of pacific colonization of the site initially described as Other, can be told, imaginarily speaking, only through the alternate route of a story, a tale of maternity.[33] It is a tale whose main effect seems to resolve the possible conflict between two discursive genres: the scientific discourse of the naturalist (the descriptions) and the fantasmatic discourse representing the story of Mother Nature (the tale). The novels each present two discourses upon woman: (1) woman as inanimate nature, the woman of the naturalist discourse—(2) woman as animate being, the woman of the fantasmatic dream. In *Le Différend*, Jean-François Lyotard, analyzing social disputes and historical conflicts, shows how "narrative fiction" appears to be the only genre that is able to reconcile the heterogeneity of conflicting discourses. Lyotard defines the tale as follows:

> Le récit est peut-être le genre de discours dans lequel l'hétérogénéité des régimes de phrases et même celle des genres de discours trouvent le mieux à se faire oublier. D'une part le récit raconte un ou deux différends et il lui impose une fin, un achèvement qui est son propre terme.
>
> [The tale is perhaps the kind of discourse in which the dissimilarity of the sentence/schemes and even the dissimilarity of the various kinds of discourse find it easiest to drop from view. On the one hand, the tale recounts one or two differend(s) and, on the other hand, it imposes on it an end, a finality that is its own term of expiration].[34]

This *différend* can only be resolved through history, the diegesis. In exotic tales the conflict is resolved, "domesticated," at two levels: first, from a retrospective perspective the drama is presented as already consumated; second, the death of the woman puts an end to the conflict itself.

Paul et Virginie and *Atala*, two stories of primitive life, are related by natives who have lived them, to European voyagers who can relive them only as *memory*. The perspective of the tale is not then only retrospective, it is the story of a kind of mourning for a past life and/or protagonist now buried in time. Everything takes place as if exotic discourse could come about only in the form of nostalgia. Exotic discourse would be, according to Chinard, the discourse that civilized man creates for himself out of a distant land but whose entire appeal would come from the fact that it could reactivate the memory of a prior life.[35]

In Bernardin de Saint Pierre's fiction, it is, in fact, in the inaugural moment of transmission of the tale by the old man, the protector and only survivor of the primitive family, to the voyager, the cosmopolite, that the latter expresses how intimate is the tie that links him to the simple inhabitants of the wild island:

> "Mon père," repris-je . . . "même le plus dépravé par les préjugés du monde aime à entendre parler du bonheur que donne la nature et la vertu."

> ["Father," I continued, "even the man who is most depraved by worldly prejudices likes to hear of the happiness provided by Nature and virtue"] (82).

But the interest of the jaded man-of-the-world in the story of the man of nature betrays not only a likeness but a sharing, a "being in common" in a group or in a certain kind of family that transcends individual specificity.[36] Trading tales, the narrator acknowledges his belonging, after a fashion, to the same community, that original community called the family of man.

It is according to this same protocol that Chateaubriand's voyager and narrator initiates the circulation of his exotic tale:

> C'est une singulière destinée, mon cher fils, que celle qui nous réunit. Je vois en toi l'homme civilisé qui s'est fait sauvage; tu vois en moi l'homme sauvage que le Grand Esprit, (j'ignore pour quel dessein) a voulu civiliser.

> [It is a strange fate, my dear son, which has brought us together. I see in you the civilized man who has become a savage; you see in me the savage whom the Great Spirit has (I know not for what purpose) chosen to civilize] (77).

This transmission of tales legitimized by the familial discourse allows the primitive story to interlock with the cosmopolitan tale. The personal, intimate history of the primitive becomes then the history of the universal. It is in the mode of the familial tale, the exchange from father to son, that the traveler, addressing the old man as a son would a father, renarrates the great story of man.

When the Exotic Becomes the Familiar: A Voyage into the "Uncanny"

The legitimizing of this familial/universal tale is not realized, in the two fictions under analysis, without a detour: the voyage to an exotic land. If it is the bewitchment of the other as Other that precipitates familial discourse, this discourse, as we have seen, can only be transmitted in the form of a voyage. It is to undertake the same kind of voyage that Freud, a century later, would invite us. This other man of science, also an expert in imaginary voyages and in family tales, initiates these new expeditions in one of his first essays on the difference between masculinity and femininity, *Some Psychological Consequences of the Anatomical Distinctions between the Sexes*. It is first a voyage in time since it concerns an analysis of the most remote periods of childhood but it is also a voyage in space, which, according to Freud, "leads us into dark regions where there are as yet no sign posts."[37]

The imaginary space of a new world, the dark continent of femininity, is also the site par excellence of the uncanny. On first thought, one might say that

Freud's approach parallels the one we just sketched above in the fictive journeys of Bernardin and Chateaubriand. The discovery of this uncannily familiar continent could only come about at the expense of a voyage that would seem by definition already finished. A nostalgic pursuit of an object, forever lost, which civilized man would undertake only because it has already been made, once and for all, in the long, immemorial night of infancy. In the beginning, then, at the origin, bliss, the attachment of the infant to its mother: the Eden of the primitive, animist universe, of the return to the original dwelling place. Then the event: the discovery of sexual difference, the separation.

Freud's *Das Unheimlich* begins, in fact, with the analysis, not of a tale, but of a *différend*, a semantic conflict.[38] The problem that initiates Freud's inquiry is that the meanings of the two terms "*heimlich*" and "*unheimlich*," seemingly contradictory, coexist in the aesthetic sense of *unheimlich*. The word *unheimlich* would refer at once to the familiar, to the intimate, to the inside as well as to the unfamiliar, the strange, the outside. But what is even more interesting perhaps, in view of my analysis, is that, as is immediately indicated by Freud and to some extent by the clumsy French paraphrase, "*inquiétante étrangeté*," in many languages the word designating this particular shade of the frightening does not exist."[39] Moreover, note that the particular characteristics of this aesthetic sense seem to express themselves most often not only in terms of paraphrases, but also in terms of place, *locus suspectus*, which summons description, a description of what cannot be said otherwise. But again this description would be defined, according to the science of dreams, in terms of "displacement." The problematics of the *unheimlich* covers, as we can see, those that I earlier defined as exotic. The analysis of exoticism as a subgenre of the *unheimlich*, uncovers, however, the secret relationship, in those revolutionary times, between exoticism and femininity: "The usage of speech has extended "das Heimlich" into its opposite "das Unheimlich": for this uncanny is in reality nothing new or foreign but something familiar and old established in the mind that has been estranged only by the process of repression."[40]

Exoticism would, in this way, amount to a history of repression. Now this repression of the *unheimlich*, the familiar and the intimate, is, in our texts, the repression or displacement of woman. Uncanny exoticism would, then, come down to coupling the oppositions of familiar/nonfamiliar, inside/outside and to collapsing them on each other. The feminine and the maternal family must be repressed by the masculine and the family of men. All the interest in the *unheimlich* obviously centers around the fact that this repression is ill-accomplished. Its proof is the experiencing of the uncanny. In *Paul et Virginie*, as in *Atala*, the repressed element of the intimate and the feminine returns in a violent and obsessional manner through the descriptions of that suspect extraterritoriality of a wild, virgin nature. I shall cite as an example just this rather poetic passage from the epilogue of *Atala*, wherein, following the spectacular burial of Atala, the voyager-depository of the tale, resuming his journey, encounters along the banks of the Mississippi a young mother. This young woman, put to flight by the white Virginian's decimation of her people, cannot "dry her son's body on the limbs of a tree," as Indian custom dictates (138). The narrator-voyager then joins these Indian exiles who set out "in search of a homeland." A long description of Niagara Falls, near which they make their camp, follows, a description evoking the sense of the uncanny, which can be read following the animate-inanimate paradigm I have already identified:

> Nous arrivâmes bientôt au bord de la cataracte qui s'annoncait par d'affreux mugissements. Elle est formée par la rivière du Niagara . . . c'est moins un fleuve qu'une mer dont les torrents se pressent à la bouche béante d'un gouffre. . . . La masse du fleuve qui se précipite au midi, s'arrondit en un vaste cylindre puis se déroule en nappe de neige, et brille au soleil de toutes les couleurs. . . . Avec un plaisir mêlé de terreur, je contemplais ce spectacle.
>
> [Soon we reached the edge of the cataract, whose mighty roar could be heard from afar. It is formed by the Niagara River, which emerges from Lake Ontario. . . . It is not so much a river as a sea whose torrents surge into the gaping mouth of a chasm. . . . The mass of water hurtling down in the south curves into a vast cylinder, then straightens into a snowy sheet, sparkling, irridescent in the sunlight. With a pleasure mixed with terror I contemplated this spectacle] (140).

Viewing the spectacle, the voyager asks the Indian woman: "What is this, my sister?" She answered: "Brother, it is the earth of our homeland. . . ."

The story of Atala and Chactas interlocks, at the end of the novel, with another story that, while similar, represents an entire people—a people driven from the colonized territory, a people repressed. This family tale of a western Oedipus has trouble assimilating, as it were, the "*différend*": the conflict between the colonized and the colonizer. A fact to which the sentiment of the uncanny gives witness. The sense of the feminine exotic, which creates the backdrop for these novels, gives similar witness to it. And yet the epilogue to *Atala* concludes upon the pacifying note of nostalgia, the nostalgia of a man born of men, for whom there now remains only the consolation of not having failed virtue: ". . . moins heureux dans mon exil, je n'ai point emporté les os de mes pères. . . . [Less fortunate than you in my exile, I have not brought with me the bones of my forefathers] (144). It is a masculine virtue, however, which is in complete contradiction with the passive virtue of the feminine heroine: Atala.

The Universal Tale of Feminine "Virtue"

The story of *Paul et Virginie* likewise turns upon a semantic conflict (a *différend de mot*): a conflict over the word "virtue." It is also symptomatically the luxurious description of the wild nature of "L'Ile de France" that brings this conflict in the foreground. This conflict on the two definitions of the word "virtue," which unexpectedly opposes the old man and Virginie, betrays in fact a larger conflict at work in the novel, the conflict between two theories of language. The transformation of the personal history of the children of nature into the universal story that the old man can transmit to the civilized voyager occurs in fact as a result of the repression of the language of the particular by the language of the universal. In the Eden provided by Mother Nature, naming is in the beginning (origin) idiodialectic. Each site takes the name of the familial memory with which it is associated:

> Rien n'était plus agréables que les noms donnés à la plupart des retraites . . . la découverte de l'amitié, la concorde, les pleurs essuyés, le repos de Virginie.

> [Nothing could be more agreeable than the names they had given to most of the charming retreats . . . 'Friendship's View . . . , 'Concord' . . . , 'Tears Wiped Away' . . . , 'Virginia's Rest.'] (p. 103).

This pleasant, natural language—the archaic language of space-naming—quickly becomes, however, the site of the universal handed down from man to man and from age to age through the expedient of humanist texts, fragments of which are carved by the old man on all the tree trunks: "Je gravais ce vers de Virgile sur l'écorce d'un tatamaque . . ." [On the bark of a tacamahac-tree . . . I carved this line from Virgil] (103).

The interlocking of the language of the particular to the language of the universal does not go unchallenged in the text. Virginie, in particular, rebels against this process of universalization:

> Mais Virginie n'approuvait point mon latin; elle disait que ce que j'avais mis au pied de sa girouette était trop long et trop savant. J'aurais mieux aimé, ajouta-t-elle: Toujours agitée mais constante . . .

> [But my Latin did not meet with Virginia's approval; she said that what I had written at the base of her weather-vane was too long and too learned, and she added: 'I would have preferred: Shaken always, but constant'] (103).

Taking her eyes from the cabin, she then looks into the distance at the restless sea at which Paul is looking at the same moment. Then, an imprudent remark to which the old man will put an end, "Cette devise, lui-répondis-je, conviendrait-mieux à la vertu. Ma réflexion la fit rougir." [A motto that would be even more fitting if applied to virtue, I replied. She blushed at this reflection] (103).

We have here a *différend*, a dispute, in point of view between Virginie and the man presented as the "citizen" of the world. A *différend* that can only be resolved, in the novel, through the death of one of the speakers: the woman's.[41] Only the death of Virginie will enable the erection of a universal language, that language in which each word has but one meaning; whence the importance of that final and spectacular ritual, the burials and feminine obsequies:

> Lorsqu'elle fut arrivée au lieu de la sépulture des négresses de Madagascar et des Cafres de Mozambique déposèrent autour d'elle des paniers de fruits . . . les indiennes du Bengale et de la côte Malabare apportèrent des cages d'oiseaux . . . tant la perte d'un objet aimable intéresse toutes les nations, et tant est grand le pouvoir de la vertu malhereuse, puisqu'elle réunit toutes les religions autour de son tombeau.

[When she had been carried to her burial-place, Negresses from Madagascar and Caffres from Mozambique placed baskets of fruit around her and draped pieces of cloth from the trees nearby, according to the custom of their countries; while Indian women from Bengal and the Malabar coast brought cages full of birds which they set free over her body. For the loss of one so deserving of love concerns every nation; and so great is the power of unhappy virtue that all religions are gathered together around its tomb] (162).

Through these funeral rites, the story of these humble two, Paul and Virginie, becomes a universal parable, a story men can recount to other men. But this passage to the universal, for want of a tribunal to decide the conflict, the *différend*, can finally be accomplished only through the alternate route of a homonymic resolution: exotic femininity becomes "exotic virginity" as if through the homonymic reflection of the word "virginity" in the word "virtue." Everything revolves around the homonymic apprehension of the root word *vir*—from the etymological sense of the Latin *vir, virtus*—as that which is credited to men only. In this sense the word virginity sums up the imaginary reinscription of the history of women as it can be understood from the point of view of the history of men.

The return of the woman to the entrails of Mother Nature parallels, in its ideological function, the sending back of the revolutionary women to the simple home of virtue by the Jacobins and later by Napoleon. In both cases, the burial of the woman's body, as well as the confinement of the virtuous woman to the home, result in an enclosure that is an expulsion from the polis. It is only this double exclusion that allows the old man, citizen of the world, to speak the universal language of citizenly virtue. In the end, as we can see, naming is a man's business, in opposition to the "local" language, muddled by Virginie's weather vane (the shiftings of the weather vane are the natural, iconic signs of the power of Nature's winds). The old man places a language that fixes and freezes once and for all: the ethical language of the universal, a language that, to the capricious voices of the winds, substitutes a voice of stone:

L'idée me vint de graver une inscription sur la tige de ce roseau. Quelque plaisir que j'ai eu dans mes voyages à voir une statue ou un monument de l'antiquité, j'en ai encore davantage à lire une inscription bien faite; il me semble alors qu'une voix humaine sortie de la pierre, se fasse entendre à travers les siècles, s'adressant à l'homme au milieu des deserts, lui dise qu'il n'est pas seul.

[I took a fancy to carve an inscription on the stem of this tall reed. In the course of my travels, I have seen many ancient statues and monuments, but whatever pleasure I experienced in looking at them does not compare with that of reading a well-conceived inscription. From this ancient stone a human voice seems to speak across the centuries, saying to man, in the midst of the deserts, that he is not alone] (102).

This language turns the animate (the moving) into the inanimate (but constant). This passage from the animate to the inanimate is initiated in the text through the expedient of a classical comparison between ancient and natural civilizations but ends in a curious amalgam wherein Nature, first described as preferable to ancient monuments, speaks as a statue of stone.

The mixture of the vocabulary of the architect and of the sculptor, and its incongruity with that of the naturalist, is a commonplace in romantic descriptions. In our analysis of "exotic femininity," however, it is legitimized by a double story: a story in which subversive young girls of the wilderness paralleling the subversive women of the revolution are transformed—as we have seen in the ruins of the Bastille—into the marble statues of Mother Nature.

Notes

All the quotes from the two novels are taken from the following: Jacques-Henri Bernardin de Saint Pierre, *Paul et Virginie* (Paris: Garnier Flammarion, 1966), trans. John Donovan, *Paul and Virginia* (London: Peter Owen Pub., 1982); René-Auguste de Chateaubriand, *Atala* (Paris: Garnier Flammarion, 1964), trans. Irving Putter, *Atala, René* (Berkeley: University of California Press, 1952/1973). They are cited parenthetically in the text by page references.

1. Cf. Jules Michelet, *Histoire de la Révolution* (Paris: Robert Laffont, 1979). For the historical information used in this analysis, I am especially indebted to Paule-Marie Duhet, *Les Femmes et la Révolution* (Paris: Julliard, 1971); L. Lacour, *Trois femmes de la Révolution* (Paris: Plon, 1900); A. Lasserre, *La Participation collective des femmes à la Révolution* (Paris, 1906); Maïté Albistur and Daniel Armogathe, *Histoire du Féminisme français* (Paris: Des femmes, 1977); Carol Blum, *Rousseau and the Republic of Virtue: The Language of Politics in the French Revolution* (Ithaca and London: Cornell University Press, 1986); Marie-Hélène Huet, *Rehearsing the Revolution* (Berkeley and Los Angeles: University of California Press, 1982); *Women in Revolutionary Paris: 1789-1795*, selected documents, trans. with notes and Commentary by Darline Gay Levy, Harriet Branson Applewhite, Mary Durham Johnson (Urbana and Chicago: University of Illinois Press, 1979); *French Women and the Age of the Enlightenment*, ed. Samia Spencer (Bloomington: Indiana University Press, 1984); and the recent book of Joan B. Landes, *Women and the Public Sphere in the Age of the French Revolution* (Ithaca and London: Cornell University Press, 1988).

2. Cf. Michelet, *Histoire de la Révolution*, 226; and Duhet, *Les Femmes et la Révolution*, 11.

3. Cf. the text of the 93 Constitution, which will be analyzed later in this chapter, in E. Laferrière, *Les Constitutions d'Europe et d'Amérique* (Paris: Cotillon, 1869); and Duhet, *Les Femmes et la Révolution*, 153.

4. Cf. the different interpretations of this type of festivities celebrating "woman as nature" in Mona Ozouf, *La Fête Révolutionnaire: 1789-1799* (Paris: Gailimard, 1976), 28–30; Blum, *Rousseau and the Republic of Virtue*, 209–12; and Sara Maza, in her article "The Rose-Girl of Salency" in *The French Revolution in Culture*, ed. Lynn Hunt, *Eighteenth Century Studies* 22, no. 3 (Spring 1989). Marie-Hélène Huet, in an article on the iconographic system of the revolutionary festival of the Supreme Being, analyzes what precisely, in the cultural unconscious of the period, will make the choice of the feminine image as allegory of Reason highly problematical. "Le Sacre du Printemps: Essai sur le sublime et la Terreur," *Modern Language Notes* 4, 1988.

5. Cf. Marina Warner, *Monuments and Maidens: The Allegory of the Female Form* (New York: Atheneum, 1985). In this comprehensive and ground-breaking study, in which Marina Warner examines "a recurrent motif in allegory, the female forms as an expression of desiderata and virtues," she shows how allegory possesses "a double intention to tell something which conveys one meaning but which also says something else" (xix). See also the study of Lynn Hunt, "The Political Psychology of Revolutionary Caricatures," in *French Caricature and the French Revolution, 1789–1799*, Grunwald Center for the Graphic Arts, University of California, Los Angeles, 1988. We will see how the motif of "exotic femininity" in the fictions *Paul et Virginie* and *Atala* conveys, in a very specific fashion, double meanings whose workings are very parallel.

6. Naomi Schor has uncovered the importance of the relation "woman, writing and stone" in her analysis of what she calls the "hieratic code" in nineteenth century realism, see "Smiles of the Sphinx: Zola" in *Breaking the Chain: Women, Theory and French Realism* (New York: Columbia University Press, 1985), 29–47. The theme of the woman/statue is also a recurrent theme in romantic literature, cf. my book, *Fictions Féminines: Mme. de Staël ou les voix de la sibylle* (Sarratoga: Anma Libri, 1987), 183–88, and the article "Voice as Fossil, Mme. de Staël's *Corinne, or Italy:* An Archeology of Feminine Discourse," *Tulsa Studies in Women's Literature* 6, no. 1 (Spring 1987).

7. For the definition of "virtue," in this political context, I am here indebted to the milestone analysis of Carol Blum. According to Carol Blum, it is precisely at this moment when we witness the consecration of the juridical equation—human/masculine/citizen—that the impact of Rousseau's republican ideas are most clearly shown to be operative in the political vocabulary and ethics of the revolution. The citizen thus defined would be but the copy of Jean-Jacques Rousseau, this "virtuous citizen," who dreamt of an ideal republic and spoke like a Plutarchan hero, Blum, *Rouseau and the Republic of Virtue*, 37–56.

8. Blum, ibid., 43–48; and Elizabeth Fox-Genovese, in her introduction to Spencer, *French Women and the Age of Enlightenment*, 5–6, has shown all the complexities of this reorganization of the social imaginary. The bourgeois revolution ended privileging the bourgeois model of womanhood at the expense of these other images of women that were emerging from the lower and higher layers of society (the working market woman of the faubourg for example or the enlightened woman of the salons). In her book, *Women and the Public Sphere*, Joan Landes gives an enlightening analysis of the various ways in which "the gendering of the public sphere" can be seen as a by-product of the passage from the society of French absolutism to bourgeois society.

9. Sigmund Freud, *The Interpretation of Dreams* (New York: Avon Books, 1965), 340–44. My analysis of the cultural imaginary of the French Revolution in the topos of the "feminine exotic" will make use, as will be evident later, of the cultural unconscious in a Freudian sense.

10. *Le Grand Larousse Encyclopédique*, vol. 4 (Paris: Larousse, 1960), 848.

11. Phillippe Hamon, *Introduction à l'analyse du descriptif* (Paris: Hachette, 1981), 6.

12. Paul Hazard, *La Crise de la Conscience Européenne: 1680–1715* (Paris: Fayard, 1961), 47–73.

13. See the analysis of the crisis of anthropological discourse in travel narratives and ethnological sciences in Francis Affergan, *Exotisme et Altérité* (Paris: P.U.F., 1987). For the problematic question of the linking and the articulation of historical discourse and ethnic discourse, I will use also the work of Jean-François Lyotard in "Notice, Déclaration de 1789" and "Notice Cashinahua" in his book *Le Différend* (Paris: Minuit, 1983), 209–13, 219–23.

14. Michel de Certeau, *L'Écriture de l'histoire* (Paris: Gallimard, 1975), 118.

15. Tzvetan Todorov, *La Conquête de l'Amérique et la découverte de l'autre* (Paris: Seuil, 1982). The parallel between the savage and the woman has also been analyzed by Josette Féral in "The Powers of Difference" in *The Future of Difference*, ed. Hester Einsenstein and Alice Jardine (Boston: G. K. Hall, 1980).

16. The word "revolution" here is taken in its astronomical sense of a turning around on axis. Jeffrey Mehlman has analyzed how this interpretation of the word could reveal some troubling aspects of the French Revolution in *Revolution, Repetition: Marx, Hugo, Balzac* (Berkeley: University of California Press, 1977).

17. Jules Michelet, as Paule-Marie Duhet reminds us, regrouped the portraits and the fragments of the *Histoire de la Révolution*, which dealt with women, in a separate volume, *Les Femmes de la Révolution* in 1854, Duhet, *Les Femmes et la Révolution*, 9.

18. To connect the writing of the law to the writing of fiction is doing something more than just placing esthetic texts in "context." In this analysis we will see that in a certain way the novel of exotic femininity functions as the cultural unconscious of the law.

19. *Le Code Civil: texte antérieur et version actuelle* (Paris: Flammarion, 1981). Whereas in the constitutions the women were only excluded by default, in the code women were assigned their place and role explicitly. According to articles 213 and 214 (1803) the wife not only "owes obedience" to her husband but is obliged to live and "follow him wherever he chooses to dwell." Lastly, since she is not recognized as having the capacity to sign a contract, she is denied any independent involvement in social and public life: her only world is the home.

20. My analysis of the romantic topos of exotic femininity takes shape, as is plain, against a horizon not only historical but also anthropological, taking into account the epistomological figures of the period. Literary investigation here becomes an archeological quest for a "site" or rather a scene in which is staged the mythical founding of a new order, the bourgeois order that would illustrate, in the aesthetic mode, the novels of exotic femininity.

21. As we have already mentioned this story has been long repressed and for too long presented under the mode of "secondary history," the *petite histoire* only worth figuring in the legendary mode of popular literature and iconography. Catherine Clément has shown how this repressed history usually haunts literature in her discussion of Michelet's writing "La Sorcière" in *La Jeune Née* (Paris: U.G.E., 1975).

22. P.-M. Duhet, *Les Femmes et la Révolution*, 152.

23. Cf. Laferrière, *Les Constitutions*, xxxiii (decree of June 24, 1793), and see Carol Blum's analysis of this decree, *Rousseau and the Republic of Virtue*, 210–11.

24. Laferriere, *Les Constitutions*, xxx.

25. Lyotard, *Le Différend*, 208–12. In her illuminating book, Joan Landes, in the chapter "The New Symbolic Politics," analyses from another perspective and in more detail, the political and sociocultural workings of this process, *Women and the Public Sphere*, 39–65.

26. Ibid., 83–86.

27. Charles Baudelaire, *Les Fleurs du Mal*, *Oeuvres Complètes* (Pléïade, Paris: 1961), 58.

28. François René de Chateaubriand, *Les Mémoires d'Outretombe* (Paris: Flammarion, 1948), Livre V.

29. Quoted by Duhet, *Les Femmes et la Révolution*, 219. See also Neil Hertz's article, "Medusa's Head: Male Hysteria under Political Pressure," *Representations* 4 (Fall 1983):27–54.

30. Christine Bucci-Glucksman, *La Raison baroque: De Baudelaire à Benjamin*

(Paris: Galilée, 1984). A section of part 2 of this book, "L'Utopie féminine" is translated as an article, "Catastrophic Utopia: The Feminine as Allegory of the Modern," in *Representations* 14 (Spring 1986).

31. Michel Foucault, *Les Mots et les Choses* (Paris: Gallimard, 1966), 136.

32. Luce Irigaray, *Ethique de la différence sexuelle* (Paris: Minuit, 1984), 97.

33. The largest part of the tale is set before the discovery of sexual difference: familial utopia corresponds to that pre-Oedipal phase characterized by Freud as an attachment of the mother. Cf. "The Uncanny" in *On Creativity and the Unconscious* (New York: Harper and Torch Book, 1958).

34. Lyotard, *Le Différend*, 218.

35. G. Chinard, *L'Exotisme américain dans la littérature française* (Paris: Hachette, 1911), 25.

36. Lyotard, *Le Différend*, 225.

37. Sigmund Freud, *Some Psychological Consequences on the Anatomical Distinctions between the Sexes*, in *Sexuality and the Psychology of Love* (New York: Macmillan Publishing Co., 1963), 183.

38. Freud, "The Uncanny," 127–29.

39. Freud, ibid., 124.

40. Freud, ibid., 149.

41. See J.-F. Lyotard, who shows how the conflict between the savage and the cosmopolitan, given their respective positioning in the discursive context of western culture, can never be resolved in favor of the "savage," *Le Différend*, p. 225.

11

The Engulfed Beloved:
Representations of Dead and Dying
Women in the Art and Literature
of the Revolutionary Era

MADELYN GUTWIRTH

No one could claim that evocations of dead or dying women were lacking in art and literature before the end of the eighteenth century. An ancient Greek genre of funerary epigrams spreads its imagery of brides perishing in the depths from antiquity to the ages beyond. An epitaph by Xenocritus of Rhodes reads,

> Your hair rushes still through the salty waters, oh/
> Lysidice, young maid perished at sea . . . /
> A bitter sorrow for your father, who, in leading you to your groom/
> has brought him neither a wife nor a corpse.
>
> Quoted in Chénier, 847

Or there is the doomed Ophelia, found in the "weeping Brooke," whose

> garments heavy with their drink/
> Pulled the poor wretch from her melodious lay/
> To muddy death./
>
> *Hamlet*, IV.vii

In France we have only to think of the grandiose death scene of Racine's guilt-ridden, incest-obsessed Phèdre, imbibing the magic potion devised by Medea, which darkens her sight forever, as the light of the world returns (*Phèdre*, V.vii). A fascination with female frailty certainly recurs in western art with some reliability over the centuries, remaining one of the stock of topoi available to it. But no glut of such foredoomed figures exists in modern times before the waning of the Age of Enlightenment and in the century that copes with this heritage. As we consider the era of Chardin, Watteau, Boucher, and Frago-nard, to cite only the most celebrated of the painters, we find no brooding preoccupation with female dismay, disease, and death. The literary works of the earlier half of the century, which often explore the tensions of female subordination with some intensity,[1] display a greater range of complexity in their portrayals of women. While Montesquieu's Roxane or Prévost's Manon

Lescaut do, of course, die, their struggles tend to center around selfhood or self-interest. No established fictional or artistic obsession with female weakness as yet asserts itself there.

It is the phenomenon of an increased concentration upon sacrificial female figures in the decades preceding and in the years following the revolution that I would like to explore here.

I will consider figures of sacrificial or sacrificed women, whether at bay, engulfed, dying, or dead interchangeably in my chapter, for I regard them as belonging to a single order of representation. The artistic phenomenon I broach here has previously been subsumed as a feature of the rise of Romanticism, or of gothicism. Such perspectives are perfectly viable, but they tend to leave out of explicit account the relationship between the gender discourse transmitted by art and that of society. This is the gulf I hope to bridge here, in a political reading for their gender implications of familiar texts. The evolution I intend to portray, which reaches from the 1760s to the start of the Napoleonic Empire, overflows the boundaries of political revolution, preceding and outlasting it. Its dynamics lie in the domain of eroticism and power, and they cannot be fully subordinated to the logics of social, political, or economic structures because they possess an illogic of their own. What I ask here is, did this evolution bear any relationship to the fate of women in the revolution? Could it, in its inherent violence, have been the sign of a more pervasive gender malaise, a factor that might even have contributed to the etiology of revolution?

The culture in question here, though it assumes a posture of universality, is essentially a male one. Though it incorporates into its fabric that pronounced female component of manners and dress that has sometimes led to the belief that women's influence was preponderant, that indeed this very era was "the reign of women," such a view does not sustain serious scrutiny. While women were invited to consume its products, the ethical and aesthetic systems of value of its works of art reflect a male consensus to which women were able to contribute only episodically, not fundamentally. Even the most eminent women in this era of superb salon figures, such as Mesdames du Deffand, Geoffrin, and Necker or Mlle. de Lespinasse, and accomplished novelists, like Mesdames de Graffigny and Riccoboni, saw themselves essentially as satellite figures to the dominant male literati. Indeed a sense of "foreignness," an extreme of alienation that even the most august women might experience within the ambience of this male-dominated culture, is expressed by Madame de Graffigny's *Lettres d'une Peruvienne*. Such a sense of alienness could only have been heightened by the restructuring of sexual passion by male artists that we witness in the rise of prestige of figurations of engulfed women.

I will focus here on this sole phenomenon: male art's fascination with sacrifice for love and/or family. In this chapter I will deliberately eschew historical nuance to dwell on the underlying mythical and psychological plane where fantasy constructs its own history. I take as a suggestive point of departure Klaus Theweleit's view that "in all European literature . . . desire, if it flows at all, flows in a certain sense *through women*. In some way or other, it always flows in relation to the image of women" (272). According to this insight, images of women may have power to reveal aspects of the history of gender that history itself shrouds from view. The desire Theweleit alludes to has been defined primarily by the male artists and authors who have been the chief shapers of experience. But as Freud has reminded us—a thing that few among us probably would be moved to deny—the *id* itself knows no gender. Nevertheless, in the absence of powerful rival articulations by women of their own experience of desire, conceptions of that free-floating charge like those proposed in the works of male artists I discuss below would be understood by women and by men alike as preconditions of a certain style of passion.

We step back momentarily to a longer perspective. The eighteenth century had witnessed so substantial a participation by women in the upper reaches of society that the Goncourt brothers were later to dub it "the century of women." From Montesquieu to Rousseau and beyond, men continued to raise the issue of women's influence as a problem to be resolved. As I've argued elsewhere,[2] a class of "social women" who lived their lives in a worldly sphere—as *salonnières* like Madame du Deffand or Madame Geoffrin, influential mistresses to powerful men like la Pompadour or la Du Barry, or simply as less clamorous actors on the social scene—had risen to prominence. The extent and effect of the influence that women actually wielded was, within this period, widely debated and either deplored or praised. In this vein, in Rousseau's *Nouvelle Héloïse* itself—that work which on the surface appears so slavishly to "worship" the female as a principle—Rousseau denounced the women of Paris. Of course he attacked them in the name of his own idea of "the feminine." Following in his wake, Restif de la Bretonne proclaimed, "It is a crime of infringement against humanity for Men to serve Women, except out of graciousness or protectiveness" (184). The sexual provocativeness of some of these insubordinate women inflamed the ire of the chevalier Feucher d'Artaize, who wrote in his 1786 *Reflections of a Young Man* that man was in fact defeating himself: in his "laughable submissiveness, his servile and self-serving compliments" to women, he was fostering the destruction of his natural right, "that devouring ardor instinctive in him to command. What a revolution!" he lamented (44).

One woman among those who tried to answer such diatribes, Madame de Coiçy, attempted to reply to the charge of female privilege by putting her own construction upon the case:

> They bruit it about that in France women enjoy all there is to be enjoyed; that they are given an excess of honor. France, they say, is the paradise of women: and yet there is no people among whom really and in point of fact, they are more unworthily scorned and mistreated, although they are superior to all the other women of Europe in their talents, their charms of nature, wit, and art. (74)

But her case could not hope to meet the level of an attack, a revealing one to be sure, like Feucher's: "the corruption of morals is caused by the sex that has most to gain by it, the sex hungriest for pleasure, the more emotional sex, the weaker sex" (1788, 13).

The ascension to social prominence of women took place in a period that was experiencing a dramatic rise in illegitimate births. It tolerated (not without guilt) massive abandonments of infants born outside marriage (of five such infants by Rousseau himself) to foundling homes or wet nurses under whose ministrations a large proportion of them died.[3] Prostitution, both cheap and expensive, was rife and on the increase.[4] Marriage in the lower classes was a laborious imperative and in the upper, largely dynastic and nominal. The concatenation of social factors has suggested to some that France was enduring serious tension around issues of natality and sexual morality,[5] and these are, of course, precisely areas that center on the relations between men and women. The apogee of the age of the libertine, of the *petit-maître*, makes its own contribution to the coming apart of the sense of the nation as a family of coherent classes with more or less stable family expectations. Women's new and as yet unintegrated social presence combined with an atmosphere of sexual predatoriness, which attracted many women as well as many men who wished to profit thereby. Together these factors came to represent an impending menace to the social fabric. This sense of menace generated, as we will see in Rousseau's novel, a moralistic backlash against both the idea of women's social power and their sexuality. For the masculinist faction, in time-honored fashion, women would 'take the rap' for human sexuality and the failure to live up to society's professed moral codes. Public reaction was then to produce a new ideology, a model of woman that was to resemble Rousseau's Julie in being selfless and sacrificial; yet unlike that *philosophe* in skirts, this new model was to be stripped of mind, of culture, of language. Akin to Julie as emblem of Nature, the new figuration would incorporate that heroine's sexually repressed aspect in her assumption of the role of medium between man and God, man and his destiny.[6]

Two eloquent pre-romantic seascapes by Joseph Vernet, both shown in the salon of 1765 and commented upon by Diderot, might serve as tokens of our theme. The *Grande Tempête* (Figure 11.1) depicts a rocky storm-washed shore, with a capsized vessel blown about by the sea and a wildly buffeted tree standing out scrawnily on its crag. On shore, a handful of survivors or rescuers, among whom we distinguish a seated woman expiring in the arms of two men. Her figure, the foundering ship, and the fragile tree bear all the burden of pathos in the work. We must think of them together, as stricken figures. Diderot remarked, "Look at this drowned woman who has just been drawn from the waters and try to prevent yourself from feeling the sorrow of her husband if you can" (*Salons*, 122). In the second Vernet book, *Shipwreck by Moonlight* (Figure 11.2), the sky is clearing. We are in the aftermath of a violent storm. Again we find the capsizing vessel bereft, and at center, a few men working in the debris of the ship's wreckage. At right, we find the human focal point in a concerned group; a man tries to support a visibly weakened white-clad female figure, as a circle of men looks on. The fireside at which they seek

Figure 11.1 Joseph Vernet, *La Grande Tempête*, Salon of 1765. *Source*: Bibliothèque Nationale, Paris.

to warm her, the tent, are, like the studied expert efforts of the men in both scenes, symbolic references to the culture men sustain in the face of nature's awesome depredations. But in both scenes, as the men struggle, the women succumb. As the "nature within culture," they alone fall easy prey to the wind and water to which they are connected as untamed powers. Woman's vulnerability has a sexual origin: it leads her to pregnancy and sometimes to death. In her study of medical tracts of this time, Jordanova writes that "women were the carriers and givers of life, and as a result, a pregnant woman was both the quintessence of life and an erotic object" (106). The affect around the female figures in these storm scenes distills masculine awe, anxiety, and ambivalence over the saving of the woman's life, or experiencing the pathos of seeing her die, a victim of nature's violent ravages from which the man, in his alliance with culture, has detached himself.

How do these factors operate within a domestic setting? Carol Duncan has written that Greuze's painting of the *Beloved Mother*, also from the 1765 Salon, emphatically affirms that motherhood is blissful ("Happy Mothers," 572) (Figure 11.3). Yet, as she has seen, the bliss of this mother, though not literally murderous, is a deeply debilitating or at the least highly equivocal state. Diderot accurately read the work: "The mother here has joy and tender-

Figure 11.2 Joseph Vernet, *Shipwreck by Moonlight*, Salon of 1765. *Source*: Bibliothèque Nationale, Paris.

ness painted upon her face along with some of the discomfort inseparable from the motion and weight of so many children upon her who overwhelm her, and whose violent caresses would end up distressing her were they to last" (*Salons*, 143). As if this were not enough to suggest an analogy with bodily assault akin to rape, Diderot stresses how, "It's that sensation approaching pain, mixing tenderness with joy, and her prone position suggesting lassitude, that half-open mouth," which provide him, a male observer,[7] with such keen pleasure. Greuze's work confronts us with a dramatic bourgeois scene, an example of this artist's departure from the predominating mythological or genre conventions. And within this milieu he sets a swarming mass of children's eyes, arms, hands, all importuning their young, yet overpowered mother. Confirming Jordanova, Duncan points out how often maternity was linked with sexual satisfaction in eighteenth century art ("Happy Mothers," 572). Here the mother's vulnerability creates the bond between sexuality and maternity. This is what warms the heart of the male viewer like Diderot. While Greuze's ideal mother is not dead, nor is she dying, she is engulfed by her procreativity. Hers is the portrayal that will become the political revolution's ideal for woman: the

Figure 11.3 Jean-Baptiste Greuze, *The Well-Beloved Mother*, Salon of 1765. *Source*: Laborde Collection, Madrid.

young mother of a large patriarchal family, seductive in her passive consent to motherhood. Greuze openly displays the *Schadenfreude* inherent in this model.

Duncan again provides the most cogent feminist reading of David's *Oath of the Horatii* ("Fallen Fathers") (Figure 11.4). The collapsed female figures seated on the right, including as she has pointed out the young boy who alone of that group is privy to the sight of the oath, form a group of helpless choral weepers, bringing their sighs and lamentations to enrich the emotions of the scene. The thrusting muscularity of male arms and legs is contrasted with the sinuous line of the downcast women. The gender schism here is complete. It could almost be seen, in fact has been seen[8] as a 1785 forecast of the Jacobins' gender policy, allocating to men the public—military, legislative, commercial, and intellectual—realms; to women, the realm of privacy, or the family. David's vision of Roman male heroism and female frailty are so little accidental that they are recapitulated in his *Brutus* of 1789, where the father muses in disarray over the sacrifice of his sons to the state, while the female figures, again ghettoized within their space, express open grief with the braided curves of their bodies and gestures, as the mother clasps her daughters, especially the pale and fainting corpselike one—an Ingresque figure—to her breast.

Despite the force of David's example, the yield of visual images of dead and dying women is small in the iconography of the revolution. This is because the

Figure 11.4 Jean-Louis David, *The Oath of the Horatii*, 1784. *Source*: The Louvre, Paris.

revolution turned massively to the use of the empowering female figure as allegory, as Lynn Hunt has theorized, to counter and discredit the potent and consecrated imagery of kingship. Gender struggle during the active years of revolution assumed a different dimension, as struggle actualized in the political arena.[9] Hunt notes two relevant points: first, that "the proliferation of the female allegory was made possible . . . by the exclusion of women from public affairs. Women could be representative of abstract qualities and collective dreams because women were not about to vote or govern ("Political Psychology," 39), and second, that as compared with the English, "French engravers were less free to express their fantasies of power" (36) during this period. Pressures upon these artists were such that they restricted themselves, in a form of self-censorship, to a ready repertoire of set allegories and symbols. Hunt has also claimed that a deliberate political decision appears to have been taken by the Jacobins in 1794 ("Engraving the Republic") to substitute the male figure of Hercules for the by then stock figures of *Liberté* or the Republic in a move against feminization of the national symbols. Visual evidence for the years 1789 to 1795 will therefore be elided here. Although these years are the eye of the hurricane of a long evolution, the revolution's use of allegory poses wholly different questions, too complex to be compassed in this chapter. Some impor-

Figure 11.5 Pierre-Narcisse Guérin, *The Return of Marcus Sextus*, 1799. *Source*: The Louvre, Paris.

tant literary examples of our theme, by Sade and André Chénier, will represent that era. (See below.)

In the period after 1795, with the Directoire, visual images of dead and dying return in force. Among a series of works apparently reflecting the guilt of returning aristocratic émigrés and the rising popularity of the Oedipus and related themes, we find Harriet's *Oedipus at Colonus*.[10] His Antigone is prostrate, an exhausted, dispirited comforter to her despairing and disabused parent: in him we find an apposite icon of postrevolutionary French manhood, baffled by fate. Guérin's *Return of Marcus Sextus* (Figure 11.5) of the same period explores a like scene of domestic tragedy awaiting the returning hero.

We discern a pattern:[11] the dispirited, dead, or dying female figure in these works, generally following the visual model of fainting lissomeness given by David, is always young, either maiden or young matron, but always in full sexual bloom. Projections of masculine fears and passions, these figures frequently lack individuation or characterization as images, are generalized, fluid, evanescent, even when depicted as full-bodied.

Three works, finally, all picturing a watery scene, round off this swift survey: Bonnemaison's rather Blake-like *Young Woman Surprised by Storm*

Figure 11.6 Chevalier Féréol de Bonnemaison, *Young Woman Surprised by Storm*, 1799. *Source*: Brooklyn Museum.

(Figure 11.6) of 1799 shows a figure more plainly Gothic in character, at bay before the storm's ravages, and rigidly clutching at herself as her flimsy gossamer draperies gracefully unfurl to the whipping of the winds: a very emblem of lostness; Gros's *Sapho* (1801) casting herself in lovelorn despair from the cliffs at Leucadia, an altogether ghostly apparition (Figure 11.7); and lastly, one of a number of postrevolutionary depictions of flood, this one by Danloux (1802), in which the father has been unable to preserve either his voluptuous young wife or his livid infant from death by drowning (Figure 11.8).

I would like to be able to argue that male artists' increased production of images of flood reflects a postrevolutionary sense of engulfment, of feeling overwhelmed by the political and natural fates, to which the female figure simply contributes her inevitable quotient of pathos as preordained victim, an allegorical projection and displacement of historically based male disarray onto the figure of the female. This logic proves inadequate, for a prerevolutionary work from 1779, Gamelin's *Flood* (Figure 11.9), also depicts a scene of deluge, with the dead beloved, not yet denuded as she will later become, her blond hair and clothing burdening her lifeless form, being dragged from the waters by strong, loving arms as the storm rages about her. So the revolution in

Figure 11.7 Baron Antoine-Jean Gros, *Sappho at Leucadia*, 1801. *Source*: Musée Baron-Gérard, Bayeux.

the depiction of women did not await the revolution: it decidedly preceded it. Could the two have had anything to do with each other?

Literature helps us make some otherwise obscure connections in this series of related visual constructs of woman. The heroine of his 1761 novel, Rousseau's powerfully emblematic Julie, who expires from a malady contracted after saving her son from drowning, is the ancestress, spiritually and in her physical fate of these doomed figures of fantasy (Figure 11.10).

The Julie who has briefly but fatally succumbed, in defiance of her father's wishes, to her passion for her tutor Saint-Preux, has spent her remaining life in a full filial obedience so great that it resembles contrition. Married to Wolmar, the older man her tyrannical father had chosen, having borne children, she has created about her an ordered circle of intimates that includes her former lover. At the moment of her death, though still in her twenties, she is no waif, but a rather imperious woman whose monitory remarks from her deathbed go on for many pages. She looks upon her accident, which decisively prevents her from falling sway once more to her enduring passion for Saint-Preux, as a happy one, upon death as a boon. Her death speech announces that her passage from life is a sublimation for her survivors, as she affirms her will to "rectification,"

Figure 11.8 Henri-Pierre Danloux, *The Flood*, 1801. *Source*: Musée Municipal, Saint-Germain-en-Laye.

to the beautification of her life as a story. "My return to God settles my soul and calms me in a painful moment. . . . Happy I was, and am still, and happy I will be . . . (*Nouvelle Héloïse*, 714–15). Although she will be massively mourned, we are invited to regard Julie's death as an ethical as well as an aesthetic good. Her children having passed beyond infancy, they are at an age when they will be removed from her authority so as to continue their education as men. Julie herself avers that her continued life would be useless to her, for having known all the bliss of passion and of domesticity she was capable of feeling, how could she find further profit from staying alive? The way she expresses this reinforces the notion that female life is disposable after sexual and reproductive use. "When once one has obtained everything, one can only lose, even if it is only that the pleasure of possession weakens with use" (714).

Two powerfully emotion-laden scenes of the novel are crucial to our theme. Saint-Preux's account of the storm on the lake in which the little company is capsized during an otherwise peaceful excursion, develops the association of passion with engulfment. "Any moment, I thought I would see the boat capsized, this touching beauty struggling amidst the waves, and the paleness of death drawing the roses from her cheeks" (499). The beloved, principle of light and purity though she is given us as being, has a killing affinity with the

Figure 11.9 Jacques Gamelin, *The Flood*, 1779. *Source*: L'Eglise Saint-Vincent, Carcassonne.

swirling waters.[12] Tormented by the impulse to redeclare his passion for her, Saint-Preux, in a mimesis of sexual desire, writes of his violent longing to throw her into the waters so as to "end his long torment in her arms" (504); but as he realizes that her own passion for him is passing through a similar trial, both become subdued. A mutual awareness of sexual passion becalms the lovers, stills their desire.

Tanner has also stressed another premonitory scene of disaster in Rousseau's fiction, that of the dream of the veil. Saint-Preux dreams of Julie's mother on her deathbed, Julie weeping disconsolately beside her. The mother turning toward Julie, says, "You will be a mother in your turn," and disappears. Saint-Preux dreams on. "In her stead I saw Julie . . . ; I recognized her although her face was covered with a veil. I gave a shriek and rushed to put the veil aside; I could not reach it. I stretched out my arms and tormented myself, but I touched nothing.

Figure 11.10 Jean-Baptiste Regnault, *The Flood*, 1789. *Source*: The Louvre, Paris.

"'My friend, be calm,' she said to me in a low voice. 'The terrible veil covers me. No hand can set it aside'" (603).

Maternity casts its fell veil over desire. Putting these two scenes side by side, we may distinguish what Tanner has referred to as "the problematical relationship (or opposition) between the dissolving liquefactions of passion and the binding structurations of marriage" (172). These are, at the core, the terms of the conflict we witness in all our other exempla of engulfed women: they play out the lover's unwillingness to confront the female object of desire at those moments when she ceases to be one, and his insistence upon her watery mutability and mortality in evasion of an awareness of her essential unsinkability.

Tanner in fact notices what he terms "a perverse element" in Saint Preux's failure, as he watches her floundering in the lake, to think of saving Julie. The drowning scene, as well as Julie's eventual death by water, convey the ambiguity of engulfment by passion. Praised by all for her goodness and purity, the beloved, by her consent to her demise—clearly a species of sacrifice—takes upon herself the task of disculpating sexuality itself of guilt or consequences. By washing them away, cleansing them in the waves, she will allow the hero's passion—for herself remembered, or for another—to be reborn after her death.

Rousseau's image of that fateful veil of motherhood comes as an antithesis to the passionate freedom of the open waters of desire. The dream condemns woman, Julie, to extinction for her indelible association with giving birth, in consecration of an ancient pattern of male anxiety.[13] In Rousseau's novel, both their conceded aptitude for passion and their biological maternity predestine women for early mortality. Drawing men, through passion, into a domesticity that spells passion's end, the persons of women are in Rousseau a site of conflict redeemable only through sentimentality. The goodness of Julie, her crown, has a leaden weight.

Julie, of all people, becomes the spokesperson for male sensuality as she tries to convince Saint-Preux to marry: "Man was not made for celibacy, and it is quite unlikely that a state so contrary to nature should not bring with it some disorder, whether public or concealed. How then to escape the enemy we carry always with us?" (656). This framing of male desire as a fractious enemy within fits the picture of the novel as a whole, in which passion, infinitely alluring, has absolutely to be transcended, for it splinters the vision of what the hero longs for even more than union: freedom from conflict, freedom for the free-ranging, desiring male subject.

For we see that despite verbalizations of fealty to domestic order, the orderliness of Clarens, the Wolmar's estate, arises far less from its dubious marital bliss than from a dream of an agricultural community that acts as a cornucopia to an intimate society of friends, among whom dangerous passionate impulses "safely" pass to and fro. This underlying layer of the work is far more consonant with Rousseau's professed views than with his fictional structures. We see these views openly displayed in the scolding he administers women in a footnote, in which he chides them for wishing to make men aspire to fidelity; that is, for him, fixity: "You are certainly mad, you women, to want to give consistency to so frivolous and fleeting a feeling as love. Everything in nature changes, everything is in continual flux, and you want to inspire constant passion! By what right do you claim to be loved today because you were yesterday! Keep the same face, the same age, the same temper, be always the same, and then you'll be loved if possible. But to change ceaselessly and wish still to be loved is to want at every moment to cease being loved; it's not to seek a constant heart, but a heart as changeable as you are yourself" (403).

This overt statement interfaces with the novel to imply that what is at stake in the symbolic image and fate of Julie is a restructuring of male passion and that of its female object that, while casting the beloved as a fount of good and—at least here—allowing her her own capacity for passion, nonetheless kills her off in her youth so that she may never grow beyond her ability to inspire it. In this system, male passion is less expressed in the male self than in his female *other* who plays out the ravages of his self-doubts, guilts, and loyalties. The representations of the engulfed beloved mirror men's desire. Yet they convey an idea of "woman" to women also, nonetheless and inevitably. Such a vision excludes maturity or power from female self-representation, no less than from male representation: reproving women's self-assertion, it tends to encamp them in self-concepts of juvenility and pathos.[14]

Nancy Miller has alluded to the eighteenth century novel's obsession with threatened female innocence and speculates, I believe accurately, that it may be a "working out of an unsaid male ambivalence on the part of male writers toward the very existence of female desire, and an unsayable anxiety over its power" (134). Rousseau very nearly exposes the core of a related hostile male response to the lack of innocence in women in Saint-Preux's remarks on the manners of city-bred women. Interestingly, he ties their verbal freedom to their sexual predatoriness: both repel him. Woman's sociability is itself a threat to confident, unstressful male dominance.

As Saint-Preux writes to Julie, in comparing the *Parisiennes* unfavorably with herself, "that charming modesty that so distinguishes, honors and embellishes your sex, seemed to them rough and loutish . . . no decent man would not lower his eyes before their self-assured glances. In this way they cease to be women; out of the dread of being identified with other women, they prefer their rank to their sex and imitate prostitutes so as not to be imitated" (245). Their speech he finds even more revolting. "It's even worse when they open their mouths. What comes out of them is nothing like the sweet and coaxing voices of you Vaudois women; it's a sort of harsh, bitter, interrogative, imperious, mocking tone, stronger than a man's" (246).

This text richly sets out Rousseau's own reaction, which he apparently assumed would be widely shared—and was certainly not widely contested—to the assumption of power in a mixed society by the women of the upper classes and their inevitable imitators as influence brokers and as vocal members of society with unrepressed eyes. That mixed society itself is a deliberate target of Rousseau's, as he strongly advocates precisely the social separation of the sexes and the concentration of their activities into the separate spheres the revolution eventually enacted. Beneath the overtly misogynous polemic, we perceive Saint-Preux's malaise in approaching such verbal and assertive women as the *Parisiennes* as objects of desire. Too characterized, too distinct, too critical, they are too much at ease in public; so much so that he characterizes them as public women. For Rousseau such women obstruct his creation of fantasy based upon his construction of their gender, thereby blasting his persistent longing for effortless fusion.[15]

One might propose that the moralized art of the revolutionary era, in its images of dead and dying women, reflects a sort of cleaned-up version of rococo eroticism, where unformed heroines in the flower of youth die amidst settings of storm or flood instead of inviting swift moments of sexual congress on clouds and in wooded bowers. What distinguishes the new mode, however, is that it prefers sublimation to embraces. As Tanner remarks of Saint-Preux, his onanism is the mark of his impotence (122). We are moving toward that *mal du siècle* that afflicts the Werthers and Renés with their loss of moral and sexual nerve. The French novel that most spectacularly exhibits that loss of nerve while pitting the older, cynical gender dispensation against the new sentimental one, is Laclos's *Liaisons dangereuses* (1782).[16]

For the worthless allegiance of the libertine Valmont a titanic struggle is waged between the wicked, manipulative, controlling, self-conscious Marquise de Merteuil and the good, dutiful, artless, manipulable Madame de Tourvel. The potent power of verbal seduction as art, as deployed in the letters of this work, reveal it as a locus of pent-up passions. Laclos is quite explicit: the Marquise has ironized and internalized the male libertine's code. In her famous Letter #81, she tells us how experience has taught her to despise spontaneity, which makes so easy a mark of so many women: her law is that of a secret mastery over circumstances, a secret necessarily, since her relentless code, even for her corrosive set, is an unseemly one for a woman. Although devoid of all sense of solidarity with women, Merteuil yet views herself as a female avenger of male tyranny. Emblematic of the woman of society (Seylaz, 89), the Marquise as phantasm reflects the terror of women as sexual predators, manipulators of men's desire. Although the novel reveals an identical mechanistic manipulativeness in Valmont, for readers of eighteenth century novels hardened to male seduction, his shock value is simply not comparable to our amazement at Merteuil.

The contrast between the two women is what makes the novel take on the aspect of a war: but the war is not really between them; rather it is a contest to see which model of woman will form a couple with the man. Madame Riccoboni and her friends saw the work as a war against their kind, the women of society. A popular novelist, Ricconi wrote Laclos protesting at the way he had made the Marquise use her cultivated arts to serve evil ends. She also assailed him for his lack of patriotism in what she saw as his slandering of French woman by his creation of Merteuil, a personage, she claimed, resembling no one she herself had ever, in her long experience, met up with (Laclos, *O. c.* 713). Laclos was immovable. While admitting there were *few* Merteuils, he insisted there were some (714–15). The reality quotient scarcely mattered. His novelistic character would remain as a cautionary figure to women of the fate of the ruthless cultured woman. Placed on the scale with the sacrificed, unworldly "natural" woman Tourvel, her arts cannot save her from flying off into oblivion, being shunned by society, exiled to Holland, and marked by the pox of her diseased spirit. She does not even have the grace to die.

Within its terrified rejection of the woman of power as the culprit for the sexual/social system, the *Liaisons dangereuses* exhibits its disarray, still mixed with male complacency, before cynical sexual plunder. Exhaustion with heartlessness finds expression in the meek, gentle figure of the innocent Tourvel, whose very name suggests the tender turtledove. The greater the pain in the surrender of the beloved, the greater the joy of the lover's conquest. Forced to feel, he thinks he loves. In arms like Tourvel's, a man might find—himself.

Sade's heroes too exhibit what Michel Camus has termed their "monosexuality" (267) in their obliteration of the object. But whereas Rousseau had sought to repress women's "culturedness" as he celebrated their bonds with nature, what Sade longs to destroy in them above all is precisely their putative "naturalness," their maternity, that very state wherein the age's dominant consensus decreed their redemptive potential must lie.[17] Jean Ehrard has written that in the late eighteenth century the concept of Nature eclipses even that of Divinity and moves from being a mere order to becoming a full-fledged power (in Camus, 273). Insofar as that sacred power was represented by the female figure—certainly it was so for the revolution until 1794—it would nonetheless end up by being felt to be "out of order" in its threat to patriarchal preeminence. The remedy Sade proposes to this trend toward celebration of the feminine lies in a system of female self-abasement exemplified in his cartoon character Justine's demands upon others to punish and debase her relentlessly. As her final speech argues, she has always been magically *in order*, submissive and ready to die: "this unhappy creature who had imbibed only snake's venom, whose unsteady feet have trod only upon nettles . . . ; whom cruel reverses have robbed of family, friends, fortune, protection and help . . . ; such a one, I say, sees death come without fear; she even welcomes it as a secure port where tranquillity may be reborn for her in the bosom of a God too good to allow innocence vilified on earth not to find a reward in the other world for having suffered so many evils" (143–44). Sexual use by her tormentors simply confirms Justine's status as *the* sacred object of nature, therefore demanding defilement. Her fantasized ironic acquiescence to her fate, even to her death, confirms the mythic locus of power as resting with those torturers. But Sade does not refuse himself, in this work, a "sentimental" resolution in which Justine does not actually die. (Since she is not *really* sacred, her sacrifice would be pointless.) The revolution is under way as this work, whose tongue-in-cheek contradictions are reworkings of the underlying sexual code, is being written.

Bernardin de Saint-Pierre's *Paul et Virginie* (1788) constitutes a sort of exact inversion of Sade's *Justine* in its gender politics: paradoxically, chastity no less than sexual use or abuse destroys young women. Its mythical and allegorical vagueness is what lent the work its unbelievable (to latter times) success: for it met with an absolute frenzy of enthusiasm in the prerevolutionary public, apparently responding to an ever more potent need for moral renewal, a renewal that would take the emblematic form of investment in the sacrifice of her life by a young and untried woman. No stereotype of female goodness has been left out of her composition. Bernardin's Virginie feeds the birds; like Cunégonde and the children of the old man at the end of *Candide* who make sherbets and sweets, she prepares cakes for the poor. With her *frère de lait* Paul, she listens avidly as her mother reads the Gospels. The shorthand depiction of Paul makes him frank, open, cordial: his soul-sister's nature is confiding, "tenderly caressing" (252). Consenting to leave their little matriarchal family's idyllic but primitive existence in Ile-de-France only so as to redress its fortunes, Virginie voyages to wicked France. Ignorant and trusting, she will be cruelly deceived by the rapacity and heartlessness of her great-aunt: she rejects the loveless match proposed for her, is disinherited, and summarily placed aboard a ship back to her island home during the hurricane season. The grandiose and/or ludicrous apogee of her life is her apotheosis as she dies in the stormy seas. Refusing to remove her clothing to plunge into the waters and be saved, she raises her serene eyes on high "like an angel who takes flight heavenward" (345).

As the phenomenal popularity of the work confirms, the description of Virginie as she prepares to leave her Caribbean home incorporates into her moral and physical attributes the topos of the young woman as chaste ideal of this time. "She was dressed in white muslin over pink taffeta. Her tall, lithe figure was perfectly visible beneath her stays, and her blond hair, braided in a double tress, admirably adorned her head. Her beautiful eyes were filled with melancholy; and her heart, agitated by contained passions, gave her complexion an animated flush and her voice an emotional pitch. The very contrast with her elegant adornments, which she seemed to be wearing in spite of herself, made her languor the more touching. No one could see or hear her and remain unmoved" (285–86). Virginity and goodness, yes: but under siege by nascent passion from within and without. Obsessed by the imperative of making of herself a gift—to the birds as to the poor—she offers the paradigm of the young woman as consumable object, in her unconscious narcissism and sensuality offering herself, while yet withholding appetite, her own or others,—at some remove; inviting desire, but only on pain, as we discover, of that death by drowning which finally allows the sensual languor of the girl's body to untense itself and release the hold of chastity's imperative.

Martyrdom is crowned in this heightened version of the paradox of female chastity by the propagandistic sanctification of Virginie that follows: "Mothers asked God for a daughter like her; young men for a mistress as constant; the poor for a friend as tender; slaves for a mistress so good" (352). The text drives home the prescriptive quality of her example for her sex as the poor young girls she had helped have to be restrained from throwing themselves en masse upon the coffin of "their sole benefactress" (353).

A compact prurience in Bernadin's prose couples budding sexuality with the pains of ignorance: his attribution to Virginie's person, in his description, of the sexual power that flows toward her, makes her an ambiguous victim: and indeed, Sade apart, in none of these literary works is the beloved less powerful than her lover, since the charge of passion is seen to be emitted by her. But in fact, such felt power is precisely what appears to be in need of control—by works of art that enact its nullification, making both men and women sense the futility of women's powers and, conversely, the utility of a model of female powerlessness to making the sexes feel a mutual attraction to each other. Sweet and innocent, the young woman struggling against the flood wrests love from the reader. The consequent acceptance of pity as the precondition for sexual passion implies the internalization, the ratification by men of a pattern of regarding women, as Rousseau had preferred to, as weak objects, hence sexually approachable; it implies for women an acceptance of themselves as needing to repress all appearance of strength so as to appear pitiable, hence desirable, approachable. This posture would then become an imprisoning precondition of their own sexual and social responses.

No author was more obsessed with the figure of the engulfed beloved than the greatest poet of the revolution, the one deriving his inspiration most directly from Greco-Roman antiquity, André Chénier. Guillotined as a moderate by the Terror in 1794 at the age of thirty-two, Chénier wrote a quantity of his finely wrought neoclassical verse in prison at Saint-Lazare where he spent the months before his execution. A remarkable medium for the taste of time, two of his poems bring him especially within our purview. Both *La Jeune Tarentine* and *La Jeune Captive*, works tirelessly anthologized, are celebrations of a young beauty facing death. *The Young Tarentine* met with immediate and eager readerly acceptance. It describes a young bride in all the splendor of her nuptial adornments as she sets out by boat to join her lover. But alone in the prow of the ship, the "impetuous wind" catches up her veils and she falls into the waves and dies. The goddess Thetis protects her body from the monsters and the Nereids carry her to the shore. The young poet's voice laments, Alas! she was never to return to her lover; never to wear her bridal dress. The mourning for her untapped sensuality can be heard as the poet alludes to the "gentle perfumes [that] never flowed through your hair" (11–12). Chénier recaptures the poetic lament for the dead bride from antiquity and hands it on to Romanticism. A recurrent theme with a resilient life, it spoke again to the revolutionary generation. The poet's other enormously anthologized work, a song of praise to an imprisoned young woman, *The Young Captive*, is a modern poem rather than a neoclassical one, which owed much of its popularity to the pathos of the Terror. Significantly, its main stanzas are spoken by the young woman herself, who compares her person to an ear of corn ripening in the summer sun, trusting not to be cut down before her time. Despite the pains of the present day, she clings to the beauty of existence, asking that she not die. "I am only in the springtime, I want to see the harvest," she tells death, pleading that it wait and let her live out her love.

The *Young Tarentine* simply evokes with the greatest economy the figure of the dead bride, clothing it in none of the overlay of moralism or sentimentality that shrouds Bernardin's Virginie. No moral burden of goodness is imposed upon her: simply, she is doomed before she can know life to the full. But her figure retains and reinforces the familiar aura of that girl most beloved of men, since so much sublime male poetry is devoted to her, who has never reached the nuptial bed, whom male desire has reached out for, but never touched. As to the *Young Captive*, unlike Rousseau's Julie who, though allowed to speak, makes deathbed reflections full of self-denial, Chénier not only has her speak her own lines, but defend her right to live (185–86). And she is not made, in the poem, actually to die. Unlike Julie or Virginie, she is not constrained by the poet to accept death as an epiphany. All the epiphanies of this poem are in its life lines.

The *Young Captive* is the single significant work of art on the theme of the dying woman that, albeit in the ambiguous tones of the popular pathos, gives expression to the revolution's own moment of aspiration for women from 1789 to 1793 by letting the captive speak as her own advocate. This moment is the one historically recorded in women's *cahiers de doléance* and in their political and street activities.[18] We ought not be surprised that it should have come from the pen of a Feuillant and a constitutionalist, for whom a speaking woman claiming her right to life was not an outrage.

Chénier's heroines have been read retrospectively as allegorically loaded emblems of the abortive French Republic, without history or roots or future. Such a political reading is plausible enough; but it remains significant, on the most overt level, that such expressions of dismay should be expressed so often by male artists via the alterity of woman, and specifically through her death before her sexuality and her maturity have flowered. When we read these works solely as allegory, we neatly efface from consciousness their brute force as gender constructs, as ideological prescripts.

Restif de la Bretonne's work lies in a journalistic gray area between gossip and the imaginary. In 1797 he published among his *Nuits de Paris* a curious account of an incident—whether actual or apocryphal we are always in doubt with Restif, so we may think of it as a construction. "At Fontenay-le-Peuple," it begins, "there was a watchmaker named Filon, who had a very beautiful wife. Two emigrés returning from England had seen her and their greatest desire was to possess her." They went to Filon's house and found her there with her husband. "Her beauty, her gentleness disarmed them; that is, they could not do violence to her before her husband as they had planned to do" (273). So they tell her her life is in danger and they've come to take her off to a safe place to protect her. But once she's in their house, they violate her, after tossing a coin to see who would begin. "They satiated themselves at length. After which, remembering how much they had desired her and how pretty she was, they were about to kill her out of a kind of jealousy when another thought came to them; it was to degrade her so that they might feel no regrets over her." So they proceed to have her raped by their valets as they watch, and then by their coachmen. They then take her home, dying; but she doesn't die. After taking leave of her senses for two months, hiding herself under beds and in the cellar, and trying to jump into a well, she is cured by being sent to a quiet place. Restif ends his story, "You can see her still, in Paris."

In this unsublimated account of male desire, class resentment is overwhelming: the returning *aristos*, thinking that everything belongs to them, have appropriated whatever falls beneath their gaze that promises to gratify their senses. They enact the ruthless sexual violence associated with the ancien régime. Yet even though Restif may tell this story to cast opprobrium on the aristocracy, certain elements of our pathetic fictional sexual fable that transcend class considerations are curiously recapitulated here: the legendary beauty, the actual goodness of the unnamed woman provoke the men's imperious desire to defile them, in Sadean fashion; with satiety comes this moment of "jealousy": She cannot be allowed to survive their desire, to be desired by others of their class, by men of lower class, or even by themselves. Is this "jealousy"? Or is it revulsion against their own desire that they turn against the one who has evoked it? In a sense, Restif's fable strips bare the mechanism of this reduction of the woman to her moment as an object of use that we find sublimated in the poeticized dying beloved. Here, for her attackers, being used (passed around), and by men of all classes, is equated with being used up. Once passion is spent, she is ready for consignment to the trash heap. Consignment to the watery deep is not so different from this fate. But in this version, though scarred, she survives. The reader is reassured by this ending, implying that rape, though dramatic, is but transitory. Male passion may be vicious at times, it suggests, but not lethal.

Transposed anew to the poetic level, we find the issue of woman as a figment of male fantasy explored by the conservative Chateaubriand in his 1801 tale, *Atala*, intended to take its place in his magnum opus, *Le Génie du Christianisme*, but so popular after its first printing that it was republished five times in that same year. Already in 1791 as he set out on his six-month voyage in America, as Chateaubriand would later tell us in his *Mémoires d'outre tombe*, the heroine of his novel dominated him. "Having attached myself to no woman, my Sylph still obsessed my imagination. I made it my happiness to traverse with her the forests of the New World" (Garnier, xxvi).

A verse makes waggish summary of Atala's fate.

> Ci-gît la chrétienne Atala
> Qui, pour garder son pucelage,
> Très moralement préféra
> Le suicide au mariage

Or roughly,

> Here Atala the Christian lies
> Who chose a virgin to remain
> And chastely gave herself to pain
> Of death instead of marriage ties.

Chactas, now a blind old Natchez Indian, recounts her tale to the young French traveler René. In his youth, Chactas had come under the protection of a Spaniard, Lopez, who had educated him as a son and a European. Nostalgic for his native forests, Chactas leaves him to return to his people: but he finds that his tribe has been defeated by the Muscogulges (or Creek) tribe, who, taking Chactas prisoner, sentence him to death. Atala, a Christian and daughter of the enemy tribe's chieftain, pities the captive. They fall in love, she liberates him, and they flee by night. Yet Atala, though deeply enamored of Chactas, refuses to let herself love. At the height of a storm, she confesses to her lover that she is Lopez's daughter; she and Chactas, finding themselves children of the same father, are then overpowered by passion, and she is close to succumbing to her desire—for it is *hers* that is dwelt upon—when a missionary, Père Aubry, discovers them and offers them shelter in his grotto. Aubry makes Chactas visit his mission so as to display to him the virtuous orderliness of the savages who have converted to Christianity. But when the two return to the grotto, they find Atala dying: sworn by her devout but ignorant mother to a life of virginity and feeling herself, in her passion for Chactas, helplessly about to betray this vow, she has chosen suicide, not realizing that such a course is a sinful one for Christians or that a bishop might have delivered her from her parent's ill-considered pledge. She agonizes through the night, dies, and is buried at dawn by the sage and her lover, as shown in Girodet's celebrated painting from the Salon of 1808 (Figure 11.11).

As Julie dominates Saint-Preux by her personality and character, even as Virginie does Paul, so does Atala outshine Chactas. Her courage saves him from death, her determination carries them safely through the forests. Her very

Figure 11.11 Anne-Louis Girodet-Trioson, *The Funeral of Atala*, 1808. *Source*: The Louvre, Paris.

conflict over her passion makes her more substantial than her passive lover. Despite this manifest vitality, Chactas reflects to René about the cloud that cast its shadow over even the lovers' very first kiss: "Alas, dear son, sorrow follows closely upon pleasure" (Delmas, 47). This lugubrious mood of *Liebestod* is sustained as Atala and Chactas visit the tomb of a child whose grieving mother addresses her dead little one: "Happy are those who die in the cradle! For they have known only the kisses and smiles of their mother" (Delmas, 49).

Yet Chateaubriand's emotionally effusive funeral dirge can also sound a note, in the context of tribal war and nationalism, of open contempt for women. Chactas taunts his Muscogulge captors: "I do not fear your torments. . . . I defy you; I scorn you more than women" (Delmas, 54). In this way, Chateaubriand's text, an emanation of the Napoleonic era, declares openly what other sentimental fiction had striven to repress or at least not to betray: a singular male ambivalence toward even the beloved, devoted, and sacrificial, but impassioned, woman. Atala is torn, palpitates with desire; but her lability of sentiment is a decidedly mitigated good:[19] "Atala's perpetual conflict between love and her religion, the abandon of her love and the chastity of her habits, the pride of her character and her deep sensibility . . . everything together made her an incomprehensible being for me. Atala could not have a feeble power over a man: full of passion, she was full of power; one could only adore or detest her" (Delmas, 59). We note Chateaubriand's candor: Atala's active desire is what dooms her. Such a woman is better adored dead.

In his retrospective dismay at having lost her, Chactas describes what might have been his fate and gives us a clue as to why their love was ill-fated: "A mud-hut with Atala would have brought me such happiness; there all my races would have been run; there with a wife, unknown to men, hiding my joy deep in the forests, I would have passed on my way as do the rivers that, in the wilderness, have no name" (Delmas, 74). In this telling version of married felicity, union with Atala is equated with subordination to her desire. Chactas's personhood would be lost to him: no more struggle, no experience except the quotidian, no name. This vision of man reclaimed by nature dissipates precisely what revolution and romanticism promised men: freedom of the imagination guaranteed by a sense of their power as individuals. Here consent to a woman's passion is the emblem of its dispersion and loss.

Atala's incipient flaw of having imposed the heat of her desire upon her lover is punished in the much admired *delectatio morosa* of her funeral scene. Every single element in it bespeaks chastisement, from the partly unclad bosom and the faded magnolia—the flower that Chactas had cast upon her bed to make her fruitful—to her ebony crucifix. The "celestial" vision is one of sleeping virginity (Delmas, 91). "The morbid sensuality with which Chateaubriand portrays the cadaver of his heroine shows what pleasure he finds in imagining the beloved woman dead," writes Lehtonen, one of his critics (95).

That this morbid obsession is not Chateaubriand's alone must now be clear. Denis de Rougemont, who has written somewhat disaffectedly about the nexus of love and death in literature, opines that on the individual level "the passion of love is at bottom narcissism, the lover's self-magnification, far more than it is a relation with the beloved" (270). One would have to argue, in the light of our survey, rather that passion has some need, fortunately not always exercised, to obliterate the object. De Rougemont stresses the notion that male sexuality in western culture tends to reassert itself according to the old formulations of redemption: "the more passionate a man is, the more likely he is to revert to tropes of the rhetoric, to rediscover their *necessity*, and to shape himself spontaneously according to the notion of the 'sublime' which these tropes have indelibly impressed upon us" (176). Hence Chateaubriand's, Chénier's, Bernardin's, and Rousseau's ready deployment, in their magnifications of the male lover's passion, of the ancient and ever renewable category of the "sublime" to deal with the encounter with woman. At the same time, there is something new and modern about the insistence upon these tropes in this specific era of human history, the age of raised bourgeois awareness of a universal human nature and condition. In his interrogation of this very idea of sublimity, Theweleit has seen it as a "(historically relatively recent) form of the oppression of women through exaltation, through a lifting of boundaries, an 'irrealisation' and reduction to principle—the principle of flowing, of distance, of vague, endless enticement" (284). In other words, the image of the sublime engulfed beloved swindles woman out of a sense of her own power and out of inclusion in universal personhood.

This confrontation of works during a forty-year span featuring the prostrate or dying woman reveals a persistent male anxiety around the issues of masculinity as dominance and of sexual fidelity during the time of gestation of the modern republic. Both of these preoccupations implied a need to police women's behavior. What currents had fed this male anxiety over the emergence of women as individuals? We may make some guesses. Anguish over the loss of human ties as witnessed in the tide of infant mortality and abandonments as rural life began its long disintegration, perhaps. Almost certainly a related uncertainty about paternity, which would produce the obsession with chastity and the great bourgeois return to paternal prerogatives. Yoked with the age-old misogynies of the combined Christian and Gallic traditions, a sullen jealousy of the confident women of high society for what was felt to be their usurpation of power and influence would play its own incalculable role. And perhaps a longing for a less brutalized model of sexuality in which their desire would not be experienced as a fractious enemy, an agent of disorder, might have contributed to men's refashioning of love and family life. In any case, the wresting of sexual order out of its chaos seemed to most of them to demand the redomestication of women and their departure from the public space. Most of this program is inherent in polemics and works of art that precede 1789, as we have seen.

Women's eruption into historical action in events like the October Days of 1789, as they formed a boisterous crowd to march on Versailles and bring the monarchs triumphantly back to Paris, in the light of the underlying gender tensions, could only reinforce a reaction of terrified consternation among the most male supremacist of the men. Women's own modest demands for change by the revolution at first met with some success, to be set aside later as militarism came to dominate national life. As the claims of women were swept aside, first Jacobin and then Napoleonic politics would finally embody those lovingly fashioned, seductive visions of sacrificial female goodness in their legislation. The long evolution from monarchical society's dominant conceptualization of woman as man's lively and energetic opposite, even when defeated or despised, had given way to the new paradigm: the feeble subordinate.[20] Who can say whether the political revolution, among the eddies of its turbulence, was not also a struggle to assure this end?

In subduing female self-affirmation, romantic culture wove other elements into its skein. The male artists of romanticism would appropriate their conception of the female principle in their own tendency to swoon with the very sensibility with which they endowed their heroines, outdoing them in "their" presumed game of dolorous sentiment and love of love.[21] Finally, the long emotional tide of male resentment adumbrated in the figures of the engulfed beloved effects a sublimation, etherealization, and sentimentalization by an influential artistic coterie of what would be given as "natural" sexual impulse. Popular fantasies, elegies of lament for the disappeared object will continue to shroud underlying sexual realities, making male sexual violence and betrayal, actualities of many women's experience, impossible to avow. By making allusions to such brute realities appear as solecisms against what attracted the sexes to each other, crude invasions of the sacred precinct of what Tanner has termed "the dissolving liquefactions of passion," this structurally coercive mode of fantasizing sexuality passed itself off as the life-force itself.

Such an alluring phantasm, so easily internalized, enabled the dominant masculinist factions to silence dispute or negotiation over sexuality among or between women and men. With this mechanism in place, the long sleep of pious sexual repression had begun. In the politics of gender, art is not on the margins: it is the arena. The arts, in their gentle, insidious way, had colluded in a "restoration" of their own, a counterrevolution of daunting consequences for humankind.

To call upon Klaus Theweleit's terms, the male desire that flowed through these images of women had the effect of stilling women's own expression of desire. Yet art has power to make a naked display even of such repression. Anaïs, the heroine of Grétry's 1797 opera, *Anacréon chez Polycrate*,[22] speaks the required words of contrition. We may envisage her as the swooning, lightly clad, distraught figure of one of our paintings:

> Enamored by a rash passion, I dared to dispose of myself in despite of the rights of my father. I have much deserved his anger. If he must avenge himself, let him punish me alone. I abandon myself to his wrath, for I owe him my life. Let him take it back, then, and forgive me . . . *Fille rebelle, et criminelle*—a daughter rebellious and guilty, I ask only to die.

Notes

1. Montesquieu's *Lettres persanes* (1721), which describes the revolt of a harem, and Marivaux's *La Colonie* (1729), a satiric drama in which the women revolt against the tyranny of the men, are two of the most searching explorations of women's consciousness of their subordination.

All translations from the French are my own unless otherwise indicated.

2. "Laclos and 'Le Sexe:' the Rack of Ambivalence," *Studies on Voltaire and the Eighteenth Century* 189 (1980); see the section "The Rise of Women and the Reaction to it," 258–69. Joan M. Landes elaborates on a closely related thesis. See also my *The Twilight of the Goddesses: Women and Representation in the French Revolutionary Era* (Rutgers University Press: forthcoming, 1992).

3. Out of a vast quantity of material, some essential studies are Claude Delasselle, "Les enfants abandonnés à Paris au XVIIIe siècle," *Annales: Economies, Société, Civilisation* 30 (1975):187–218; Micheline Boulant, "La Famille en miettes," *Annales:Economies, Sociétés, Civilisations* 27 (1972):959–68; Edward Shorter, "Illegitimacy, Sexual Revolution, and Social Change in Modern Europe," in *Marriage and Fertility, Studies in Interdisciplinary History*, Robert I. Rotberg and Theodore K. Rabb, eds. (Princeton: Princeton University Press, 1980); Roger Mercier, *L'Enfant dans la société française du XVIIIe siècle* (Dakar: Université de Dakar, 1961); George D. Sussman, *Selling Mother's Milk—The Wet-Nursing Business in France 1715–1914* (Urbana: University of Illinois Press, 1982). Note also titles by J.-L. Flandrin in the bibliography below.

4. See D. A. Coward, "Eighteenth Century Attitudes to Prostitution," *Studies on Voltaire and the Eighteenth Century* 189 (1980):363–99.

5. Note Michel Vovelle's statement: "If we approach the realm of attitudes to life at the first, most elementary and at the same time most basic level—that of life given or received—we come across a cluster of surprisingly converging data for several specific and important tests: contraception, illegitimacy, premarital conceptions and abandoned children." In "Le tournant des mentalités en France 1750–1789: la 'sensibilité' pré-révolutionnaire," *Social History* 5 (1977):611.

6. For an account of Germaine de Staël's unobtrusive withdrawal of approval of this role that, following Rousseau, she had initially embraced in the course of her successive fictions, see my "Woman as Mediatrix: From Jean-Jacques Rousseau to Germaine de Staël." In *Woman as Mediatrix—Essays on Nineteenth Century Women Writers*, ed. Avriel H. Goldberger. New York: Greenwood Press, 1987.

7. The politics of the gaze has enjoyed wide discussion. I cite here, Teresa de Lauretis, John Berger, and Norman Bryson for their penetrating treatments of the implications of this question.

8. See Françoise d'Eaubonne's confusing but intriguing Jungian polemic, *L'Histoire de l'art et lutte des sexes*.

9. Note Marina Warner's summation: "The interpenetration of actual and symbolic planes has rarely been as full as during the revolution's early years, and such a convergence can present tremendous possibilities for emancipation. But the emphasis in the female allegories of 1794 and afterwards returned to Rousseau's ideals of virtue, purity and decorum, even bashfulness, to motherhood and nubility; and so women were not enfranchised by them." *Monuments and Maidens—The Allegory of the Female Form*, 291.

10. Readers may consult the catalog, *French Painting 1774–1830: The Age of Revolution* for discussions of the works by Harriet (145), Bonnemaison (155), and Gamelin (53) referred to in the text.

11. Jules Renouvier originally posited that a "new type" of representation of woman arose in visual works around 1800. He saw this phenomenon manifest specifically in images of women mourning at a tomb. I see this set of images as related to earlier pre-romantic ones of women giving the occasion for mourning. The identification of women with death here provides the continuum.

12. Tony Tanner in fact finds Julie, who describes her mind as "a moving wave," "watery at the center, fluid, labile, potentially 'thalassic'" (172).

13. See Wolfgang Lederer's and Erich Neumann's rich documentation of this ancient tradition, as well as Karen Horney's analysis of it.

14. There has been a good deal of discussion over the value of Rousseauism to women. Gita May, for example, argues reasonably enough, that the "most intelligent and strong-willed" women readers of Rousseau largely embraced his ideas. Unlike present-day feminists, "earlier readers thought [Julie and Sophie] admirable, moving women characters, capable of ennobling their lives and of endowing courtship, marriage and motherhood with a new moral seriousness and dignity" (311). The question arises, however, whether these women had any genuine choice, given the emotional skewing and rigging of the issues by the emergent ideology of the sexual/maternal sphere that was imposed upon them and to which they were not asked to contribute their own conceptions, or even to lend their consent. There are monstrous dumb-shows of self-repression evident in the self presentations of Manon Phlipon and Germaine de Staël, to cite two of the most "expressed" women of the time, who professed, in the virtually ritualistic mode prevalent in enlightened circles, their obeisance to Rousseau. There is no question, however, as May points out, that certain features in the Rousseauist dispensation, in their apparent softening of the rough heartlessness of

current mores, did seem to offer women a kind of immediate release from a continuing posture of relentless conflict between the sexes. Rousseauism at least promised an accommodation between the sexes, albeit one ultimately demeaning to women, and paternalistic.

15. This longing for fusion I assimilate to what Jean Starobinski alludes to as Rousseau's recurrent evocation of the state of *transparence*.

16. I treat Laclos's various texts on women together in my article "Laclos et 'le Sexe': The Rack of Ambivalence." *Studies on Voltaire and the Eighteenth Century*, 189, 1980, 247-96. Dominique Aury's essay "La Révolte de Madame de Merteuil," is for me the most satisfying of the myriad readings of the novel.

17. The physician and *Idéologue*, P. J. G. Cabanis (1757–1808) argued that women's heightened sensibility functioned to assure successful uterine gestation, first physiologically, and then in terms of nurturance of the child. Brain work was contraindicated for women as harmful to their own and their children's physical welfare. See Jordanova, 99.

18. See works by Marie Cerati, Paule-Marie Duhet, Darline G. Levy, Harriet B. Applewhite and Mary D. Johnson, Dominique Godineau, and Annette Rosa for accounts of women's activities from 1789 to 1799.

19. Father Aubry actually tells Atala that her passion is excessive, her transports "unworthy of her innocence" (Chateaubriand, François-René de. *Atala-René*. Paris: Delmas, 1956, 79). Realizing she is dying, he comforts her by saying that she should as soon regret a dream as her life. "Do you know the heart of man, and could you count on the constancy of his desire? You could sooner calculate the number of waves roiled by the sea in a tempest" (Chateaubriand, 83).

20. "In adding to the gentle seductiveness of the female sex and to its beauty, has nature not foreseen the suitability of placing women in a habitual state of relative weakness?" Georges Cabanis, "Ve Mémoire sur les Rapports du Physique et du Moral de l'Homme, 1795–96," *Oeuvres philosophiques* I:292.

21. Vital, for example, writes of the Byronic hero, "in his attempt to rebel against the violence in male-dominated history, in his attempt to realize in his own life the cherished values of the feminine, [he] is embarked, if the nature of sentimental language is kept in mind, on an enterprise tragically quixotic." Vital, Anthony Paul. "Lord Byron's Embarrassment: Poesy and the Feminine," *Bulletin for Research in the Humanities*, 86, 1983–85, 269–290.

22. Text courtesy of the Aston Magna Music Academy, Great Barrington, Massachusetts.

Works Cited

Applewhite, Harriet B., and Darline G. Levy, "Women, War and Democracy in Paris, 1789–94." *French Women and the Age of Enlightenment*. Samia I. Spencer, ed. Bloomington: Indiana University Press, 1984.

Aury, Dominique. "La Révolte de Madame de Merteuil," in *Les Cahiers de la pléiade*. 1951.

Berger, John. *Ways of Seeing*. London: Penguin Books, 1972.

Bernardin de Saint-Pierre, Jacques-Henri, *Paul et Virginie*. Ed. Jacques van den Heuvel. Paris: Poche, 1974.

Bryson, Norman. *Vision and Painting: The Logic of the Gaze*. New Haven: Yale University Press, 1983.

Cabanis, Pierre-Jean-Georges. *Oeuvres philosphiques*. Eds. Claude Lehec and Jean Cazeneuve. Paris: PUF, 1956. 2 vols.

Camus, Michel. "L'Impasse mystique du libertin." In *Sade: Ecrire la crise*. Colloque de Cerisy, 1981. Paris: Pierre Belfond, 1983.

Cerati, Marie. *Le Club des Citoyennes républicaines révolutionnaires*. Paris: Editions sociales, 1966.

Chateaubriand, François-René de. *Atala-René*. Paris: Delmas, 1956, and *Atala-René*, ed. Letessier. Paris: Garnier, 1962.

Coiçy, Madame de. *Les femmes comme il convient de les voir*. London, Paris: 1785.

Chénier, André. *Oeuvres complètes*. Ed. G. Walter. Paris: Pléiade, 1958.

De Lauretis, Teresa. *Alice Doesn't*. Bloomington: Indiana University Press, 1984.

Diderot, Denis. *Oeuvres complètes*. Paris: Club français du livre. 15 vols., 1969-73. VI, "Salons."

Duhet, Paule-Marie. *Les Femmes de la Révolution*. Paris: Julliard "Archives," 1971.

Duncan, Carol. "Fallen Fathers: Images of Authority in Pre-Revolutionary French Art." *Art History* IV (1981):186-202. See also "Happy Mothers and Other New Ideas in French Art." *Art Bulletin* (1973):570-83.

Feucher d'Artaize, le Chevalier. *Réflexions d'un jeune homme*. London, Paris: 1786. *Lettre à Mme Gacon-Dufour, auteur du mémoire pour le sexe féminin contre le sexe masculin*. Paris: 1788.

Flandrin, Jean-Louis, "Contraception, mariage et relations amoureuses dans l'Occident chrétien." *Annales* XXIV (1969):1370-90, and *Les amours paysannes*. Paris: Gallimard, 1975.

Godineau, Dominique. *Citoyennes tricoteuses*. Aix-en-Provence: Alines, 1988.

Gutwirth, Madelyn. "The Representation of Women in the Revolutionary Period: The Goddess of Reason and the Queen of the Night." *Proceedings—Consortium on Revolutionary Europe, 1983*. Athens: University of Georgia Press, 1985, pp. 224-41; "Laclos and 'le Sexe': the Rack of Ambivalence." *Studies on Voltaire and the Eighteenth Century* 189 (1980):247-96; and "Woman as Mediatrix: From Jean-Jacques Rousseau to Germaine de Staël." In *Woman as Mediatrix—Essays on Nineteenth Century Women Writers*. Ed. Avriel H. Goldberger. New York: Greenwood Press, 1987.

Horney, Karen. "The Dread of Women." *International Journal of Psycho-Analysis* 13 (1932):348-60.

Hunt, Lynn. "Engraving the Republic—Prints and Propaganda in the French Revolution," *History Today*. October 1980:11-17; "The Political Psychology of Revolutionary Caricatures." In *French Caricature and the French Revolution*. Wight Art Gallery, University of California: 1988; and *Politics, Culture and Class in the French Revolution*. Berkeley: University of California Press, 1986.

Jordanova, Ludmilla. "Naturalizing the Family: Literature and the Bio-Medical Sciences in the Late Eighteenth Century," in *Languages of Nature*. Ed. L. Jordanova. New Brunswick: Rutgers University Press, 1986.

Laclos, Pierre Choderlos de. *Oeuvres complètes*. Ed. M. Allem. Paris: Pléiade, 1943.

Landes, Joan B. *Women and the Public Sphere in the Age of the French Revolution*. Ithaca: Cornell University Press, 1988.

Lederer, Wolfgang. *The Fear of Women*. New York: Harcourt Brace Jovanovich, 1968.

Lehtonen, Maija. *L'Expression imagée dans l'oeuvre de Chateaubriand*. Helsinki: Société néophilologique, 1964.

Levy, Darline Gay, Harriet B. Applewhite, and Mary D. Johnson., eds. *Women in Revolutionary Paris, 1789-1795*. Urbana: University of Illinois Press, 1979.

May, Gita. "Rousseau's 'Antifeminism' Reconsidered." In *French Women and the Age of Enlightenment*. Ed. Samia I. Spencer. Bloomington: Indiana University Press, 1979.

Miller, Nancy. *The Heroine's Text—Readings in the French and English Novel, 1722-1782*. New York: Columbia University Press, 1980.

Neumann, Erich. *The Great Mother*. Princeton: Princeton University Press, 1974.

Renouvier, Jules. *Histoire de l'art pendant la Révolution*. Paris, 1860.

Restif de la Bretonne, Nicolas-Edmé. *Les Nuits de Paris*. Paris: Hachette, 1960, and *Les Gynographes*. The Hague, 1977.

Rougement, Denis de. *Love in the Western World*. Trans. Montgomery Belgion. New York: Doubleday, 1957.

Rousseau, Jean-Jacques. *Julie ou la Nouvelle Héloïse*. Paris: Garnier, 1960.

Rosa, Annette. *Citoyennes—Les Femmes et la Révolution française*. Paris: Messidor, 1988.

Sade, Donatien, marquis de. *Justine ou les malheurs de la vertu*. Paris: Soleil Noir, 1950.

Shorter, Edward. "Illegitimacy, sexual revolution and social change in Modern Europe." In *The Family in History*. New York: Harper Torch Books, 1973.

Starobinski, Jean. *Jean-Jacques Rousseau—La Transparence et l'obstacle*. Paris: Plon, 1958.

Sussman, George D. *Selling Mother's Milk: The Wet-Nursing Business in France 1715-1914*. Urbana: University of Illinois Press, 1982.

Tanner, Tony. *Adultery in the Novel*. Baltimore: Johns Hopkins University Press, 1979.

Theweleit, Klaus. *Male Fantasies. Vol. I. Woman, Floods, Bodies, History*. Minneapolis: University of Minnesota Press, 1987.

Trahard, Pierre. *La Sensibilité revolutionnaire 1789-1794*. Paris: Boivin, 1936.

Vital, Anthony Paul. "Lord Byron's Embarrassment: Poesy and the Feminine," *Bulletin for Research in the Humanities* 86 (1983-85):269-290.

Vovelle, Michel. "Le Tournant des Mentalités en France 1750-1789: La Sensibilité Pre-Révolutionnaire," *Social History* 5 (1977):605-629.

IV

The Birth of Modern Feminism
in the Revolution
and Its Aftermath

12

"Equality" and "Difference" in Historical Perspective: A Comparative Examination of the Feminisms of French Revolutionaries and Utopian Socialists

CLAIRE GOLDBERG MOSES

It has become common practice among today's feminists to speak of two opposing tendencies within the movement. One tendency—that of a so-called equality group—emphasizes the similarities between women and men, affirms androgyny, and argues that an equal rights, gender blind strategy is the sensible way to achieve women's freedom and equality. A second tendency—that of a so-called difference group—emphasizes the differences between women and men, affirms the female, and argues that sex-differentiated policies may be necessary to achieve gender justice.[1] Although most feminists have aligned themselves clearly with one or the other of the two tendencies, some others are now suggesting that we must accept contradiction and argue from one or the other position as circumstances warrant. Few, however, recognize that the positioning of these two tendencies in opposition, one to the other, is a construct that we might—and, I urge, that we should—challenge.[2]

This essay is intended to shed light on the two tendencies in feminist thought and open up the possibility of an alternative understanding of their seeming opposition. I begin by briefly chronicling the construction of this opposition in contemporary feminist theory and politics, for it is within our movement that the questions we ponder have been constructed. I then examine the two tendencies in early French feminism—the "equality" tendency among feminists of the 1789 Revolution and the "difference" tendency among utopian socialist feminists of the next generation. By looking at these two moments in the history of the development of feminist thought we can explore these tendencies in the context of their initial articulation and reflect on the circum-

I would like to thank the General Research Board, Office of Graduate Studies and Research, of the University of Maryland and the National Endowment for the Humanities Travel to Collections Fund for their support for the research for this paper.

Several people read and commented on an earlier version of this article. I would like especially to thank Gay Gullickson, Joan Scott, and the anonymous readers for their suggestions.

stances that explain the emergence of divergent discourses and on their significance and political consequences both for earlier feminists and for us. Finally, by comparing these two feminisms, this essay will make clear that the construction of "equality" and "difference" in opposition is mistaken.

Equality versus Difference in "Second Wave" Feminism

The ideas of theorists of the "equality" tendency, like Shulamith Firestone, Kate Millet, and Elizabeth Janeway, dominated feminist debate in the early 1970s.[3] Drawing for their inspiration from Simone de Beauvoir's *The Second Sex* and Betty Friedan's *The Feminine Mystique*, they examined the social and historical construction of gender-distinct "roles" and upheld a universalistic, or androgynous, ideal in its stead. Historians writing at the same moment confirmed—or reflected—their stance. Following the lead of Barbara Welter, whose germinal article had identified a nineteenth-century "Cult of True Womanhood,"[4] they came to link the failure of nineteenth-century feminists to challenge notions that women were innately different from men—for example, that they were more moral or more nurturing—to their failure to complete the revolution of women's liberation.

The "difference" tendency emerged as a second stage in the recent history of feminism, beginning in the late-1970s, but especially in the 1980s. Theorists like Adrienne Rich, Mary Daly, Carol Gilligan, and Jean Bethke Elshtain affirmed gender differentiation and celebrated qualities considered traditionally feminine, particularly those associated with nurturance and mothering.[5] The "difference" tendency also had its counterpart among historians. Nancy Cott and Carroll Smith-Rosenberg, who examined the psychologically sustaining relationships developed among nineteenth-century middle-class women in their separate culture, reconceptualized the view of separate spheres and women's culture, identifying it as a source of women's power rather than an explanation for their powerlessness.[6]

The emergence of the "difference" perspective made many feminists uneasy. Not only was the "equality" tendency the one with which we were most familiar, but the historical record that had been created seemed to "prove" the wisdom of this stance. The "difference" tendency was regarded as either a departure from the ideological tradition or a step backward; it puzzled us and called for explanation. *Feminist Studies* published a special symposium that examined the significance of the work of women's culture historians like Smith-Rosenberg; *Signs* published an interdisciplinary forum examining the significance of Gilligan's work.[7]

But time and reflection did not resolve the disagreements within feminism. On the contrary, tensions have recently become more charged as feminists aligned with one or the other of the two tendencies have taken opposing sides on issues like pregnancy benefits, maternity leave, and custody and divorce law reforms; argued on different sides in the recent *EEOC v. Sears, Roebuck* case; and fashioned quite different justifications for affirmative action and comparable worth policies.[8] Clearly, our scholarship has had political ramifications.

The tensions in the American movement may explain the discomfort that many Americans have experienced with recent feminist theory that comes to us from France. Because early translations into English of French feminist writings emphasized writings from the "difference" tendency, Americans quickly came to the conclusion that "difference" and "French feminism" were one and the same.[9] But actually both tendencies exist in France, where theorists like Christine Delphy, Colette Guillaumin, and others associated with the periodical *Nouvelles Questions féministes*, the group that wrote for *La Revue d'en face* before its demise, and the group that is associated with APEF (Association pour les Etudes Féministes) have continued the tradition associated with de Beauvoir; the "difference" tendency is most evident in the writings of Annie Leclerc, Hélène Cixous, Luce Irigaray, and the group Psychanalyse et politique (familiarly called "psych et po"). And in France, as in the United States, it is actually the "equality" group that is the more visible and the one whose ideas are most likely to underpin struggles in the political arena (e.g., abortion rights, anti-rape, and anti-battering struggles and government initiatives for equal pay and affirmative action). Also in France—sadly, much more so than in the United States—the tensions between the groups (and especially between the "equality" group and the theorists now or once associated with psych et po) is bitter, perhaps because it is fueled not only by ideological differences (which certainly play a role) but also by struggles for power.[10]

Just as it is now clear that the two tendencies are not simply "American" and "French," it is also now clear that both tendencies, not just the "equality" one, have a history. Already in 1964, Aileen Kraditor, in *The Ideas of the Woman Suffrage Movement, 1890–1920*, examined the "two major types of suffragist arguments"—one that she labeled the justice argument, based on "the ways women were the same as men and therefore had the *right* to vote," and a second, the expediency argument, based on "the ways [women] differed from men, and therefore had the *duty* to contribute their special skills and experience to government."[11] Karen Offen, in her recent article "Defining Feminism: A Comparative Historical Approach," seemed to concur with Kraditor in identifying "two distinct modes of argumentation or discourse"— which she terms "individualist" and "relational"—but she differed from Kraditor in suggesting that not only their modes of arguments but also their goals diverged. ("Instead of seeking unqualified admission to male-dominated society, [relational feminists] mounted a wide-ranging critique of the society and its institutions.")[12] But neither of these two studies are adequate to resolve our disagreements today. Kraditor's focus was on suffrage only; she made no attempt to reflect on the many other issues feminists have addressed. And Offen, by identifying the "relational" tendency as "couple-centered"—one that endorses traditional family structures and accepts the sexual division of labor—offered little to challenge the view that "difference" is indeed opposed to "equality."[13]

An examination that compares and contrasts feminist discourse during the French Revolution to that of the next generation of feminists—utopian socialist feminists active in the 1830s and 1840s—opens up the possibility of deconstructing the "equality/difference" dichotomous pair. Feminists of the revolutionary era were Enlightenment rationalists. They argued that individuals of both sexes were born similar in capacity and character and ascribed male/female differences to socialization. Feminists of the next generation were utopian socialists. They argued that women and men were innately different, but they actually prized the feminine nature over the masculine. Revolutionary feminists grounded their arguments for sexual equality in their claims that women and men were alike. They thus equated identity and equality and opposed this particular definition of equality to inequality (equated with difference). Utopian socialists, however, challenged this equating of identity with equality and challenged the opposition of equality to difference. They, too, championed equality but argued that only through the association of differentiated sexes and classes would women (and workers, as well) be able to attain full equality. Although some aspects of their discourse were adopted by some quite timid feminists in a later period, utopian socialist feminists in the 1830s actually offered a far-reaching vision of liberation that is more akin to the feminism we today call radical. It is in this respect that the French historical record is different from the American. Although both tendencies can be identified in both historical traditions, the French historical experience includes a tradition of *radical* "difference" that challenged the separate spheres doctrine and the traditional family and permits us to challenge the construction of equality and difference in opposition.

Revolutionary Feminism

Already during the years immediately preceding the storming of the Bastille, a number of pamphlets and brochures on the woman question were circulated throughout France.[14] In 1787, Madame de Coicy published *Les Femmes comme il convient de les voir*, and Madame Gaçon-Dufour issued her *Mémoire pour le sexe féminin contre le sexe masculin*. In 1788, *La Très Humble Remontrance des femmes françaises*, *La Requête des femmes à Messieurs composants l'Assemblée des Notables pour leur admission aux Etats-Généraux*, and Olympe de Gouges's *Lettre au peuple* appeared. A document of January 1, 1789, addressed to the king—*Pétition des femmes du Tiers Etat au roi*—demanded improved educational opportunities for women. The *Cahier des doléances et réclamations des femmes*, signed Madame B . . . B . . . , went further, to demand political rights for those who had fiscal responsibilities: "Since [women] are required, like men, to pay royal taxes and commercial fees, we believe that it is only justice to collect their grievances, at the foot of the throne, and to collect their votes as well." The author demanded not only a better education ("do not raise us as if we were destined for the pleasures of the harem") but also that the Estates General recognize women's right to marry according to their individual desires.[15]

The *cahiers de doléances*, prepared in 1789 by the primary electoral assemblies to inform their representatives to the Estates General of their concerns, reveal the demand for improved female education was widespread. According to one study of the several hundred edited *cahiers*, thirty-three recommended schooling for girls.[16] The third estate of Chatellerault went so far as to argue for equality of the sexes.[17]

Women's active participation in the revolution furthered the emergence of a collective female consciousness. In early October 1789, a crowd of 4,000 women—mostly from the Paris market districts, but evidently others joined them along the way—marched off to Versailles to demand that the royal family, the court, and the National Assembly be moved to Paris and that the king assure a steady supply of bread to the city.[18] Months later, the feminist newspaper, *Etrennes nationales des dames*, calling for representation of women in the National Assembly, would remind readers that "last October 5, Parisian women proved that they were as brave and enterprising as men."[19]

The predominately male political clubs that proliferated throughout France after 1789 excluded women,[20] but women did take part in politics through the "mixed fraternal societies" created to inform and instruct "passive" citizens. In the provinces, clubs of entirely female membership became quite popular. For the most part, the women in these provincial clubs seemed to understand their role to be that of auxiliary supporters of the male makers of the revolution. But some women in the clubs demanded the right to fight with the armies, and according to Paule-Marie Duhet, about thirty women actually did so before this was expressly forbidden in 1793.[21] The *Société des Républicaines-Révolutionnaires*, a Parisian women's club founded in the spring of 1793 by Pauline Léon and Claire Lacombe, was distinctly feminist, although it saw its role mostly as defending the revolution. On June 2, 1793, *Le Moniteur* reported that a deputation from this group demanded the right to deliberate with the Revolutionary Committee, and after the Constitution of 1793 granted universal male suffrage, they protested the exclusion of women.[22]

These revolutionary years were more a time for organizing and activity than for reflective writing, analysis, and theorizing, but writings of three important feminist publicists, Condorcet (Marie Jean Antoine Nicolas Caritat, Marquis de Condorcet), Olympe de Gouges, and Etta Palm d'Aelders, illustrate the "equality" tendency embedded in revolutionary discourse. Condorcet's "Essai sur l'admission des femmes au droit de cité," which appeared in 1790, called for "equality of rights" for both sexes. "Either no individual of the human race has genuine rights, or else all have the same." In this short document (about the length of a speech), he specifies the right to assist "in the making of laws," the "right of citizenship," and "the franchise" for women as well as men, and states also that the "tyranny of the civil law," which "subjected wives to their husbands," should be destroyed.[23]

Condorcet based his argument on the claim that women have the same natural rights as men. These so-called natural rights, or "rights of man," derive from our human capacity to reason and to acquire moral ideas. Women have "these same qualities," but people have become so accustomed to women's oppression that "nobody thinks to reclaim [their rights]." Sexual inequality, then, is the triumph of the "power of habit" over reason.[24]

To those who would deny that women have the same capacity to reason as men, Condorcet countered that educational disabilities and legal discrimination alone explain the seemingly different reasoning of women and men.

> It is not nature, it is education . . . which is the cause of this difference. . . . Banished from affairs, from everything that is settled according to rigorous justice and positive laws, the matters with which they occupy themselves are precisely those which are ruled by natural amiability and feeling. It is hardly fair, therefore, to allege as a ground for continuing to deny women the enjoyment of their natural rights, reasons which only possess a certain amount of substance because women do not enjoy these rights.[25]

The differences are not natural, then; indeed, they are more apparent than real, for both sexes are using their reasoning capacities to secure happiness. Women may, perhaps, "aim at a different end," but "it is not more unreasonable for a woman to take pains about her personal appearance than it was for Demosthenes to take pains with his voice and his gesticulation."[26]

Olympe de Gouges constructed similar arguments to achieve similar goals. Her *Déclaration des droits de la femme et de la citoyenne* was based on the *Declaration of the Rights of Man*, to which she demanded the inclusion of the word "woman."

> All women are born free and equal to men in rights. . . .
>
> All female citizens, like all male citizens, must participate personally or through their representatives in the formulation [of laws]. . . .
>
> All female citizens and all male citizens, being equal in the law, must be equally eligible for all dignities, positions, and public offices, according to their abilities, and without any other distinction than that of their virtue and their talents.
>
> Woman has the right to mount the scaffold; she must equally have the right to mount the rostrum.
>
> Property belongs to both sexes . . . ; for each it is an inviolable and sacred right.[27]

Gouges was, of course, specifying just those gains that the revolution had conveyed to men: equal rights of citizenship, equal access to political offices and public employment, liberty to speak out publicly, equal property rights. In a postscript, she added to these demands the access to public education, which was at that moment being debated in the National Assembly, and legal equality between wife and husband (a "social contract between man and woman").

Like Condorcet, Gouges based her arguments on natural rights theory. Equality was not something to be granted, like a gift; equality was "natural" and had only to be recognized ("Woman, wake up; . . . discover your rights"). And the law "must be the same for all" because natural rights are the same for all: "What is there in common between [women] and [men]? Everything." Only "prejudice, fanaticism, superstition, and lies" and perhaps also some "non sequitur in contradiction to principles" have denied women their "inalienable" rights.[28]

The same claims were put forth by Etta Palm. She wrote that "justice . . . calls all individuals to the equality of rights, without discrimination of sex; the laws of a free people must be equal for all beings. . . . The powers of husband and wife must be equal. . . . Girls [must have] a moral education equal to that of their brothers; for education is for the soul what watering is for plants."[29] According to the reporter for the *Archives parlementaires*, when Palm addressed the Legislative Assembly in 1792, she asked "that women be admitted to civilian and military positions and that the education of young people of the feminine sex be set up on the same foundation as that of men."[30] And always she, too, based her claims on a "natural" equality: "Nature formed us to be your equals." Equality is "a natural right of which [women] have been deprived by a protected oppression."[31]

The language of these revolutionary feminists—two hundred years old now—sounds familiar to us, still, today. This is because it emphasizes values that we think of as traditionally American, reminding us that equality and fairness and goals such as property rights, education, and sovereignty vested in an independent citizenry were codified in our eighteenth-century revolutionary documents as well as the French ones. Placing this discourse back into the moment of its original articulation helps us to understand its appeal to feminists: Both the American and the French revolutions were the culmination of a centuries-long process by which sovereignty was redefined in public rather than private terms. With the growth of national bureaucracies and the economic transformations we associate with mercantile capitalism, people came to value education and independence, for bureaucrats, diplomats, and merchants required these attributes in ways that those who exercised power in feudal times did not. Equal rights of "citizenship," as defined in the new *Declaration of the Rights of Man and of the Citizen*, and equal access to newly promised national educational programs were important, then, to revolutionary feminists because the intense political debate of that historic moment had made these goals important to all the French.

That revolutionary feminists borrowed their goals from the dominant culture is evident. What is less evident is that the very stand upon which they based their claims—the "essential" or "natural" equality of all humans—was borrowed as well. *Revolutionaries*, not just revolutionary feminists, argued for equality on this basis. It was on this basis that the feudal "orders" were destroyed and that political outsider groups like peasants, Blacks, and Jews made their case for equality. Not surprisingly, feminists did so as well.

In doing so, they borrowed from a discourse of equality that had even included women. That such a discourse existed has now been shown in the works of Erna Hellerstein, Londa Schiebinger, and Thomas Laqueur—each of whom has examined the medical literature on this question and made clear that a view stressing the essential similarities of women's and men's bodies was widespread still at this time.[32] In fact, from the time of the ancient Greeks, scientists had held the view that women's and men's bodies, skeletal frames, and reproductive organs were essentially the same "under the skin."[33] True, most scientists in the eighteenth century probably had no trouble reconciling their "knowledge" that the sexes were physiologically rather similar with the view that women were inferior to men (even physiologically, since their reproductive organs, although identical, were interior and therefore cooler).[34] But seventeenth- and eighteenth-century feminists—Erna Hellerstein identifies Chevalier de Jaucourt, Claude Adrien Helvétius, and Antoine Leonard Thomas, as well as Condorcet;[35] Londa Schiebinger identifies Poullain de la Barre[36]—cited "scientific" evidence to support their claims for women's rights. Just as there was no basis in nature for inequalities among men, there was no basis in nature for the inequality of man and woman. Thus, by appealing to the professed beliefs of the dominant culture in "natural" equality and "natural" rights, feminists made their case as had other political outsider groups and hoped, not unreasonably, for the same successful outcome. Perhaps not surprisingly, "science" will shift at about this time to a new view of the sexes—one that Thomas Laqueur has labeled "the biology of incommensurability"—to justify better the exclusion of women from citizenship.[37] Interestingly, feminists will also shift their view—although with a different end in mind.

Utopian Socialist Feminism

The next generation of feminists challenge the binary oppositions—sameness/difference, equality/inequality—and especially the equating of sameness with equality, and difference with inequality, that was implicit in revolutionary ideology. As we shall see, they too argued for the equality of the sexes—no less fiercely than had revolutionary feminists. But they charted a sharply divergent path from their revolutionary predecessors. Indeed, they inveighed against revolution, which they associated with violence and terror. They were romantics rather than Enlightenment rationalists. They challenged the universalizing of human experience in revolutionary discourse—but not to limit, rather to further, equality. The groups with which these feminists identified had invented the word "socialist" for themselves as a way of emphasizing that their concern was the "social"—that is, the way humans related to each other—rather than the individual. Their focus shifted away from the individual rights of citizenship, including political rights, to new ways of organizing enduring social networks, intimacy, sexuality, and reproduction,[38] as well as production. Their social change strategy was to create a New World Order of alternative communities intended not only to collectivize households and production but also to provide a peaceful means for change in contrast to revolutionary means. The New World would be constructed alongside the Old, and people—

merely by observing the far preferable utopian life—would be won over to join with them and create more of these alternative communities.

The most visible and active of these feminists were Saint-Simonians. Beginning in the late 1820s, these Saint-Simonians organized themselves into a community somewhat on the model of a religious community. Prosper Enfantin and Saint-Amand Bazard were the Fathers of the Church. Then, after a schism, Enfantin alone bore the title of pope; an empty seat alongside him signified the awaited Female Messiah who would rule one day as "popesse." The inner circle of Saint-Simonians lived collectively in several *maisons de famille* (at rue Taitbout and at rue Monsigny) and pooled their financial resources. Their work was for the movement—lecturing and other propaganda efforts and organizing among workers in their neighborhoods and at their workplaces. Income needs were covered by contributions. Meals were collectively prepared and served for an even larger group of adherents.

Among these Saint-Simonians were significant numbers of women. In my earlier examinations of the Saint-Simonians I have identified many ways in which the feminism developed by the male Saint-Simonian leadership, especially Prosper Enfantin, differed from the feminism of a particularly interesting group of women among these Saint-Simonians—working-class women who, in 1832, created a separatist feminist movement and began to publish their own newspapers and other pamphlets.[39] But both the women and the men were in full agreement in grounding their feminism in a view of women that stressed their difference from men.

Throughout Saint-Simonian writings one finds the recurrent image of the male who represents "reflection" and the female who represents "sentiment." Women and men were, by nature, different. Men were rational—the time of their leadership in the Saint-Simonian movement is likened to "the phase of the doctors"; it is they, for example, who have "made theory."[40] But men are "somber like the solitude, . . . heavy and cold like the marble of a tomb, . . . harsh like a cross."[41] In contrast, "*nature* [emphasis in original] provided [women] a soul that is tender, sensitive, exalted; . . ."[42] Women have "emotions that are gentle and poetic, a warm imagination, and fire in their hearts—they announce the reign of peace and love,"[43] the "phase of sentiment."[44]

Like revolutionary feminists before them, these feminists also were agreeing with and appealing to the widely held beliefs of the dominant culture, although—again like revolutionary feminists before them—they came to conclusions that most found unwarranted. By the 1830s, the view that the sexes were essentially or "naturally" similar had been fully superseded in science by the view that stressed sexual difference. Erna Hellerstein has studied the medical texts of Pierre Roussel and Antoine Camus; Thomas Laqueur has discussed the work of F. A. Pouchet and Achilles Chereau, as well as several German researchers, on spontaneous ovulation; Londa Schiebinger has examined the drawings of the French anatomist Marie-Genevieve-Charlotte Thirous d'Arconville and the German anatomist Samuel Thomas von Soemmerring. All of these nineteenth-century scientists advanced the view that women were different from men—not just inferior, "an incomplete man,"[45] as had been taught since the time of Aristotle, but different in the sense of "a being apart,"[46] organized around their reproductive systems, which were no longer viewed as identical to men's.

It is interesting to remember here that the scientific view emphasizing difference had existed in the seventeenth and eighteenth centuries alongside the contradictory view emphasizing the inherent similarity of the sexes, but that the "difference" view came to predominate only in the nineteenth century. Hellerstein, Laqueur, and Schiebinger conclude from this that science was not transformed simply by the force of its own "objective" research. The shift in knowledge happened in the context of a political *need* to construct a new justification for sexual hierarchy. It was as if "science" agreed with equal rights feminists that the logical conclusion to the view stressing the inherent similarity of women and men in nature was sexual equality; but rather than argue for equal rights, science opted instead for a new view of nature.

Hellerstein, Laqueur, and Schiebinger are convincing in locating in politics the explanation for a new construction of scientific meaning. The new view of woman served well to "prove" that women and men were governed by different natural laws and that women's natural role was in childrearing and not in intellectual work or in the exercise of public rights. It was this view of women that was expressed in the 1793 order that women be excluded from political clubs

> because they would be required to sacrifice to them [the clubs] the more important cares to which Nature calls them. Private functions to which women are destined by Nature are necessary to the general order of society; social order results from the difference between men and women.[47]

It was this view of women that was expressed in the Napoleonic Code's treatment of women, for by recognizing the equal rights of all citizens, but excluding women from the definition of citizenship, the code enshrined not only the subordination of women to men but also the rigid differentiation of women from men. And it was this view of women—self-sacrificing, subordinating themselves to men's interests—that was expressed in romantic literature.

But if the dominant discourse of sexual difference served to justify sexual inequality, what possible appeal could it have had for feminists? To answer this perplexing question requires a reexamination of that discourse in the context of a historically specific moment, for the feminist potential of the discourse of difference related to its particular meaning in the romantic era and to its explanatory power for an historically specific social reality.

The influence of Romanticism was especially important. Unlike rationalists, romantics valued difference above sameness, the particular and the unique above the uniform or the universal. That Romanticism may be conservative—especially, but not only, in its view of women—is widely understood. There is, after all, a reactionary strain within Romanticism that longed for the old feudal order, the old religious order, and, of course, the old sexual order. But Romanticism was also exploited for its emancipatory potential. For example, socialists of this period, borrowing from Romanticism its valorizing of difference, held that the French Revolution's espousal of universal rights had actually masked a policy of entrenched inequality. It was necessary, they believed, to recognize the differences between classes. This, rather than some false sense of shared universal interest, would emancipate workers from employers. As one *Saint-Simonienne* warned: beware "a unity that will merge (*confondre*) the worker and the master; we must recognize that both have their particular interest."[48] Understandably, it was feminists associated with these socialists who developed the new kind of sex analysis based on "difference." The example of socialist class analysis held out the promise of a more effective challenge to inequality than the universalizing now associated with the dominating classes.

The Saint-Simonian archives include a record of a debate over "sameness" and "difference" that illustrates the feminist potential of the discourse of "difference." The occasion was the creation of the ruling hierarchy for the new Saint-Simonian "Church" and in question was Prosper Enfantin's proposal that the Church be headed by a woman and a man—a "couple-pope." Philippe-Joseph-Benjamin Buchez argued against the proposal, from the "sameness" position: "I know of no being who has deep feelings, [whose feelings are] not accompanied and served by the greatest rational strength. . . . Then, why have two individuals compete in order to obtain an integration of that which each possesses integrally?" His feminism—and his words do seem incontrovertibly feminist—is within the familiar Rationalist tradition: "Truly great revelations . . . are neither male nor female. . . . It matters little if [the pope] is . . . male or female. . . ."[49] But when viewed in the specific circumstances of this particular debate, his argument takes on a meaning by no means so incontrovertibly feminist. Buchez was in fact arguing for one head of the Church—"it is unnecessary that the sexes share in [the papacy]"[50]—to be chosen from among the current leadership, which at that moment (1829) was entirely male. It was Enfantin, therefore, who was actually arguing for women's participation in the governance of the Saint-Simonian movement. He carried the day: The New World Order would be ruled by a couple-pope, who together incarnated the attributes of God—"HE" who "is not only *good* like a FATHER, [but also] SHE [who] is . . . *tender* like a MOTHER; for HE *is* and SHE *is* the FATHER and the MOTHER of all [men] and all [women]."[51] Each of the institutional structures of the new Church would be directed by a female and male couple— the *maisons de famille* by a "sister" and a "brother" and the workers' associations by a "directress" and a "director."

Saint-Simonian women welcomed this politics and theology of "difference":

> [Woman] is no longer drawn from a rib of man; she no longer is confounded with his glory; she descends, like him, directly from *her* God, father and mother of all [*tous et toutes*]. . . . In the future, she will find her own place; she will have her own life . . . ; she will no longer, like in the past, be merged into another's existence.[52]

They clearly thought of the theory of difference as a recuperation of the feminine and found it inspiring. "Woman, discovering her model and guide in *her God* [emphasis in original], can now develop *active* virtues; no longer will she be reduced to a passive role as was the ideal of Christian perfection."[53]

Moreover, Romanticism not only valorized difference, it valorized women. True, romantics valorized—even idealized—women only in certain settings and in certain roles. But with all its evident limitations, women—feminists included—responded positively to the ideal woman depicted in romantic literature. Likely they recognized in the romantic idealization of women a means to challenge eighteenth-century negative views of women. As Joan Landes has so skillfully described, revolutionary discourse was not simply patriarchal, it was also strongly misogynist. The aristocratic state was associated with women: Power, it was claimed, was exercised in private settings where women had undue influence and where "men were unmanned."[54] Thus, the revolutionaries' aim to make power more "public," less "private" and therefore less elitist, took on, by force of the logic of their own misogynist discourse, the complementary aim of "empty[ing] out the feminine connotations (and ultimately, the women as well) of absolutist public life."[55] Although revolutionary feminists protested the revolution's exclusion of women from public life, they did not seem to understand and certainly did not challenge the misogyny embedded in the new discourse of public rights. They, too, associated the aristocratic state with some illegitimate, manipulative "empire" of women. Condorcet, for example, was bowing to this misogyny in holding out the promise that "this empire would diminish if women had less interest in preserving it; if it ceased to be their sole means of defense and of escape from persecution."[56]

Saint-Simonians used the romantic idealization of women to allay the fear of women's power. After all, the power of women who are "loving," "conciliatory," and "inspiring"[57] could be neither threatening nor illegitimate. In fact, the future direction of the new age could be entrusted only to those who were especially endowed with the particular quality of women—sentiment—for only sentiment and not reason could provide a strong and solid bond for a peaceful society. "In a religion that is about *love*, the most *loving* becomes the most *capable*."[58] This is not, of course, what romantics intended. Their ideal woman was a disempowered, domesticated woman—literally confined to the domestic sphere. But Saint-Simonians empowered women and called for their full participation in public life. This runs like a leitmotif through their writings: women should recognize "the power that is in them";[59] "they should sense their force."[60] "We must understand our power";[61] "we have a powerful act to accomplish."[62]

But the appeal of "difference" to utopian feminists was not only in its particular meaning in the Age of Romanticism; "difference" also had an explanatory power that was especially useful for addressing the issues that most concerned 1830s' feminists. Most important was their focus on sexuality.

Sexual liberation became central to Saint-Simonism in the early 1830s. According to Enfantin, the New World Order of sexual equality necessitated a new sexual morality. Building on the principle that woman's nature was defined by "love," Enfantin argued that the emancipation of women required the "rehabilitation of the flesh." He proposed that morality be regulated by a complicated system based on three different but equally valid codes: that of the "constants," that of the "mobiles," and that of the synthesizing love of the couple-priest who were charged with harmonizing all social relations by "rekindling the numbed feelings of the first and moderating the 'unruly appetites' of the second."[63]

These sexual issues were very controversial within the movement. Many found Enfantin's proposal immoral, but many others—women as well as men—chose to "put the words of the Father into practice."[64] Saint-Simonian women who would proclaim their adherence to the new morality by engaging in nonmarital sexual relationships agreed to wear a flame-colored ribbon "as a sign of communion among us."[65] Clorinde Rogé asked her husband for "all her liberty" in order to be able "to act without lies or remorse." She wrote: "I threw myself onto the new path of the female apostle . . . putting no barrier in the way of my heart or my acts. Never did any woman search with such zeal for the secret of liberty of women!"[66] Claire Démar criticized Enfantin's proposed system for regulating morals as too restrictive.[67] Eugénie Soudet was of like mind: "There are no laws in the heart," she wrote.[68] Joséphine Félicité and Isabelle also attacked the timidity of some Saint-Simonian men who had apparently called the sexual radicals immoral.[69] And even Suzanne Voilquin, who never considered herself a sex radical, "divorced" her husband in a Saint-Simonian ceremony (divorce was not then legal in France) explaining that their marriage was false because love no longer existed between them.[70]

Saint-Simonians understood that a liberated sexuality required new structures of intimacy to replace the traditional family. Some, like Marie-Reine Guindorf, borrowed from Charles Fourier and argued that isolated households and indissoluble marriages enslaved both women and men. If the work of the home, including the socialization of children and housekeeping tasks, were collectivized, love alone would bind couples. Their union need last only so long as their attraction joined them. Sexual liberation would be possible.

Several other *Saint-Simoniennes*, like Claire Démar and Pauline Roland, called for a new kind of family defined by the mother—"woman alone is the family"[71]—and especially an end to a definition of legitimacy based on paternal recognition: "Be gone, man! . . . and with you the principle of paternity!"[72] "The *monstrous power*—paternity—must be destroyed. No more paternity, always in doubt and impossible to prove."[73]

The concern with family structure and sexual issues that characterized French feminism in the 1830s contrasts with the concerns of revolutionary feminists and relates to changes in women's daily lives that were unsettling, sudden, indeed revolutionary. First was the increased importance given to property in the initiation of marriages. William Sewell has shown how a conception of property, born with the French Revolution, "gave rise to a new set of social conflicts that culminated in an attempt to abolish private property in the Revolution of 1848."[74] The feminist attempt to abolish the family is a similar challenge to the institution of private property. Because property matters had become the basis for forming marital unions among the urban middle and upper classes and among the peasantry, 1830s' feminists, generally from the unpropertied classes, contested this role for property by proclaiming that love alone should be the basis for forming personal unions.

And just as changing theories about how to initiate marriages were being resisted, so too were changing theories about the appropriate role for married women. It was just at this moment, the 1830s, when the so-called cult of domesticity became popularized in the burgeoning women's press and in the works of Pauline Guizot, Claire de Remusat, Albertine Necker de Saussure, and Nathalie Lajolais. The 1830s' feminists—generally young, unmarried, and self-supporting—saw little to recommend in a life of economic dependency. They compared their own financial insecurity—subject as their jobs were to the vagaries of the market—to that of rich women who could just as easily find themselves, Saint-Simonian women warned, on the streets, following a stock-market reversal.[75] Only collectivized production and housekeeping offered real security.

But most importantly, the ideology of 1830s' feminists reflected the breaking of the link between sexuality and reproduction—a revolution in human experience that came earlier to France than elsewhere. Traditionally, a married woman had expected to spend the major portion of her adult life bearing or nursing children. Children were born at regular intervals of from twenty-five to thirty months, and the only processes holding down the average number of births per family to about four or five were late marriages and the fact that one or the other partner commonly died before menopause.[76] In France, beginning early in the nineteenth century, however, in the space of merely one generation, this traditional pattern changed suddenly and completely.[77] By the mid-nineteenth century, the two-child household was commonplace throughout France.

Family limitation—the possibility that childbearing could be chosen or not—resulted in a new consciousness about sexuality. In sorting out sexuality from reproduction, a context in which sexual pleasure may be pursued as an end in itself came into being. The 1830s' feminists reflected this new consciousness by promoting their right to have nonmarital sexual relationships and to have children without being married.

A developing consciousness of women's sexuality led also to a developing consciousness of women's bodily specificity. This was reflected not only in the issues that 1830s' feminists discussed, but also in the kind of analysis and the very language they employed to express their feminism—that of "difference." Attention has shifted to that which is indeed innately different between women and men, our bodies. It is interesting to note that sexual, reproductive, and other issues related to women's bodies are central to those feminists in contemporary France and the United States who are generally called "radical"—the Psychanalyse et politique group, Hélène Cixous, Luce Irigaray, Adrienne Rich, Mary Daly, to name only the best known of this group—and that these radical feminists are in the "difference" camp as well. The discourse of "difference," apparent in the feminism of the 1830s and again in more recent times, relates to the focus on sexuality. Indeed, it not only reflects sexual and/or bodily difference, it is perhaps even necessary for allowing a consciousness of women's sexuality to develop.

For Americans, whose revolutionary tradition is almost completely in the one strain of politics that is radical individualism, the use of a rhetoric valorizing difference appears quite conservative. Moreover, the history of U.S. feminism seems to confirm this judgment, for in the nineteenth century, feminists who affirmed rather than challenged sexual difference were often timid feminists who feared to challenge men and men's power directly. In affirming women's culture and women's domestic activities, they failed to recognize the power of men in defining women's sphere.

In France, however, among socialists who had already rejected revolutionary individualism and developed in its stead class analysis, a rhetoric valorizing difference coexisted with radical views. For example, 1830s' feminists did not argue that essentially different natures of women and men should dictate different roles or separate spheres for them. Nor did these feminists fear to challenge men and male power. On the contrary, among these Saint-Simonians a developing consciousness of the political significance of sex led, not to the hoped-for harmonious association of the sexes, but, rather, to increased tensions among women and men Saint-Simonians. In what was likely the first politically self-conscious separatist venture in feminist history, women Saint-Simonians, in early 1832, responded to continuing sexism within their own movement, by founding a newspaper "that would publish articles only by women."[78] They held weekly meetings, for all of the Saint-Simonian *femmes prolétaires*, at which theoretical issues were first presented and developed. They organized also a Société d'Instruction Populaire to teach poor women, explaining their purpose thus: "that which men have not done it is up to us to do."[79]

Freed to write, think, and act, "each according to her own inspiration,"[80] the women of this collective actually transformed Saint-Simonian feminism. First—as suggested above—they transformed feminist politics by organizing, not the universal association called for by Saint-Simonians earlier, but rather sororal association, a self-consciously political women's culture. They recognized not only that women's experience and nature differed from men's but also that their interests differed from and were in conflict with men's and that political and social change required that women join together across male-constructed barriers to emancipate themselves, by themselves ("women alone shall say what kind of liberty they want").[81]

Their next theoretical innovation was in the way they blended sex analysis with class analysis. Whereas Saint-Simonians' earliest experimentation with class analysis and sex analysis had the two coexisting in such a way that suggested that all workers were male and all women were bourgeois, the editors, who themselves were workers, brought the two together, proclaiming: "The woman question is fundamentally connected to that of women workers."[82] In their writings, the Saint-Simonians explored the differing realities of women of different classes and sought to work out a politics to achieve unity across a reality of division.

Finally, these women changed the priorities of feminism. They spoke less and less about sexual radicalism, focusing instead on expanding women's educational and work opportunities and reforming marriage laws that prohibited divorce and subjugated wives to husbands. The demise of the more radical sexual program related to changes in daily existence that working-class women in general, and these women in particular, were living through in these years: skyrocketing illegitimacy rates, coupled with increasing unemployment among women of their class and declining wage rates. Birth control was still too unreliable, the possibility for women's sexual pleasure was still too commonly limited by bodily injury incurred in childbirth or by venereal disease, and women's ability to support themselves on their own was still too fragile to sustain their sexual radicalism. In fact, the appropriateness of the terms "radical" and "conservative" to define the earlier and the later sexual politics is questionable. Seemingly more conservative than Enfantin's "rehabilitation of the flesh," the new politics of the *femmes prolétaires* was actually more radical, for by linking sexual emancipation to economic, intellectual, and legal emancipation, they had placed the sexual question into the larger context of the political relationship of the sexes.

Were there, then, no dangers to this ideology of "difference"? Certainly there were. First, the closeness of this kind of analysis to traditional patriarchalism led easily to co-optation, particularly in later decades when "difference" was used to extol maternity and usually a separate role and place for women as mothers. Second, this kind of theory, which in its essentialism would serve to unify women, actually divided women when it denied the very real differences of women's lived experience. This was not so among the class-conscious Saint-Simonian feminists. But painful and counterproductive splits along class lines and religious lines did occur among later nineteenth-century feminists, and among feminists today, similar splits along lines of race, class, ethnicity, and sexual orientation have erupted. The biological unity of women has not been sufficient to construct a true sisterhood; feminists need to understand the diversity of women's social situations and work to coordinate multiple struggles.

Deconstructing the "Equality-versus-Difference" Debate

In recent years, it has become commonplace to view the two different tendencies within feminism that I have been discussing here as a debate and to label the opposing sides "equality" and "difference." I suggest, though, that this is unhelpful on two counts: first, because this wrongly suggests that only one side argued for equality and that only one side recognized that there are biological differences between the sexes; second, because it wrongly suggests that there is one right way to explain the social and political relationship of the sexes and only one right way to articulate our claims for change. In a debate, two sides oppose each other; one side will win. The two tendencies I have discussed here, however, are not mutually exclusive, although their emphases are divergent.

Nor should they be viewed as opponents; both have proved useful in addressing quite different issues.

It is important to recognize that feminism varies across time and place, and that feminist ideology is shaped by historically specific phenomena—some social, some economic, some conceptual. It is this historical specificity of feminism that explains that there is not one unified feminist discourse. At various moments, under one or another set of circumstances, feminists' preoccupations have shifted. And when feminists have reordered their priorities, their view of the causes of the status quo and their strategies for change, including their rhetorical strategies, have also shifted.

At the time of the revolution, it was the universality of rights that preoccupied feminists. Revolutionary ideologues had stressed the universality of rights in challenging the ancien régime system of particular rights. Indeed, it was this challenge to the old order that shaped feminist and nonfeminist ideology alike. Gone were the ancien régime's caste-like "estates." Instead, the revolution proclaimed that one's belonging to the human race determined one's rights. What mattered was that which all humans had in common and that separated humans from the animal species—not humans' reproductive organs but their brains, not their different procreative roles but their shared capacity to reason. Differences between human beings were never denied, only their relevance to the exercise of citizenship.

It is important to keep in mind that revolutionary feminists did not deny the biological differences between women and men. This point is strongly argued in Joan Scott's reading of the works of Olympe de Gouges: "While [Gouges] maintained that equality, and not special privilege, was the only ground on which woman could stand, she nonetheless (unsuccessfully) sought special advantage by claiming that she was pregnant in order to avoid . . . the death sentence conferred on her. . . ."[83] Moreover, revolutionary feminists did not even challenge the sexual division of labor; on the contrary, in order to save jobs for women, they sometimes stressed women's particularity. But the differences between women and men were irrelevant to their claims to the rights of citizenship. Citizenship rights were based on the capacity to reason, and because there was no biological difference between women's and men's brains, there could be no difference between their capacities to reason.

To revolutionary feminists, women's exclusion from a new regime based on universally applicable laws was untenable once the rule of law replaced the rule of the arbitrary tyrant and once reason replaced superstition. Utopian socialists, in contrast, were little interested in the rule of law and placed little hope in the power of reason. But they never denied the importance of equality.[84] Saint-Simonian women argued for an equal place in the direction of the New World Order and challenged Saint-Simonian men to practice what they preached in the construction of the New Order alongside the Old. Still, as part of a generalized challenge to Enlightenment values, they did challenge the universalizing of human experience in revolutionary discourse—not, however, to reinstate the feudal order of particular rights, but, rather, to extend the very notion of equality.

The priorities of 1830s' femininsts had changed. Social relationships of intimacy, reproduction, and production mattered to them, not the formal rights of citizenship. Although the universalistic discourse of revolutionaries had been useful for arguing for the rule of law, it was inadequate to the task of reordering relationships of production between workers and capitalists or in reordering the sexual relationships between women and men. For this, it was necessary to pull apart the component parts of relationships and to identify the particularities of class and sex.

The argument that feminist discourses of "equality" and "difference" are neither right nor wrong but relate to historically specific concerns or opportunities is further strengthened by noting the instability of these categories. Just as Olympe de Gouges had to stress women's difference when arguing for matters that touched on women's maternity, Saint-Simonians stressed sameness when arguing for the revolutionary goal of educating women. Although education had not been their primary concern, an 1833 law establishing publicly funded compulsory schooling for boys (but ignored girls) piqued their rage. In arguing, however, for the development of girls' reasoning capacity—a "revolutionary" goal—they borrowed revolutionary rhetoric. Moreover, their borrowing even included the misogynist element in revolutionary discourse: women, due to the impoverishment of their education, are described as frivolous and untrustworthy![85]

Today, when feminists have found themselves locked into debates over the relevant merits of seemingly oppositional rhetorical strategies, it is useful to look back to earlier moments to examine these different strategies in historical contexts from which we have some distance. In so doing, it becomes clear that neither discourse was intrinsically the more radical or conservative; neither was the only right way to argue for sexual equality. Revolutionary feminists' claims to equal rights formalized in the laws determining citizenship are not today viewed as radical, and especially are not viewed as a challenge to the liberal state. Yet, in the late eighteenth century, this was not the case, and feminists were punished as subversives.[86] Nor have we, two hundred years later, been fully successful in convincing others that women's claims to equal rights are in accordance with the values of the liberal state, as the recent failure to ratify an Equal Rights Amendment to the U.S. Constitution attests. Feminists today also note that the revolution's universalizing view of human nature masked the many real differences between women and men resulting from biology and socially constructed roles and masked as well the many differences among women due to class and ethnicity. At that moment in history, however, revolutionary feminists in fact spoke for all women, for all women were excluded from that which had just been granted all men.[87]

A rhetoric valorizing difference may also appear conservative, more likely to legitimate separate spheres for women and men than to challenge them. But in the 1830s this was not the case. Saint-Simonians used "difference" to give expression to new concerns—concerns like sexual liberation, which today we would label radical. And Saint-Simonians used "difference" to argue that women must be involved in all of the kinds of activities that were usually reserved for men. They even experimented, for a time, with a domestic role for men.[88]

Further, their analysis of "difference" served to create the collective consciousness that we today call sisterhood. That all women—defined by the biological fact of being born women—share an experience of political significance is basic to this kind of feminist analysis. The language of "difference" identifies the unity that exists already among women; it also calls women to unity. In a frequently cited article, historian Elizabeth Fox-Genovese has linked the concept of sisterhood to liberalism and revolutionary individualism,[89] but this is not correct. Rather, it is when women's bodily specificity, either as sexual beings or as mothers, is foregrounded that sisterhood or woman-bonding—both in ideology and in the reality of separatist organizing— is most significant. The language and reality of sisterhood was important to 1830s' feminists—socialists not liberals—and their concept of sisterhood (again, this challenges Fox-Genovese) did not preclude class analysis.[90]

This examination of two separate moments in feminism's history is intended to clarify the relationship between ideology and social reality. It is easier here to see this relationship because the two moments under consideration are limited to a few number of years. In the case of revolutionary feminism, government repression precluded the movement's development. Utopian socialist feminists, however, were active in Paris until the early 1850s. An examination of their discourse over a longer period of time would show changing priorities and changing forms of analysis. At some moments, as their program widened and shifted, they would even argue from both kinds of analysis at the same time. They had discovered that to articulate the very different needs of women sometimes required them to stress that which defines women's difference from men (and from other women), sometimes that which defines women's similarities with men. To argue *for equality* requires the capacity to accept this seeming contradiction.

Notes

1. At the "Women and the French Revolution" Conference, held at UCLA in October 1989, the so-called equality perspective was termed the "universalistic" perspective and "difference" was termed the "particular." In the field of women's history, the difference perspective is often referred to as the women's culture perspective. In this article, I use all of these terms.

2. Joan W. Scott's "Deconstructing Equality-versus-Difference: Or, the Uses of Poststructuralist Theory for Feminism" (*Feminist Studies* 14 (Spring 1988):33–50) was most useful for my working through this deconstruction. She writes (44): "equality-versus-difference cannot structure choices for feminist politics; the oppositional pairing misrepresents the relationship of both terms."

3. Shulamith Firestone, *The Dialectic of Sex: The Case for Feminist Revolution* (New York: Bantam Books, 1970); Kate Millet, *Sexual Politics* (New York: Avon Books, 1970); Elizabeth Janeway, *Man's World, Woman's Place: A Study in Social Mythology* (New York: Dell Publishing, 1971). Firestone went the furthest in the direction of

"equality," envisioning that scientific advances in artificial reproduction would make possible the liberation of women even from childbearing—and that this was desirable.

4. Barbara Welter, "The Cult of True Womanhood, 1820–1860," *American Quarterly* 18 (Summer 1966):131–75.

5. Adrienne Rich, *Of Woman Born: Motherhood As Experience and Institution* (New York: W. W. Norton, 1976); Mary Daly, *Gyn/Ecology: The Metaethics of Radical Feminism* (Boston: Beacon Press, 1978); Carol Gilligan, *In a Different Voice: Psychological Theory and Women's Development* (Cambridge: Harvard University Press, 1982); Jean Bethke Elshtain, *Public Man, Private Woman: Women in Social and Political Thought* (Princeton: Princeton University Press, 1982).

6. Nancy Cott, *Bonds of Womanhood: "Woman's Sphere" in New England, 1780–1835* (New Haven: Yale University Press, 1977); and Carroll Smith-Rosenberg, "The Female World of Love and Ritual: Relations between Women in Nineteenth-Century America," *Signs* 1 (Fall 1975):1–29.

7. Ellen DuBois, Mari Jo Buhle, Temma Kaplan, Gerda Lerner, Carroll-Smith-Rosenberg, "Politics and Culture in Women's History: A Symposium," *Feminist Studies* 6 (Spring 1980):26–64; and Linda K. Kerber, Catherine G. Greeno, Eleanor E. Maccoby, Zella Luria, Carol B. Stack, and Carol Gilligan, "On *In a Different Voice:* An Interdisciplinary Forum," *Signs* 11 (Winter 1986):304–33.

8. See Sylvia Ann Hewlett's *A Lesser Life: The Myth of Women's Liberation in America* (New York: William Morrow, 1986) for a demand for preferential treatment instead of "equality." Lenore Weitzman, *The Divorce Revolution: The Unexpected Social and Economic Consequences for Women and Children in America* (New York: Free Press, 1985) is the source most quoted against gender-neutral, no-fault divorce laws that have hurt homemakers and their children. *California Federal Savings & Loan* v. *Guerra*, the Supreme Court case involving preferential maternity benefits found NOW in the uncomfortable position of arguing against California's law guaranteeing maternity leave to Lillian Garland. *EEOC* v. *Sears, Roebuck* found historians Rosalind Rosenberg and Alice Kessler-Harris on opposing sides (Rosenberg for Sears; Kessler-Harris for EEOC), basing their arguments on these divergent tendencies.

9. See especially Elaine Marks and Isabelle de Courtivron, eds., *New French Feminisms, An Anthology* (Amherst: University of Massachusetts Press, 1980).

10. See Claire Duchen's *Feminism in France: From May '68 to Mitterrand* (London: Routledge & Kegan Paul, 1986); also Michele Blin-Sarde, "L'Evolution du concept de difference dans le Mouvement de Liberation des Femmes en France," *Contemporary French Civilization* (Fall/Winter 1982):195–202.

11. Aileen Kraditor, *The Ideas of the Woman Suffrage Movement, 1890–1920* (New York: Columbia University Press, 1965), 52.

12. Karen Offen, "Defining Feminism: A Comparative Historical Approach," *Signs* 14 (Autumn 1988):119–57, esp. 121, 124.

13. Note especially that Offen's way of conceptualizing a feminism that acknowledges women's difference—as "relational" or "couple-centered" and accepting of the sexual division of labor—conceptualizes a difference perspective that would be unable to address some of today's most pressing issues. First, this "couple-centered" feminism would fail to challenge compulsory heterosexuality. Nor would it permit feminists to challenge racism, or at least to challenge the view that failure to adopt a particular family structure that accords with white, middle-class experience *explains* the status of poor people of color in the United States. Nor, finally, would it permit feminists to challenge the "Mommy track" or other work structures that justify women's economic inequality by blaming women rather than patriarchal capitalism.

14. Paule-Marie Duhet, *Les Femmes et la Révolution, 1789–1794* (Paris: Juillard, 1971), 41.

15. Ibid., 37.

16. Elizabeth Racz, "The Women's Rights Movement in the French Revolution," *Science and Society* 16 (1952):153.

17. Edwin Randolph Hedman, "Early French Feminism from the Eighteenth Century to 1848" (Ph.D. diss., New York University, 1954), 47.

18. Duhet, *Les Femmes et la Révolution*, 47–48.

19. Evelyne Sullerot, *Histoire de la presse féminine en France, des origines à 1848* (Paris: Armand Colin, 1966), 48.

20. Only the Cordeliers permitted women a public role; but here, too, their participation was limited. When Théroigne de Méricourt asked to be admitted with voting rights, she was refused. The other clubs, including the Jacobins, denied women even the freedom to speak.

21. Duhet, *Les Femmes et la Révolution*, 117.

22. Ibid., 130.

23. Translated and reproduced in Susan Groag Bell and Karen M. Offen, *Women, the Family, and Freedom: The Debate in Documents*, vol. 1, *1750–1880* (Stanford: Stanford University Press, 1983), 99–103.

24. Ibid.

25. Ibid., 100–101.

26. Ibid., 100.

27. I have translated these passages from the text that is reproduced in Hubertine Auclert, *Le Vote des femmes* (Paris: V. Giard & E. Brière, 1908), 78–79. The entire text is translated and reproduced in Darlene Gay Levy, Harriet Branson Applewhite, and Mary Durham Johnson, *Women in Revolutionary Paris, 1789–1795* (Urbana: University of Illinois Press, 1979), 87–96.

28. The text here is from Levy, Applewhite, and Johnson, *Women in Revolutionary Paris*, 92, 89.

29. Translated and reproduced in Levy, Applewhite, and Johnson, 75–77.

30. Ibid., 123.

31. Ibid., 77.

32. Londa Schiebinger, "Skeletons in the Closet: The First Illustrations of the Female Skeleton in Eighteenth-Century Anatomy"; and Thomas Laqueur, "Orgasm, Generation, and the Politics of Reproductive Biology," both in *The Making of the Modern Body: Sexuality and Society in the Nineteenth Century*, ed. Catherine Gallagher and Thomas Laqueur (Berkeley: University of California Press, 1987); and Erna O. Hellerstein, "Women, Social Order, and the City: Rules for French Ladies, 1830–1870," (Ph.D. diss., University of California at Berkeley, 1981).

Actually, the three historians examine *contending* scientific views—again, one that stressed the similarity of the sexes and another that stressed the difference. Although we are more familiar with scientific views that stressed difference, less aware of the view that stressed similarity, it was this latter view stressing similarity that predominated in the seventeenth and eighteenth centuries. The "difference" view was heard, of course—think of Rousseau; but feminists like Condorcet, Palm, and Gouges were as able to find scientific evidence to support their claims as were the patriarchalists.

33. Schiebinger, "Skeletons," 48.

34. Laqueur, "Orgasm, Generation," 4. Laqueur explores these theories through the works of the second-century medical writer, Galen, still influential at this time.

35. Hellerstein, "Women, Social Order, and the City," 67.

36. Schiebinger, "Skeletons," 46–47.

37. Laqueur, Schiebinger, and Hellerstein. Both Hellerstein and Schiebinger are clear that the medical, biological, or anatomical view of women that stressed their difference from men did not predominate until the nineteenth century. Laqueur gives more weight to early views, which already in the mid-eighteenth century had articulated a biology of "difference." He believes that the new biological views grounded both the antifeminism of the revolution and the new feminism emerging with the revolution and continuing into the next century. I maintain, however, that he has conflated two quite different feminist tendencies, ignoring revolutionary feminists' arguments from "sameness" and misplacing—in time—a feminism of difference.

38. Although we can see here the historical origins of "the personal is political," it is interesting to note the conceptual difference between Saint-Simonian theory and that of the 1970s. Saint-Simonians, unlike 1970s' radical and socialist feminists, accepted the binary oppositions of public versus private and political versus personal. They never defined their challenge to personal relations of inequality as "political"—even a new kind of politics—for they agreed that politics was about the same kind of public activities and rights that liberals thought the realm of politics. Accepting the public/ private opposition, however, they reversed the usual hierarchy and accorded to the private sphere the higher value.

39. See my *French Feminism in the Nineteenth Century* (New York: State University of New York Press, 1984), 41–87, and "Saint-Simonian Men/Saint-Simonian Women: The Transformation of Feminist Thought in 1830s' France," *Journal of Modern History* 54, no. 2 (June 1982):240–67.

40. *Tribune des femmes* 1:106.

41. Ibid., 1:193.

42. Ibid., 1:131.

43. Ibid., 1:160.

44. Ibid., 1:106.

45. Hellerstein, "Women, Social Order, and the City," 67.

46. Ibid., p. 67.

47. Duhet, *Les Femmes de la Revolution*, 155.

48. *Tribune des femmes* 1:166.

49. Phillipe-Joseph-Benjamin Buchez, letter to Enfantin, [October 1829], "Archives," 1:509–10, Fonds Enfantin, Bibliothèque de l'Arsenal, Paris.

50. Ibid., 508 verso.

51. These words are Enfantin's, uttered at his trial and reprinted in the *Tribune des femmes* more than once (1:193, 194, 222).

52. *Tribune des femmes* 1:222.

53. Ibid., 1:223. The author continues: "Mary has influence but no power, and no action, in the government of heaven; her prayer is all powerful upon her divine son, but she prays, she intercedes; by herself she does not act."

54. Joan Landes, *Women and the Public Sphere in the Age of the French Revolution* (Ithaca: Cornell University Press, 1988), 87.

55. Ibid., 40.

56. Ibid., 116.

57. *La Femme libre* (*Tribune des femmes*, 1, no. 1), 1, 3, 6.

58. *Tribune des femmes* 1:107.

59. Ibid., 1:43.

60. Ibid., 1:156.

61. *La Femme libre* (*Tribune des femmes*, 1, no. 1), 1.

62. Ibid., 1:2–3.

63. Prosper Enfantin, "Enseignements fait par le Père Suprême," *Réunion générale de la famille: Séances des 19 et 21 novembre 1831* (Paris: Bureau du Globe, 1832).

64. Pauline Roland to Charles Lambert, January 1834, Fonds Enfantin 7777.

65. *Tribune des femmes* 1:65–66.

66. Clorinde Rogé to Prosper Enfantin, June 20, 1845, Fonds Enfantin 7776, no. 52.

67. Claire Démar, "Ma loi d'avenir," in *Textes sur l'affranchissement des femmes*, ed. Valentin Pelosse (Paris: Payot, 1976), 80.

68. Eugénie Soudet, "Une Parole de femme!" Fonds Enfantin 7627, no. 57.

69. *Tribune des femmes* 1:127–31.

70. Ibid., 2:169–79.

71. Pauline Roland to Gustave Le Français, May 25, 1851, quoted in Edith Thomas, *Pauline Roland* (Paris: Marcel Rivière, 1956), 172.

72. Ibid., 155.

73. Démar, "Ma loi d'avenir, 88.

74. William H. Sewell, Jr., "Property, Labor, and the Emergence of Socialism in France, 1789–1848," in *Consciousness and Class Experience in Nineteenth-Century Europe*, ed. John Merriman (New York: Holmes & Meier, 1979), 45.

75. *Tribune des femmes* 1:95.

76. See Louis Henry, "The Population of France in the Eighteenth Century," and Pierre Goubert, "Recent Theories and Research in French Population between 1500 and 1700," both in *Population in History*, ed. D. V. Glass and D. E. C. Eversley (Chicago: Aldine, 1965).

77. Etienne Van de Walle, *The Female Population of France in the Nineteenth Century* (Princeton: Princeton University Press, 1974), 9, 136–44.

78. Marie Reine, *La Femme libre* (*Tribune des femmes* 1, no. 1), 8; repeated in the second, third, and fourth issues.

79. *Tribune des femmes* 1:146.

80. Suzanne Voilquin, *Souvenirs d'une fille du peuple ou La Saint-Simonienne en Egypte* (1866; reprint ed. Paris: François Maspero, 1978), 119.

81. Joséphine-Félicité, *Tribune des femmes* 1:45–46.

82. *Tribune des femmes* 2:167.

83. Joan Scott, "'A Woman Who Has Only Paradoxes to Offer': Olympe de Gouges Claims Rights for Women," in this volume.

84. The masthead of each issue of *La Tribune des femmes* carried this slogan: "Equality among all in rights and duties." See also, ibid., 1:62: "The Saint-Simonian religion declares that woman is free and the equal of man"; ibid., 1:132: "We preach the equality of man and woman"; ibid., 150: "We demand social equality between the two sexes."

85. For example, Marie-Reine Guindorf (see *La Tribune des femmes* 1:114), in calling for "equal opportunity . . . in education" explains that women should not be excluded from a career in science just because of their "flightyness," since they are "flighty" and (later) "frivolous" only because of their inferior education. Depicting women as flighty or frivolous is typical of revolutionary rhetoric—one is reminded here of Mary Wollstonecraft—but rare among the *Saint-Simoniennes*. However, Marie-Reine could not express a "revolutionary" goal without using the revolution's discourse; it was as if it was a package deal.

86. Olympe de Gouges was tried and found guilty of treason for publishing a pamphlet calling for a popular referendum on the form of government; she was

guillotined on November 1, 1793. On October 20, 1793, the Société des Républicaines-Révolutionnaires was shut down, along with all the other clubs of female membership. Other feminists, not discussed here, were also punished. Théroigne de Méricourt was publicly whipped, and her breakdown following this painful humiliation resulted in her incarceration in an insane asylum. Claire Lacombe and Pauline Léon were imprisoned in the spring of 1794.

87. The class of these feminists to whom I am granting this role of representing the interests of the totality of human kind (à la Georg Lukacs)—or, at least, the interests of the totality of womankind—is noteworthy. The women were rather marginal, "Bohemian" types. Although Condorcet was aristocratic, Olympe de Gouges's and Etta Palm d'Aelders's titles of nobility were fabricated. Olympe de Gouges's father was a butcher, although she claimed to be the illegitimate daughter of the poet Le Franc de Pompignan. She married and was widowed at a quite young age and then moved to Paris where she wrote plays, one of which was performed at the Comédie Française in 1789. Etta Palm was from Holland; her life before coming to Paris is unknown, although assuredly not noble.

88. The occasion was the celibate, all-male, retreat to the Enfantin family home (Ménilmontant) on the outskirts of Paris. There, Saint-Simonian men attempted to create a new kind of community in which all men would do all of the different kinds of work, including the "domestic" work, required for daily life concerns.

89. Elizabeth Fox-Genovese, "The Personal Is Not Political Enough," *Marxist Perspectives*, no. 8 (Winter 1979–80):94–113.

90. Again, the class of the women speaking on behalf of all womankind is noteworthy. The particular standpoint of working-class women may explain their success in blending class analysis with a sex analysis that stressed the essential unity of all women.

13

English Women Writers
and the French Revolution

ANNE K. MELLOR

Following the fall of the Bastille, at the height of the Terror and afterward, during the Napoleonic campaigns and the reign of Bonaparte, a few intrepid Englishwomen crossed the Channel and experienced at first hand the events and the consequences of the French Revolution. Recording their impressions in letters, memoirs, and published prose, they developed out of the initiating ideology of the revolution—the battle cry of *liberté, egalité, fraternité*—a new vision both of the ideal government and of the nature and role of women. For these English women writers—and here I propose to discuss only three who visited France between the years 1790 and 1815, a formidable trio composed of Mary Wollstonecraft, Helen Maria Williams, and Mary Shelley—the French Revolution became a contradictory symbol, representing both the possibility of freedom for women and at the same time the potential liberation of monstrous evil.

The Enlightenment ideals of the French philosophes, of Voltaire, Diderot, and Rousseau, opened up a discourse of equality—between the classes, between the sexes—in which women could participate. Inspired by Condorcet and Thomas Paine, Mary Wollstonecraft, Helen Maria Williams, and Mary Shelley all came to advocate what we would now call liberal feminism, an argument for the equality and even the potential sameness of men and women. All three located this demand for equality within the structure and practices of the bourgeois family, arguing that men and women should assume equal responsibility for governing the family, nurturing the young, and promoting moral virtue, benevolence, and justice within the household. Their belief in the value of the domestic affections for both sexes produced their extreme revulsion from the blood-thirsty executions of the Montagnards during the Terror. They saw these assassinations not only as the breaking up of individual families but as the destruction, through sibling rivalry, of the family-politic itself. But only Mary Shelley recognized that the demand for equality and hence sameness could finally *produce* oppression, that the Terror followed directly from the insistence that all citizens must think and act alike.

In December 1790, Mary Wollstonecraft published an impassioned defense of the ideals of the French Revolution, *A Vindication of the Rights of Man*, in

255

which she directly attacked Edmund Burke's rhetorically inspired affirmation, in his *Reflections on the Revolution in France* (1790), of the French monarchy, of the hereditary principle of succession, of the necessary alliance between church and state, and of the restriction of political power to men "of permanent property." Responding to Burke's insistence that we "derive all we possess as an *inheritance from our forefathers*" and that men have equal rights "but not to equal things," as well as to his inflammatory images of revolutionary France as a female prostitute and of Marie Antoinette as an innocent and pure young damsel, forced to flee "almost naked" from her bed, pursued by "a band of cruel ruffians and assassins," from a palace "swimming in blood, polluted by massacre and strewed with scattered limbs and mutilated carcasses,"[1] Wollstonecraft insisted instead that all political authority should rest on the grounds of reason and justice alone. She demanded that every person be entitled to enjoy and dispense the fruits of his or her own labors, that inequality of rank be eliminated, and that in place of an exaggerated respect for the authority of "our *canonized forefathers*" be subsituted the cultivation of an independent understanding and sound judgment. For Burke's image of the nation as a ravished wife in need of virile protection, Wollstonecraft substituted the image of the nation as a benevolent family educating its children for mature independence and motivated by "natural affections" to ensure the welfare of all its members. In such an enlightened nation, Wollstonecraft concluded, love would engender love, the poor would be relieved by "the fostering sun of kindness, the wisdom that finds them employments calculated to give them habits of virtue," and "domestic comfort, the civilizing relations of husband, brother, and father, would soften labour, and render life contented."[2]

Since she believed that the French Revolution would quickly establish such an enlightened republic, one that would respect the natural rights of every person, Mary Wollstonecraft was appalled when she read in 1791 that the French minister of education for the new Constituent Assembly had proposed a state-supported system of public education for *men only*. She immediately composed a lengthy response to the former Bishop of Autun, Citizen Charles Maurice de Talleyrand-Perigord, and his *Rapport sur L'Instruction Publique, fait au nom du Comité de Constitution* (Paris, 1791). That response, *A Vindication of the Rights of Woman*, went through two editions in 1792. Independently of the French feminist thought of the time, Mary Wollstonecraft perceived that the gender inequality at the core of both the revolutionary French nation and of British society threatened the development of a genuine democracy. She recognized that the denial of education to women was tantamount to the denial of their personhood, to their participation in the natural and civil rights of mankind.

Wollstonecraft therefore initiated her own revolution, what she explicitly called "a *REVOLUTION* in female manners."[3] Appealing to the Enlightenment rationalists of her day, she grounded her social revolution on a rigorously logical argument, proceeding from the premise that if women are held morally and legally responsible for their sins or crimes (as they were in both England and France), then they must have both souls and mental capacity to think correctly or ethically. And if women are capable of thinking, they must have a rational faculty. And if they have a rational faculty that is capable of guiding and improving their character and actions, then that rational faculty should be developed and exercised to its greatest capacity. Here Wollstonecraft explicitly attacked both Talleyrand's and her own society's definition of the female as innately different from the male, as emotional, intuitive, illogical, capable of moral sentiment but not of rational thought.

From this logical argument for the equality of women, Wollstonecraft launched a passionate plea for women's education, for only if women are educated as fully as men will they be able to realize their innate capacities for reason and moral virtue. Calculatedly appealing to male self-interest in order to effect her revolutionary reforms, Wollstonecraft argued that more highly educated women will not only be more virtuous, but they will also be better mothers, more interesting wives and "companions," and more responsible citizens. Because Wollstonecraft assumed a society in which most women would marry, she devoted a large portion of her *Vindication* to describing the ideal marriage, a marriage based on mutual respect, self-esteem, affection, and compatibility. It is a marriage of *rational love*, rather than of erotic passion or sexual desire.

Wollstonecraft advocated other rights for women: the vote (which she insisted should be given to both working-class men and all women), the civil and legal right to possess and distribute property, the right to work in the most prestigious professions, in business, law, medicine, education, and politics. Above all, she demanded for all children between the ages of five and nine a state-supported, coeducational public school system that would teach reading, writing, mathematics, history, botany, mechanics, astronomy, and general science.

Wollstonecraft not only articulated a utopian vision of the rational woman of the future. She also described in detail the errors and evils of the prevailing British and French gender definition of the female as the subordinate helpmate of the male, insisting throughout that the historical enslavement of women has also corrupted men. By being forced to assume the social role of the master, men are taught to be demanding, self-indulgent, arrogant, and tyrannical. The habit of treating their women as inferior dependents has undermined men's ability to understand the needs of others, to act justly or compassionately, to be good leaders. While Wollstonecraft's attack on men is muted (after all, they comprise the audience whom she must persuade), she nonetheless makes it clear that the existence of a master-slave relationship between husband and wife creates evils on both sides. "How can women be just or generous, when they are the slaves of injustice?" (189), she asks rhetorically.

The revolution in female manners demanded by Wollstonecraft would, she insists, dramatically change both women and men. It would produce women who were sincerely modest, chaste, virtuous, Christian; who acted with reason and prudence and generosity. It would produce men who were kind, responsible, sensible, and just. And it would produce egalitarian marriages based on compatibility, mutual affection, and respect. As Wollstonecraft concluded, we shall not see women affectionate till more equality be established in society, till ranks are confounded and women freed, neither shall we see that dignified domestic happiness, the simple grandeur of which cannot be relished by ignorant or vitiated minds; nor will the important task of education ever be properly begun till the person of a woman is no longer preferred to her mind (191).

The rational woman; rational love; egalitarian marriage; the preservation of the domestic affections; responsibility for the mental, moral, and physical well-being and growth of all the members of the family—these are the cornerstones of Wollstonecraft's liberal feminism, a feminism committed to a model of equality rather than difference. Her political ideology diverged profoundly from that of the Girondist leaders of the French Revolution in its insistence on the equality of the female and on the primary importance of the domestic affections and the family. By advocating the model of the egalitarian family as the prototype of a genuine democracy, a family in which husband and wife not only regard each other as equals in intelligence, sensitivity, and power, but also participate equally in child-care and decision making, Wollstonecraft introduced a truly revolutionary political program, one in which gender and class differences could be erased.

In 1792 Wollstonecraft continued to look to the leaders of the French Revolution for the institution of this ideal democracy. In December 1792 she sailed to Paris, arriving on the eve of the Terror. From her window at White's Hotel, she looked down on the procession taking Louis XVI to his trial for treason on December 26. As she movingly described the event to her publisher and employer Joseph Johnson:

I . . . wished to wait till I could tell you that this day was not stained with blood. Indeed the prudent precautions taken by the National Convention to prevent a tumult made me suppose that the dogs of faction would not dare to bark, much less to bite, however true to their scent; and I was not mistaken; for the citizens, who were all called out, are returning home with composed countenances, shouldering their arms. About nine o'clock this morning, the king passed by my window, moving silently along (excepting now and then a few strokes on the drum, which rendered the stillness more awful) through empty streets, surrounded by the national guards, who, clustering round the carriage, seemed to deserve their name. The inhabitants flocked to their windows, but the casements were all shut, not a voice was heard, nor did I see any thing like an insulting gesture.—For the first time since I entered France, I bowed to the majesty of the people, and respected the propriety of behaviour so perfectly in unison with my own feelings. I can scarcely tell you why, but an association of ideas made the tears flow insensibly from my eyes, when I saw Louis sitting, with more dignity than I expected from his character, in a hackney coach going to meet death, where so many of his race have triumphed. My fancy instantly brought Louis XIV before me, entering the capital with all his pomp, after one of the victories most flattering to his pride, only to see the sunshine of prosperity overshadowed by the sublime gloom of misery. I have been alone ever since; and, though my mind is calm, I cannot dismiss the lively images that have filled my imagination all the day.—

Nay, do not smile, but pity me; for, once or twice, lifting my eyes from the paper, I have seen eyes glare through a glass-door opposite my chair, and bloody hands shook at me. Not the distant sound of a footstep can I hear. My apartments are remote from those of the servants, the only persons who sleep with me in an immense hotel, one folding door opening after another.—I wish I had even kept the cat with me!—I want to see something alive; death in so many frightful shapes has taken hold of my fancy.—I am going to bed— and for the first time in my life, I cannot put out the candle.[4]

Further horrified by the execution of the king and the numerous deaths that followed at the hands of the Jacobin Convention, Wollstonecraft reflected bitterly on the *Present Character of the French Nation* in early 1793. In contact only with the English-speaking community in Paris, most notably Helen Maria Williams and Ruth and Joel Barlow, she condemned the Parisians as people "rendered cold and artificial by the selfish enjoyments of the senses," as "men vicious without warmth." She feared that the golden age of which she had dreamt for France, a time when "strong virtues might exist with the polished manners produced by the progress of civilization," a time when "men would labour to become virtuous, without being goaded on by misery," was forever lost. Instead, she reluctantly confessed,

every thing whispers me, that names, not principles, are changed, and when I see that the turn of the tide has left the dregs of the old system to corrupt the new. For the same pride of office, the same desire of power are still visible; with this aggravation, that, fearing to return to obscurity after having but just acquired a relish for distinction, each hero, or philosopher, for all are dubbed with these new titles, endeavours to make hay while the sun shines; and every petty municipal officer, become the idol, or rather the tyrant of the day, stalks like a cock on a dunghill.[5]

Despite her disgust with the Montagnards, whom she described as the generator of "a race of monsters, the most flagitious that ever alarmed the world by the murder of innocents, and the mockery of justice,"[6] Mary Wollstonecraft continued to support the democratic ideals of the Girondists. In February 1793, she responded to a request delivered by Thomas Paine from Condorcet, whom she never met, by "writing a plan of education for the Committee" on Public Instruction,[7] a plan for coeducation which was not adopted. In 1795, after her tempestuous and distracting love affair with the American speculator Gilbert Imlay and the birth of her daughter Fanny, she published an overview of the French Revolution in which she condemned the ancient régime as "a deadly disease" and justified the overthrow of the monarchy as necessary to the progress of liberty and equality in France. Again blaming the cruelties and excesses of the revolution on the French character, with its "disposition to intrigue, and want of sincerity," she nonetheless supported the general direction of recent events in France as "progressive." "It was," she concluded, "a revolution in the minds of men; and only demanded a new system of government to be adapted to that change," a new system that she—still blissfully happy in her own domestic situation—would ground on the model of the egalitarian family and "the family affections, whence all the social virtues spring."[8] For Wollstonecraft, then, the French Revolution was simultaneously a movement toward human perfectibility and a monstrous terror, a contradictory image that would later inform her second daughter's most famous work.

For the other English woman writer who went to France in 1790, Helen Maria Williams, the French Revolution was a less complicated sign: it was liberty itself. Arriving with her sister in Paris on July 13, 1790, Helen Maria Williams was just in time to attend the great anniversary celebration of the Federation at the Champs de Mars on July 14. Described in detail by Mona Ozouf,[9] this fete was designed to manifest to the citizens of France their universal participation in the community of man, without distinction of rank, age, or sex. The festival overwhelmed Helen Maria Williams by its communality, its seriousness of purpose, its sheer grandeur. Impressed by the absence of all social distinctions, by the fusing of the people and the king, by the festival's rationally ordered processions and spatial configurations—in which the National Assembly and royalty together wound through the level field and then ascended to the top of the pavilion—Williams enthused,

> How am I to paint the impetuous feelings of that immense, that exulting multitude? Half a million of people assembled at a spectacle, which furnished every image that can elevate the mind of man, which connected the enthusiasm of moral sentiment with the solemn pomp of religious ceremonies; which addressed itself at once to the imagination, the understanding, and the heart.[10]

Even though she was a foreigner, Williams was at once swept up in a wave of emotion, experiencing an almost sacred bonding with the mass of humanity around her, convinced then and for years to come that the French Revolution had brought genuine freedom to the people of France. So committed was she to this revolutionary ideal that she eagerly volunteered to play the role of liberty at a private fete celebrated three months later at the chateau of her friend Madame du Fossé. She appeared in the last scene as the statue of liberty, wearing a Phrygian cap; she was then draped with a tricolor scarf, the signal for the audience to break into a rousing chorus of *Ça ira*. Thus, she records in her *Letters from France*,

> do the French, lest they should be tempted, by pleasure, to forget one moment the cause of liberty, bind it to their remembrance in the hour of festivity; with fillets and scarfs of national ribband; connect it with the sound of the viol and the harp, and appoint it not merely to regulate the great movements of government, but to mould the figure of the dance (I:205-6).

Seeing in both these festivals the visible and transparent representation of the achievements of the National Assembly and the beginning of a golden era of French democracy, Helen Maria Williams embodied in her very person the founding ideology of the revolution. As an icon of female liberty, she persuaded herself that women had indeed achieved a new freedom and dignity under the revolutionary Republic. But one could argue, as have several contributors to this volume, that Williams here was naive, failing to see the ways in which the representation of Liberty as female actually functioned ambiguously, enabling the male leaders of the revolution to control their female compatriots by making them the objects of masculine representation rather than active, equal partners in the building of the new nation.

Williams's eight volumes of *Letters from France*, describing the events in France from July 1790 through 1795, unfold a narrative of spectacular if necessarily uneven triumph over tyranny. She grounds her affirmation of the revolution simultaneously in her sense of communion with the freed workers of France and in her direct experience, through her friends, the du Fossés, of the evils of the ancien régime. More aware of the sufferings inflicted on the French in the past and hence more accepting of present excesses than Mary Wollstonecraft, Williams presents the tale of the du Fossé family as the paradigm of the political tyranny of the ancien régime, enforced collectively by church and monarchy in both the private and the public realm.

In brief, Augustin François Thomas du Fossé, the eldest son of the wealthy Baron du Fossé, fell in love with the virtuous daughter of a local bourgeois farmer, the paid companion of his mother. Their relationship, founded on mutual esteem and extensive knowledge of each other's character and temperament, promised the highest domestic happiness. But the snobbish Baron du Fossé objected to the match and issued a *lettre du cachet*, which authorized the imprisonment of his oldest son and heir, to prevent the marriage. The young couple, now secretly married, fled to England where they barely survived by giving French lessons. Augustin, now a father unable to feed his growing family, was persuaded to return to France by the promise of a reconciliation with his father and an allowance. As soon as he entered his father's house, he was arrested and imprisoned in the monastery of Les Frères de Sainte Charité where he was held, unable to communicate with his wife and daughter, for three years. He finally managed to escape from prison, seriously injuring himself in a leap from the monastery walls, and would have been reinterred had not the townspeople of Beauvais protected him from the priests and his father and shipped him back to London. Reunited at last with his family, sick, in dire poverty, he was eking out a minimal existence when the Williams sisters, eager to learn French, hired him as their teacher.

The day after the fall of the Bastille, du Fossé returned to France with his family, claimed his rightful share of his inheritance, gave up his aristocratic title, and became—with the Williams sisters—an ardent supporter of the revolution. His history became for Helen Maria Williams the narrative of the ancien régime itself, a story of unrelenting and arbitrary cruelty, ending only with the advent of revolutionary freedom and the new regime instituted in the du Fossé household, a regime of mutual benevolence, rational action, gender equality, justice, and "domestic felicity" (II:2).

The du Fossé story was also for Williams the narrative of the abuses of patriarchy, of the excessive power of the father in the domestic sphere. Repeatedly she portrayed the cruel behavior of Baron du Fossé as the dereliction of paternal responsibility. Commenting on Augustin's imprisonment, she exclaimed:

> Is it not difficult to believe that these sufferings were inflicted by a father? A
> father!—that name which I cannot trace without emotion; which conveys all
> the ideas of protection, of security, of tenderness; that dear relation to which, in
> general, children owe their prosperity, their enjoyments, and even their
> virtues!—Alas, the unhappy Mons. du Fossé owed nothing to *his* father, but
> that life, which from its earliest period his cruelty had embittered, and which he
> now condemned to languish in miseries that death only could heal (I:156–57).

The arbitrary authority of the father over his sons and daughters would, in
Williams's view, end with the revolution. Like Wollstonecraft, Williams saw
the revolution as an opportunity for women to gain greater domestic and
public power. She enthusiastically applauded those female aristocrats who
with "a spirit worthy of Roman matrons" willingly gave up "titles, fortune and
even personal ornaments, so dear to female vanity, for the common cause" and
who became the "secret springs in mechanism, by which, though invisible,
great movements are regulated" (I:27, 37–38). She commented approvingly on
the French practice of instructing the wife of a merchant in arithmetic and
insisting that she act as her husband's first clerk in his countinghouse, thus
training her to carry on the business in his absence or after his death. In
addition, she urged the English to adopt the new French institution of the
lycée, a place where bourgeois men and women of Paris gathered to hear
lectures by the most celebrated professors on natural philosophy, chemistry,
natural history, botany, history, and belles lettres, and where Greek, Italian,
French, and English languages were taught (II:130–31). Like Wollstonecraft,
Williams saw in the practices of the new revolutionary era in France a model
for the equality of women, for the education and vocational training of females
on a par with males.

Helen Maria Williams suffered the reign of Robespierre and the Jacobins in
an extreme form; under the edict that forbade all foreigners to remain in Paris,
she was arrested and incarcerated in Luxembourg Prison for six months. But
even here, her enthusiasm for the possibilities of the revolution remained
undiminished; she comments feelingly on the numerous acts of bravery, sacrifice, generosity, and personal courage manifested by the other prisoners,
whether former aristocrats, Girondists, or innocent bystanders like herself.
Despite her fear, disgust, and outrage at Robespierre and the Montagnards,
and her horror at the unending massacre in which the guillotine becomes "the
minister of finance" (I:224), beheading innocent persons solely so the Convention can appropriate their property, she remained convinced that the noble
ideals of the revolution would finally win out. As she commented,

> no people ever travelled to the temple of Liberty by a path strewed with roses;
> nor has established tyranny ever yielded to reason and justice, till after a
> severe struggle. I do not pretend to justify the French, but I do not see much
> right that we at least have to condemn them" (IV:227).

She ended her account of the events in France with the death of Robespierre (in her eyes the ultimate betrayer of revolutionary ideals), the joyous release of all those unjustly imprisoned by the Convention, the defeat of the Jacobin factions in the countryside, the successes of the French armies fighting at the borders, and an affirmation of the new constitution, the Declaration of the Rights of Man. Unlike Wollstonecraft who returned to England repulsed by the September massacres and the reign of Terror, Williams remained in France for the rest of her life, committed to the new French nation and the sophistication of its culture. Writing from abroad for an English audience, she preserved during the ministries of Pitt and Burke the enthusiasm of the Enlightenment philosophes for a democratic government and the equality of women.

Living with another English émigré John Hurford Stone, raising two nephews, and earning a modest income from her writing, Helen Maria Williams became famous for hosting parties at which the ideals of the Girondists were kept alive. At first she ardently supported Napoleon Bonaparte, believing that he possessed not only the desire and the will to unify France under the democratic ideals of the revolution, but also the soul of a poet. In 1798 she publicly hailed Bonaparte as "the benefactor of his race converting the destructive lightning of the conqueror's sword into the benignant rays of freedom."[11] Not until the coronation of Napoleon the Great, Emperor for Life, by Pope Pius VII, on December 2, 1804, did Helen Maria Williams undergo the crisis of the true believer. In her *Narrative of the Events which have taken place in FRANCE* published in London in 1816, Williams tracked not only the career and downfall of Napoleon Bonapart after April 1815, but also the path of her own disillusion. Chronicling Napoleon's hypocrisies, vanities, cruelties to women (whom he forced into financially advantageous marriages), and military defeats, she sardonically portrayed the too easily duped French as the instruments of a malevolent despot.

So outraged was she by Napoleon that she could finally portray the restoration of the Bourbon monarchy as "the pure effusion of real happiness,"[12] a happiness registerd in the faces of the Parisians themselves. Although she remained a devotee of political liberty and continued to call for the establishment of a Congress of Europe that would create a constitutionally guaranteed democracy not only for France, but for all the countries invaded by Napoleon, this second narrative subtly reveals that her primary values were those of domestic tranquillity and the preservation of the civilized arts. As she detailed the disposition of the works of art captured by Napoleon, temporarily housed in the Louvre, and finally reclaimed by their respective homelands, she passionately decried the damage done to Venice's winged lion and Titian's *Transfiguration* during the process.

Her deepest emotions appeared when she was asked to describe the future fate of France.

> Are the French people, after all the mazy wanderings of the Revolution, are they approaching an asylum . . . ; are they going home at last?—This is

indeed a momentous question. It is not made by me, as perhaps it may be by yourself, in the spirit of speculative investigation; to me it comprehends all that can awaken solicitude, all that can interest the heart; all chance of personal tranquillity towards the evening of a stormy life, and all hope of felicity for the objects most dear to me, and to whom life is opening. France is to me also the country of my friends—of persons endeared to me by the tie of common suffering. We have passed through the tempest, to use the words of M. de Boufflers, "sous la même parapluie." How should I have lived so many years among the French without loving that amiable people, to apply the term in their own sense, who so well know the art of shedding a peculiar charm over social life! How much better than others they understand the secret of being happy! happy at a cheap rate, and without being too difficult, and too disdainful as we are in England, about the conditions; while they bear misfortunes with a cheerful equanimity, which if it does not deserve the proud name of philosophy, is of far more general use; the former being common property, belonging to all, and not, like the latter, the partial fortune of an enlightened few (302–4).

Here we can see all the tenets of Williams's mature ideology: a commitment to the domestic virtues, to home, to the equality of men and women, to the living of a good and happy life at modest expense. Even within the devastations and sufferings of the Terror and the Napoleonic campaigns, the French have in her eyes sustained a capacity to value that which is truly worthwhile, a humanitarian impulse for benevolent social relationships. At bottom, then, Williams remains optimistic, convinced that the French people will emerge uncorrupted by the cruelties of the Terror and the civil wars that have raged in France for the previous twenty years.

Both the positive image of the revolution as the birth of a new freedom, a movement toward human perfection, and the negative image of the Jacobin reign as a monstrous terror were literally embodied in the most famous novel written by Mary Wollstonecraft's daughter, Mary Godwin Shelley. Growing up in the Godwin household where the events in France were eagerly followed by the leading liberals of the day, obsessively reading and rereading the writings of the mother who had died giving birth to her, Mary Godwin was fully aware of the history of the French Revolution. Eloping at the age of sixteen with the married poet Percy Shelley in 1814, Mary fled to France where she recorded in her Journal the suffering brought to the French peasants by fifteen years of civil and foreign wars. Horrified by what she found, Mary described the village of Echemine as

a wretched place . . . [which] had been once large and populous, but now the houses were roofless, and the ruins that lay scattered about, the gardens covered with the white dust of the torn cottages, the black burnt beams, and squalid looks of the inhabitants, presented in every direction the melancholy aspect of devastation."[13]

The following winter, Percy Shelley read aloud to her both from Mary Wollstonecraft's *View of the French Revolution* and from the works of the Jacobin editor and publisher Louis-Marie Prudhomme.[14] Looking through Prudhomme's *Révolutions de Paris*, an influential radical journal dedicated to the ideal of popular sovereignty that was republished in book form in 1797, Mary Shelley encountered the symbolic image which the National Convention in Paris had publicly proclaimed for the new French Republic in November 1793. That image, invented by the painter David, was a colossal statue of Hercules to be erected on the Pont-Neuf and depicted on the new seal of the Convention: "This image of the people *standing* should carry in his other hand the terrible club with which the Ancients armed their Hercules!"[15] As Lynn Hunt has shown, Hercules was thus intended to represent, as transparently as possible, the strength, courage, labors, and unity of the common man (or sans-culottes) as he destroyed the many-headed Hydra of monarchical, aristocratic, and clerical tyranny.[16] As the image of Hercules developed in revolutionary French discourse, it came to embody both a gigantic liberating energy, the power of the people incarnate, and a potential monster, the Terror embodied in the strength and fury of the maddened Hercules.[17]

The ambivalence of the image of Hercules was graphically captured in an engraving for *Révolutions de Paris* in 1793 entitled "Le Peuple Mangeur de Rois" (Figure 13.1), which Mary Shelley may well have seen. Here the giant Hercules, clad "sans-culottes" in rolled-up trousers and Phrygian cap, bare-chested, club in hand, roasts the child-sized figure of the king over an open Regency pyre. This image graphically prefigures key elements in Mary Shelley's novel *Frankenstein:* the creation of a giant who plays with fire and who strangles a defenseless child by the throat.

When Mary Shelley passed through Paris a year later, en route to Switzerland to visit Lord Byron in the summer of 1816, she perceived a radical deterioration in the morale and manners of the Parisians as a result of Napoleon's recent defeats on land and sea: "the discontent and sullenness of their minds perpetually betrays itself."[18] In Geneva, she found Byron passionately writing about Napoleon's defeat in the third canto of *Childe Harold*. Byron had visited the fields of Waterloo only a few weeks earlier, on May 4, and was overwhelmed by this melancholy sign of human fallibility and the fall of empires:

> Stop!—for thy tread is on an Empire's dust!
> An Earthquake's spoil is sepulchred below!
> Is the spot mark'd with no colossal bust,
> Nor column trophied for triumphal show?
> None; but the moral's truth tells simpler so,
> As the ground was before, thus let it be;—
> How that red rain hath made the harvest grow!
> And is this all the world has gained by thee,
> Thou first and last of fields, king-making Victory?
> *Childe Harold*, Canto III, stanza xvii

It is not surprising, then, that when Mary Shelley was asked to compete in Byron's ghost-story writing contest on June 16, 1816, she included the recent history of France in her tale of *Frankenstein*. Her novel tells many other

Figure 13.1 Anonymous, "Le Peuple Mangeur de Rois." Engraving. *Source*: Musée Carnavalet, Paris.

stories, which I have discussed elsewhere[19]—the story of science gone berserk, the story of what happens when a man tries to have a baby without a woman, the epistemological story of the problematic relation of seeing to knowing. Here I wish to focus on the way in which it represents her response to the French Revolution.

Mary Shelley pointed to the political dimensions of her novel when she titled it "Frankenstein, or The Modern Prometheus." For the romantic poets Byron and Percy Shelley, Prometheus was the symbol of political revolution, of a just rebellion against the tyranny of reigning monarchs, of a belief in human perfectibility. By sending her protagonist Victor Frankenstein to the University of Ingolstadt for his scientific training, she further associated him with the hotbed of Jacobin thought in Germany, the home of the Illuminist sect founded by Ingolstadt's most famous professor, Adam Weishaupt. And she specifically dated Victor Frankenstein's creation to "a drear night in November" 1792, midway between the September Massacres and the execution of Louis XVI on January 21, 1793, thus figuratively identifying Frankenstein's animation of a dead body with both the birth and death of the revolutionary French nation. Like the Girondists, Victor Frankenstein is originally inspired by the desire to perfect human nature, to create a "new species" of mankind able to triumph over death and corruption. In fact, the being he creates explicitly voices the basic tenet of Jacobin ideology, the belief in the innate goodness of human nature. As the creature proclaims throughout the novel, echoing Rousseau's *Social Contract*, "I was benevolent and good; misery made me a fiend."[20]

But Victor Frankenstein flees in horror from the eight-foot tall, discolored child he has created, abandoning his newborn son, refusing to mother it. His creature at first seeks desperately to become part of the human community: he saves a drowning girl, only to be shot at by her father; for two years he brings gifts of firewood to the De Lacey family, only to be finally rejected by Felix De Lacey. Unable to obtain the human sympathy he craves, Frankenstein's disfigured and gigantic creature is finally driven to violence and even murder by the constant suspicion, fear, and hostility he encounters. In a senseless rage, he burns down the De Lacey cottage and murders the five-year-old William Frankenstein. Once again frustrated by his maker in his desire for female companionship (Victor Frankenstein first agrees to make a female monster for his creature and then destroys her half-finished body), he finally murders Frankenstein's best friend Clerval and his bride Elizabeth.

The life of this fictional Creature thus rewrites the history of the French Revolution. As Mary Shelley had learned from her mother's account of the origin and progress of the French Revolution, and as she could see clearly for herself in 1816, the French Revolution that had originated in a democratic vision propounded by the idealistic Girondists had not found the parental guidance, control, and nurturance it required to develop into a rational and benevolent state. Unable to find a legitimate place in the new revolutionary social order for the dispossessed aristocrats and clergy, unable to create the egalitarian family-politic that Mary Wollstonecraft had advocated, the Girondists had unleashed a political movement that had finally resorted to brute force to attain its ends, beginning with the violence of the September massacres, continuing with the executions of Louis XVI and Marie Antoinette and the Terror, and ending with the Napoleonic wars.

In personifying the French Revolution as a gigantic monster, Mary Shelley relied on prior inscriptions of the revolution as a monster. Abbé Barruel, the fierce critic of Illuminism, had warned the readers of the final volume of his *Memoirs, Illustrating the History of Jacobinism*, published in 1797 and read by Mary and Percy Shelley in August 1814: "Meanwhile, before Satan shall exultingly enjoy this triumphant spectacle [of complete anarchy] which the Illuminizing Code is preparing, let us examine how . . . it engendered that disastrous monster called Jacobin, raging uncontrolled, and almost unopposed, in these days of horror and devastation."[21] Helen Maria Williams had lamented that the reign of the Montagnards had "dragged our reluctant steps into dens of undescribed and unknown monsters, whose existence we had never till now believed" (*Letters from France*, VII:51). Closer to home, Mary Wollstonecraft had condemned the Girondists for "peevishly" retiring from the leadership of the revolution and thereby hurrying "into action a race of monsters, the most flagitious that ever alarmed the world by the murder of innocents, and the mockery of justice" (*View of the French Revolution*, 300). That Mary Shelley intended her readers to associate Frankenstein's gigantic monster with the French Revolution is further suggested by the account she later gave of her father's radical politics in 1789:

The giant now awoke. The mind, never torpid, but never rouzed to its full energies, received the spark which lit it into an inextinguishable flame. Who can now tell the feelings of liberal men on the first outbreak of the French Revolution. In but too short a time afterwards it became tarnished by the vices of Orleans—dimmed by the want of talent of the Girondists—deformed & blood-stained by the Jacobins. But in 1789 & 1790 it was impossible for any but a courtier not to be warmed by the glowing influence.[22]

By representing in her Creature both the originating ideals and the vicious consequences of the French Revolution, Mary Shelley offered a far more negative assessment of the revolution than had Helen Maria Williams or her mother. Twenty years after Wollstonecraft's death, Mary Shelley had come to believe that an abstract ideal or political cause (e.g., the creation of a just society), if not carefully nurtured within a tolerant social environment, can become an end that justifies any means, however cruel. As Victor Frankenstein worked to conquer death by creating a living being out of dead human and animal parts, he never paused to consider how his alien, freakish child would be regarded and treated by others. By 1816, Mary Shelley believed that the Girondists, in their eagerness to end the social injustice of the ancien régime, had given insufficient thought to the fates of the aristocrats, clergymen, and peasants who would necessarily be hurt, even killed, during the process of political revolution. Looking back on this period of French history in 1839, she criticised Condorcet, in her *Lives of the Most Eminent Literary and Scientific Men of France*, for his failure to recognize the probable consequences of the political enactment of his beliefs:

> Condorcet . . . showed his attachment to all that should ameliorate the social condition, and enlarge the sphere of intellect among his fellow-creatures. He did not, in his reasonings, give sufficient force to the influence of passion, especially when exerted over masses, nor the vast power which the many have when they assert themselves, nor the facility with which the interested few can lead assembled numbers into error and crime.[23]

Reflecting on the Terror and the rise and fall of the Napoleonic empire as she wrote her novel in 1817, Mary Shelley concluded that political means often become ends in themselves. A political cause cannot be detached from its modes of production. For a revolution to succeed, she argued, it must balance the abstract goals it seeks against the moral obligation to preserve the welfare of every living individual.

Mary Shelley's novel clearly implies that if Victor Frankenstein had been able to love and care for his creature, to give his newborn child the nurturing it required to develop into a healthy and well-adjusted adult, he might indeed have created a race of immortal beings that would in future times have blessed him. Similarly, if the Girondists had been able to reconcile the king, the nobility, and the clergy to their new republic and to control the suspicion, hostility, and fears of the people, the French Revolution they engendered might have become the just and benevolent democracy of which they dreamed. In a passage that functions in Mary Shelley's novel both as authorial credo and as

the moral touchstone from which we can judge his errors, Frankenstein confesses:

> A human being in perfection ought always to preserve a calm and peaceful
> mind, and never to allow passion or a transitory desire to disturb his tranquil-
> lity. I do not think that the pursuit of knowledge is an exception to this rule.
> If the study to which you apply yourself has a tendency to weaken your
> affections, and to destroy your taste for those simple pleasures in which no
> alloy can possibly mix, then that study is certainly unlawful, that is to say,
> not befitting the human mind. If this rule were always observed; if no man
> allowed any pursuit whatsoever to interfere with the tranquillity of his
> domestic affections, Greece had not been enslaved; Caesar would have spared
> his country; America would have been discovered more gradually; and the
> empires of Mexico and Peru had not been destroyed (51).

Having learned the lessons of the Terror and the accession to power by the
Bonaparte dynasty, Mary Shelley perceived a danger that for her was inherent
in the ideology of the French Revolution: commitment to an abstract good can
justify an emotional detachment from present human relationships and family
obligations, a willingness to sacrifice the living to a cause whose final consequences cannot be fully controlled, and an obsession with realizing a dream
that too often masks an egotistical wish for personal power. As she later
commented on Condorcet,

> like all French politicians of that day, he wished to treat mankind like
> puppets, and fancied that it was only necessary to pull particular strings to
> draw them within the circle of order and reason. We none of us know the laws
> of our nature; and there can be little doubt that, if philosophers like Con-
> dorcet did educate their fellows into some approximation to their rule of
> right, the ardent feelings and burning imaginations of man would create
> something now unthought of, but not less different from the results he
> expected, than the series of sin and sorrow which now desolates the world.[24]

In *Frankenstein* Mary Shelley followed both her mother and Helen Maria
Williams in promoting an alternative political ideology based on the trope of
the peaceful, loving, egalitarian family. She too suggests that if political actions
are based on the "domestic affections"—on a genuine concern to protect the
legitimate interests and welfare of every member of the family politic, no
matter how different from one another—then tyranny, war, and cultural
imperialism can be prevented and the historical examples of national enslavement and military destruction that she specifically cites—Greece, Rome, native
America, Mexico, Peru—will not recur. By unveiling the pattern of psychological desire, self-delusion, and egotism that informed Frankenstein's revolutionary goals, a pattern I have traced in greater detail elsewhere,[25] she drew our
attention to something that Helen Maria Williams overlooked, to the extent to
which any given political ideology serves the psychic as well as the economic
interests of a specific class: in the case of Frankenstein, Talleyrand, and the
male Girondists, the class of the male bourgeois capitalists who would profit
from the overthrow of the aristocracy and monarchy. She thus disclosed the

gender bias implicit in the Declaration of the Rights of Man and subverted its claim to have served the *universal* interests of humanity.

Her own political ideology would serve instead the interests of the family and thus allows both for the equality of women and for the participation of women in the body politic. From a modern feminist perspective, however, the commitment of Wollstonecraft, Williams, and Shelley to a political ideology based on the model of the egalitarian bourgeois family is highly problematic. For such a model necessarily replicates the hierarchical structure of the bourgeois family—if not based on gender, then based on age and ordinal position. Implicit in the trope of the polis-as-family promoted by these three women writers is the constitution of certain political groups as "children" who must be governed. While neither Wollstonecraft nor Williams confronted this structural inequality directly, Mary Shelley's acceptance of such a hierarchy is tellingly revealed both in her revulsion from the lower classes, particularly those of foreign nations—the German peasants whose "horrid and slimy faces" she found "exceedingly disgusting" during her voyage along the Rhine in 1814[26]—and in her unquestioned later assumption that she belonged to "society," the upper-middle-class world of her husband's gentry ancestors, rather than to the artisanal lower-middle classes of her own parents.

The ideological contradiction between freedom and domination exposed by the development of the French Revolution thus cracks apart the writings of these three English women. Indeed, the text of *Frankenstein* can be read as the locus of this fracturing. Here, contradiction is embodied in the very figure of the French Revolution—Frankenstein's Herculean creature who represents both the possibility of human divinity and the monstrous havoc of universal destruction. For as the Creature tells his maker, "Remember that I have power; . . . I can make you so wretched that the light of day will be hateful to you. You are my creator, but I am your master;—obey!" (165).

Moreover, the trope of the egalitarian family promoted as the model of good government by Wollstonecraft, Williams, and Shelley alike can function as a trope of oppression. Inherent in their celebration of domestic tranquillity and the family-as-polis is an affirmation of the power of parents over children, an affirmation that implicitly endorses the preservation of a class system. In Mary Shelley's view, parents have the right, even the obligation, to control as well as to nurture and protect their children. When she voices her belief that America should "have been discovered more gradually," (51) she implicitly casts America in the role of a newborn child-continent that should have been cautiously developed under the loving parental care of its new explorer-rulers. Significantly, she does *not* say that America should have been left undiscovered, uncolonized, unexploited; but only that this process of imperial conquest should have occurred more gradually, perhaps less painfully.

More important, the model of gender equality proposed by Wollstonecraft, Williams, and Shelley can too easily become a model of sameness imposed on both women and men. All three women argued that men should be more like women, more nurturing, more committed to the domestic affections, while women should fulfill the roles outside the home traditionally assigned to men.

But their argument failed to acknowledge the possibility of difference, both between and *within* the gender categories of man and woman—differences of age, temperament, physical capacity, ethnicity, race, sexual preference, and so forth.

Their failure to articulate a model of human development and political organization that would embrace the full complexity of human *difference* as well as human equality should not be seen as a dismissive criticism of Wollstonecraft, Williams, or Shelley, since no current feminist theory has yet adequately constructed such a model. But their historical engagement in the discourse of the Enlightenment, with its conceptual reliance on natural rights, the equality of man, systematic benevolence, and the possibility of progress toward human perfection, significantly restricted their feminist program to a model of liberal equality, both within and without the domestic sphere. And such a model, insofar as it implicitly identifies equality with sameness and thereby coerces every individual to conform to an abstract norm (historically grounded on a paradigm of *male* experience) necessarily—and often violently—produces the Other, the outcast, and even the monster.

Notes

1. Edmund Burke, *Reflections on the Revolution in France, and on the Proceedings of Certain Societies in London, relative to that Event* (November 1790), ed. Thomas H. D. Mahoney (New York: Liberal Arts Press, 1955), 35, 67, 82.

2. Mary Wollstonecraft, *A Vindication of the Rights of Men* (November 1790), A Facsimile Reproduction with an Introduction by Eleanor Louise Nicholes (Gainesville, Fla.: Scholars' Facsimiles & Reprints, 1960), 41, 52, 146, 147.

3. Mary Wollstonecraft, *A Vindication of the Rights of Woman* (1792), ed. Carol H. Poston (New York: W. W. Norton & Co., Inc., 1975), 45 and 192. Further citations from this edition will be given parenthetically in text.

4. Mary Wollstonecraft, *Collected Letters of Mary Wollstonecraft*, ed. Ralph M. Wardle (Ithaca and London: Cornell University Press, 1979), 227.

5. Mary Wollstonecraft, "Letter on the Present Character of the French Nation," in *A Wollstonecraft Anthology*, ed. Janet M. Todd (Bloomington, Indiana and London: Indiana University Press, 1977), 122–24.

6. Mary Wollstonecraft, *An Historical and Moral View of the Origin and Progress of the French Revolution and the Effect it Has Produced in Europe* (1795); a facsimile reproduction with an Introduction by Janet M. Todd (Delmar, New York: Scholars' Facsimiles & Reprints, 1975), 300.

7. Mary Wollstonecraft, *Collected Letters*, 230.

8. Wollstonecraft, *Origin and Progress of the French Revolution*, 63, 297, 396, 406.

9. Mona Ozouf, *Festivals and the French Revolution*, trans. Alan Sheridan (Cambridge: Harvard University Press, 1988), Chapter One and passim.

10. Helen Maria Williams, *Letters written in France, in the Summer 1790, to a Friend in England, containing Various Anecdotes relative to the French Revolution; and Memoirs of Mons. and Madame Du F——* (London: T. Cadell, 1796); republished as *Letters from France*, Eight Volumes in Two, facsimile reproductions with an

Introduction by Janet M. Todd (Delmar, New York: Scholars' Facsimiles & Reprints, 1975), I: 5-6. All further citations from these two volumes are given in the text, by original volume and page.

11. Helen Maria Williams, *A Tour in Switzerland; or, a View of the Present State of the Governments and Manners of those Cantons, with Comparative Sketches of the Present State of Paris* (London: G. G. & J. Robinson, 1798), II: 55-56.

12. Helen Maria Williams, *A Narrative of the Events which have taken place in FRANCE, with an account of the Present State of Society and Public Opinion* (London: John Murray, 1816; 2nd edition), 271. Further references to this volume will be cited in the text.

13. Mary Wollstonecraft Shelley, *History of a Six Weeks Tour through a part of France, Switzerland, Germany and Holland, with Letters descriptive of a Sail round the Lake of Geneva, and of the Glaciers of Chamouni* (London: T. Hookham, Jr., and C. and J. Ollier, 1817), 22-23.

14. Mary Shelley, *The Journals of Mary Shelley 1814-1844*, ed. Paula R. Feldman and Diana Scott-Kilvert (Oxford: The Clarendon Press, 1987), I: 49, 55, & n. 1.

On Prudhomme's career as editor and journalist, see Jack Richard Censer, *Prelude to Power—The Parisian Radical Press 1789-1791* (Baltimore: Johns Hopkins University Press, 1976), 22-6 and *passim*.

15. M. J. Guillaume, ed., *Procès-verbaux du Comité d'Instruction publique de la Convention Nationale* 2 (17 brumaire an II) (Paris, 1894), 779.

16. Lynn Hunt, *Politics, Culture, and Class in the French Revolution* (Berkeley: University of California Press, 1984), Chap. 3.

17. See Joseph Fouche, "Déclaration aux Citoyens de la Départmente de L'Aube," June 29, 1793, *Archives Parlementaires* (Troyes) 68, 73.

18. Mary Shelley, *Six Weeks Tour*, 86.

19. Anne K. Mellor, *Mary Shelley—Her Life, Her Fiction, Her Monsters* (New York and London: Methuen and Routledge, Chapman & Hall, 1988), chaps. 2-7.

20. Mary Wollstonecraft Shelley, *Frankenstein, or The Modern Prometheus* (The 1818 Text), ed. James Rieger (Chicago and London: University of Chicago Press, 1974, 1982), 95. All further quotations from this edition of *Frankenstein* will be cited parenthetically in the text.

On Mary Shelley's indebtedness to Rousseau in *Frankenstein*, see Paul A. Cantor, *Creature and Creator: Myth-making and English Romanticism* (New York: Cambridge University Press, 1984), 119-28; Jean de Palacio, *Mary Shelley dans son oeuvre* (Paris: Klincksieck, 1969), 209-11; and Milton Millhauser, "The Noble Savage in Mary Shelley's *Frankenstein*," *Notes and Queries* CXC (1946), 248-50.

21. L'Abbé Augustin Barruel, *Memoirs, Illustrating the History of Jacobinism*, trans. Robert Clifford (London, 1797-98), III: 414.

22. Mary Wollstonecraft Shelley, "Life of William Godwin," 151 (Bodleian Library, Oxford: Abinger Shelley Collection, Abinger Dep. c. 606/1); Mary Shelley never completed or published her biography of Godwin.

23. Mary Wollstonecraft Shelley, *Lives of the most Eminent Literary and Scientific Men of France*, for *The Cabinet Cyclopedia*, ed. Rev. Dionysius Lardner (London: Longman et. al., 1838-39), II: 179.

24. Mary Shelley, *Lives of the . . . Men of France*, II: 186.

25. Anne K. Mellor, *Mary Shelley—Her Life, Her Fiction, Her Monsters*; see especially Chaps. 4-7.

26. Mary Shelley, *History of a Six Weeks Tour*, 50, 56.

14

Flora Tristan: Rebel Daughter of the Revolution

DOMINIQUE DESANTI

The nineteenth century is the second wave of the French Revolution. Utopian socialists extended its ideas to the people the revolution had forgotten—women and workers—and thereby deepened those ideas. At this time, one woman, Flora Tristan (1803–44), acting alone, cast upon the political scene a flash of brilliance that lasted but a few years. Through her life and her work, inseparable from each other, she appears the emblematic figure of this second revolutionary wave.

Even more than other feminists of the age, she was erased from the history of ideas and deeds. Then finally, in 1925, the scholar Jules Puech consecrated a serious study to her[1]—then silence. In 1946, some excerpts from her writings on socialism were published by Lucien Scheler.[2] Then silence again until 1972. Since that year, on the other hand, theses, studies, and publications on her life and work have multiplied both in France and the United States.[3] And so she is now recognized as perhaps the most vivid, or in any case, the most romantic and talented of the pioneers and founders of French Socialist Feminism. Second to George Sand, you might say? Yes, second to her for talent and renown, but not for conviction or tenacity, in furthering this second wave of the French Revolution.

Flora's writings about her own life—memoirs, a diary, letters—make it seem a novel composed by destiny to illustrate woman's marginality in the early nineteenth century. The gradual recognition of these writings has allowed us to discern behind the blinding sun of George Sand the figure of Flora. Her daily experience, as it appears in the introduction to her memoirs, *Peregrinations of a Pariah*,[4] sums up all the dramas of the feminine condition, all the denied rights, and all the unfinished tasks of the French Revolution with respect to women—all of them. First, she is an illegitimate child. Then she is unhappily married in a period that outlawed divorce, deprived the mother of all rights concerning her children, and made the father the sole head of the family. She is impoverished in a period that refused to provide trades or

Translated by Judith Pike and Leslie W. Rabine.

education to girls without money. She is a wife who leaves her husband and so becomes a delinquent, since the Civil Code of 1803 specifies that the woman is required to live in the conjugal domicile, which belongs to the husband.[5] She is a fugitive sho takes her daughter, Aline, with her, and so becomes in addition a "thief." A liberalization, slight but essential, the right to divorce, accorded by the revolution had been taken away by the restoration.

But, you will say, isn't all this the case for George Sand as well? Did these two women have parallel destinies? Yes, they did, but George had the estate of Nohant, powerful friends, illustrious lovers, and a very early fame, all of which helps to lessen the crushing weight of these restrictions. Flora's fate bears witness to the fate of thousands, even tens of thousands, of her contemporaries. She was, in fact, one of the extremely rare women who spoke out and took up the pen precisely in order to bear witness; and to draw from this fate the logical decision: not resignation, but struggle. Yet, the writers who studied the Utopian Socialists, Saint-Simon (1760–1825), Charles Fourier (1772–1837), and their disciples, hardly cited her name although she left behind a significant body of social criticism and theory.

Her works, *Peregrinations of a Pariah* (1836 in periodical form, 1838 in book form), *Promenades in London* (1840), and *Worker's Union* (1843),[6] show first that Flora recognizes the source of her ideas in the French Revolution and the Declaration of the Rights of Man; second, that she wants to include in these basic rights those people—women and workers—forgotten by the revolution; and third, that in order to do so, she finds it necessary to go beyond the Revolution of 1789. She is unquestionably a *rebel daughter* of the revolution, which she criticizes and at times rejects because of its inadequacies, but which she reveres for its profound upheaval and fundamental subversion of an entrenched order.

The Saint-Simonians and Fourierists also sought to revive and deepen the gains of 1789 and above all of the never-executed Constitution of 1793.[7] In Flora's first book of sustained social theory, *Promenades in London*, she distinguishes herself from these other socialists, but without denying them as sources from which her ideas developed. She had visited Fourier while she was beginning to gain social awareness in 1835; she had spoken at length with Owen, whose followers guided her through her investigations of London; and she did not lack contacts—probably stormy—with the Saint-Simonians. But this rebel daughter of the revolution remained alone, outside of any group or movement, except the "Committees of the Workers' Union," which she organized in several cities of France, in 1844 during the last months of her life.

Her work is strewn with evocations of, denunciations of, and appeals to prolong the revolution. For example, in 1840, under the reign of Louis Philippe, she writes in *Promenades in London:*

> [I]f the principles which triumphed in 1789 and 1830 have not yet been
> realized anywhere, and if arbitrary rule raises its arrogant head everywhere,
> the man of faith, contemplating the triumphs of thought, nevertheless feels
> his confidence in God doubled. He rests assured that the freedoms pro-

claimed by the Constituent, the Legislative, the Convention and all assemblies born of the universal suffrage of the people . . . will be realized because thought never dies . . . (*Promenades*, 227).

On the other hand, one of her very last written utterances, just before her death during her "tour of France" to organize the Workers' Union, is a long bitter cry against the shortcomings of political revolution. Having just been harassed and threatened by the police of Agen at her hotel after a meeting with local workers, she writes in her private diary, called the *Tour of France:*

It is in the name of the king that they operate, exactly as in 88. Good grief, what's the use of guillotining two or three—of expelling 4 or 5—just to return 56 years later to the old formula, "in the name of the king". . . .

It must be admitted that political revolutions are first-rate farces! . . . . But it's more than a farce.—It's stupid, atrocious!—Fight, workers, go ahead and kill yourselves in order to change governments. Yes, you'll be repaid handsomely! Oh how governments must laugh at the workers![8]

This disillusioned denunciation appears in her diary on September 23, 1844, during one of her many despairing moments in the days of police harassment, physical exhaustion, and failing health before her death on November 14 of that year. By contrast, two months before, in Avignon, it is the heiress of the Jacobins who expresses anger with those "proletarians" who wanted to speak "patois" (that is to say Occitan) as opposed to French: "It is a misunderstanding of the great and sublime idea of the Revolution of 89 to thus disrupt the unity of the country. What was our fathers' motto? 'The French Republic, one and indivisible'" (*Tour*, 177). She goes on to praise the Convention for its desire to establish schools so that all children "would speak the same language." For Flora, the illegitimate daughter of a Spanish father, half foreign wherever she went, language was the homeland. And so she laments that "since the fall of the glorious Revolution, no government has set itself the task of realizing this idea, the most urgent of all, of the national Convention." Flora is thus truly a daughter, both loyal and rebellious, of the revolution.

In *Promenades in London* Flora develops explicitly the foundation of her social ideas in the principles of the revolution as well as the need to go beyond them. If the people, she says "are raised in the principles of liberty and equality," they will have "learned to consider that not only is the resistance to oppression the *natural right* of man, but also that when the people are oppressed, insurrection becomes a *sacred duty*" (*Promenades*, 50). She tells the French workers: "The English people have not, like your fathers and yourselves, begun to win equality and freedom through glorious revolutions" (*Promenades*, 51). Yet she goes on to warn them of the limitations of revolutions modeled on 1789: "you should consider political rights uniquely as a *means* through which you can put yourself in a position to attack legally the ill at its source. . . . It is with the social order, the foundation of the edifice, that you should be concerned, and not with politics, which is only a factitious power . . ." (*Promenades*, 51). Flora shared this view with all the socialists before Marx. Like them, she believed: "Until the present, politics have been an egotistical science which governments have used more or less skilfully to exploit the people, while social science embraces in its entirety the interests of humanity" (*Promenades*, 51).

Her words comprise at the same time a criticism of the laws instituted by Louis-Philippe "the bourgeois king," a criticism of the lack of social measures taken by the revolution itself, and a foresight of the importance that the theory of "social revolution" would have. "Social science," which Saint-Simon's disciple August Comte will call "sociology," and which Flora practices in her investigations of London, presages the philosophical system founded upon the analysis of social classes and their struggle that Marx would soon construct. But it is Flora who first articulates the notion of proletarian class struggle. She bases this, moreover, on the goal of accomplishing for the "working class" what 1789 had accomplished for the bourgeoisie: "to constitute the working class" as a powerful entity "through a compact and indissoluble Union," and "to have the working class represented before the nation."[9] As early as 1832 in Lyon, striking workers had used the expression "universal union among workers." But in 1843, Flora's title *Workers' Union* still sounded new and scandalous, as a vehicle for organizing a comprehensive revolution.

One of the main ways that Flora both criticized and sought to deepen the principles of the revolution was by seeking to extend them to women. She wrote shortly after the time that a group of Saint-Simonian feminists had published *La Tribune des femmes* (1832–34), and during the time that another feminist group was intermittently publishing *La Gazette des femmes*.[10] This latter journal sought to expand the famous "Declaration of the Rights of Woman" of Olympes de Gouges (guillotined in 1793) and the demands of the "Society of Revolutionary Republicans" (banned also in 1793). Through articles and petitions it set out to realize the idea that "women have the same civil and political rights as men." Saint-Simonian women like Suzanne Voilquin and Fourierist women like Désirée Veret-Gay were fighting for the same ideas by organizing working women.[11]

Yet the autodidact Flora Tristan attracts our attention for the unique way in which, remaining unattached to the teachings of any of the prophets of socialism, she created a body of deeds and writings that draw her ideas, ambitions, and courage from the struggles she went through in her daily life. She both incarnates her ideas in her lived experience and composes her life through her writing. Thus a knowledge of her life is inseparable from a knowledge of her ideas if we are to hear the unique, feverish, poetic, but precise vibration of her appeal for a new kind of revolution, a social revolution through a pacifist union. Like these prophets, she knew that strength lay in union, and she ultimately sought to unite women, all of whom were oppressed because of their sex, and workers, oppressed as a class. But the journey of this heiress of the revolution was long.

Born November 7, 1803, Flora will later see the conditions of her birth and early life as a result of the revolution, its upheavals and its clashes between the new and the old. On the one hand, her mother, Thérèse Laisney (or Lainé), a dressmaker, emigrated to Bilbao, "to flee the horrors of the revolution,"[12] as

Flora says, where she met a Peruvian aristocrat, Don Mariano Tristan de Moscoso. On the other hand, her father, as a Spanish cavalier, in the service of the king of a country where no revolution had as yet swept away the old regime, needed the personal permission of the Spanish king to marry. Flora's parents thus "married clandestinely, and it was a French émigré priest who performed the marriage ceremony in the house where my mother was living" (Intro. to *Per.*, xxxvi). The marriage would not be recognized as valid. The father's death in Paris when Flora was four plunged mother and daughter into dire poverty. Flora passed from the aristocracy to the working class without ever experiencing bourgeois life. She knew about "the poor" not through hearsay, but because she did not have wood to keep herself warm. At fifteen, in love and beloved, she was rejected by the young man's family because of her "illegitimate" birth.

At the age of fifteen, therefore, this adolescent knew a triple marginality— as "bastard," foreigner, and destitute—from a society that rejected her. Before the age of eighteen she was married to an engraver, André Chazal, for whom she worked as a "colorist." Although her letters to her fiancé show her trying to persuade herself that she loves him while her body refuses him (*Letters*, 43), she later writes in *Peregrinations of a Pariah:* "my mother *compelled* me to marry a man I could neither love nor respect. I owe to this union all my misfortunes" (Intro. to *Per.*, xxxvi). Chazal rapidly proved to be an alcoholic, a gambler, lazy, and no doubt, violent. In less than four years, Flora was three times a mother, first of two sons . . . and then when she discovered herself pregnant for a third time at the age of 20, she fled.

Her flight completes her marginality, and forces her to live according to the double standard of a society whose laws compel her to lie in order to survive. According to the Napoleonic Civil Code: "The wife is obligated to live with the husband and follow him everywhere" (article 214). It is the husband alone who determines the "conjugal domicile" of the wife and children. Leaving this domicile is a crime. Flora thus calls herself a "fugitive slave" (Intro. to *Per.*, xxxviii), living a life that has become a series of violent scenes. Chazal continually tries to take the children and set the police upon his delinquent wife, until she finally wins her struggle against him and the regime he represents, in 1838. But from 1827 to 1838, she must transform herself from a fugitive slave into a prophet of the new revolution.

In this process, she cannot fail to link her personal drama to the need for broad social reform through the mediation of the Revolution of 1789. For instance, on December 20, 1837, she formulates her position on marriage, often expressed in her books and her letters, in a "Petition for the Reestablishment of Divorce" submitted to the Chamber of Deputies: "The ills produced by the indissolubility of marriage are generalized in a way that is strikingly clear to everyone. God has not granted continuity to any but a very small number of our affections, and yet we wish to impose immutability upon the most variable of them all" (*Letters*, 74). These remarks, which bear the influence of Charles Fourier, are shortly followed by a reference to the only historical model for the establishment of divorce, the Revolution of 1789:

Gentlemen, our glorious revolution had as its goal the emancipation of thought, and it was greeted by an acclamation of the people . . . divorce by mutual consent or by the desire of one of the parties was instituted, separation in deed was followed by legal separation, and the legislator was no longer forced by dogma to recognize a fictive paternity" (*Letters*, 74).

Addressing herself to men elected under a royalist regime (although it is bound by a Charter), Flora knows that she will be heard only by the "liberals," those for whom the constitutions of revolutionary governments represent a lost progress. She adds: "Despotism needs merely obedience. Napoleon wanted to make divorce a royal prerogative. . . . He made it almost the exclusive right of the husband" (*Letters*, 74). Yet, as Flora says, Napoleon did "not dare abolish" (74) divorce. Not until the Restoration did the kings dare do so "in opposition," she says, "to the freedom of religion." Turning back the clock on the progress of the revolution, this "anti-social law" had the effect of creating chaos. Invoking the "annual declaration of illegitimate but legally recognized children," Flora says: "In France there exist more than 300,000 disunited marriages" (*Letters*, 75). Exposing the condition of women with neither profession nor money, burdened with children and either forced to leave their husbands or abandoned by them, she argues that "the illicit unions they form must be attributed to the law itself" (*Letters*, 75).

In this same official petition, filled with logical arguments and statistics, she makes a brief allusion to her own destiny between the ages of twenty-one, when she had fled from Chazal's home and thirty-four, when she is beginning to write her memoirs, saying: "Gentlemen, I have undergone the severe trials resulting from the indissolubility of marriage. Forced to separate from my husband, although I had no financial resources, I was obliged at a very young age to provide for my needs and those of my children all by myself" (*Letters*, 75).

The memoirs, *Peregrinations of a Pariah*, recount an arduous and adventurous journey to Peru, which begins with her desire to better her personal situation, and which results in her decision to engage in the second wave of the revolution. On her thirtieth birthday, April 7, 1833, having confided her daughter Aline to the care of a friend, she embarks upon an ocean journey of 133 days, without having said anything to her mother, who continues to act as informant to Chazal. Flora describes herself hiding her marital state from the ship's captain Chabrié, whose amorous feelings for his passenger both protect and discomfit her, as she goes from port to port, learning first hand about the stark reality of slavery, the slave trade of blacks, and the condition of women slaves.

She reports seeing two black women condemned to death for infanticide and feeling that the gaze of one of them "seemed to say to me: 'I let my child die because I knew he would not be free like you; I preferred him dead to enslaved'" (*Per.*, 352). For Flora, these two slaves become the epitome of every servitude that, imperceptible or horrifying, symbolizes the condition of woman, especially in their will to "die without being bent to the yoke" (*Per.*, 352). According to her narrative, she tells a slave owner: "Monsieur, a revolution whose motives were the most generous had to be roused to indignation by the existence of slavery. The Convention decreed the emancipation of Blacks, out of enthusiasm, and without appearing to suspect that they would need to be prepared to make use of their liberty" (*Per.*, 349). For the entire gamut of problems from her personal confinement in indissoluble marriage to the most extreme forms of oppression in slavery, the Revolution from 1789 to 1793 arises as the historical model for solutions.

According to *Peregrinations*, it is this voyage to Peru, these twenty-two months of discoveries that transform Flora's world view in this way. The book recounts her first-hand experiences with a feudal despotism ruled by her uncle Don Pio. He reigns over plantations, factories, and workers, even over the monks in a convent located on his property, and he rules doubly over a whole kinship of poor women, aunts, cousins, unmarried daughters, and poorly married widows who surround him with a docile court. He grants a fifth of the Tristan inheritance to his brother's "bastard" and invites her to stay with him, where he will arrange her marriage. As on Chabrié's ship, Flora once again confronts the fear of bigamy. To no one does she reveal her true situation, preferring to pass as a spinster, or in France even as an unmarried mother, since this is at least not a criminal offense. The necessity of living a false role in the luxurious and medieval microsociety of Arequipa gives her such a horror for life that in the process of her personal transformation to revolutionary apostle, she more than once contemplates suicide.

Flora's despair thus reaches its depth in this world where neither ideas nor morals were changed by the revolution or even by the generously liberal inspiration of her father's friend, Simon Bolivar the "Liberator," whose letters to her parents Flora will later publish.[13] She begins to climb out of this despair through the excitement of an event, not exactly a revolution, but a coup d'état and resulting siege at the end of January 1834. Because this Parisian has experienced the July Days of 1830, she is, as she describes it, treated as a kind of strategic counselor. Yet it is after her uncle's party is defeated and he immediately allies himself with the winners that Flora undergoes the strange adventure, which will lead her through a tortuous path to become the revolutionary writer of *The Peregrinations*.

Among the victors, Flora meets Colonel Escudero, Spaniard, journalist, musician, and above all, political counselor and intimate companion of "La Presidente" Doña Pencha de Gamarra, the adventurous and repudiated wife of the former president, and leader of Don Pio's party. From the moment of Escudero's first visit, Flora is attracted to him, and it seems she has finally met a man with whom she falls in love. "He was ugly in the eyes of the world, but not in my own" (*Per.*, 290), she writes, and even goes so far as to admit: "I have the deep conviction that had I become his wife, I would have been very happy" (*Per.*, 290).

But the amorous attraction is fed by another kind of attraction. Writing in 1838, she makes a revolutionary admission about her frame of mind in 1834: "the desire to contribute to the public good had been the constant passion of my soul and an active, adventurous career one of my lifelong preferences"

(*Per.*, 290). Speaking of the "ambitious projects" that are born in her, she confesses: "I believed that if I inspired Escudero's love, I would have a great influence on him" (*Per.*, 290).

But to do this, she must turn him away from her rival, Doña Pencha de Gamarra, a "woman with Napoleonic ambition" (*Per.*, 289) and an "extraordinary . . . power of will" (*Per.*, 360), who wielded considerable political power, galloped at the head of the troops, and maintained discipline over them with a cruel hand. Flora's rivalry combines her newfound passion for fame and her passion for love. With Escudero, she has the frankness to write, she imagines that together the two of them could win fame and reports herself thinking: "What do I care if I succeed since I have nothing to lose?" (*Per.*, 290). Her desperation here foreshadows Marx's famous revolutionary phrase to the workers: "you have nothing to lose but your chains." Was Flora sexually attracted to Escudero? We cannot know, nor even if he repaid her attraction, but she admits to experiencing "the strongest temptation" (*Per.*, 290) of her life.

One of the most memorable passages of *The Peregrinations* recounts the scene in which Flora finally meets Doña Pencha, who is en route to her exile in Chile. Epileptic, feverish, and domineering, Doña Pencha seems nonetheless heroic to the narrator, even though she is horrified by her former rival's humiliation. She gives as her reasons for renouncing her rivalry with Doña Pencha the fear of bigamy, her extreme longing to return to her daughter Aline again, and above all Virtue, the Revolutionary Virtue inherited from the National Convention of 1793: "I dreaded that moral depravation to which the enjoyment of power generally subjects us" (*Per.*, 290). She writes that after meeting Doña Pencha, she experiences "a feeling of shame of having been able to believe for one moment in the happiness of ambition," and remarks: "Ah! how my poverty and obscure life lived in liberty seemed preferable and more noble" (*Per.*, 367). Although she tells us that she has always chosen independence, it is this encounter, her unfulfilled love for Escudero, and her analysis of this woman of power that give birth to a new resolution, one faithful to the moral tradition of the revolution, to become a Woman-Guide spreading the new ideas—a prophet, but not a despot. She obtains from her uncle the promise of a small pension that will allow her to return to France.

Her return plunges her into her old humiliations, as Chazal continues to harass her and takes away Aline. But Flora, determined to pursue her goal as a fighter for women and all oppressed people, writes her first social essay: *On the Necessity of Extending a Warm Welcome to Foreign Women*,[14] which in the spirit of utopian socialism proposes the creation of a haven for women who are traveling or in flight. She enters into friendly relations with Charles Fourier and plans to create a new feminist newspaper with Eugénie Niboyet, one of the founders of the *Gazette des femmes* (see *Letters*, 56–59, and 64). Accepted into the circle of Parisian social reformers, Flora begins, in September 1836, to publish parts of her future *Peregrinations of a Pariah*, "The Women of Lima" and "The Convents of Arequipa: The Story of Dominga" in *La Revue de Paris*, edited by George Sand's friend François Buloz.[15] The Fourierist Victor Considérant publishes a long letter from her in his newspaper *La Phalange*, and in his lengthy response calls her "one of the women the most gifted in love, intelligence and zeal for the cause of social reform," but questions her ideas on organization.[16]

When her *Peregrinations of a Parish: 1833–1834* appears as a two volume work in 1838, its combination of autobiographical revelation and appeals for social reform produce dramatic effects. In Peru, her uncle allows her book and portrait to be burned in the public square and takes away her pension (see *Letters*, 88). André Chazal, who has been drinking more and more and whose guardianship over their children had been revoked by the courts, is enraged upon seeing the story of their harrowing marriage in print. Delirious, he writes threatening letters, buys a pair of pistols, and on September 10, 1838, wounds Flora in broad daylight, in the middle of the street. A bullet lodges itself near her lung and cannot be extracted. That night the rumor spreads through Paris that George Sand has been murdered by her husband, but the *Journal des débats* puts the rumor to rest on September 12 by reporting that Sand had been at the theater on that fateful night.[17] Flora becomes famous.

The shooting and the dramatic trial that followed made the book a commercial success, and a new edition was published. While Flora is busy writing articles, publishing Bolivar's letters to her parents, having her portraits painted by Jules Laure, and writing her only novel, *Méphis or the Proletarian*,[18] she also prepares for Chazal's trial, by, among other things, presenting a petition against the death penalty to the Chamber of Deputies, on December 19, 1838 (*Letters*, 91).

From Chazal's failed attempt at murder comes her liberation. His trial, before a full house, receives lengthy, detailed reports in *Le Droit* and *La Gazette des Tribunaux*.[19] Chazal's attorney, the soon to be famous Jules Favre, brandishes Flora's *Peregrinations* and reads from it truncated passages as proof of her guilt, as he turns the victim into the accused. The misconduct of this bad wife, claims Favre, pushed his client to crime. Flora's sudden appearance in court creates a sensation. She cries out that the work is a novel and faints at the bar. In a letter to an unknown correspondent, Flora writes that "my wretched assassin" had tried "to assassinate me morally after putting a bullet in my chest. . . . He posed not as an assassin of Flora Tristan, but as the *defender of husbands* attacked by Flora Tristan" (*Letters*, 96). Chazal is, however, condemned, the marriage is annulled, and the children take their mother's name. Flora is finally free.

Now finding herself among the celebrated queens of Paris, Flora could choose to play the role of an elite woman of letters. But the rebel daughter of the revolution remains faithful to herself. Preferring to serve the cause of the oppressed, she leaves for London. Although she had been a "female companion," or really lady's maid, in London before her voyage to Peru, she returns to investigate the social conditions in the capital of the most advanced industrial country in Europe. She prepares a book, *Promenades in London*, which will describe the atrocious poverty of the workers, the degradation of the poor, and the depravity of wealth.

In spite of a strong personal, emotional aversion for England, in all likelihood born of her previous humiliations as a servant there, Flora succeeds in tracing a striking sociological tableau of London. She depicts the horror of working people defenselessly handed over to an all-powerful capitalism, which exploits the new Third Estate, a "Fourth Estate" called the proletariat. With a style marked by a strong, romantic subjectivity, she describes all the "alienations"—of proletarians, prostitutes (including children of both sexes), prisoners, the mentally ill, and what we would call "ethnic minorities." Among these are the Jews, whom she describes with an edge of contempt, and the Irish, whom she describes with admiration.

Although Flora is escorted into every social milieu—sweat shops, slums, haunts of vice and prostitution, Bedlam, prisons, and even the House of Lords, where she is disguised as a man—by the Owenites, especially Anna Wheeler, and although she has great admiration for Robert Owen, whom she had met in Paris in 1837, she maintains her independence. Just as she is a rebel daughter of the revolution, she is a sort of rebel sister to its heirs, the utopian socialists of the 1830s. Influenced by all of them, she also criticizes them all and joins with no movement, preferring to organize on her own.

While *Promenades in London* aroused indignation in certain British social spheres, French social reformers took the book seriously. The Fourierist Jean Czynski wrote enthusiastically and at length about it in *Le Nouveau Monde*, as did the proletarian writer Vinçard in *La Ruche populaire* and in *La Revue du Progrès*, published by Louis Blanc.[20] From this time forward, Flora Tristan counts among the social reformers. After its first two editions in 1840, and a third edition in 1842, *Promenades in London* is republished in a low-cost format in 1842, with a new "Dedication to the Working Classes."[21] Here she writes that the purpose of her book is to "instruct" the workers "on *the causes of their suffering and the means to remedy it*" (*Promenades*, 54, emphasis in text), and announces the principle of class struggle: "Proletarians, my work is the exposition of the great drama that England is going to play out before the eyes of the world. . . . It prepares you for the appearance of the great events of this terrible struggle that is forming between the proletarians and the nobles of this country" (53). As remedy, the book calls for a social, rather than a political, revolution. Commenting on her impressions of the English factories, Flora says:

> If at first I felt humiliated upon seeing man annihilated, reduced to operating like a machine himself, I soon saw the immense improvements which would one day come from these discoveries of science: brute force abolished, material work performed in less time, and more leisure time for man to cultivate his intelligence; but the realization of these great benefits requires a social revolution. It will come! for God has not revealed to man these wonderful inventions in order to reduce them to mere slaves of a few manufacturers and landowners (*Promenades*, 116–17).

In his excellent introduction to the modern edition of *Promenades*, François Bédarida, is struck, as I am, by the "cross references" between this book and Friedrich Engels's *Conditions of the Working Class in England* of

1845. But Bédarida believes I am wrong to think that young Engels had read Flora. "Engels," he says, "researched his book with recourse to exclusively English documentation" (Intro. to *Promenades*, 44). Given the bulimia of reading that Engels shared with Marx, who read the French publications, as well as the troubling similarity between the two books and the respective dates of their publication, I maintain that Engels was familiar with Flora Tristan. I also maintain my hypothesis that if this great quoter does not quote her, it is because a "lady's work" would not be considered a serious reference. Yet in their first collaborative work, *The Holy Family*, Engels and Marx mention Flora Tristan favorably in their critique of the German socialist Bruno Bauer, thus showing that they knew of her existence and her ideas.[22]

After writing *Promenades in London*, Flora feels endowed with the mission to disseminate her ideas. She considers herself the "Woman-Guide" she had written about in her novel *Méphis*, much as the Saint-Simonian leader Prosper Enfantin had proclaimed himself the Messiah and the Supreme Father ten years earlier.[23] Going beyond the revolution of the bourgeois Third Estate, Flora tells the workers, in her manifesto *Workers' Union*, as Marx would later tell them, to take their cause into their own hands.

In so adopting her new messianic identity and crossing the line from bourgeois to proletarian revolution, Flora enters a dilemma that her forebears of 1789 did not have to face, but that neither Marx, Engels, nor Lenin will escape. She is the leader of a movement for autonomous proletarian power but is not herself a worker. Indeed, as she organizes the workers, she is on more than one occasion insulted by the proletarian wives because she is a "lady" and turns their husbands towards politics. She thus opens the insoluble combat between the "workerism" of revolutionary formations and the intellectuals as bearers of doctrine.

The agonies of this experience do not befall her, however, until after months of disappointed hopes, she finally succeeds in publishing her *Workers' Union* by subscription at the end of 1843, and sets off on her "tour of France." Her book creates an original synthesis of the current reformist ideas that only through association among themselves and through recognizing the equality of women will workers gain freedom. In their excellent introduction to the modern edition of *Workers' Union*, Daniel Armogathe and Jean Grandjonc, from whom I will borrow several points of analysis, cite the article from *The Encyclopedic Review* of 1832 in which Jean Reynaud defines the "proletarians": "I call proletarians men who produce all of the nation's wealth, who possess nothing but the daily earnings of their labor, and whose work depends on causes outside of their control."[24]

Stressing repeatedly that it is addressed to workers of both sexes, *Workers' Union* enlarges the proletariat to include not only the 7 or 8 million factory workers, but also the 25 million or so artisans, whom Flora calls upon to constitute themselves as a class and elect a defender to represent their interests and demand their rights before the nation. To a critic who called her project too utopian and impractical, Flora responded by presenting herself as a savior carrying the tradition of the French Revolution to its next historical level:

Before effecting its realization, one must first posit the law.—Catholicism was not definitively established until the sixth century, but Christ had posited the law 600 years before.—The constitution of the bourgeois class was not established until 89, but the law had been posited in the first Estates General.—I bring you the law, and as to its realization, Gods [Dieux] will sound its hour" (*Tour*, 12).

But why "God*s*"? This plural signifies that God "is father, mother and embryo."[25] Flora's new trinity fits in with the religious ideas of the utopian socialists. Just as the Revolution of 1793 had replaced the old mystical gods with its rationalist Supreme Being, the social movement of the 1830s replaced the old male gods with new bisexual gods. Flora's friend, the sculptor Simon Ganneau, preached a "Mapa," a mama-papa god. The Saint-Simonians under the leadership of Enfantin preached that god is both *"father and mother."* (*La Tribune des femmes*, 193, emphasis in text). But Flora conceived her "Gods" as a family triangle, with the embryo providing "the germ as indefinite progress" (Postface to *Testament*, 19), the promise of the future. In her 1838 novel *Méphis* it is neither the proletarian hero nor the rebellious heroine Marequita who holds the key to liberate humanity, but their daughter, the future "Woman-Guide."

"Gods" then will realize this Law through a union between woman, the oppressed sex, and the most oppressed class, the proletariat. Therefore, according to Flora, all women, even the most privileged, must ally with the working class. The notion of the link between women and the proletariat had been expressed many times by the Saint-Simonians. In 1833, for instance, the Saint-Simonian Claire Démar had written: *"the emancipation of the proletariat, of the poorest and most numerous class*, is possible, I am convinced, only through *the emancipation of our sex."*[26] Flora develops this concept in both theory and practice. *The Emancipation of Woman and the Testament of the Pariah*, published posthumously from her notes by Abbé Constant, and doubtless revised, contains the phrase: "The most oppressed man finds a being to oppress, his wife: she is the proletarian of the proletarian." Thus forty years before Engels she articulates in more developed form the thought for which he is more famous: "Within the family he is the bourgeois, and the wife represents the proletariat."[27]

In this analysis, *Workers' Union* sees the liberation of women and workers as a continuation of the incomplete work of the French Revolution:

What happened for the proletarians [in '89] augurs well, it must be agreed, for women when their '89 will sound.—A very simple calculation makes it obvious that the wealth of society will grow indefinitely from the day that women (half the human race) are called upon to bring to social activity the sum total of their intelligence, strength and ability. . . . But alas, we are not yet there, and as we wait for this felicitous '89, let us see what is happening in 1843" (*WU*, excerpt in *OVM*, 403).

In order to bring about this new feminine 1789, *Workers' Union* sets forth a detailed plan of action, and its author travels from city to city setting up "Committees of Correspondence" that are to be joined in a tight network.

And where the revolutionaries of 1789 sought to establish the nation, Flora's new 1789 is conceived in the name of internationalism. As an eternal foreigner, a French woman in Peru and England, and always exotic and out of place in France; a lady among the workers, while too passionate and intolerant a militant among the intellectuals, Flora believes in a "Universal Union of working men and women" (WU, excerpt in OVM, p. 389). In her study of 1918, "An Unknown, Flora Tristan, the True Founder of the International," the feminist pacifist Helen Brion sees Flora as the precursor of the First International.[28]

Paradoxically, however, those qualities which make her an internationalist also make her a loner, and her "tour of France" is the mission of a solitary messiah. Although she does not explicitly call herself the "Woman-Messiah," whose coming was preached by Prosper Enfantin in the early 1830s, she does frequently compare herself to Christ in her journal, where she writes, for instance: "Faith makes me perform wondrous things" (*Tour*, 27). But at this time, such a belief was in a sense her only alternative. If a woman refused to ally herself with existing groups, she could not then speak in her name alone. Who would listen to her? She would have to tell herself and make herself believe that she is sent by something that transcends groups and schools: a divinity, "Gods."

Thus from April 12, 1844, until her death from "cerebral congestion" on November 14, 1844, at the age of 41, she will travel through almost twenty towns south of the Loire with a trunk full of *Workers' Union*s. The diary of spontaneously recorded impressions, *The Tour of France*, recounts the harassing police investigations, landlord problems, and petty rivalries among the socialists, but also the exaltation of large meetings with enthusiastic workers, while it also offers a gripping and profound tableau of class struggle in France just before the Revolution of 1848. The diary records in detail Flora's discouragement and anger, alternatively against selfish bourgeois and passive workers, as well as the mortal suffering that pushes her to her death.

In certain cities, such as Lyon, Toulon, and Marseille, she will stir up great enthusiasm and form committees. Even after her death, she has a lasting influence, for instance in Toulon in 1845, when striking arsenal workers according to Maurice Agulhon, cite her teachings.[29] But by the time her grandson, Paul Gauguin, grows up, she will have been erased from history. He will know very little about his grandmother:

> Proudhon said she had genius in her. . . . She invented a heap of socialist stories, *Workers' Union* among others. . . . It is probable that she did not know how to cook. A socialist blue-stocking, an anarchist. . . . What I do know for sure, however, is that Flora Tristan was a very beautiful and noble lady. . . . I also know that she used her whole fortune for the workers' cause, traveling nonstop.[30]

In the past twenty years she has won a more deserved place in history. Flora Tristan, imbued with the principles of the Revolution of 1789 and aware of their inadequacies, was the most romantic and the most lucid of the "utopian socialists." Among those men and women who had understood the necessity of bringing into the light of history those people who had been left underground, proletarians and women of every class, she was a messiah, that is to say a person ready to die for her message.

Notes

1. Jules L. Puech, *La Vie et l'oeuvre de Flora Tristan* (Paris: M. Rivière, 1925).

2. Lucien Scheler, *Flora Tristan: Morceaux choisis. Précédés de la Geste romantique de Flora Tristan* (Paris: Bibliothèque française, 1947).

3. Dominique Desanti, *Flora Tristan la femme révoltée* (Paris: Hachette, 1972), development in depth of details of Flora's life briefly mentioned in this essay; and D. Desanti, *Flora Tristan: Oeuvres et vie mêlées* (Paris: U.G.E., coll. 10/18, 1972). All further references to this text will appear in parentheses after the citation as "OVM." See also Jean Baelen, *La Vie de Flora Tristan: Socialisme et féminisme au XIXᵉ siècle* (Paris: Le Seuil, 1972); Sandra Dijkstra, *Flora Tristan: Pioneer Feminist and Socialist* (Berkeley: Center for Socialist History, 1984); Stéphane Michaud, ed., *Flora Tristan, 1803–1844* (Paris: Editions ouvrières, 1984); S. Michaud, ed., *Un Fabuleux Destin: Flora Tristan*, actes du premier Colloque international Flora Tristan (Dijon: Editions universitaires de Dijon, 1985); and Leslie W. Rabine, *The Other Side of the Ideal: Women Writers in Mid-Nineteenth-Century France* (Ph.D. diss., Stanford University, 1973).

4. Flora Tristan, *Les Pérégrinations d'une Paria (1833–1834)* (Paris: Arthus Bertrand, 1838; modern edition, Paris: Maspero, 1979). Unfortunately the Maspero edition omits Flora's introduction. Therefore, references to this text that appear in parentheses after the citation will refer to the out-of-print 1838 edition for the introduction, and to the 1979 edition for the body of the text.

5. For information on the Civil Code of 1803, see Claire Goldberg Moses, *French Feminism in the 19th Century* (Albany: State University of New York Press, 1984), 18–22.

6. Flora Tristan, *Pérégrinations*; *Promenades dans Londres ou l'Aristocratie et les Prolétaires anglais*, with an introduction by François Bédarida (Paris: Maspero, 1983); *Union ouvrière* (Paris: Chez tous les libraires, 1843, 1844; Lion, 1844), modern edition reprints 1844 version, Daniel Armogathe and Jacques Grandjonc, eds. (Paris: Des femmes, 1986). Lengthy excerpts of *Union ouvrière* are reprinted in Desanti, *Oeuvres et vie mêlée*, 389–435.

7. See Dominique Desanti, *Les Socialistes de l'utopie* (Paris: Payot, 1971).

8. Flora Tristan, *Le Tour de France: Journal inédit 1843–1844* (Paris: Editions Tête de feuille, 1973).

9. Flora Tristan, *Union ouvrière*, excerpt in Desanti, *Oeuvres et vie mêlée*, 344. Citations in this essay are taken from these excerpts and will be referred to in parentheses after the citation as "*WU* [Workers' Union] in *OVM*."

10. *La Tribune des Femmes*, journal of the Saint-Simonian feminists, founded and coedited by Désirée Veret-Gay and Marie-Reine Guindorf, and then edited by Suzanne Voilquin, Paris, 1832 to April 1834. Its first title was *La Femme libre*, its second title *L'Apostolat des femmes*, and its final title *La Tribune des femmes*. *La Gazette des femmes*, edited by Frédéric de Mauchamps, Paris, July 1836–April 1837; and December 1837–April 1838.

11. Suzanne Voilquin, *Souvenirs d'une fille du peuple ou la Saint-Simonienne en Egypte* (Paris: Maspero, 1978); *Mémoires d'une Saint-Simonienne en Russie* (Paris: Edition des femmes, 1977); editor of *La Tribune des femmes*. Désirée Veret-Gay, founder and first co-editor of *La Tribune des femmes*.

12. Flora Tristan, *Lettres*, collected, presented, and annotated by Stéphane Michaud (Paris: Seuil, 1980), 44. (Cited hereafter parenthetically in text as *Letters*.)

13. "Lettres de Bolivar," published and commented by Flora Tristan, *Le Voleur*, 31 juillet 1838.

14. Flora Tristan, *Nécessité de faire un bon acueil aux femmes étrangères, par Mme F. T.* (Paris: Delaunay, 1836).

15. Flora Tristan, "Les Femmes de Lima," *La Revue de Paris*, XXXIII, 25 septembre, pp. 209-16; "Les Couvents d'Arequipa, histoire de Dominga," *La Revue de Paris*, XXXIII, 27 novembre 1836, 225-48.

16. Victor Considérant, *La Phalange*, no. 6, 1 septembre 1836, 182-88, cited by Michaud in Tristan, *Lettres*, 64.

17. Puech, *La vie et l'oeuvre*, 93.

18. Flora Tristan, *Méphis* (Paris: Ladvocat, 1838).

19. *Le Droit*, 1 and 2 février 1839; *La Gazette des tribunaux*, 1, 2, and 4 février 1839.

20. Jean Czynski, *Le Nouveau Monde*, 21 mai, 11 juillet 1839; Jules Vinçard, *La Ruche populaire*, août 1840, 8-19; *La Revue du Progrès*, Louis Blanc, ed., 1 octobre 1840.

21. Flora Tristan, *Promenades dans Londres* (1st ed., Paris, H. L. Delloye; and London: W. Jeffs, 1840; 2d ed., same as first). The third edition is published as *La Ville monstre* (same publishers as first, 1842). The fourth edition is *Promenades dans Londres ou l'Aristocratie et les Prolétaires anglais* (Paris: Bocquet/Prévot, 1842). Bédarida's 1978 edition reprints the 1842 Bocquet/Prévot version.

22. Karl Marx and Friedrich Engels, *The Holy Family: or Critique of Critical Criticism: Against Bruno Bauer* (Moscow: Foreign Languages Publishing House, 1956).

23. J. P. Allem, *Enfantin: Le prophète aux sept visages* (Paris: Pauvert, 1963). P. Enfantin appointed himself "Supreme Father of the School, College and Family of the Saint-Simonian Men and Women" to whom he pledged to search for the "Supreme Mother." He instituted the "Call to Woman" and predicted the future government of the "Supreme Couple." But he excluded women from the organization of the Saint-Simonian hierarchy. His relations with Flora were temporary and not very cordial.

24. Jean Reynaud, cited in Armogathe and Grandjonc, *Union ouvrière*.

25. L'abbé Constant, "Postface," in *L'Emancipation de la femme ou le Testament de la paria*, posthumous work by Flora Tristan completed according her notes and published by A. Constant (Paris: 1845), 18-19. A. Constant combines his own writing with passages that maintain Flora's tone.

26. Claire Démar, *Ma Loi d'Avenir*, posthumous work published by Suzanne [Voilquin] (Paris: Bureau de La Tribune des femmes, 1834), 25. Emphasis in text.

27. Frederick Engels, *The Origin of the Family, Private Property and the State* (New York: International Publishers, 1972), 137.

28. Hélène Brion, "Une méconnue, Flora Tristan, la vraie fondatrice de l'internationale," in *L'Avenir social* (Epône [Seine-et-Oise]: Société d'édition de librairie, 1918).

29. Maurice Agulhon, *Une Ville ouvrière au temps du socialisme utopique. Toulon de 1815 à 1851* (Paris: Mouton, 1970).

30. Paul Gaugin, *Avant et après* (Paris: 1923), 133, cited by Bédarida, *Promenades*, 14.

INDEX